Reflections in a Bloodshot Lens

Also by Lawrence Pintak

BEIRUT OUTTAKES: A TV CORRESPONDENT'S PORTRAIT OF AMERICA'S ENCOUNTER WITH TERROR (1988)

SEEDS OF HATE: HOW AMERICA'S FLAWED MIDDLE EAST POLICY IGNITED THE JIHAD (2003)

Reflections in a Bloodshot Lens

America, Islam and the War of Ideas

Lawrence Pintak

Pluto  Press

LONDON • ANN ARBOR, MI

First published 2006 by Pluto Press
345 Archway Road, London N6 5AA
and 839 Greene Street, Ann Arbor, MI 48106

www.plutobooks.com

ISBN 0 7453 2418 5 hardback
ISBN 0 7453 2419 3 paperback

Library of Congress Cataloging in Publication Data applied for

10 9 8 7 6 5 4 3 2 1

Designed and produced for Pluto Press by
Chase Publishing Services, Fortescue, Sidmouth, EX10 9QG, England
Typeset from disk by Newgen Imaging Systems (P) Ltd, India
Printed and bound in the United States of America by
Maple-Vail Book Manufacturing Group

For my Dakini and our rootless tribe:

Marshall McLuhan once wrote. "'Time' has ceased, 'space' has vanished. We now live in a global village."

He must have had us in mind.

We don't see things as they are, we see things as we are.

Anaïs Nin (1903–1977)

O would that God the gift might give us
To see ourselves as others see us.

Robert Burns (1759–1796)

Contents

Preface

During a whirlwind tour of Asia in the fall of 2003, President George W. Bush met with Indonesian Muslim leaders on the island of Bali. Emerging from the three-hour session, Bush turned to his aides and expressed amazement that his hosts seemed to believe that Americans saw all Muslims as terrorists. "He was equally distressed," *The New York Times* reported, "to hear that the United States was so pro-Israel that it was uninterested in the creation of a Palestinian state living alongside Israel, despite his frequent declarations calling for exactly that."[1]

It was a moment reflecting the yawning gap in worldview, perception and communication that has fed the rise of anti-Americanism in the post-9/11 era. The encounter was revealing not so much for the fact that Indonesian Muslims felt that way, but that this came as a surprise to the president of the United States. *He* genuinely believed his policies were fair and even-handed; the idea that others might see things differently did not appear to have entered his mind. Aboard Air Force One en route home, Bush told reporters that he tried to explain to the Indonesians that his Middle East policy wasn't anti-Muslim, but "I didn't really have time to go in further than that."

America had lost another battle in the war of ideas.

LOST OPPORTUNITIES

There are two tragedies of September 11, 2001: the deaths of more than 3,000 innocent human beings on the day itself and the squandering of a unique opportunity in the months and years that followed, which contributed to the loss of countless additional lives. Never in modern times had there been such sympathy for the United States in the Islamic world. Beyond the relatively isolated celebrations of America's pain, and a certain level of quiet satisfaction among mainstream Muslims that the United States had proven vulnerable, the majority in the Islamic world condemned the attacks. There was also recognition among Muslim "moderates" that the forces of extremism posed a threat to them as well. "We unequivocally condemn acts of international terrorism in all its forms and manifestations, including state terrorism, irrespective of motives, perpetrators and victims," the Organization of the Islamic Conference declared in the wake of the bombings.[2]

Within months of the disaster, America had lost the chance to build a new relationship with the Muslim world. Instead, the nation began marching down a path that would systematically alienate sympathetic Muslims and play into the hands of the extremists by setting up precisely the "clash of civilizations" that the bin Ladens of the world had long sought. What was, at heart, a war between the forces of moderation and the forces of extremism for the soul of Islam was soon transformed into a confrontation between the world's Muslims and the United States.

Beginning with his off-the-cuff comment about a "crusade" against terror, President Bush presided over a series of policy statements and actions perceived by many around the world as anti-Muslim, pro-Israeli and imperialistic. As a direct result, America's favorability rating in the Muslim world is today essentially zero. We can't even buy friends. Nowhere are Americans more unpopular than in Egypt, the second-largest recipient of U.S. aid. Emblematic of the alienation of would-be Muslim allies was the dramatic turnaround on the part of Malaysian prime minister Mahathir Mohamad. One of America's most outspoken supporters in the Muslim world in the months after 9/11, by early 2003 Mahathir was accusing Washington of trying to "out-terrorize the terrorists."[3]

Another legacy of this alienation is the shift in attitudes toward Americans as individuals. Any U.S. citizen who has visited the Arab world in past decades has his/her own version of the ubiquitous story of the taxi driver, bellhop or waiter who says, "You're American? I love Americans. But tell your president to go to hell." In the past, there was a clear distinction between U.S. policy and the American people. No longer. As recently as 2002 more than 50 per cent of Jordanians said they had a favorable view of the American *people*, as distinct from the U.S. *government*. By 2004 that was down to 21 per cent. Asked the best thing about the United States, more than half of Saudis said "nothing." The worst? America's proclivity to "murder Arabs" was the most common response across the region.[4] Goodwill toward the United States has disappeared like a desert mirage. And most Americans still don't understand why. "How do I respond when I see that in some Islamic countries there is a vitriolic hatred of America?" Bush asked rhetorically in a prime-time news conference shortly after 9/11. "I'll tell you how I respond: I'm amazed. I'm amazed that there is such misunderstanding of what our country is about." The world's Muslims were amazed as well – amazed that Americans are, in their perception, so blind to the obvious.

Note that I have repeatedly used the word "perceive." It is the key to understanding the relationship between America and the Muslim world. This book is not about policy per se. It will not examine the rights and wrongs of the invasion of Iraq, U.S. support for Israel or America's relationship with the House of Saud. Rather, it is about how the *perceptions* of policy (which could easily have been the title of the book) have colored the relationship; for how a given policy is perceived can sometimes be as important as the policy itself.

Osama bin Laden instinctively knew that.

URBAN RENEWAL IN THE GLOBAL VILLAGE

"How can a man in a cave out-communicate the world's leading communications society?" former UN Ambassador Richard Holbrooke famously asked after 9/11.[5] The short answer was, "al-Jazeera." Bin Laden was a charismatic figure who arrived on the world stage at a unique moment in history. Americans heard in his messages the rantings of a murderous maniac; for, from their perspective, the man responsible for 9/11 could hardly be anything but that. Yet, however horrified they may have been at his actions, many Arabs and Muslims heard someone who was finally speaking truth to power. Timing is everything. The controlled media of the Arab world had long quashed such dissenting ideas. With the launch of al-Jazeera, the first largely independent cross-border television station in the Middle East, the muzzle was removed and bin Laden had his bully pulpit.

Back in the 1960s, media prophet Marshall McLuhan described how the "new electronic interdependence recreates the world in the image of a global village."[6] By the early years of the new century, urban renewal had come to the global village. No longer was all the world gathered around the same electronic hearth. Instead, a series of media strip malls replaced the global public sphere, with international audiences naturally turning to those outlets that reinforced their own worldview, much as increasingly fragmented domestic American audiences were switching to sources – such as Fox News or *The Daily Show* – in step with their own ideological agendas.

Most critically, regional satellite television and the Internet meant the developing world could scrap the global narrative so long authored in the West and write its own script. In Arab countries, the chains of government information control were broken. All eyes turned to al-Jazeera, al-Arabiya and the newly risen constellation of Arab and Muslim satellite stations. Western channels like CNN, the BBC, MSNBC and Fox News were available to those with satellite dishes, some even in Arabic, but the percentage of Arabs who watched them as their primary source of news was tiny. Arabs could now see the world through an Arab lens, why would they turn anywhere else? The al-Jazeera effect was also felt beyond the Middle East, as TV stations rebroadcast footage from the Arab channels and, inspired by this new perspective on the world, print journalists exhibited an aggressive new sense of Muslim solidarity. American audiences were largely oblivious to this shift in Arab and Muslim perspective. Arab television channels were simply not available to those who did not speak Arabic. The Arab and Muslim viewpoint could be glimpsed by Americans who went to the effort of seeking out the English-language websites of news organizations in the Muslim world, but few bothered. After all, life was so much simpler in black and white.

The result was a set of information ghettos whose inhabitants – in the United States and the Muslim world – saw dramatically different versions of the same reality. "Surgical strikes" versus dead babies; the "oppressed" being "liberated" versus civilians under siege. Even when the words and pictures were they same, they carried completely different meanings depending on the audience. U.S. officials failed to fully recognize the implications; but bin Laden instinctively knew how to make this media revolution his own.

US AND THEM

"Why do they hate us?" American acquaintances inevitably ask when they learn that I have spent much of my career living in Muslim-majority countries. Part of the answer can be found in the question itself: *Us* and *Them*. With its twin, *Self* and *Other*, it is the fundamental dichotomy of human existence; a concept embedded in psychology, anthropology, political science, communications and a host of other disciplines. Since 9/11, it has been the defining characteristic of global affairs; each side viewing the other through the prism of its own immutable worldview, amplified by the rhetoric of religion and ideology and further distorted by the bloodshot lenses of their respective media.

For Americans, Islam has emerged as the quintessential "Other," replacing the Soviet Union as the touchstone against which U.S. citizens measure their collective sense of Self. It has become a cliché to say that the attacks of September 11, 2001 "changed everything." On one level, that is true. The nation's illusion of security was shattered; its relationship with terror as something that happened somewhere else was unalterably transformed. But on another level, 9/11 simply made overt a worldview that had long been present but little acknowledged. Since a *keffiah*-clad Rudolph Valentino first strode across the silent screen, Arabs and Muslims have been Othered in U.S. society, the subject of stereotype and differentiation. Blinded by their view of Self, most Americans knew – or cared – little about what the rest of the world thought of them. Meanwhile, Arabs and non-Arab Muslims harbored a host of clichés and preconceived notions that shaped their view of the United States, set against the overarching perception that the United States is intrinsically linked tó, and responsible for, the policies of Israel, the ultimate Other. The years since 9/11 have only confirmed the stereotypes on both sides.

This book sets out several intersecting arguments about the relationship between the United States and the world's Muslims – particularly focusing on those living in Muslim-majority countries – in the post-9/11 era:

- that the conflicting worldviews of Americans and Muslims led each to perceive events in fundamentally different ways;

- that the polarizing rhetoric of leaders on each side was shaped by, and reinforced, those fundamentally different worldviews;
- that the prevailing worldview in the Bush White House – and the country at large – produced a failure to understand the impact that U.S. policy statements and actions had among Arabs and non-Arab Muslims;
- that the media on each side framed coverage in a manner that reinforced the dichotomy and inflamed opinion;
- that this impact was dramatically enhanced by the growth of satellite television and non-traditional media outlets in the Muslim world; and
- that the above factors led to the enhancement of a global community of Muslims, or *ummah*, that is far more cohesive than ever before.

DEFINITIONS

If you are confused when talking heads on TV start spouting jargon about Islam and terrorism, you are not alone. So polarizing is the entire topic of America's relationship with the world's Muslims that the many parties to the discussion cannot even agree on key terminologies. It is important to establish these definitions so that readers are all, as it were, on the same page.

The very process of defining – and labeling – terror is a political minefield. Of the many definitions used by the U.S. government, one of the more common describes terrorism as "premeditated, politically motivated violence perpetrated against noncombatant targets by subnational groups or clandestine agents."[7] The failure to leave space for the idea that some acts carried out by governments can be considered terrorism embodies the very essence of the difference in worldviews. To much of the globe, state-sponsored terrorism is a far greater threat than terrorism carried out by individuals or loose-knit organizations. As will be explored elsewhere, this difference in definition sparks a cascade of other questions: who is a "terrorist" and who is a "martyr?" When does a "martyr" become a "terrorist?" Seeking middle ground, I have adopted the definition of terrorism offered by Bruce Hoffman of the Rand Corporation: "[T]he deliberate creation and exploitation of fear through violence or the threat of violence in the pursuit of political change."[8]

Then there is the equally thorny definition of "political Islam." This has become media shorthand for bin Laden and those who share his philosophy. In reality, militant groups "constitute only a small minority among political Islamists."[9] Using terms like *political Islam*, *Islamists*, *Islamic revivalism*, and *Islamic activism* interchangeably fails to acknowledge the vast range of attitudes and opinions among Muslims engaged in politics. It is also important to remember that the Prophet Muhammad was both a religious leader and the founder of the first Muslim state. As Khalid bin Sayeed points out, "[a] Muslim cannot treat his politics in [a] piecemeal fashion. His active political life does not cease after he has recorded his vote in an election. For him, politics represents a whole movement which follows an elaborate socio-political program."[10]

For the purposes of simplicity, this book will employ the following definitions:

- An *Islamist* will be defined as a Muslim who shares the vision of Maulana Maududi (1903–1979), the revered founder of the South Asian Islamic revivalist organization Jamaat-e-Islami, for whom Islam was "a revolutionary concept and ideology which seeks to change and revolutionize the world social order and reshape it according to its own concept and ideals."[11]
- *Islamic* will refer to the religious and spiritual dimensions of the faith and *Muslim* to one who practices that faith or

considers him/herself to be Muslim (for a Muslim may not necessarily actively pray five times a day or attend mosque).

- The definition of *political Islam* will draw on Graham Fuller's description of the broad movement that believes "Islam as a body of faith has something important to say about how politics and society should be ordered in the contemporary Muslim world and who seeks to implement this idea in some fashion."[12]
- The term *Islamic fundamentalist* will also adhere to another of Fuller's definitions, as Muslims "who follow the literal and narrow reading of the Qur'an and the traditions of the Prophet, who believe they have a monopoly on the sole correct understanding of Islam and demonstrate intolerance toward those who differ."[13]

However, not all Islamists are fundamentalists, nor do all fundamentalists support violent action. *Islamist militant*, *extremist* and *radical* will be used interchangeably to define those Islamists who follow or endorse the path of violence as distinct from those Islamists who do not. The term *Muslim world* is borrowed from Eickelman and Piscatori to define the collection of countries stretching from Northwest Africa to Southeast Asia in which Muslims form the majority or a significant minority.[14] The Muslim world is not a monolith, it is neither a cohesive political unit nor home to all the world's Muslims; but it *is* the focal point of any discussion of post-9/11 global affairs.

BEYOND LABELS

Definitions are important, but they also get in the way. There is no cookie cutter that produces an "Islamist militant;" no template for a terrorist. "Moderate" Muslims come in all shades and colors. In the decades I have wandered through the Muslim world, I have known communists who have become nationalists and have then evolved into Islamists as the winds of change blew. I have seen subtle developments produce dramatic reversals in regional alliances. And I have watched friends who loved America lose hope. Not long ago, a Lebanese colleague from the American University of Beirut emailed me in despair. "Anti-American sentiment in the region is building up. America is even losing the modicum of sympathy it once garnered among moderate and liberal Arab thinkers," wrote this former Ivy League professor. "I don't know what can be done to avert the collective mood of anger, heightened by feelings of impotence and indignity. Finding shelter in radical Islam seems the only venue."

That growing anger and despair on both sides has been the hardest thing to witness from my sometimes strange and frustrating vantage point: until recently, a visitor in my own country, one foot in the United States, one foot in the Muslim world. No longer a full-time journalist but not quite an academic. Perhaps, in some twisted way, it was the only place from which to chronicle the disconnect that has characterized this era; trapped inside Alice's looking glass, where no one can quite agree on what they see.

Lawrence Pintak
Cairo, Egypt
July 2005

Introduction: Worldview, Identity and the Other

At the core of every moral code there is a picture of human nature, a map of the universe, and a version of history.

Walter Lippmann

In the late 1980s, the *New Yorker* magazine published its classic cover depicting the United States from the point of view of a resident of Manhattan. The Saul Steinberg painting showed Tenth Avenue, the Hudson River and a slice of New Jersey. Beyond that lay a desert wasteland separating the east coast from the Pacific Ocean. Immortalized as a poster and recreated from the perspective of a dozen international capitals, it has become the classic representation of worldview.

As the image so vividly illustrated, our perspective on the world is shaped by our environment, by our family, our culture, our religion. These and a host of influences together determine our worldview, which is, simply put, the orientation from which we view the world. "For what you see and hear depends a good deal on where you are standing; it also depends on what sort of person you are," wrote C.S. Lewis in *The Magician's Nephew*, the story of how two groups viewed very differently the creation of the land of Narnia.[1]

I have spent most of my career living outside the United States. It is my job as a journalist to understand how people about whom I am reporting perceive events, so I have done my best to see the world from the perspective of someone living in Africa, the Middle East, Europe and Southeast Asia. In the process, my own perspectives have changed; my worldview today is very different from that of the majority of Americans. My wife, meanwhile, is the daughter of an Indonesian diplomat. She was born in Jakarta, but spent many of her formative years in Britain and New Zealand. Her perspective was, likewise, shaped by that experience. In many ways, the worldviews that she and I hold are much closer to those of each other than to those of the majorities in our respective native lands. Yet, I am constantly reminded of how different they are as well. Each of us holds a unique worldview that is the product of our unique experience.

People have, of course, always had worldviews, they just didn't know it until German philosophers formalized the concept more than a century ago and dubbed it *Weltanschauung*, from which the English "worldview" is translated. This codification of the idea that we each see the world in a different way had a significant impact on the work of Kant, Nietzsche, Freud and other European philosophers of the day. The notions of good and bad, moral and immoral, acceptable and unacceptable are all shaped by our worldview. So, too, is our sense of Self and Other. It is, wrote anthropologist Anthony Wallace, "the very skeleton of concrete cognitive assumptions on which the flesh of customary behavior is hung."[2] The gradation of differences in worldview can be subtle, as in those of a New Yorker and a Bostonian or between the English and the Welsh; or they can be more dramatic, as in the difference in how a European software engineer and a tribesman in Borneo view the world.

The concept of worldview is anchored in religion and can be traced to the emergence in the first century A.D. of the Christian – in contrast to Jewish and pagan – worldview. While the various branches of Christianity are today separated by their doctrinal differences, it is their common schema of the creation, fall and redemption – with the resurrection of

Christ as the central theme – that unites them in a worldview distinguished from that of Jews and Muslims. Yet at the same time, those three traditions are united in a broad Biblically based Abrahamic worldview that differentiates them from polytheist and non-theist Eastern religions, such as Hinduism and Buddhism.

So what does all this have to do with relations between America and the Muslim world after 9/11? A great deal. This religious underpinning can lead to what has been termed "worldview exclusivism," the dogmatic claim by a particular in-group to possess Truth with a capital "T."[3] In other words, the conviction that God is on *my* side. And where one culture becomes dominant, in either a local or global context, that worldview exclusivism can lead to what the experts call the psychological colonization of others. The Crusades, the Spanish conquest of the Americas, the British Empire; each marched beneath the banner of God and Truth. As David Naugle noted in his history of the concept of worldview, this physical and psychological colonization is driven by an even deeper conviction:

> From the perspective of Christian theism, a clash of worldviews also assumes a crucial role in the hidden, spiritual battle between the kingdom of God and the kingdom of Satan in which the very truth of things is at stake. Between these regimes a conflict of epic proportion rages for the minds and hearts, and thus the lives and destinies, of all men and women, all the time . . . it is not surprising that a worldview warfare is at the heart of the conflict between the powers of good and evil.[4]

Just such a self-ordained divine mission has molded American foreign policy in modern times. The script for the modern rhetorical war on terrorism was written at the turn of the twentieth century, as a wave of anarchist terrorism swept Europe and reached across the Atlantic. Four years after anarchist Leon Czolgosz assassinated President William McKinley, Theodore Roosevelt declared the "evil" of anarchy to be the "foe of liberty," telling Congress, "The anarchist is the enemy of humanity, the enemy of all mankind; and his is a deeper degree of criminality than any other." Roosevelt affirmed America's right to strike out at any nation guilty of "[c]hronic wrongdoing, or an impotence which results in a general loosening of the ties of civilized society."[5]

Both world wars were portrayed as battles against evil and it was not long after the fall of Berlin that U.S. leaders were pointing to communism as the next threat to the forces of good. In his inaugural address, President Dwight D. Eisenhower, the victorious general of World War II, proclaimed America's divine right to lead the new battle against the evil of communism in a conflict in which there were no shades of gray:

> At such a time in history, we who are free must proclaim anew our faith. . . . This faith defines our full view of life. . . . The enemies of this faith know no god but force, no devotion but its use. . . . Freedom is pitted against slavery; lightness against the dark.[6]

Speaking against the Cold War backdrop of mutual assured annihilation, Eisenhower's successor, John F. Kennedy, sought to forge a new worldview, forcefully arguing that "[n]o government or social system is so evil that its people must be considered as lacking in virtue,"[7] but his assassination – which many viewed as a manifestation of evil – ushered in a return to a foreign policy of stark confrontation, in which good and evil battled for the hearts and minds of the peoples of Southeast Asia and stood turret to turret along what the West styled the Iron Curtain. Once more, the United States was sharpening its sword on the sacred mantle of God. Quoting Thomas Jefferson, who had enshrined in the Declaration of Independence a "firm reliance on the protection of divine Providence,"[8] President Lyndon Johnson told Congress that, "Our efforts on behalf of humanity" meant the nation must "accept the necessity of choosing 'a great evil in order to ward off a greater'"[9] as it pursued the Vietnam war.

The black-and-white foreign policy of the 1960s was somewhat moderated by the realpolitik of Richard Nixon and Henry Kissinger, who pursued a more nuanced "triangular diplomacy" as they sought to play the Soviet Union and China against each other; but with Ronald Reagan's so-called Evil Empire speech in 1987, the forces of light and darkness were once more joined in battle. While the collapse of the Berlin Wall brought the symbolic death of the good versus evil dichotomy of the Cold War, it only confirmed the dominant American self-view as the "City Upon a Hill" with, in the ageless lines of John Winthrop's 1630 poem about the first settlement in the New World, "the eies of all people" upon them.[10] That sense of manifest destiny remained deeply embedded in the American psyche two-and-a-half centuries later when Ronald Reagan reprised Winthrop's words in his now-famous speech named for the poem:

> We cannot escape our destiny, nor should we try to do so. The leadership of the free world was thrust upon us two centuries ago in that little hall of Philadelphia. In the days following World War II, when the economic strength and power of America was all that stood between the world and the return to the dark ages, Pope Pius XII said, "The American people have a great genius for splendid and unselfish actions. Into the hands of America God has placed the destinies of an afflicted mankind." We are indeed, and we are today, the last best hope of man on earth.[11]

Such a self-image leaves little room for nuance or complexity. If *we* represent the forces of light, those who do not share our worldview must inevitably represent the forces of darkness. "Evil," linguist Geoffrey Nunberg has observed, is "a corrective for the excesses of moral relativism, it cleaves neatly between us and them, and it simplifies the business of explaining why we fight, and no less important, why they do."[12] John F. Kennedy pointed to the dangers of such an absolutist worldview when he warned Americans "not to see only a distorted and desperate view of the other side, not to see conflict as inevitable, accommodation as impossible, and communication as nothing more than an exchange of threats."[13] The cost of ignoring such advice has been witnessed in the rice paddies of Vietnam, the rubble of Beirut and on the killing fields of Afghanistan; historically complex conflicts that involved a clashing array of political, ideological, ethnic, economic and religious forces, reduced to black and white by a parade of U.S. administrations. Yet to admit that each of us embodies shades of gray is, in this worldview, to cede the moral high ground. The lower *they* are, the higher *we* are. To accept that our opponent might embody some good, that his/her arguments might have a basis in validity, is to open to the possibility that *we* might have faults.

This "good versus evil" dichotomy is an extension of the more elemental *Us* and *Them* comparison. As human beings, we measure ourselves against the Other. I am white, she is black. I am a member of a certain club, he is not. I am American, she is Russian. It is true of individuals, of communities, of racial and ethnic groups, of nations and of entire peoples: Democrats and Republicans, Harvard and Yale, the British and the French. The boundaries between *Us* and *Them* are constantly shifting, as with siblings who bicker incessantly but instantly unite in the face of a challenge from outside the family. Former president Ronald Reagan jokingly used to say that all it would take for the Arabs and Israelis to set aside their differences was an alien invasion.[14]

This Othering is the basis of the nation-state and it is also the root of much of the world's violence: the Hatfields and the McCoys of the hills of Tennessee, the Crips and the Bloods street gangs of South L.A., the skinheads and the South Asians in Britain, the Maronites and the Druzes of Lebanon, the Hutus and the Tutsis of Rwanda, Washington and Moscow. In short, in order for us to be *Us*, we need to create *Them*. Serbia was a classic example of this. There, psychiatrist and nationalist leader Jovan Raskovic consciously fostered "the fatal salience of in-group–out-group images" to "systematize, compartmentalize, and deindividualize the image" of Bosnian Muslims in order to create the cultural conditions for genocide.[15]

"War begins in the mind, with the idea of the enemy," Vietnam veteran William Broyles once wrote.[16] The psychological manipulation that makes violence possible is not limited to Serbian war criminals. Former diplomat George F. Kennan notes that the creation of this "enemy system" seems essential to America's sense of Self:

> There is a substantial, politically influential, and aggressive body of American opinion for which the specter of a great and fearful external enemy, to be exorcised only by vast military preparations and much belligerent posturing, has become a political and psychological necessity.[17]

As in Serbia, that idea of the Other as enemy is often a chimera manufactured by unseen hands to serve goals that are not truly our own. It is an old trick of leaders under siege. Faced with divisiveness and dissent at home, create an external threat to distract and unite the nation. "[T]he attitude of one people towards another," wrote Harvard psychiatrist John Mack, who was involved in private diplomacy efforts between the Israelis and Palestinians in the 1980s, "is usually determined by leaders who manipulate the minds of citizens for domestic political reasons which are generally unknown to the public."[18]

ORIENTALISM

When it came to America and Islam, the historical frame in which this Othering took place was that of Orientalism, a legacy of colonialism that Edward Said, in his classic work of the same name, described as "a dimension of modern political-intellectual culture" that sees the world divided into two unequal halves, one of which is "manifestly different."[19] In this worldview, the Orient is a semimythical construct used to define that which is "other" than the Occident (or West). In practical terms, Orientalism was also the patronizing mechanism through which the West sought to dominate the East. Intrinsically linked to Western colonialism, Orientalism, as Said defined it, is "the corporate institution for dealing with the Orient . . . in short . . . a Western style for dominating, restructuring, and having authority over the Orient." He went on:

> Orientalism is a style of thought based upon an ontological and epistemological distinction made between "the Orient" and (most of the time) "the Occident." Thus a very large mass of writers . . . have accepted the basic distinction between East and West as the starting point for elaborate theories, epics, novels, social descriptions, and political accounts concerning the Orient, its people, customs, "mind," destiny, and so on.[20]

By framing "Islam" as a monolithic entity, Said wrote, "[l]ocal and concrete circumstances are thus obliterated." Any discussion or examination of Islam becomes "a one-sided activity that obscures what *we* do, and highlights instead what Muslims and Arabs by their very flawed nature *are*."[21] As a result, he argued, the label "Islam" distorted and ideologized Western perceptions of the region and its people. Central to this approach was what Foucault, who heavily influenced Said, called the "truth games" played by those in positions of power, giving them the ability to dictate what is truth and define the sense of Self among all parties to the game.[22]

Said and the other anti-Orientalist voices came under much criticism from traditional Orientalists in academia who argued that it was the crisis of the East, not the crisis of the Orientalist approach to *studying* the East, that was at fault.

The "right" and "wrong" of that debate is largely irrelevant in this context of this book. What *is* relevant is that Said's view of the West's attitude toward the East represents a common perception among Muslims, contributing to the suspicion and resentment that would play such an important role in how Bush administration statements and actions were seen post-9/11. Making matters worse was the arrival of yet another philosophical approach to the Middle East, known as postmodernism. It rejects absolutes and embraces plurality, thus, its critics charged, erasing cultures and creating, in the words of David Lloyd, "[A] global narrative which allows for only one version of human history, [and] the gradual incorporation of all nations by a Western notion of development or modernity."[23]

That same set of accusations, in far less academic language, would be heard in the rhetoric of Osama bin Laden and other radical Islamists.

MUSLIM IDENTITY

The post-9/11 encounter of opposites came as Muslims around the world were struggling with their own sense of identity. Various authors have chronicled the sense of frustration and malaise that has accompanied the failure of Arab nationalism, the neutering of democratic impulses and the anger at the inability of Arab governments to successfully confront Israel. Although flowery rhetoric of Arab unity resounds from Morocco to Oman, a half-century after the colonial powers ceded authority to Arab governments the region remains rife with animosity, intrigue and conspiracy that plays itself out in repression, hidden plots and, occasionally, open conflict.

The highly controversial Fouad Ajami, for one, has built a career pointing out the faults and foibles of the Arab world, a place where he writes, "triumph rarely comes with mercy or moderation."[24] The disdain with which the expatriate Lebanese academic views the Arab world would likely prove fodder for the psychologists. However, it does reflect the struggle within the Middle East to come to terms with the political and economic decay that has left the region and its people awash in "despair and hopelessness" and powerless in the face of the new unipolar world.[25] At a gathering of Muslim leaders in 2004, the secretary-general of the Organization of the Islamic Conference, Abdelwahed Belkeziz, contrasted the unity of the precolonial Islamic Caliphate to the present day, when, he said, the Muslim community is dispersed, divided, diminished and debased, overwhelmed by a debilitating feeling of "powerlessness."[26] Many of these same observations apply equally to the non-Arab Muslim world, a collection of nations ruled largely by generals and dictators (benign or otherwise) or plagued by instability (and frequently both), characterized by disunity and fragmented by nationalism.

As Said and others have rightly pointed out, to speak of "Islam" or "the Muslim world" as a monolith is beyond misleading. The world's 1.2 billion Muslims are "as diverse as humanity itself" and reflect a host of competing religious, political and ideological schools of thought.[27] The domestic challenges of a Malaysia or a Bangladesh are far different from those of a Nigeria or a Somalia. So too are the priorities of their ordinary citizens. Yet one thread binds them together: a reverence for Islam. Islam is, first and foremost, a religion. But, by its very nature, it is also "a complete way of life."[28] An introductory text published by the Muslim International Trust described Islam this way:

> It covers all the things people do in their lifetime. Islam tells us the purpose of our creation, our final destiny and our place among other creatures. It shows us the best way to conduct our private and public affairs, including social, political, economic, moral and spiritual activities.[29]

In his seminal text on Islam, *Milestones*, Sayyid Qu'tb, the Egyptian Muslim Brotherhood ideologist considered the spiritual godfather of modern Islamists, called Islam a "complete system of life for the Muslim community in all its details."[30] Qu'tb went on to explain:

> In this community the beliefs and ideas of individual persons, and their devotional acts and religious observances, as well as their social system and their laws, are all based on submission to Allah alone. If this attitude is eliminated from any of these aspects, the whole of Islam is eliminated.[31]

To be sure, the degree to which individual Muslims – and individual societies – follow the tenets of Islam varies widely. From the doctrinal disagreements over the line of descent from the Prophet Muhammad and the role of the clergy that separate the two largest schools within Islam, the Sunnis and the Shi'ites, to the bitter debates between those who interpret the Qur'an literally and those who favor a more liberal reading that adapts the teachings to the modern world, to the ongoing struggle over whether nations will be governed by religious or secular law, those who call themselves Muslims represent a broad spectrum of opinion, culture and spirituality. There are, simply put, many faces of Islam. Qu'tb insists this is Islam's strength:

> The forms of Islamic civilization constructed on these fixed principles depend on actual conditions and are influenced by or modified according to the level of industrial, economic, or scientific progress of a society. These forms are necessarily different and show that Islam possesses flexibility and can penetrate any system to modify it and use it for its own objectives. But this flexibility in the outward forms of Islamic civilization does not mean any flexibility in the basic Islamic belief.[32]

No matter their cultural mores or political ideologies, even those Muslims who do *not* bow toward Mecca five times a day subscribe to an abiding philosophy first relayed by the Angel Gabriel 1,500 years ago: *la ilaha illa Allah*, There is no god but God; and *Muhammad al-Rasul Allah*, Muhammad is the messenger of Allah.[33]

Arab and non-Arab Muslims thus share a basic worldview that transcends local culture, ethnicity and nationalism. Just as a Judeo-Christian worldview is, at some level, a unifying force among North American and European countries, the Muslim worldview represents "an implicit consciousness of common notions"[34] and unites "a great variety of local cultures more or less embedded in a single great civilization."[35] Scholars have observed that the "Muslim nationalism" of the Ottoman Empire reflected a "corporate identity that was primarily religious."[36] Religion thus becomes a "cultural system"[37] and "religious nationalism" emerges as a political force.[38]

Ernest Gellner has posited that nationalism is primarily a political principle fashioned by a confluence of factors including culture, social and political processes, economic structures, education, geography, religion.[39] But nationalism and its sister, ethnicity, are also "highly complicated and variable phenomena that resist simple diagnoses of any kind."[40] At its core, nationalism represents "an expression of the primordial attachments of an individual to a group . . . which existed long before the group to which such passionate loyalty was attached became the modern nation-state,"[41] a description not much different than that of a worldview.

Thus, a common Muslim worldview served as the foundation from which there arose in the post-9/11 era a resurgent form of Islamic nationalism that reinforced the connection between Muslims across the geographic and political spectrum by reemphasizing their essential sense of Muslim identity in the face of the American Other.

Section I

Foundations of the Relationship

1

In the Eye of the Beholder

Empathize with your enemy. We must try to put ourselves inside their skin and look at us through their eyes just to understand the thoughts that lie behind their decisions and their actions.

Robert McNamara, architect of the Vietnam War

It is impossible to understate the degree to which the Othering of the United States in the Middle East and broader Muslim world was the result of a deep and widespread resentment for what was, and is, seen as decades of biased and misguided policies toward Arabs and Muslims. The essence of this worldview disconnect was encapsulated in the question that rose like a collective moan from the U.S. body politic after 9/11, "Why do they hate us?" and was mirrored by an equally bewildered "Why can't they see?" Much of the answer is found by examining the way in which America's long engagement with the Middle East, and particularly the Israeli–Palestinian conflict, has shaped Arab and Muslim perceptions of the United States. The naiveté of the post-World War I King–Crane Commission that carved up the old Ottoman Empire; the cynicism of Dean Acheson and John Foster Dulles in manipulating regimes in Iran, Egypt, Syria, Jordan and Iraq; and America's increasingly overt pro-Israeli tilt since the 1967 Arab–Israeli war.

After World War I, Woodrow Wilson "followed his idealistic predilections, his chums, and his views of political prudence" and allowed himself to be convinced to support the controversial Balfour Declaration, a British-drafted document calling for the establishment of a homeland for the Jews in Palestine,[1] which a Zionist slogan at the time misleadingly characterized as "A land without people for a people without land."[2] In 1948, America presided over the creation of the state of Israel on what was, to Arabs, undisputedly their land, recognizing the existence of the new state 11 minutes after it declared independence and leaving Arabs wondering "why they had been selected by the West for this particular treatment."[3] Domestic politics was one reason. Responding to State Department advisors who warned that recognizing Israel would have long-term foreign policy implications, Truman said, "I'm sorry, gentlemen, but I have to answer to hundreds of thousands who are anxious for the success of Zionism; I do not have hundreds of thousands of Arabs among my constituents."[4] For posterity, he would write that guilt over America's failure to prevent the Holocaust had left him determined to "make the whole world safe for Jews."[5]

In subsequent decades, Arab bewilderment would turn to anger and then rage as they watched America's relationship with Israel evolve into one of, in their view, blind support. "The United States has a special relationship with Israel comparable only to that which it has with Britain," John F. Kennedy told Israeli foreign minister Golda Meir, expressing a sentiment that would be repeated by American presidents for the next half-century.[6] "The United States is foursquare behind Israel," Lyndon Johnson later confirmed, adding, "[it is] a friend in the truest sense."[7] With Arabs already deeply suspicious of the United States, the so-called Six Day War of 1967 had a "devastating, negative impact on Arab views" of the United States,[8] coming as it did on the heels of several years of disintegrating relations between Washington and Egyptian president Gamal Abdel Nasser, the leading Arab nationalist at the time. When Israel launched its preemptive strike on June 5,

> Arab nationalists . . . felt overwhelming resentment and anger for the Johnson administration, fueled initially by official Egyptian

and Jordanian accusations that the United States had participated alongside Israel in the first air attacks against the Arab forces. Although unfounded, these accusations served to confirm a widely held Arab stereotype of American hostility . . . Egyptians pointed to the fact that although the United States had secured from Egypt a commitment not to fire first, it failed to extract a similar pledge from Israel.[9]

It was an example of the kind of double standard about which Arabs and Muslims would still be complaining in the years after 9/11 as George W. Bush vowed to rid the Middle East of weapons of mass destruction, while failing even to mention Israel's nuclear arsenal.

The 1967 war polarized the region, enmeshed the conflict in the *Us* against *Them* dichotomies of the Cold War and sent the protagonists – reluctantly or not – deep into the waiting arms of their respective patrons. Up until then, the United States had been wooing then-Egyptian president Nasser, while the Israelis received most of their weapons from Moscow. Now, roles were reversed and there began the flow of U.S. weapons and technology to Israel that would give it vastly overwhelming military power. Billions of dollars in military and economic aid and America's veto of 38 UN resolutions criticizing Israel between July 1972 and March 2004 left Arabs with no illusions of U.S. neutrality.[10]

"American domestic politics became a principal component in the events leading to the outbreak of the Arab–Israeli wars,"[11] British historian Ritchie Ovendale wrote of Truman's role in the formation of Israel after World War II. Meanwhile, Israel would likewise become a principal component of U.S. domestic politics. Richard Nixon, for example, was so supportive of Israel during his first term in office that Israeli ambassador Yitzak Rabin openly campaigned for him.[12] That same electoral muscle was also used against politicians and policies perceived as challenging Israel's vital interests. In his controversial 1985 book about those who tried to oppose the Israel lobby, *They Dare to Speak Out*, former Congressman Paul Findley charged that pressures from Israel frequently caused "damage in our relations with Arab states."[13] One example was the 1986 Congressional defeat of a $354 million arms sale to Saudi Arabia, which marked the first time in history that Congress rejected a presidential proposal to sell weapons to a foreign country. "Because of the [Israel] lobby's influence," said Donald McHenry, America's UN ambassador under Jimmy Carter, "our government is unable to pursue its own national interests in the Middle East."[14] American political support for Israel would become so complete that U.S. policymakers would, at Israel's behest, ultimately ban all official contact with Yasser Arafat and his Palestine Liberation Organization, recognized by the UN as the legitimate representative of the Palestinian people, a move, Arabs were fond of pointing out, that the United States did not even take against its own enemy, the Vietcong. Even when the White House did criticize Israeli actions – as when President Reagan suspended shipments of jet fighters in the wake of the Israeli invasion of Lebanon – the Israelis themselves recognized the empty nature of such gestures. "Here is the final irony," wrote Michael Oren of the Shalem Center in Jerusalem, "on those occasions when Israel has asserted, and exercised, its right to self-defense, the American reaction, after an initial burst of anger, has almost always been one of heightened respect."[15] In the case of Reagan and the jets, shipments resumed within months.

By the time George W. Bush began to contemplate a run for the White House, support for Israel was the sine qua non of U.S. presidential politics. "America's special relationship with Israel precedes the peace process," Bush declared in a 2000 campaign appearance. "And Israel's adversaries should know that in my administration, the special relationship will continue, even if they cannot bring themselves to make true peace with the Jewish state."[16] John Kerry would take up that refrain during the 2004 campaign, vowing in an opinion piece written for the New York Jewish newspaper *The Forward*, "We will never compromise America's special relationship with our ally Israel."[17] When their respective vice presidential candidates, Richard Cheney and John Edwards, debated in October 2004, the two men argued which presidential ticket was more committed to defending Israel. The words "Palestine" or "Palestinian" crossed neither man's lips. Such performances were the reason many Muslims saw little distinction between the United States and Israel, which, as one Pakistani writer put it, had become "so intertwined . . . that they exchange roles often, with America becoming Israel's surrogate, indeed proxy."[18]

Resentment of Israel produced a deep vein of anti-Jewish hatred in the Arab world, erroneously called "anti-Semitism" (both Jews and Arabs are Semitic peoples, tracing their lineage back to the prophet Abraham). While the anger was primarily aimed at the state of Israel, not the Jewish people per se, Israel's self-proclaimed status as "the Jewish state" and the proclivity of Israeli officials to equate Israel with Judaism – as in Prime Minister Ariel Sharon's references to terrorism in Israel as attacks "on the Jewish people" – meant that the two often blurred. Jewish financier George Soros observed, "The policies of the Bush administration and the Sharon administration contribute to that. It's not specifically anti-Semitism, but it does manifest itself in anti-Semitism as well."[19] Anti-Zionist sentiment in the Arab world, therefore, was often indistinguishable from anti-Jewish sentiment. There were many ugly products of this anger. *The Protocols of the Elders of Zion*, a Czarist tract alleging a Jewish conspiracy to control the world, was available in many Middle East bookstores (rich Saudis financed the translations). During the Muslim holy month of Ramadan in 2002, an Egyptian satellite channel, Dream TV, ran a television serial entitled

Horseman without a Horse, based loosely on the *Elders of Zion* fabrication. Long-time Syrian defense minister Mustafa Tlass published a book, *The Matzah of Zion*, perpetuating the lie first spread in Europe that Jews use Christian blood to make matzos during Passover.[20] Abu Dhabi's royal family helped fund, and Libyan leader Muammar Qaddafi presented a human rights prize to, a French revisionist historian who was put on trial in France for denying the reality of the Holocaust. But more rational voices could also be heard. As *Horseman* was airing, Egyptian presidential advisor Osama el-Baz told the *al-Ahram* newspaper:

> We must uphold the correct perspective on our relationship with the Jews, as embodied in the legacy of Arab civilization and in our holy scriptures. This legacy holds that ours is not a tradition of racism and intolerance, that the Jews are our cousins through common descent from Abraham and that our only enemies are those who attack us.[21]

THE ISRAELI–AMERICAN "US"

Domestic American politics was one reason for the "special relationship" between the United States and Israel, but the connection also went deeper, inextricably linked to the concepts of worldview and Othering – tinged with racism – that so colored U.S. relations with the Muslim world. America's suspicion of Islam stretched back to the dawn of the republic. Cotton Mather, the famous minister of Boston's Old North Church, had railed against "Mahometan Turks and Moors, and Devils" when reports of the imprisonment of North Americans by the Barbary pirates trickled back to the colonies in the late 1600s. He took pride in the fact that "we are afar off, in a Land, which never had (that I ever heard of) one Mahometan breathing in it."[22] Mather and other American Protestant religious leaders commonly equated Muhammad with the Antichrist and linked Islam to

Armageddon, a theme still heard in the sermons of televangelists like Pat Robertson and Franklin Graham. Aaron Burr wrote of the "Rise of that false Prophet and great Impostor Mahomet,"[23] and from the earliest days, Islam became an epithet in American politics. John Adams was accused of being the new Muhammad and John Quincy Adams compared Jefferson to "the Arabian prophet."[24] Benjamin Franklin's Poor Richard wondered aloud, "Is it worse to follow Mahomet than the Devil?"[25] In fact, it was the confrontation with the Barbary pirates over the taking of American slaves that became the young republic's first foreign policy challenge – and its first real encounter with Islam.

In contrast to this history, many Americans felt a natural affinity with the people of Israel. They were, after all, "like us," citizens of a Western-style democracy whose leaders, through much of the twentieth century, were largely born in the West (Israeli image-makers downplayed the fact that by the mid-1970s Oriental, or non-Western Jews, were the majority).[26] Israeli prime minister Golda Meir, everybody's grandmother, grew up in the United States and taught school there before emigrating to Israel. Prime minister Benjamin Netanyahu went to high school in Philadelphia and spoke American-accented English. There was a sense of shared identity because, after all, many Israelis *were* Americans; the law of *aliyah* gave every Jew the right to claim Israeli citizenship upon setting foot on the soil of the Promised Land. This connection was assiduously cultivated. Each summer, planeloads of American students enjoyed all-expenses-paid trips to Israel, grassroots organizations like B'nai Brith made Israel's cause their own, and, whenever possible, the spokespeople the Israeli government made available to American reporters had American accents (as those with British accents often appeared on British TV). All this was bolstered by the fact that American reporters gave Israel a relatively free ride. "The American media is far less critical of Israeli policies than we in the Israeli press," says Nathan Guttman, Washington correspondent for the Israeli daily *Ha'aretz*.[27]

This careful crafting of Israel's image as an outpost of Western democracy – some would say America's 51st state – helped to produce a gut-level sympathy for the Israeli cause on the part of many Americans. Madeleine Albright admits that it was not until she met with a group of students on the West Bank while serving as secretary of state in the Clinton administration that she began to understand the Palestinian point of view: "I was brought up completely seeing the Israeli side."[28]

The Arabs spent millions of dollars on public relations firms in an effort to make their own connection with U.S. opinion leaders and the body politic, to no avail. They remained the Other. "Israel sends its best people to interact with the policy and opinion makers in Washington, while the Arabs host parties and indulge in public relations exercises which fail to convey much," Benjamin Bradlee, the former managing editor of *The Washington Post*, told a 2002 gathering in Dubai.[29] Nor did efforts to organize the Arab vote meet with any more success. "Arab Americans do not vote as a block," explains James Zogby, president of the Arab American Institute, the main Arab lobbying group. "They come from many different countries with many different ideologies and outlooks. They are Republican businessmen and Democratic factory workers. There is no one issue that unites their vote."[30]

A LOVE–HATE RELATIONSHIP

The Arab–Israeli conflict may have been the root of Muslim – and particularly Arab – anger at the United States, but a host of other issues also fueled resentment: restoring the father of the Shah to his throne after a coup in the 1950s; the dispatch of the U.S. Marines to Lebanon to shore up minority

Christian governments in both the 1950s and the 1980s; unquestioning support for the feudal rulers of Saudi Arabia and the Gulf states, and authoritarian leaders like Anwar Sadat and Hosni Mubarak of Egypt; the cynical, secret arming of Saddam Hussein during the Iran–Iraq war. Arabs point to these and a host of other examples of American oppression and hypocrisy that produced "a pervasive sense of external, Western, manipulation of the politics of the region."[31]

Yet historically, hatred of American policy has not automatically meant hatred of Americans. Very little serious public opinion research was conducted in Muslim-majority countries until recent years. However, those surveys that were carried out showed "a strong dislike for American foreign policy but much more nuanced, and often quite positive, attitudes toward Americans society and culture and toward the American people."[32] It is a finding backed by widespread, street-level experience, producing such seemingly bizarre encounters as my conversation with a member of Hizbullah, the radical Shi'ite militia responsible for a string of suicide attacks against American interests in Lebanon, who both denounced "the Great Satan" and wished aloud he could qualify for a U.S. visa. "It is a love–hate relationship, of course," explained Jordan's then-foreign minister Marwan Muasher. "Culturally, American music is popular, American food is popular, American clothes are popular. People still wear jeans with American flags on them. And they don't see any contradiction in that despite the animosity towards America."[33]

With the so-called "war on terror," that distinction began to disappear. An ignorance of global affairs on the part of the U.S. public, coupled with what veteran diplomat Barry Zorthian called a "disdain for 'the opinions of mankind' "[34] on the part of the nation's leaders, began to erase the distinction between individual Americans and U.S. policy. Feeding the resentment were the images of themselves that

Arabs and Muslims saw reflected in the lens of the Western media. All this threatened to make the so-called clash of civilizations a self-fulfilling prophecy. Writing from Cairo in early 2002, journalist Emad Mekay noted that as the question "Why do they hate us?" was reverberating through U.S. society, "Arabs and Muslims ask the same question – only here, 'they' refers to the West."[35] Many Arabs and Muslims charged that the Western media's use of white Western "experts" on Islam, rather than Muslims themselves, further distorted American perceptions. "The real question is not who hates who," another Arab journalist wrote, "It is in fact, 'Why the West hates us so much?'"[36]

"There is little doubt that stereotypes of Americans as arrogant, self-indulgent, hypocritical, inattentive, and unwilling or unable to engage in cross-cultural dialogue are pervasive and deep rooted," reported the Council on Foreign Relations.[37] For the majority of Arabs and Muslims who are not fluent in English, there was a dearth of information to help counter those stereotypes. Few serious and balanced books about the United States were available in Arabic, and – despite hundreds of millions of dollars spent by the U.S. government on international public diplomacy efforts over the decades – fewer still translations of the basic documents and seminal thinkers of American democracy. As a result, according to Middle East scholar Juan Cole, "most of what ordinary Middle Easterners know about the U.S. is via Hollywood."[38]

Ziauddin Sardar and Merryl Wyn Davies frame the contrast between America's self-image and the image many Muslims have of America in the language of the quintessential Hollywood western:

> American political rhetoric may circle its wagons around old familiar idea of national self-identity, with clear and certain recognition of the need for self-preservation and security. But beyond the comforting wood-smoke and firelight, outside that circle, the meaning is plain: other people will have to die.[39]

After a half-century of Othering, most Arabs and non-Arab Muslims had no illusions about either the truth of those words or who those "other people" might be.

THE ECONOMICS OF ALIENATION

It wasn't just Arabs and Muslims who felt alienated. There were plenty of other people in the world with reason to be suspicious of the United States. "U.S. actions over the last 55 years have contributed, directly and indirectly, to the slaughter of over 10 million Asians," read the very first words of Indian author Patwant Singh's 2004 book.[40] While his precise figures were open to dispute, Singh's sentiments were shared by many in what has been called the "South." Economics were one cornerstone of this view. With the collapse of the Soviet Union, Bush Senior's New World Order emerged, "crafted largely in America's image and likeness."[41] The implications of this new unipolar world were quickly felt by the Arabs as the elder Bush sent U.S. forces pouring into the Middle East to repulse Saddam Hussein's invasion of Kuwait, leaving many Arabs frustrated "at the way their destinies are being manipulated within the framework of the 'new world order.' "[42] That sense of alienation was shared by the poor masses and their spokespeople among the "progressive" intelligentsia of places like India, the Congo and Bolivia, who felt abandoned and exploited by a New World Order that dangled the fruits of progress just out of reach on the far side of the television screen. "In today's globalized world, America is seen as the prime cause of everything. Nothing seems to move without America's consent; nothing can be solved without America's involvement," wrote Sardar and Davies, thus creating "the cosmological grounds for resentment."[43]

In many important ways then, Bush Sr. effectively set the stage for his son's "monumental struggle of good versus evil."[44] This view was at the core of an essay by Indian writer Arundhati Roy published just after 9/11, which posited bin Laden as Bush Junior's dark doppelganger:

> He has been sculpted from the spare rib of a world laid to waste by America's foreign policy: its gunboat diplomacy, its nuclear arsenal, its vulgarly stated policy of "full-spectrum dominance," its chilling disregard for non-American lives, its barbarous military interventions, its support for despotic and dictatorial regimes, its merciless economic agenda that has munched through the economies of poor countries like a cloud of locusts, its marauding multinationals who are taking over the air we breathe, the ground we stand on, the water we drink, the thoughts we think.[45]

The article streaked across the Internet, eliciting shock and excitement in "progressive" intellectual circles. Did they really think that of us? It was a revelation – and a commentary on how ignorant Americans were about how they were percieved by much of the globe.

ISLAMIST PERCEPTIONS

If Arab fans of Big Macs and Nikes harbored a love–hate relationship with the United States, conservative elements in the Muslim world had a far more black-and-white view. For them, the American consumer culture was a corrupting influence that threatened to engulf their traditional societies. The battle over the "indiginisation of American culture"[46] said as much about the conflicts within Arab and Muslim society as it did about the relationship between the inhabitants of those societies and the West. An example was the reaction of conservative clerics to the popular Arabic versions of Western-style reality shows that began airing on television stations in the Middle East. One program, a remake of the European-American show *Big Brother*, was cancelled after more than 1,000 protesters took to the streets in Bahrain, where it was being filmed. Unlike in the Western versions, where the housemates shared rooms and much more, the sexes were strictly segregated in the Arab version. But that was not enough for some. "I have watched the show and it must be stopped," said 34-year-old teacher Shahnaz Rabi'i, an organizer of the demonstration. "Our religion has strong values which say boys and girls should not mix together. This programme is a threat to Islam. This is entertainment for animals."[47] A similar program on another channel prompted a sharp reaction from the Kuwaiti Ministry of Islamic Affairs. When the cast of *Star Academy*, a combination of *Big Brother* and *American Idol*, came to Kuwait to perform after a Kuwaiti won the contest, the ministry, under pressure from the Islamist faction in parliament, issued a *fatwa* banning all concerts by the producers "as long as they include practices forbidden by Islam" such as "women singing to men not related to them, mixing between the sexes when women are revealing part of their body, and the use of vulgar words and dancing."[48] The ruling came as the prime minister announced plans to launch another effort to pass legislation giving women the vote, a move previously defeated by the conservative Islamist faction.

No worldview was more completely at odds with that of the majority of Americans than that of the Islamists who sought the implementation of Islamic – or Divine – law, known in Arabic as *shari'a*. For them, the world was divided into *dar-ul-Islam*, the lands of Islam, and *jahiliyya*, the lands of barbarism. To the more extreme among them, not only were Western infidels the enemy, but so too were fellow Muslims who did not subscribe to their worldview. "Many thought I meant the Communist party when I wrote 'the Devil's party,'" Egyptian Islamist Wail Uthman said after publication of his book *The Party of God in Struggle with the Party of Satan*. "The Party of Satan is that group of people who pretend to believe in Islam but in reality

are Islam's first enemies."[49] To the head of Pakistan's
Jamaat-e-Islami party, those enemies included the leaders of
many Muslim countries who were "under control of Jews
and Christians who have now joined hands all over the
world to subjugate and coerce Muslim people."[50]

Islamism is a reaction to a host of developments: Ataturk's
elimination of the Caliphate in 1924, the disempowerment
that came with the West's creation of nation-states in the
Arab world after World War I, the demonization of Islam by
Western leaders and media, the sense of victimization at the
hands of Western Christians, the double standard, hypocrisy
and duplicity of U.S. policies toward the Middle East and
Muslim countries, and the hegemony of the New World
Order. One of the most intriguing in the blizzard of Western
theories of what drives the Islamists is that offered by
Islamic historian Yvonne Yazbeck Haddad, who argues that
"Islamism can be said to be a kind of mirror image of
Zionism . . . an attempt to emulate what is perceived as a
winning Israeli formula in which religious zeal, divine
justification, scriptural prooftexting, and victimization are
employed to mobilize" support.[51]

Maulana Maududi (1903–1979), a seminal figure in
Islamist thinking, first proposed the idea that the West was
the modern incarnation of *jahiliyya*. His spiritual heir, the
late Egyptian Islamist ideologue Sayyid Qu'tb, regularly
preached against "the rubbish heap of the West" after
spending a year in the United States in the late 1940s.
In *Milestones*, Qu'tb wrote of how he told Americans he
encountered that he was repulsed by

> . . . this individual freedom, devoid of human sympathy and
> responsibility for relatives except under the force of law; this
> materialistic attitude which deadens the spirit; this behavior, like
> animals, which you call "free mixing of the sexes"; this vulgarity
> which you call "emancipation of women"; these unfair and
> cumbersome laws of marriage and divorce . . . .[52]

Upon returning home to Egypt, he was equally incensed by "the evil and dirty materialism of the East." This led him to conclude that it was up to "true" Muslims to struggle against *jahiliyya* without compromise wherever they found it.

> The chasm between Islam and *jahiliyya* is great, and a bridge is not to be built across it so that the people on the two sides may mix with each other, but only so that the people of *jahiliyya* may come over to Islam.[53]

Such views represented the hard right of Islamist politics. They were anathema to the majority of Muslims. Yet buffeted in the swirling eddies between these two currents of thought was what Pakistani scholar Akbar Ahmed calls "the restless generation" now coming of age in Muslim societies:

> It has grown up with the media and feels familiar with American culture. It is ambiguous about what it sees: it cannot live by the American standards it observes, yet paradoxically, it wants them. It also feels contempt for much of what it sees on television (particularly sex and violence) and believes it to be representative of American society. Frustrated, it finds its only legitimate sense of identity in its own traditional civilization, which is Islam. This generation therefore emphasizes its Islamic identity by rejecting the West.[54]

This trend was given new impetus in the rhetorical cacophony of the post-9/11 world, amplifying the core messages and influence of the Islamists, simultaneously alienating and drowning out moderate voices, creating a heightened sense of Muslim identity and speeding a shift in opinion within the broad Muslim body politic toward opposition to U.S. hegemony and support for political change.

2
U.S. Coverage of Islam

If [the media] is to serve and survive, it must hold a mirror up to the nation and the world . . . The mirror must have no curves, and be held with a steady hand.

Edward R. Murrow

I n the eyes of its critics, the U.S. media has had a long and inglorious relationship with the world's Muslims, characterized by stereotype, distortion and oversimplification. That cliché-ridden history created the frame through which Americans viewed Islam and those who practiced it in the wake of 9/11: dehumanizing Muslims, creating the cultural ground for violence and fueling the subsequent polarization of attitudes between the U.S. and the Muslim world.

First published in 1981 in response to coverage of the Palestinian–Israeli conflict and the Iranian revolution, the late Edward Said's now-classic work, *Covering Islam*, criticized both academics and reporters for the "patent inaccuracy" that he claimed has historically characterized U.S. media coverage of Arabs and Muslims, an approach that he charged has been driven by "unrestrained ethnocentrism, cultural and even racial hatred."[1] Such coverage, Said and the other early authors on the subject wrote, reflected the Arab stereotypes that had become common currency on television, in political cartoons and in popular works of fiction, and were reinforced by the so-called "talking heads" who play a critical role in shaping news coverage. Jack Shaheen's landmark studies of Arab images on television and in Hollywood concluded that the entertainment media perpetuates four basic myths about Arabs: " . . . they are all fabulously wealthy; they are barbaric and uncultured; they are sex maniacs with a penchant for white slavery; and they revel in act of terrorism."[2]

As a result of such conditioning, Arabs are "dehumanized"[3] in the minds of many Americans, which thus leads some reporters to "think restrictively and reductively in us-versus-them dichotomies,"[4] presenting a one-dimensional version of the Middle East conflict in which the Arabs are cast in a negative light. Equally criticized is the journalistic shorthand that distorts peoples, nations and religions. "Ill-equipped" in terms of education or experience, reporters substitute cliché for knowledge and "raid the Orientalist cupboard for alimentation, picking up old prejudices and scatological bits of information."[5] The notion that U.S. journalists report on the Middle East and Islam through the "fundamentally, . . . [and] radically, fractious"[6] worldview of Orientalism lies at the heart of Edward Said's thesis.

In *Split Vision*, journalist-scholar Edmund Ghareeb endorsed Said's premise, arguing that "the residual culture gap between Arabs and the West"[7] is at the root of flawed U.S. reporting of the Middle East. This tendency to frame the region within the constructs of the colonial legacy, combined with an "ignorance"[8] of its complexities on the part of those covering it, contributed to the creation of the "pro-Israeli and anti-Arab bias"[9] in the media. This argument was supported by several content analyses of the U.S. newspapers in the period from the 1940s through the 1970s, which concluded that U.S. reporters generally dehumanized and largely ignored the Palestinians.[10] Interestingly, those who conversely claim the media embodies an *anti*-Israeli bias, such as Ze'ev Chafets, spokesman to then-prime minister

Menachim Begin, likewise point to a failure of U.S. reporters to know and understand the *Arab* world.[11]

Another key theme woven through such critiques of U.S. coverage of Arabs and Muslims is the tendency to blur the line between the two, as well as the media's reliance on scholars (or those who position themselves as scholars) who generalize about "the Arab mind,"[12] "the lands of Islam,"[13] and "Islamdom"[14] as a place, thing, or a state of mind. In an observation that still resonates two decades later, Said argued that the very notion of "Islam" as "some real and stable object out there"[15] was flawed; a situation he found unchanged a decade-and-a-half later when he wrote the introduction to the 1996 edition of *Covering Islam*:

> . . . [R]easoned, well-researched, alternative views have been barely in evidence; the market for representations of a monolithic, enraged, threatening, and conspiratorially spreading Islam is much greater, more useful, and capable of generating much more excitement, whether for purposes of entertainment or of mobilizing passions against a new foreign devil.[16]

"Islam" is thus reduced to "a commodity"[17] peddled by self-appointed experts who "pontificate on formulaic ideas about Islam on news programs and talk shows."[18] Against this background, critics say, the media first built the frame for Islam that would ultimately be used in the 9/11 era. One content analysis of news reporting about the Middle East in *The New York Times* between 1917 and 1947 concluded that "overall coverage had set the ground for a conflict-oriented image for the Arabs prior to 1948."[19]

Historically, the critics say, the media has treated Islam "as very backward and medieval. There was an arrogance [on the part of the media] that the idea of an effective, modern form of Islam was inconceivable, and that in order to be modern, it had to be a carbon copy of the West."[20] As a result, complained one Egyptian journalist, "When the foreign media direct their attention to the region, they do so with a preconceived idea of what the Arab world is like. Few come with an open mind to find a different image."[21]

Much of the analysis of U.S. coverage of the Middle East is critical of the failure of U.S. news organizations to allow their reporters to put down roots in order to gain expertise in the region, much less learn the language. Said contrasts them with European journalists such as Eric Rouleau of *Le Monde* (who later became a French diplomat) and David Hirst of the *Guardian*, who spent three decades covering the Middle East. However, as low as is his regard for print reporters, Said reserves his greatest scorn for their television colleagues: "The odds against adequate reporting by the network reporter, who is likely to be even more itinerant than the print journalist, makes the latter seem like an encyclopedia of knowledge and serenity in comparison."[22]

As a former Middle East correspondent for CBS News, this writer can attest that there is more than a kernel of truth to the allegation. Like their print colleagues, TV correspondents based in the Middle East worked hard to ground themselves in the complexities of the region. But that often comes only after we arrive. I was a young freelance reporter in Africa when CBS hired me for the Middle East. I was chosen not for my regional expertise, but because I had a track-record covering wars. The dictates of what has come to be called "parachute journalism" meant that though my beat was the Arab world, I was just as likely to find myself metaphorically parachuting into a story in South Africa or India. Likewise, when a big story broke in the region, the Middle East-based correspondent was likely to be supplanted by a star correspondent sent in from London or even New York, who knew little more about the situation than what s/he read in the background files on the flight.

Rouleau himself highlighted another criticism of the Western media's coverage of Islam, the tendency to use generic photographs of Muslims praying, mosques or women in chadors to illustrate stories about extremism and terror. At a 2002 Arab media summit in Dubai, the former journalist and diplomat told of picking up a special issue of a French newsweekly which carried the title 'Fanaticism" in bold red letters on the cover. "I opened the magazine to find that all the articles were on Islam. But what did the reader see? He saw that Islam had a relationship with fanaticism!"[23]

Although built on a firm foundation of historical documentation, the work of Said and some other critics does, however, reflect a certain naiveté about how the media works. One Canadian Muslim group released an 'anti-Islam' glossary listing scores of terms, such as "radical Muslim faction" and "Muslim extremist," which it insisted should not be used by the media. But it offered no viable alternatives.[24] Said would have reporters use the terms "Islam" and "Islamic" only "with great restraint and many qualifications," while Canadian scholar Karim Karim argues that even acts of terrorism carried out by a group that called itself Islamic Jihad "cannot be considered 'Islamic'. . . [or] . . . even considered to be expressions of 'Muslim terrorism.'"[25] Instead, he endorses the argument that "Islam" should be reserved for "the 'metaphysical, religious, spiritual' dimension of the faith," while the term "Muslim" should be used "in a qualified sense, for 'the second level of signification, [which] is the sociohistorical space in which human existence unfolds.'"[26] Such ivory-tower arguments are greeted with derision by working reporters and undermine the many valid criticisms embodied in these books. Covering the 1985 TWA hijacking, I was not inclined to challenge the hijackers on the choice of their organization's name, Islamic Jihad, or point out to my audience that the word "Islamic" really shouldn't be used because the drama was unfolding in a sociohistorical, rather than metaphysical, space. They called themselves Islamic, they had the guns. Who was I to argue? Likewise, Iran, Saudi Arabia and other Muslim-majority countries define themselves in terms of Islam. As Malaysian political scientist Farish Noor has written:

> While it is true that the international media has done some damage to the understanding of 'jihad,' it is also important for Muslims to realise that the term itself has been used and abused by the very same people who have resorted to the use of violence in their name.[27]

TERRORISM AND THE MEDIA

While Said and his contemporaries concentrated their attentions on how U.S. reporters covered Arabs and Muslims, a second set of media critics emerged who focused on the coverage of terror and terrorist acts. The latter included both academics and politically motivated individuals.

Societies are shaped by media. So, too, has been the world's relationship with terrorism, which could not have emerged in its present form and influence without television. As far back as 1979, a demand that the media "deny them publicity" was made at the First International Conference on Terrorism, a gathering in Jerusalem that brought together Americans, Europeans and Israelis, but notably, no Muslims, to discuss the "special relationship" between terrorism and Islam.[28] This demand was based on the belief that terrorists had become "the master of ceremonies at a media spectacle."[29]

The 1972 Munich Olympics was frequently cited by those who espoused this view. It has been called "the premier example of terrorism's power to rocket a cause from obscurity to renown."[30] There, Palestinian gunmen operating under the banner of the Black September faction, held hostage a group of Israeli athletes for 24 hours before a worldwide television audience estimated at 900 million. Though all of the hostages and all but three of the gunmen were killed in the ensuing gun battle with German commandos, and none of the Palestinians' demands were met, Munich was an unequivocal success for Black September because it vaulted the Palestinian cause to the top of the international agenda. "Before Munich, we were a forgotten people; afterwards, everyone knew our plight," a Palestinian official involved in Black September once told me, with a mixture of pride and regret. The – inevitable – massive coverage of terrorist acts against U.S. and Israeli targets that followed ushered in an era of mass-mediated terrorism that fed a cycle of violence. Carlos the Jackal, Abu Nidal and other terrorists became the Che Guevaras of their age.

The Munich Olympics, the circus-like atmosphere of the 1985 TWA hijacking and similar events were examples of what critics called "terrorist theater" and "media terrorism"[31] in which the goal "was not revenge, it was airtime."[32] Reporters, such critics charged, served as "card-carrying participants who helped to shape and direct the unfolding drama"[33] in partnership with the now media-savvy terrorists, who were "aware of the particular frames designed for news stories"[34] and frequently "design their atrocities for television."[35] For those of us involved in covering terrorism, such criticism stings. Yet a reality check is in order. There inevitably exists a symbiotic relationship between the news media and groups that stage dramatic acts – terrorist or otherwise. This was particularly true before a sense of patriotism began to color U.S. reporting post-9/11. Simply put, such acts could not be ignored. Any reporter who tried would quickly be out of a job. For example, as the sole CBS News correspondent in Beirut in the first days of the TWA hijacking referred to above, I was under tremendous pressure from my bosses in New York to report every minor development. That pressure was particularly intense since my competitors at ABC News had, through one of their local staffers, a direct line to Shi'ite militia figures close to the hijackers. By providing ABC with exclusive access to the hostages in carefully stage-managed settings, such as a seafront hotel restaurant, the hijackers and their allies effectively manipulated America's image of the crisis. CBS management in New York decried this incestuous relationship, but it was not long before I was asked whether money would buy us access. I made it clear I would have nothing to do with such an offer, but the incident is indicative of the degree to which terrorist theater is as valuable to the networks as any other form of entertainment that drives ratings. In short, terror sells, which is why any working definition of terrorism includes publicity as a key component. The act itself is not enough. It must strike fear in a broader public. And to do that, it must be widely reported by the media.

The Information Age reality that "the report of the event is as important as the event itself"[36] is reflected in the fact that the majority of Americans firmly identify suicide terrorism with the Middle East[37] despite the fact that almost half of all suicide bombings between 1983 and 2000 were carried out in connection with the conflict in Sri Lanka.[38] Some media critics claim this is the result of "the anti-Muslim, anti-Islamic feelings that permeate American newsrooms,"[39] but the real explanation lies in the parochial nature of the U.S. media, its ethnocentric, nationalistic bias and the high level of identification with Israel among the American public.[40]

The U.S. media caters to the appetite of its audience and until the growth of alternative media sources in the late 1990s, mainstream media organizations, in the form of the television networks and a handful of influential newspapers, had a near monopoly on the U.S. public's perception of the world (and, in fact, the world's perception of itself). These elite U.S. organizations had the power to define what is news. In the infamous words of former NBC anchorman David Brinkley, "News is what I say it is."[41] The public's lack of awareness of Sri Lankan terrorism had nothing to do with some journalistic bias that emphasized Middle East terrorism to make Arabs or Muslims look bad. The Sri Lankans were, for the most part, killing other Sri Lankans or Indian troops, which put their actions far outside the U.S. media's very limited radar screen. Bottom line: the U.S. audience didn't care, so neither did the media. But when suicide bombers blew up U.S. embassies and cafes full of Israelis, they *did* care.

However guilty it may be in sensationalizing terrorist actions aimed at people with whom the U.S. public identifies, the media is ultimately caught in the classic Catch-22. ABC *Nightline* host Ted Koppel (a beneficiary of terrorism, since the Iran hostage crisis made his career) summed up the conundrum:

> Without television, terrorism becomes rather like the philosopher's hypothetical tree falling in the forest: no one hears it fall and therefore it has no reason for being. And television without terrorism, while not deprived of all the interesting things in the world, is nonetheless deprived of one of the most interesting.[42]

FRAMING

Media theory holds one clue to why the media in the United States and the Muslim world covered post-9/11 events from such different perspectives. Journalists rely upon "news frames"[43] that simplify and prioritize news to fit existing societal concepts, values and knowledge. These frames "convey dominant meanings" and "provide contextual cues, giving meaning and order to complex problems . . . by slotting the new into familiar categories or storyline 'pegs.'"[44] In short, they put the story in a context the audience can understand. News frames are based on the prevailing societal narratives about people, places and events and "reflect the power relations of the general society."[45] They are often established, at least in part, by the public statements of political leaders and, in turn influence public opinion and the policy process: "Reporters can . . . 'tell it like it is' within 60 seconds, or within brief newspaper headlines, rapidly sorting key events from surrounding trivia, by drawing on reservoirs of familiar stories to cue readers."[46]

With 9/11, the U.S. media immediately fell back on the prevailing – and stereotyped – narrative about Arabs and Muslims and reverted to its historic tendency to present the world, in Henry Kissinger's words, as "a morality play between good and evil."[47] The crisis was reported from within a clearly delineated good guy/bad guy frame, set out in President Bush's now-famous "either you are with us, or you're with the terrorists"[48] dichotomy. The terms "Islam," "Muslim," and "terrorist" were intrinsically linked and became what the psychologists call "labels of primary potency,"[49] terms that grabbed the audience's attention and held it. Islam took the Soviet Union's place as America's new "Other" and "Islamic violence" became the new threat. That message had been driven home as early as 1996 with an Elaine Sciolino *Week in Review* article in *The New York Times* entitled "Seeing Green; The Red Menace is Gone. But Here's Islam."

In her lead, Sciolino wrote:

> When Americans consider the safety of the world these days, many still seem conditioned to look for end-of-the-world threats that must be confronted. The end of the cold war sparked a kind of intellectual contest to identify the biggest and most credible new enemy . . . [O]ne threat has resonated in the public mind: Islamic holy war.[50]

The veteran foreign affairs writer went on to punch holes in the argument that Islam constituted the new "green menace," rhetorically asking whether Sheikh Omar Abdel Rahman, who had just been convicted for the first World Trade Center bombing, was "the emissary of a global threat to America and its allies, or just another opportunist with a claim to God's truth, a band of followers and not much of a future?" But, as Sciolino documented, the notion that Islam itself constituted a vicious new challenge resonated with many Americans; here was the ultimate Other, the little-understood force against which Western Christendom had repeatedly clashed through the ages. Rather than having to construct a new paradigm, clash theorists simply replaced the communist East with an older, and more primal enemy, the Islamic East.

No wonder then, that in the wake of 9/11, American reporters – consciously or not – tapped the perennial and deep-seated Western fear of resurgent Islam with reporting focusing on *what* "they" were rather than *why* they were doing it. Some of the images associated with this coverage, particularly on certain editorial pages, were darkly reminiscent of the anti-Nazi propaganda of World War II, epitomized by ubiquitous cartoons of the bloodthirsty Saracen wielding "the sword of Islam." One such panel, first published in the *Montreal Gazette*, summed up this Othering. It depicted a vicious dog, fangs bared, wearing an Arab headscarf. The headline read: "In the name of Islamic extremism." A cartoon balloon below the image added this note: "With our apologies to dogs everywhere."[51] Dogs are considered dirty in Islam, adding to the insult. It is difficult to conceive of a North American newspaper running such a cartoon with the headline: "In the name of Jewish extremism," or "In the name of Christian extremism." This was not the work of some isolated racist. The man responsible has been called Canada's premier editorial-page cartoonist. While among the more egregious examples, the cartoon was one of many post-9/11 media images offensive to North American Muslims.

In much of the mainstream U.S. media, there was only the most cursory of efforts to understand the motivations of those who had carried out the attacks, or even the perspectives of the world's 1 billion-plus Muslims. The plaintive cry of "Why do they hate us?" rose from the U.S. public, but few waited to hear the answer. A handful of writers for the nation's largest newspapers touched on the roots of anger – but it was often only in the most tentative of ways. After listing all the positive things the U.S. was doing for the world's Muslims, as evidence of why they should feel positively toward the U.S., the *Wall Street Journal's* Gerald Seib, a former Middle East correspondent, gingerly added, "This isn't to say there aren't legitimate complaints about America in the Islamic world. Surely, there are."[52]

One notable exception to this pattern was Peter Jennings, anchor of the ABC *World News Tonight* and himself a former Middle East correspondent. But such attempts to explain that there might be another perspective worth hearing were soon drowned out in the national chorus of "America the Beautiful." The White House wrote a script that left little room for dissent. Events were described in the language of war and a "rally-round-the-flag impulse" took hold, with television newscasts draped in red, white and blue, orders given to "tie facts to a pro-U.S. perspective,"[53] and talk of a rising terror threat from militant Islamists feeding on what has been called the nation's culture of fear. It was as if the American body politic had been consciously primed: "Almost entirely ignorant of global politics, devoid of any understanding of the Islamic world, educated primarily by Hollywood movies featuring Arnold Schwarzenegger, Bruce Willis, and Sylvester Stallone, Americans were ideally prepared for a paranoid and hysterical response."[54]

CNN offered one example of this pro-American bias draped in a cloak of objectivity. During the invasion of Afghanistan, CNN reporters and producers were instructed to "balance" any reporting of Afghan civilian casualties with reminders that the carnage of 9/11 prompted the invasion, because, CNN Chairman Walter Isaacson told his staff, it "seems perverse to focus too much on the casualties or hardship in Afghanistan."[55] A memo distributed by CNN's head of standards and practices actually gave on-air reporters suggested language to insert into their stories. Such phrases, he told them, might include: "We must keep in mind, after seeing reports like this from Taliban-controlled areas, that these U.S. military actions are in response to a terrorist attack that killed close to 5,000 innocent people in the U.S." The memo went on to say, "though it may start sounding rote, it is important that we make this point each time."[56] But even with such caveats, according to *New York Times* foreign editor Roger Cohen, the public wasn't much interested in hearing about what was widely considered the "collateral damage" of America's war on terror, therefore "to get a story about five Afghan villagers being killed in apparently misdirected attacks . . . onto the front page was extremely difficult."[57]

JIHAD JOURNALISM

The U.S. government does not overtly control the American media. However, a tendency on the part of the media to rely on official sources and repeat prevailing wisdom means that official Washington plays an important role in shaping the broad themes reflected in coverage and helping to direct where the media spotlight will shine at any given time.

In his theory of media effects, Robert Entman sketched a "cascading model" of public policy communications flow in which the initial White House framing of a given issue acti-vates "thoughts and ideas" in the minds of elite journalists and other power-brokers, cascades down through the media pecking order, then resonates back up the network. In some instances, according to this theory, a cacophony of dissent among those elites will undermine the administration's attempt to frame policy. Hence, the practice of unnamed sources releasing trial balloons to see whether particular policy approaches will fly. However, after 9/11, there was near unanimity of sentiment among the elites and, as a result, "the news made little room for any but official, government-sanctioned interpretations."[58]

Patriotism, which in times of national crisis becomes the glue that binds what political scientist Benedict Anderson has called the "imagined political community,"[59] emerged as the dominant narrative post-9/11, no less in the media than in society at large. Terrorism itself became the "imagined" landscape on which the nation's future would be written. "Patriotism was the administration's ally, building a protective wall around its policy," veteran network correspondent Marvin Kalb and media scholar Stephen Hess later observed.[60] Individual reporters who sought to rebel against the prevailing good-guys and bad-guys news frame were labeled unpatriotic. Even before 9/11, the Bush administration had set out a vision of a New World Order undergirded by "American nationalism, new forms of racism, and the appropriation of Middle Eastern histories."[61] Now the White House embellished on the theme, dividing the world into the forces of good and the forces of evil. Ronald Reagan's Evil Empire was back, but now it was wearing green.

The vast majority of the U.S. media proceeded, in the words of journalism scholar Silvio Waisbord, to "march behind and sustain hawkish patriotism after September 11" and in the process, helped to "prepare the cultural ground for violence,"[62] building on television's well-documented ability to provoke violent behavior. The media became a funnel for the official version of reality, rather than a filter. A study of U.S., European and Middle East newspapers in the lead-up to the invasion of Iraq, conducted by a team from the Department of Defense, concluded that the U.S. media "primed its audience to support the war" while opposition voices "were silenced by the media as the fervor for war coverage grew."[63] Reporters themselves would look back at what CNN's Christiane Amanpour called "a climate of fear and self-censorship"[64] that pervaded the post-9/11 era, during which, in the view of NPR senior foreign editor Loren Jenkins, "we were manipulated."[65]

The stage for this journalistic jingoism was set by none other than Dan Rather, the venerable anchor of the *CBS Evening News*, when he appeared on Dave Letterman's CBS late-night talk show just days after 9/11. At times fighting back tears as he spoke about the country's anger at the terrorist attacks, Rather declared: "George Bush is the president. He makes the decisions and . . . wherever he wants me to line up, just tell me where."[66] It was a watershed moment; one of the most important reporters in America was jettisoning the sacred principles of post-Vietnam journalism – objectivity and independence – and reverting to the era of media as propaganda tool. This jihad journalism would become the hallmark of the post-9/11 era and have a profound impact on the polarization of the nation and the world. Ironically, less than two years later, Rather himself would tell the BBC that "patriotism run amok" was threatening the freedom of American journalists. Rather used the analogy of the South African practice of "necklacing" suspected traitors: "The fear is that you will have a flaming tire of lack of patriotism put around your neck . . . it's that fear that keeps journalists from asking the toughest of the tough questions."[67] Absent was any acknowledgment of the role he had played in creating such an atmosphere. But the numbers told the story. A content analysis of the network newscasts by the conservative Center for Media and Public Affairs concluded that CBS's coverage of the invasion of Iraq was the "most supportive" of official policy, with less than 10 per cent of the individuals interviewed on the *CBS Evening News with Dan Rather* conveying an "anti-war" message – findings that indicated CBS was far more "pro-war" than even Fox News, which had been founded on the principal that the other networks were "too liberal" and was seen as the "headquarters for patriotic fervor."[68] Yet CBS was not alone. When asked why his network was interviewing so few critics of Bush administration policy, Erik Sorenson, president of MSNBC replied that there wasn't enough dissent in the country "to warrant coverage."[69]

"Since 9/11, there is a general feeling among many media outlets that they need to stay away from anything that could be interpreted as disloyal to the country," wrote *Los Angeles Times* media critic Howard Rosenberg. His colleague, foreign editor Simon K.C. Li, later recalled the backlash against early attempts to explore the reasons behind the 9/11 attacks:

> The reaction that we all got to those stories was . . . as if somehow we were not explaining a reality but justifying the 9/11 attacks. And I think that sort of super-patriotism does cause us to hesitate a little bit and perhaps pull our punches sometimes.[70]

Media theorists call this the "spiral of silence."[71] At times when a particular sentiment or message dominates society, individuals "avoid speaking out to avoid isolating themselves."[72] "The more clear-cut the majority and the minority are in the climate of opinion, the more it may be assumed that this will influence the willingness to speak out or keep silent in public."[73]

In the post-9/11 era, the "climate of opinion" could not have been more clear-cut. Whether driven by a professional or personal fear, a pack mentality, or, as in the case of Dan Rather, personal conviction, coverage quickly conformed to the dominant sentiment in the body politic. As one network correspondent, who understandably didn't want his name used, told this writer, "You know where the lines are. They never tell you 'don't say this, or say that,' but you know the piece simply isn't going to get on the air if you do. You save your ammunition for the big battles and concede the small ones."[74] A *Columbia Journalism Review* article examining editorials written in the nation's top newspapers in the six weeks leading up to the Iraq war documented an "astonishing failure" to "exercise skepticism" of administration claims.[75] In a postmortem of its coverage of the alleged presence of weapons of mass destruction in Iraq, *The New York Times* itself acknowledged a failure to sufficiently question what was later revealed to be a "pattern of misinformation" from the Bush administration and anti-Saddam Iraqis. Reporters and editors were

> too intent on rushing scoops into the paper . . . information that was controversial then, and seems questionable now, was insufficiently qualified or allowed to stand unchallenged . . . Articles based on dire claims about Iraq tended to get prominent display, while follow-up articles that called the original ones into question were sometimes buried. In some cases, there was no follow-up at all.[76]

Within the nation's elite media organs, the notions of objectivity, independence and the traditional commitment to "comfort the afflicted and afflict the comfortable" – the hallmarks of American journalism in the post-Vietnam era – had largely been abandoned. The journalistic "they" was traded for an inclusive "we." As one U.S.-based British correspondent wrote:

> [T]he mindset that has dominated the American media since the collapse of the twin towers . . . illustrates a tendency to . . . circle the wagons around nationhood, leaving on the outside questions about what is being done in the nation's name and why . . . The problem is not so much that such views are unavailable as that they have been effectively marginalised.[77]

Tough questions were ignored, debate over whether the nation should go to war was largely absent from the pages of the nation's largest newspapers and the broadcasts of the major networks. Instead, the media became a mouthpiece for the Bush administration; and some editors appeared proud of their new role. "This nation is now at war. And in such an environment, domestic political dissent is immoral without a prior statement of national solidarity, a choosing of sides," declared the editor of the *New Republic*, once considered a liberal publication.[78] Those who strayed from the party line – primarily smaller fringe publications and web sites – paid the price. Matthew Rothschild, editor of the *Progressive*, which opposed the war on terror, was buried in hate mail. "Call me when you're in New York," one reader wrote. "I'll take you to the local firehouse and we will all take turns bouncing your head off the sidewalk. We could call it '*Progressive* basketball.'"[79] Writing in the September 24, 2001 issue of the *New Yorker*, novelist Susan Sontag asked, "Where is the acknowledgement that this was not a 'cowardly' attack on 'civilization' or 'liberty' or 'humanity' or 'the free world' but an attack on the world's self-proclaimed super-power, undertaken as a consequence of specific American alliances and actions?"[80] In the next morning's *Washington Post*, Sontag was labeled "belligerent, self-righteous and anti-American,"[81] while the conservative *Weekly Standard* responded by creating the Susan Sontag award for "inanity by intellectuals and artists in the wake of the terrorist attacks."[82]

Bill Maher, the controversial host of ABC's *Politically Incorrect* talk show became a lightning rod for conservative – and White House – criticism when he questioned those who had been calling the 9/11 terrorists "cowards." "*We* have been the cowards lobbing cruise missiles from 2,000 miles away," he said on the air during the early stages of the Afghan war. "*That's* cowardly. Staying in the airplane when it hits the building, say what you want about it, it's not cowardly." Despite his subsequent apologies, Maher's comments was apparently *too* politically incorrect for the reigning sense of patriotism in the country and, after an exodus of advertisers, his show was canceled. Nationalism, not candor, was the order of the day.

One of the most vivid examples of journalistic self-censorship involved the way in which the media framed the president. Prior to 9/11, George W. Bush's proclivity for fracturing the English language was a constant media target. In fact, as I drove to work on 9/11, the first NPR bulletin about a

for the most part did not disagree. "Objectivity can come back into fashion when the shooting is over," Macdonald Hastings, a British correspondent in World War II, once said.[92]

There has been a symbiotic relationship between the media and the war effort since the days of the first foreign correspondents. Circulation soars in time of conflict. Echoes of the U.S. media's coverage of the so-called war on terror and the invasion of Iraq are heard throughout journalistic history; embedded journalists, jingoistic fervor, self-censorship, and the race for ratings. The symbiotic relationship is epitomized by a story from World War I: after listening to a journalist's dinner-table account of the situation on the Western Front, Britain's then-prime minister, Lloyd George, told a newspaper editor, "If people knew, the war would be stopped tomorrow. But of course they don't know and can't know."[93]

The media's well-documented "capacity to drum up violent feeling"[94] has been adeptly used through history by politicians and greedy publishers alike. As he and fellow publisher Joseph Pulitzer fanned the flames of jingoism to fuel their circulation war in the run-up to the Spanish–American War, William Randolph Hearst is reported to have had the following cable exchange with photographer Frederick Remington in Cuba: "Everything is quiet. There is no trouble here. There will be no war. I wish to return," Remington wrote. To which Hearst famously replied: "Please remain. You furnish the pictures. I will furnish the war."[95]

"Remember the *Maine*." "Remember Pearl Harbor." "Remember 9/11." American politicians have historically used such slogans, designed to exploit public outrage over apparent attacks on the nation's honor, to further their own geopolitical goals. To this day, many experts believe the sinking of the *Maine*, which served as pretext for the American invasion of Cuba, was caused by an exploding boiler, not Spanish sabotage. President Johnson's Gulf of Tonkin Resolution, which dramatically escalated U.S. involvement in Vietnam, was passed in response to a supposed attack on U.S. Naval forces that later proved fictitious.[96] Truth, as Sen. Hiram Johnson said during World War I, is the "first casualty" of war.[97]

Veteran Australian journalist John Pilger recalls his shock on discovering that U.S. correspondents in early days of Vietnam knew all about the systematic slaughter and abuse of civilians at the hands of American forces. Visiting the offices of the major U.S. news organizations, he saw bulletin boards covered with pictures of dismembered bodies, soldiers holding up severed ears and testicles, and actual scenes of torture.

> The question came up whenever visitors caught sight of these pictures: why had they not been published? A standard response was that newspapers would not publish them, because their readers would not accept them. And to publish them, without an explanation of the wider circumstances of the war, was to "sensationalise."[98]

The shift in the media framing of the Vietnam War from support of the government's position to open criticism midway through the conflict reflected the fact that "truth" in journalism is at best a relative term; news is "at most a provisional kind of truth, the best that can be said quickly."[99] Faced with the stark contrast between the military's version of events and the reality they witnessed in the rice paddies of Vietnam, the media turned on the administration and the nightly images of body bags and gore in America's first "living room war" eventually drove public opposition. It culminated in CBS anchor Walter Cronkite's broadcast concluding that the conflict was unwinnable, which led President Johnson to declare that if he had lost Cronkite, he had lost the country.[100]

A decade later, an unfettered media would again bring into America's living rooms the spectacle of U.S. troops being driven out of a country by a largely unseen enemy, this time

Even conservatives like columnist William Safire of *The New York Times* decried the failure of his fellow journalists to "expose the broadcast lobby's pressure on Congress and the courts to allow station owners to gobble up more stations and cross-own local newspapers, thereby to determine what information residents of a local market receive."[107] Disney controlled ABC; Walt Disney Pictures and Miramax Films; ESPN, A&E, Lifetime, Disney, History and other cable channels; radio stations; and numerous Internet operations. AOL-Time-Warner, which called itself a "fully integrated media and communications company," brought together Time Inc., the largest magazine publisher in the world; AOL Online, the country's largest Internet provider; Time-Warner cable; CNN; Home Box Office; and Warner Brothers Entertainment. General Electric, meanwhile, controlled NBC and its fleet of cable offshoots, as well as Universal Studios and, in the spring of 2004, announced a merger that created NBC Universal, which called itself "a global media and entertainment enterprise"[108] and generated $12 billion in revenues in its first full year of operation. Media scholar Robert McChesney painted a dark picture of the result of such media incest:

> Media fare is ever more closely linked to the needs and concerns of a handful of enormous and powerful corporations. . . . These firms are run by wealthy managers and billionaires with clear stakes in the outcome of the most fundamental political issues, and their interests are often distinct from those of the vast majority of humanity. . . . [Meanwhile] media fare is subjected to an ever-greater commercialization as the dominant firms use their market power to squeeze the greatest possible profit from their product.[109]

The impact of consolidation was felt particularly at the three major U.S. broadcast networks. Massive cutbacks in the 1980s – when the first mergers and takeovers began – left the networks shadows of their former selves and set the stage for reduced international coverage in all the major media. As a CBS News correspondent in the 1980s, this writer was one of 18 staff correspondents permanently based overseas, including nine in Western Europe, two in Moscow, two in the Arab world, one in Israel, one in Africa and two in Asia. Twenty years later, the foreign staff was less than half that and concentrated primarily in London.[110] The networks were relying on what one ABC News executive called "Just-in-Time News," in which the next available correspondent – not necessarily the most-knowledgeable – was dispatched when a story broke, sometimes from the other side of the world. An article in the *American Journalism Review* recounted an example of this "flexible response" approach, which occurred when the ABC News foreign editor called New York-based correspondent Bill Blakemore and asked whether he would go to Moscow, where Chechen rebels were holding 700 people hostage in a theater.

> "Sure," said Blakemore. "Why me?"
> "Because you're the only ABC correspondent on the planet who can get there in time to do a live report for *Good Morning America* tomorrow."[111]

Many hours later, Blakemore landed in Moscow and was rushed to the scene, where he went live on *Good Morning America* just ten minutes later; he was, quite literally, "Just-in-Time."

A 2004 poll by the Pew Research Center for the People and the Press found that two-thirds of U.S. journalists working for national news organizations "have come to believe that increased bottom-line pressure is 'seriously hurting' the quality of news coverage," that reporters are "too timid" and that "the media is paying too little attention to complex stories."[112] When, in 1985, CBS decided to close its remaining bureau in the Arab world, this writer was told by the CBS News vice president in charge of news coverage that "the American Marines are gone, so there's no story there anymore." The bureau in Israel, meanwhile, remained open and fully staffed. By the spring of 2005, CBS News had two full-time correspondents based in Israel and – despite the war on terror and the occupation of Iraq – still had no correspondent permanently based in an Arab or Muslim-majority country. It had been twenty years and counting. Might that have something to do with America's failure to understand why "they" hated "us"?

Exacerbating the bottom-line mentality that had taken over in the media was the lack of interest in international news on the part of the American body politic. A 2002 Pew survey reported that while the number of Americans who said they were "generally interested in foreign news" had increased slightly since the previous year, these people represented a narrow, highly educated segment of the public. The overwhelming majority said they "lack the background" to understand overseas news. Concluded Pew: "The survey offers powerful evidence that broad interest in international news is most inhibited by the public's lack of background information in this area."[113]

It was a vicious cycle fed by the corporate appetite for profits: if Americans didn't have the basic knowledge to understand international news, they psychologically and physically tuned out, the media had no incentive to cover such issues, and the public therefore was never exposed to the basics they needed to understand. Even 9/11 didn't have much impact. Viewership of television news was actually *lower* in the summer of 2002, *after* 9/11, than in the summer of 2001, *before* the tragedy. As journalist-scholar Philip Seib has observed, "Relatively few news executives appear willing to gamble that the American news audience might be interested in the rest of the world."[114] On top of that, the good/bad dichotomy of the Cold War had given way to a far more complex world, "and many news organizations have not made the effort needed to understand a system of politics that is more shaded with nuance than was the stark face-off between superpowers."[115]

The implications of the U.S. media's failures in its approach to Islam went well beyond the issue of how Muslims were being framed in the mind of the average American. The fallout extended into the Muslim world as well. The American media was a global media; Arabs and Muslims saw themselves reflected in the lens of the Western media and they did not like the images they saw. "In the 1990s America and its cultural allies (like countries of Europe) appear to dominate the world," Akbar Ahmed wrote from the perspective of that time. "They do so through the media. That is why the media is seen as hostile by the Muslim world."[116]

Those words were written nearly a decade before the tragedy of 9/11; before the unblinking lens of the U.S. media shifted to the Muslim world and framed a storyline every bit as black and white as the newsprint on which it was published.

3
The Arab and Muslim Media

"There's the King's Messenger. He's in prison now, being punished: and the trial doesn't even begin till next Wednesday: and of course the crime comes last of all."
"Suppose he never commits the crime?" said Alice.
"That would be better, wouldn't it?"
Lewis Carroll, Alice Through the Looking Glass

When it began reporting on America's so-called "war on terror," the media of the Arab and non-Arab Muslim world was in the throes of change. Since the end of World War II, government control had been the hallmark of media in Arab countries, where "muzzling and suppression . . . manipulation and co-option"[1] by regimes that "claimed a monopoly on truth"[2] became the norm, many journalists saw themselves as defenders of Arab nationalism or national honor, and the media was traditionally viewed with suspicion and little respect. Much the same was true of major non-Arab Muslim nations, such as Indonesia, where the media had been a partner of the state until the late 1990s.

Looking at the Middle East in the 1970s, William Rugh, a former U.S. ambassador in the region and expert on the Arab media, divided the Arab print media into three classifications: the "mobilization press," controlled by revolutionary governments like those in Libya, Syria, Iraq and Sudan; the "loyalist press" of Saudi Arabia, the Gulf and Palestine, which was largely privately owned but beholden to the government; and the "diverse press" of Lebanon, Kuwait, Morocco, and Yemen, which reflected a diversity of views but was subject to more subtle pressures.[3] A fourth category of Arab print media was the offshore pan-Arab press. Up until the early 1970s, Beirut was the media capital of the Arab world. Its rough-and-tumble mix of politics and religion covered the entire spectrum of Arab opinion, from the Arab nationalism and socialism of the Nasserites, Ba'athists and Palestinians to the Saudi-backed monarchists and Islamist sympathizers of the Egyptian Muslim Brotherhood. All these views were represented in the pages of the country's lively media. But the same political crosscurrents that fed the debate also fueled the communal violence that would take hold in the early 1970s and tear the country asunder for the next two decades. Journalists were among the countless victims. Assassinations of editors, newsroom bombings, kidnappings and threats from the plethora of competing factions and the governments that sponsored them, silenced the voices of debate. Many newspapers shut down.

Beirut's loss was London's gain. The Arab world's most respected newspaper, *al-Hayat* (*Life*), stopped publishing in 1976 after 13 bomb attempts on its offices (its founder had been assassinated in 1966). Eleven years later, it reopened in London, joining the Saudi-owned *Asharq al-Awsat* (*The Middle East*), which had been edited in Britain since 1977 and printed in the Arab world. The Saudi royal family soon bought a controlling interest in *al-Hayat* via Prince Khaled bin Sultan, the Saudi military commander during the 1990–91 Gulf War. London was also base for the third of the leading pan-Arab dailies, the Palestinian-operated *al-Quds al-Arabi* (*Arab Jerusalem*). Reflecting the Arab media's reliance on political sponsors, the paper carried few advertisements and received funding directly from various Arab sources.[4]

While it maintained a broadly pro-Saudi line, the opinion pages of *al-Hayat* were "among the most varied and open fora for debate in the Arab world."[5] And although the move from Beirut to London took *al-Hayat* out of the direct line of fire of the Lebanese conflict, it did not shield its staff of some 300 journalists from other pressures faced by their colleagues at papers based in the Arab world. In early 1997, *al-Hayat's* offices in New York, Washington, London and Riyadh were the target of letter bombs ordered by Egyptian Islamist Ayman al-Zawahiri. The militant, who would later emerge as Osama bin Laden's right-hand man, was apparently upset that the paper did not run an interview it had conducted with him, something that would have likely upset Egyptian authorities and could have had repercussions for the paper's distribution in Egypt. Militants weren't the only threat. Governments could also reach out and touch the offshore papers. In the spring of 2004, the Beirut bureau chief of *Asharq al-Awsat* was convicted in absentia (he had fled the country) and sentenced to a year in prison for "disturbing national security and harming the president's dignity" after the paper reported that there had been an assassination attempt on the life of then-president Emil Lahoud.[6] In a telling commentary on the state of the Arab media, *al-Hayat* saw fit to note in its article about the conviction that, "Despite occasional pressure from authorities in recent years, the Lebanese press remains one of the Mideast region's freest."[7]

The offshore print media and their counterparts in a few Arab countries may have enjoyed some modicum of leeway, but radio and television remained firmly in government hands and, according to a leading Arab media scholar, "the concept of television journalism, as a set of distinctive professional values and practices, was virtually nonexistent in Arab world television."[8] Most broadcasting laws barred criticism of the head of state and carried penalties for such vague offenses as undermining public order or defaming religion. The system kept authoritarian regimes in power by stifling dissent. As Rugh told a Senate panel in the spring of 2004, the oft-cited prextext for muzzling the media was the Arab–Israeli conflict:

> Arab governments have been able to justify explicitly and implicitly their influence over the mass media as necessary either while the country is "at war" with Israel, or politically confronting Israel's policies. Because of the degree to which the Arab–Israeli dispute has become the central issue in Arab foreign policy and a matter of Arab patriotism, this justification is difficult to oppose.[9]

Steeped in a culture of perennial confrontation shaped by the conflict with Israel, the patriotic fervor so often seen among reporters in countries at war became a permanent fixture of the Arab media. Many journalists voluntarily subscribed to the concept of "responsible freedom,"[10] in which the interests of the state – and the Arab nation – superseded all other considerations. To stray from the party line was unpatriotic; firing was the least of the penalties. Dissenting journalists were fined, imprisoned, or, in some cases, executed. Publications were regularly shuttered. As Ibrahim Nawar, head of the Arab Press Freedom Watch (APFW), has observed, "Freedom of expression is not something on offer in the Arab world. It has to be fought for."[11] Hoda al-Mutawa, who worked for a time as a presenter on Bahrain television, recalls being summoned by the minister of information and ordered to stop discussing some of the issues she had raised on the air. When she tried to object, the minister waved his hand to silence her, sighed and said, "Hoda, why do you want to make life difficult for yourself? Just say, 'OK' like everyone else." The conversation was over. "They speak to you as a father to a child," she says.[12]

As *al-Hayat* had discovered, the pressure came not only from governments. "Clans in Yemen and Kuwait, criminal gangs in Algeria and Egypt and Islamic fundamentalists in Algeria all took part in the offensive against the freedom of speech [which was] a common denominator in all Arab countries" in 2001, according to the APFW.[13] That was underlined by the organization's list of more than 50 "free speech victims" the previous year, a litany of assassinations, attempted assassinations, imprisonments, interrogations, beatings and fines. The list was accompanied by a compendium of 15 publications in Morocco, Egypt, Yemen, Jordan and Sudan that had been forcibly closed, confiscated or taken to court.[14] The resulting self-censorship that pervaded the Arab media was exacerbated by the fact that, according to Hussein Amin, chair of the department of journalism at the American University in Cairo (AUC), "most Arab authorities do not publish a list of subjects that they do not want to be covered, leaving the reporter in a state of confusion."[15]

The Arab–Israeli conflict may have been the cover, but for many governments, survival was the real issue in attempting to control what their populations saw, heard and read. In May of 2004, as the Bush administration was unveiling its blueprint for democracy in the Middle East and Arab leaders were preparing to gather for a summit to discuss, among other things, political reform, the APFW held its third annual conference under the telling title, "Freeing the Arab Media from State Control." The final communiqué was stark reading for supporters of press freedom, highlighting "the strong linkage between the hostile attitude of the state towards the freedom of expression and the press, and its deep rooted tendencies to resist public pressure for change and democratic reform of Arab societies in response to the wide democratization in the whole world."[16]

Beyond the issue of government control was the existence of a cash culture in which reporters – particularly in the "diverse press" of Lebanon and a handful of other Arab countries – were paid to write certain stories by competing political or business interests. "One of the major problems here is that conflict of interest is not considered to be a problem," Magda Abu Fadil, the director of the Beirut-based Institute for Professional Journalists (IPJ), told an interviewer. "This is a major, major problem. Journalists cannot be credible if they accept money, free trips, gifts and favors."[17] This same phenomenon existed in many non-Arab Muslim countries (as well as elsewhere in the developing world), and was reflected in the common practice of companies handing out envelopes of cash at news conferences just to get reporters to show up. In its 2005 budget, for example, the city of Jakarta allocated more than $300,000 to pay for interviews with Indonesian journalists. Half a world away, the king of Morocco annually hosted a television broadcast on which he ostentatiously handed over government subsidy checks to executives of the major newspapers.

For those members of the economic elite who owned satellite dishes, the only real alternatives to the local media were the news broadcasts of CNN International and the BBC, while less-privileged citizens were left to rely on the shortwave broadcasts of the Arabic service of the BBC World Service, the Voice of America and a few European broadcasters, thus ensuring that Arabs and Muslims saw not only the world, but their own region, through the dominant frame of the Western media. To a large extent, this was even true for those relying on domestic news sources. With few exceptions, the Arab and non-Arab Muslim media was historically dependent on Western news organizations when it came to covering the rest of the world – and their own region. Carefully vetted wire copy from news agencies such as the Associated Press (AP), Reuters and Agence France Press (AFP) provided stories from Washington, Moscow, and Beijing, as well as other Arab capitals, while television viewers saw the world through the prism of the major U.S. networks,

CNN, BBC, and a few other Western television news agencies, such as Reuters Television and Associated Press Television, that supplied the videotape for Arab broadcasts.

This then was the situation when, in the 1990s, Saudi entrepreneurs close to the government set up the first private cross-border Arab satellite television operations. The goal was to counter the influence of the Western broadcasters then beaming signals into the Middle East, as well as smuggled videocassettes of Western programs and movies, which offered the only alternative to government-controlled television. While illegal in many countries, satellite dishes – which had been shrinking in size – began to appear on rooftops across the region in the late 1980s, even as "state broadcasting monopolies and strict government censorship remained the norm in most Arab states and Iran."[18] Just how strict was demonstrated with Iraq's invasion of Kuwait in 1991. Viewers relying on Saudi state television for their news were not told war had broken out. The state broadcaster failed to mention the invasion of the neighboring emirate for more than 48 hours. It was the equivalent of a French TV station ignoring a German occupation of Belgium. For those with satellite dishes, all eyes turned to CNN.

Egypt was the first to introduce Arab satellite broadcasting in order to convey its official position during the Gulf conflict, but Nilesat was a government-controlled operation, little different from the fare on terrestrial state-run TV. Nine months later, two well-connected Saudi entrepreneurs flipped the switch on the Middle East Broadcasting Center (MBC), ushering in the era of private satellite broadcasting in the Arab world. While MBC was "very serious about Arab news," according to a consultant who worked with the owners at the time, and brought in a group of "first-class" British and Lebanese news people,[19] coverage of Saudi affairs was handled with kid gloves. MBC was soon joined by the Arab Radio and Television Network (ART) and Orbit, both originally based in Rome, and Lebanon's LBC International and Future Television. But when it came to news, these new channels were anything but independent operations. One of the two Saudi partners in MBC was King Fahd's brother-in-law; the other Saudi partner later joined with another member of the royal family to found ART. Orbit was controlled by the son of the Saudi crown prince; LBC was founded with the help of another Saudi sheikh; and Future Television was created by Lebanese businessman Rafiq Hariri, who made his fortune in Saudi Arabia and was related by marriage to the Saudi royals (he would later become the Saudi-backed prime minister of Lebanon, helping that nation recover from 15 years of civil war, before his 2005 assassination).

Critics of Saudi domination of the region's media denounced the "eunuch-like condition" of Arab journalists and other Muslim intellectuals who had sold out to high salaries. This "media control," observed Sudanese scholar Abdelwahab el-Affendi, was not confined to the Middle East, but rather

> it constitutes a malaise that is most acutely manifested in the Arab heartlands of Islam, but which has gripped the whole Ummah (the World Muslim Community) in its tentacles. The impact of this phenomenon reverberates all over the land of Islam . . .[20]

Nowhere in the Muslim world did there exist a truly free press. In Nigeria, Pakistan, Turkey and Bangladesh decades of military coups and varying levels of authoritarian rule had left the media at the mercy of those in power. The media in Pakistan was the product of "parasitic landlordism;"[21] in Malaysia, a combination of draconian press laws and widespread ownership of media interests by state-owned holding companies led one U.S. press group to rank it among the ten worst places to practice journalism;[22] while in Suharto's Indonesia, the world's most populous Muslim country, the print press was independently owned, but the ministry of information and the armed forces held a vast portfolio of shareholdings in media companies and, according to a 1989 report by the human rights group Asia Watch, the media was "very much a partner of the government, and not an independent or autonomous institution."[23]

Goenawan Mohamad, founder of the groundbreaking Indonesian newsweekly *Tempo*, recalls that editors during the Suharto era received direction from government officials on how to report sensitive stories and practiced a large degree of self-censorship.[24] Mohamad himself was an example of what happened when the media crossed the invisible line. *Tempo* was shut down in the waning years of the Suharto era when it ridiculed the government's purchase of a large portion of the former East Germany's out-dated navy. "Most Indonesians have long resigned [themselves] to the fact that the pen is often mightier than the sword, but is absolutely no match for the gun," *Indonesia Business Weekly* wrote in 1992.[25]

There was then, compelling evidence for el-Affendi's grim portrait of the state of the Muslim media in 1993:

> They have managed to force independent voices from the Muslim world using market manipulation, bribery and sheer intimidation . . . The result is a blanket dark age extending from Indonesia to the Atlantic with long shadows falling over London, Paris, New York and other centers of Muslim exile. Debate is stifled, publishing is stymied and free thinking all but eliminated in the Muslim world.[26]

This dominance of the channels of communication by the political and economic elite affected the ways in which information spread in the Arab and non-Arab Muslim world and the very nature of the information itself. Since they worked for organizations seen as government mouthpieces, journalists commanded little respect among the public or from the governments they served. For the most part, investigative reporting was non-existent; challenging official statements or policies was unheard of. Indeed, with the rare exceptions of publications like *Tempo*, journalism in the Western sense did not exist. There were no awards for uncovering government malfeasance and few journalism schools. Rather, according to AUC's Amin, "The central purpose of mass communication programs in the Arab world is to prepare generation after generation of semi-educated journalists whose job it is to promote the 'achievements' of the state."[27]

With media quality suspect, the public turned to quantity. It is difficult to convey to those who have not visited the Arab world – especially places like Beirut, Damascus, Amman and Cairo – the degree to which a hunger for information pervades all discussion. Many Arabs skim several newspapers a day as they try to piece together a coherent picture of the news; the radio is always on, switching from one newscast to another. In past decades, the distinctive jingle of Radio Monte Carlo's Arabic newscast quite literally echoed through the streets. With the advent of satellite TV, the television provides constant background noise in coffeehouses and grocery stores. To a degree seen in the United States only during times of national crisis or catastrophe, Arabs are fixated on the events that constantly buffet their turbulent region. In Jordan, for example, 83 per cent of people say they watch TV news. That's more viewers than entertainment programs attract, the exact reverse of the United States.[28]

The manner in which the media reflected official thinking, along with the absence of formal training, meant there was little space for Western-style notions of journalistic accuracy and objectivity to take root. Thus even coverage of issues of no consequence to the government was frequently rife with innuendo and falsehood – some bought and paid for, some the result of sloppy or lazy journalism. Put simply, if a reporter was expected by the government to print articles he or she knew were not true, there was little impediment to adopting a similar approach on other stories. However flawed it may have been in the years after 9/11, Western journalistic culture was built on a foundation that gave at least lip-service to objectivity. In the Middle East and other parts of the Muslim world, the most respected journalists had traditionally been known not for unbiased reporting, but for their opinions. This was because while the news stories on the front page could not be trusted, the opinion columns offered insights garnered from the writer's access to the corridors of power. For example, the Arab world's best-known journalist, the former editor-in-chief of the Egyptian daily *al-Ahram*, Mohammed Heikel, was a close friend of Gamal Abdel Nasser at a time when the Egyptian president dominated Arab politics. Heikel's columns thus offered a window on the thinking of the region's most powerful leader.

Given the local media's lack of credibility and the general suspicion of Western sources, a counterculture of unofficial news channels emerged, in which rumors and conspiracy theories ran rife. As a result, countless unsubstantiated stories – some worthy of the *National Enquirer* – ricocheted through the Middle East every day. After a spate of bombings in Baghdad, for example, a story circulated that "John Kerry is behind this so Bush will lose his Presidency and look bad in front of the world."[29] Other rumors were based on long-standing myths, such as the story that the Wahabi sect of Sunni Islam was an invention of the British as part of a divide-and-rule strategy.[30] An American professor living in Saudi Arabia in the mid-1980s wrote that one was "likely to feel he lives amid a vast rumor, whose centre is nowhere and whose circumference is everywhere."[31]

Many of these rumors, frequently repeated and given new life in the press, reflect a set of stereotypes about the United States that are, in many ways, the mirror image of those that Americans hold about Muslims. Central is that of the "crusader–Zionist conspiracy" in which "the Western demon [is] bent on the eradication of Islam."[32] Though relatively little scholarly work has been done on portrayals of the United States in the media of Arab and Muslim countries, there is substantial anecdotal evidence of bias for anyone who has ever picked up a newspaper in the Muslim world. Writing in an Israeli publication, journalist Adel Darwish argued that anti-Americanism in the Arab language media is "all-encompassing," and includes selective showing of negative images of the U.S., selective language, exaggerated headlines, use of rumor and conspiracy theories in the place of facts, selective reporting, and the selective editing of translated articles from the Western media.[33]

In a study of Arab media coverage of the Arab–Israeli wars, William Rugh noted that while there was "less politically motivated distortion in the Arab media" in 1973 than 1967, a key theme involved U.S. support for "the Zionist entity."[34] Likewise, an examination of post-9/11 political cartoons from the Muslim world revealed a pattern of themes that include the U.S. as "deceptive" and the moral equivalent of bin Laden.[35]

ARAB SATELLITE BROADCASTING

If Osama bin Laden had launched his assault on America on September 11, 1991, it is unlikely he would have attained the mythic status he would come to enjoy. The al-Qaeda leader's actions would certainly have commanded headlines, but he would not have had the direct conduit to the people of the Muslim world that has made him such a political force. No Arab government would have given bin Laden's revolutionary views a forum in their own media and all television coverage would have come through a Western filter. Without the Arab media, bin Laden might have been a security threat, but he would have been denied his primary tool for inspiring the Muslim body politic.

Unfortunately for the West, the coming-of-age of Osama bin Laden coincided with the coming-of-age of al-Jazeera.

Founded in 1996 in the tiny Gulf emirate of Qatar, the news and information satellite channel was part of the liberalization effort launched by the new British-educated emir, Sheikh Hamad bin Khalifa al-Thani, who had ousted his father in a bloodless coup the previous year. As the fireside radio chat was President Franklin Delano Roosevelt's "bully pulpit" during World War II, so too the Qatar-based satellite channel served as bin Laden's electronic podium as he launched his military and propaganda assault on the United States. Under any circumstances, the bombing of the World Trade Center would have shaken America at its foundations. But, as the roundups of top bin Laden lieutenants and the dismantling of much of al-Qaeda's infrastructure would later demonstrate, the Saudi exile's greatest threat lay not in individual terrorist operations, but in his role as an icon around which the forces of anti-Americanism could rally.

Ironically, given later accusations of bias and unprofessionalism, al-Jazeera's original news team were almost all veterans of the BBC's Arabic television service, which had just withdrawn from an ill-fated joint venture with Orbit TV when it became clear that the BBC and the Saudi royal family – not surprisingly – had different ideas about what constituted journalism. The emir gave al-Jazeera a $140 million subsidy and a mandate: launch an independent television station free from government scrutiny, control, and manipulation. The staff proceeded to do just that. According to author Naomi Sakr, "It soon made up for lost time, astonishing viewers with uncensored political coverage quite different from any Arabic-language television programming previously seen."[36] The channel's staff saw themselves as agents of democratic change in a region trapped in the grip of autocracies. One official in the Clinton White House called it a "beacon of light,"[37] and Israeli cabinet minister Gideon Ezra told the *Jerusalem Post*, "I wish all Arab media were like al-Jazeera."[38]

Not everyone was enamored. "Using the Western style, we have broken many taboos," said Ibrahim M. Halal, al-Jazeera's chief editor; "[o]f course, we upset most other Arab countries."[39] To say the least. Arab rulers across the region were shocked by this new, largely unfettered approach that was considered "nothing short of heresy."[40] Virtually every Arab government criticized al-Jazeera. The Saudis were particularly incensed. Al-Jazeera not only impinged on their near-monopoly of pan-Arab media, but the station had the temerity to give voice to those who would question the House of Saud. As one Saudi newspaper wrote:

> The poisonous ideas that are conveyed via the Western satellite channels are easy to handle because the viewer knows the thought they are trying to convey in advance. However, when this poisonous thought is conveyed via an Arab satellite channel, it becomes all the more dangerous because it is concealing itself behind our culture.[41]

Morocco, Jordan, the Palestinian Authority, Bahrain and Kuwait all closed al-Jazeera offices, denied its reporters visas or temporarily withdrew their ambassadors from Qatar. Al-Jazeera exhibited a "lack of professionalism and neutrality when dealing with Kuwaiti issues," a senior Kuwaiti official explained when that country expelled the channel's reporters for the second time.[42] Egypt boycotted an Arab summit in Qatar because of its anger at al-Jazeera over interviews with Egyptian Islamists. Across the region, governments and individuals alike were shocked when al-Jazeera began to interview Israeli officials to hear their side of the Israel–Palestine conflict. Such an approach was in keeping with the station's motto: "Opinion, and other opinion."[43]

The impact on the average viewer was profound. London-based Egyptian novelist Ahdaf Soueif recalled the first time she happened upon al-Jazeera while channel-hopping in a Cairo hotel room at 2 a.m., and "suddenly there was a channel, speaking in Arabic, but in a way I had only ever heard people speak in private – away from the censorship and the various state security services that dominate our public discourse."[44] For Soueif and millions of others, the arrival of al-Jazeera was a political and psychological watershed:

> Within the Arab world, this channel has made censorship of news and opinion pointless. For us outside, it provides the one window through which we can breathe. It also provides reassurance against the negative or partial image of ourselves constantly beamed at us every day from the media of whatever country we happen to find ourselves in. It's not that we want to hear our own opinions; rather that we want to hear a variety of opinions of which ours is one.[45]

Where Arabs once patched together their view of current events through a plethora of news media, al-Jazeera became the touchstone. As Palestinian journalist Salwa Kaana told me, "People now say, 'I'm just going to go out for a cup of coffee and al-Jazeera.'"[46]

THE NEW INFORMATION GHETTOS

The age of government monopoly of information and Western media imperialism was coming to an end. The Arabs – and their non-Arab Muslim brethren – now had their own independent lens through which to view the world. And for them, the world would never look the same again.

Marshall McLuhan's global village had been subject to massive urban renewal. No longer did the world gather around the same television screen. Al-Jazeera and its clones had seen to that. In its place, Americans and those living in the Muslim world inhabited separate Information Ghettos, each seeing a view of the world largely at odds with that of the other. Just as news coverage of 9/11 affected domestic U.S. opinions about American domestic and foreign policies, so too was international opinion impacted as television "mediated" the events of September 11 for audiences around the world. This emerging new world news order meant that presidential rhetoric shaped for a domestic audience in the wake of 9/11 was likewise heard by international audiences, but through a very different filter. Where U.S. media imperialism meant America's narrative once dominated the global discourse, the international channels of information were now increasingly fragmented, in turn polarizing the respective audiences.

This then, was the electronic stage upon which Bush and Osama bin Laden – and the cultures they represented – embraced in a colossal Othering. A president steeped in a born-again Christian worldview and convinced of the righteousness of his cause shaping government policy and public attitudes toward an adversary he had been conditioned by culture to view with deep suspicion; an equally committed Islamist tapping into the deep vein of resentment toward America's cultural and political domination that ran through the Muslim world. In the ensuing confrontation, the respective media of the two cultures fed the confrontation, reinforcing pre-existing stereotypes, giving voice to the most inflammatory messages, and enhancing the mutual perceived threat as they reported on the same events through their contrasting ideological/ethnic/nationalistic prisms.

Thus was created a Rashomon effect, in which "truth" became a relative term, and, as in Akira Kurosawa's 1950 film of the same name, each witness was left convinced his version was the *real* story.[47]

Section II

The Framing of an Era

4

Rhetoric, Religion and Righteousness

In great contests, each party claims to act in accordance with the will of God. Both may be, and one must be wrong. God cannot be for and against the same thing at the same time.

Abraham Lincoln

E ven before the smoke began to clear on September 11, 2001, a chorus of voices rose across the Muslim world to denounce the attacks. "Brutal,"[1] "inhumane,"[2] "cowardly"[3] and "insane"[4] were some of the adjectives used by leaders and editorial writers from North Africa to Southeast Asia. The suicide hijackings were "crimes against humanity whose ugliness and barbarism exceed all imagination," declared Jordan's ambassador to Washington.[5] The decision to target civilians was "gruesome" said the Grand Imam of Egypt's al-Azhar University;[6] "un-Islamic and immoral," agreed Pakistan's *Khabrain* newspaper.[7] "No religion, particularly Islam, which is a religion of peace, allows such wanton attacks on innocent men, women and children," the vice president of the Pakistan Muslim League told reporters.[8] A declaration published in a leading Arab newspaper and signed by 46 Muslim leaders from 19 countries denounced the "killing, demolition, [and] destruction" and expressed "deepest sorrow and grief" for the actions, which they disavowed "on humane and Islamic principles."[9] Yusuf Qaradawi, a prominent Islamist and host of an influential al-Jazeera talk show on *shari'a* law joined with other clerics to issue a fatwa condemning the attacks.[10] Even the Taliban refrained from endorsing the bombings.[11]

But such is the power of images that, for many Americans, far more memorable than those condemnations was the scene of a small group of Palestinians in East Jerusalem dancing, cheering and passing out chocolates in celebration. The videotape, repeated frequently on American television in the days after 9/11, was an early indication of how the U.S. media would frame subsequent events, leaving American commentators shaking their heads at a Muslim reaction that "seemed inexplicable."[12] It also produced two enduring urban legends. From the U.S. side, the footage of the small and isolated Palestinian celebration visually reinforced the suspicion that most Muslims supported the attacks of September 11. From the Arab and Muslim side, the wide exposure the footage received immediately increased suspicion that a biased U.S. media was setting the stage for a war against Islam. Feeding this belief was a story that quickly circulated claiming the tape was not a reaction to 9/11, but actually showed a pro-Saddam rally recorded by CNN more than a decade before during the Gulf War.[13] Clearly, according to this view, it was part of a conspiracy to smear the reputation of Islam and the Palestinians.

Both misperceptions were based on fallacies but both framed the relationship that was to follow, providing an early glimpse of the bloodshot lens through which Americans and the people of the Muslim world would view each other in the coming months and years. It also demonstrated the impact that the media revolution would have in polarizing attitudes on both sides. The truth was that a Reuters TV crew had shot the footage of the small Palestinian demonstration on September 11. But the story that it was a fake streaked around the world on the Internet after a graduate student in Brazil sent an email to a Listserv in Britain claiming that his professor had videotapes of CNN stories "with the very same images" from 1991.[14] Despite the company's repeated denials, the story took on a life of its own, playing directly into Arab and Muslim stereotypes about U.S. media bias and anti-Muslim conspiracies. Meanwhile, the idea among U.S. viewers that the Palestinians – and Arabs and Muslims in general – were celebrating the attacks belied the reality that most Palestinians, like others in the region, were shocked by the bombings and fearful of what they might bring.[15] Arafat himself issued a statement on September 11 condemning the attacks and declaring, "It's not only against the American people and against America, it's against the international humanity."[16]

"How few cameras have caught the spontaneous sorrow, despair, tears and heartache of the vast majority of Palestinian people," Rev. Sandra Olewine, the Jerusalem liaison for the United Methodist Church, later recalled. "My phone rang and rang as Palestinians from around the West Bank called to express their horror and their condolences."[17] The U.S. consul general in Jerusalem received a 12-inch-thick stack of condolences from Palestinians – which he ordered sent to CNN.[18]

The incident illustrated the depth of the perception gap. A Gallup poll conducted in December 2001 and January 2002 found that only 5 per cent of those surveyed in seven predominantly Muslim countries believed the attacks on the World Trade Center and the Pentagon were "morally justified."[19] Yet 54 per cent of Americans surveyed in a separate poll in early 2002 said they believed "all or most people in the Muslim world admire Osama bin Laden."[20] A complex mix of lived experience, history, religious beliefs and world-view produced a highly nuanced vision of the events of 9/11 in the Muslim world. Not so among Americans, whose knowledge of the Middle East and the effects of U.S. Middle East policy was negligible. Within 48 hours of the bombings,

George W. Bush would declare that America was now engaged in "a monumental struggle of good versus evil."[21] That conclusion seemed obvious to most U.S. citizens, yet even America's strongest supporters in the Muslim world believed the U.S. shared responsibility for the culture of hate that led to the disaster. "No sane person supports terrorism or fanaticism. It is important to identify the source of terrorism. Isn't the U.S. arrogance a factor in provoking this type of terrorism?" asked one Pakistani columnist.[22] While the "regrettable" attacks could not be justified, agreed a writer in Beirut's leftist *as-Safir*, the "unimaginable hostility . . . reflects the degree of the masterminds' despair, despondence and hatred for the United States." The U.S. should remember, he added, "that violence breeds violence, and that however mighty a country is, it cannot be safe from violence."[23]

As noted earlier, there are two great tragedies of 9/11: the deaths of more than 3,000 human beings in the attacks themselves and the subsequent missed opportunities for a new relationship between the United States and the world's Muslims, which produced even more bloodshed. As horrified as most Arabs and Muslims were at the carnage, they saw in America's inevitable search for explanations the possibility of a new dialogue in which Americans would finally begin to hear their frustration and, perhaps, feel their pain. As the question "Why do they hate us?" echoed across the United States, Arabs and Muslims offered not just an answer, but also a formula for change. The London-based Palestinian paper *al-Quds al-Arabi* recommended "A rational, objective, and careful review of U.S. foreign policy and the adoption of a new course that supports issues of rights and justice and is based on the resolutions of international legitimacy and human rights charters." These steps, said the paper, "will definitely lead to the creation of a better international climate of peace and stability."[24]

These were not calls for America to abandon Israel or topple the House of Saud, but rather, carefully reasoned arguments acknowledging the inevitability of military action against the terrorists themselves, but urging that a measured and highly targeted military response be combined with a constructive new attitude toward the Middle East and other Muslim countries. "Such a policy should dry up the sources of terrorism," Jordan's *al-Ra'y* said in an editorial published just 12 hours after the first plane hit the World Trade Center, "and at the same time put an end to the oppression and aggression carried out by certain states against other nations with the aim of subjugating and humiliating them and occupying their territories."[25]

With each condemnation of the attacks came new signs of the depth of Arab and Muslim resentment of U.S. policy, reminders that "America is reaping what it has sowed"[26] after years in which it had operated as "the judge and the executioner."[27] In many cases, there was also a guarded aspiration that the tragedy might serve as a watershed. "I hope that the incident of the U.S. suicidal planes will be an occasion for a pause by the Americans," said a columnist for Egypt's government-owned *al-Akhbar*. "I hope that this pause will prompt them to follow a new policy of self-restraint, not a policy whereby the United States would continue its onslaught and encirclement of other peoples and the looting of their resources."[28] For some, there was an unspoken sense of satisfaction that America got what it deserved:

> Whether those responsible for the attacks are Saudi dissident Usamah Bin-Ladin, or extremist organizations opposed to the unjust globalization, or domestic U.S. organizations complaining of racial discrimination and social, political and economic marginalization, the common denominator among all these parties is their deep sense of being victims of inequity resulting from the U.S. domestic or global policy.[29]

However, where a minority felt quiet satisfaction, most Muslims shook their heads in horror. "Whatever the resentments, this has to have been an insane – and ultimately doomed – way to combat Washington," said the *Arab News* of Jeddah on September 12. "None of those who died yesterday could have been responsible for the tragedies elsewhere."[30]

In the coming days, several themes emerged in the region's media that built on long-standing resentments and stereotypes and would shape the relationship between the United States and the Muslim world in the years ahead. These included:

The centrality of the Israel–Palestine conflict: "A prerequisite for success in countering terrorism is to remove the injustices suffered by Arab and Islamic peoples, and above all the Palestinians," wrote an *al-Akhbar* columnist, expressing a view held by many Arab opinion leaders.[31] "The whole campaign against international terrorism will fail if [the United States does] not solve the Palestinian–Israeli problem," Jordan's King Abdullah told President Bush in a late September White House meeting.[32] To many commentators there was "absolutely no difference between the unacceptable bloody terrorism that struck the United States and the savage daily practices of the Israeli forces against the unarmed Palestinian people who are allowed by all relevant international treaties and agreements to fight against occupation."[33]

The anti-Muslim nature of American policy: "September 11 was not mindless terrorism for the sake of creating terror," according to one Pakistani writer. "It was a reaction and revenge, even retribution, for the systematic injustice against Muslims, often descending into genocide."[34] The head of a Pakistani Islamic youth group told the *Nation* newspaper, "the Islamic world shared the grief of Americans but they also should take into account the sufferings of the Muslims of Kashmir and Palestine."[35] Others spoke of the U.S. policy of neglect for Muslims in Sudan, Bosnia, Chechnya and elsewhere.

The economic hegemony of the United States: "The globalization process has created the invisible enemy as perceptions such as poverty, inequality and injustice, have created new dilemmas and pains for mankind," warned the political columnist of Turkey's *Milliyet* newspaper.[36] America, numerous commentators charged, was driving the gap between the haves and the have-nots through a hegemonic policy of economic imperialism.

Punctuating such arguments were long-held stereotypes such as that of "a Zionist-dominated media" that sought "to make Arabs and Muslims the new enemies of human civilization."[37] As the United States pointed the finger of blame at Osama bin Laden, many demanded evidence. Pakistani Gen. Lt. Javid Nasir was certain of bin Laden's innocence: "I personally know that he, being of a puritan religious mind and practicing Muslim, could not have been a party to such a non-Islamic act."[38] Others saw a sinister anti-Muslim motive in the U.S. targeting of the Saudi exile. "The United States wants him because of his liberation posture," said an editorial in Beirut's generally moderate *an-Nahar*. "It appears to us that in the U.S. view, he is part of the Arab and Islamic resistance camp that must be destroyed before the new world order can be established."[39] Added *The Star* in Jordan: "The U.S. has been after bin Laden for years. Even if he had nothing to do with this latest atrocity, for now he is the perfect villain, the model enemy for the U.S. and its grieving people."[40]

Conspiracy theories once more came to the fore. On September 17, Lebanon's al-Manar television reported that 4,000 Jews "remarkably did not show up in their jobs" on September 11.[41] The story was repeated by numerous Arab news organizations, each time becoming more elaborate, including details such as the "fact" that "no Jew was present in the World Trade Center on 11 September, and not a single Jew was killed or wounded in the devastating attack."[42] Those stories blamed the Israeli intelligence agency Mossad for the bombings. Others pointed to the CIA, the Palestinians, the Japanese Red Army Faction, supporters of former Serbian President Slobodan Milosevic, the drug mafia, and even a shadowy unnamed group seeking world domination "like those portrayed in science fiction films."[43]

TRAGEDY AND OPPORTUNITY

A few Islamists saw the attacks as "divine revenge,"[44] the "wrath of Allah"[45] or "the wrath of heaven brought about by the wails and cries of the oppressed nations."[46] One former Pakistani government official told an Islamist newspaper that "if the United States did not change its attitude toward the Muslim world, God could further destroy it."[47] However, for the most part, comments from Arab and Muslim leaders and in the region's media focused on how the tragedy might serve as an opportunity for Americans to reassess their relationship with the Muslim world, coupled with prescient warnings about the danger of making the situation even worse. "The world does not doubt America's military might," observed Jordanian commentator Osama el-Sharif. "It surely has the technological capability to turn Afghanistan into a black hole. But this will only undermine America's standing and turn it into the very evil it wants to rid the world of. What America needs to do now is to launch a political offensive; one that examines the disease not grapples with the symptoms. The world will surely rally to join such a coalition."[48]

Some of those early warnings accurately anticipated the events to come. "It is easy to send land forces to invade or liberate a country but it is at the same time difficult to keep these forces and protect them from a long war of attrition that is costly in political, human, and financial terms,"[49] the chief editor of London-based *al-Quds al-Arabi* wrote on September 14. "Indiscriminate revenge," an Indonesian Muslim leader warned, would "increase animosity against the U.S."[50] Self-preservation was the chief concern for many. Osama bin Laden may have wanted to precipitate a clash of civilizations, but few except the most radical of Islamist militants believed such a confrontation with the remaining superpower was in their best interest. "The world is in trouble when America is hit and in bigger trouble when America does the hitting. The world is waiting for where the missiles will land," a Lebanese journalist wrote two days after the New York and Washington attacks.[51] "If 20,000 Americans die," asked a Pakistani columnist as the bodies were being counted in New York, "how many Afghans will balance the equation? 100,000? 200,000?"[52] Many pleaded for a rational response. "Bush said they would be patient," Derya Sazak wrote in Turkey's *Milliyet*. "But would not the real catastrophe occur if he launches an attack motivated by purely emotional reasons?"[53] For some in the political mainstream, the potential danger went far beyond the immediate physical peril, threatening to undermine the very stability of the region. "What will the reverberations be?" asked another Turkish columnist of the expected U.S. military response. "Could the United States' retaliation in Afghanistan put new wind into the sail of 'Islamic radicalism' in the region or the Arab world?"[54] "As America prepares to retaliate and as it prepares for more possible strikes against it," Rafiq al-Khuri wrote in Beirut's *al-Anwar*, "the world wishes that America would tackle the root causes of terrorism rather than merely fight against its tools."[55]

How they approached this fundamental question of motives was a key difference between reporting in the Muslim world and the United States in those early days. While newspapers and television broadcasts in Muslim countries chronicled the litany of reasons for the hatred that drove some Muslims to kill themselves and thousands of innocents, many in the American media preferred to characterize the attacks as "unfathomable."[56] A level of defensiveness permeated U.S. coverage. Even the respected ABC News anchor Ted Koppel felt compelled to open a special broadcast entitled *Why the Hate? America, from a Muslim Point of View* by running a lengthy and emotional interview with the emergency services operator who had spoken by cell phone with the American who, uttering the now-famous line "let's roll," led the passenger revolt aboard the hijacked jet that crashed in a Pennsylvania field. It was as if Koppel – or his network – felt the need to fortify his viewers with a dose of red, white and blue before examining Muslim attitudes. Inherent in this mindset was the notion that any true attempt to understand the motives of the September 11 hijackers implied that America was to blame – and such reporting was thus unpatriotic.

And so, from the earliest days of the post-9/11 era, the Rashomon effect took hold. Americans and the world's Muslims perceived very different messages in the billowing smoke of the World Trade Center. For both sides, this epic tragedy was a watershed: to the majority of Muslims, an opportunity for America to begin to understand their pain and craft a new relationship based on mutual respect; to Americans, evidence that, in the words of their president, the United States was engaged in "a monumental struggle of good versus evil"[57] and it was America's "responsibility to history"[58] to confront a *Them* who were so unlike *Us* that they think "in ways that we can't possibly think in America."[59]

In short, when the majority of Americans turned on their televisions in the days after 9/11, they saw a world painted in black and white; for most Muslims, the camera lens was swathed in shades of gray.

THE LANGUAGE OF AMERICAN EXCEPTIONALISM

John Winthrop's "City Upon a Hill" was under attack; the nation's manifest destiny had been challenged. This was not the time for nuance. "The great purpose of our great land . . . is to rid this world of evil and terror," the president told the nation. "The evil ones have roused a mighty nation, a mighty land. And for however long it takes, I am determined that we will prevail."[60]

It was a classic elucidation of American exceptionalism, the paternalistic notion that the United States somehow knows what is best for the rest of the world. Based on "the myth of virtuous American power,"[61] this belief in the "mystical significance of America as a special nation with an exemplary world mission"[62] held a fitful place in American foreign policy in the late twentieth century. Dealt a body blow by the Vietnam War, American exceptionalism was revived and repackaged in less imperialistic garb with Jimmy Carter's universal human rights initiative, only to crash and burn in the ill-fated hostage rescue attempt in the deserts of Iran. Shorn of any pretense of universality and restored to its original form by Ronald Reagan's "denial of American sin and bluff reassertion of traditional American values,"[63] American exceptionalism was then among the casualties of the Beirut disaster, which saw American forces driven out of a country they had come to save.

The New World Order of George H.W. Bush gave this self-view new life, particularly in his prosecution of the 1990–91 Gulf War. The United States saw itself leading the charge in a good-versus-evil shoot-out with the tyrant Saddam, even as others viewed the conflict as a self-interested war to control the Middle East's oil. Under Bush's successor, Bill Clinton, that shoot-out ended badly for the United States in the slums of Somalia, leaving Americans once more unsure how to exercise what they saw as their God-given strength and virtues, until the attacks of 9/11 "reknit the sundered marriage partners of the American myth."[64]

"God has placed us together in this moment," George W. Bush grimly told his fellow Americans hours after the attacks, dusting off the mantle of divine destiny upon which so many previous presidents had leaned in times of crisis. "Our country is strong. And our cause is even larger than our country. Ours is the cause of human dignity; freedom guided by conscience and guarded by peace. This ideal is the hope of all mankind."[65] Yet no matter how much they sympathized with America's pain, it was precisely this "impression that he is talking from a pulpit – a moral high ground,"[66] as one Bangladeshi writer put it, that so offended Arabs, Muslims and many others.

This disparity between how America saw itself and how it was seen by the rest of the world was, in part, the product of a conflict of visions that had been inherent in U.S. foreign policy since the founding days of the Republic. The belief in the inherent goodness of man evinced by Thomas Paine and Thomas Jefferson embodied an unconstrained American vision that saw all problems as solvable "with sufficient moral commitment."[67] Alexander Hamilton enunciated a far more constrained worldview in *The Federalist Papers*, observing that actions "unbiased by considerations not connected with" self-interest are "more ardently to be wished than seriously to be expected."[68] Bush administration policy in the months after 9/11 was a textbook example of self-interest wrapped in the flag of American exceptionalism. Americans saw themselves through the prism of Jeffersonian ideals, while the view from the Muslim world was obscured by the physical and emotional fallout of America's self-interested Hamiltonian trade-offs. Some critics claimed that Bush administration rhetoric was nothing more than a cynical exploitation of the nation's emotions. To others, this "almost theological conviction that American power is by nature good"[69] was genuine, but no less frightening. "Visions," writes Thomas Sowell, "are indispensable – but dangerous, precisely to the extent that we confuse them with reality itself."[70]

In November 2001, as he unveiled the new U.S. "vision" for Middle East peace – a pragmatic set of trade-offs designed to placate America's would-be Muslim coalition partners without alienating its Israeli ally – Secretary of State Colin Powell concluded with a line seemingly inspired by the biblical "Great Commission" to "go therefore and make disciples of all the nations." Said Powell: "We welcome the opportunity to use our power and influence to make the world a better place for all of God's children."[71]

RHETORICAL BORDERS

From his first solemn comments on September 11, George W. Bush began constructing the rhetorical borders that would soon be transformed into walls of animosity protecting palaces of hate. In a brief statement early that afternoon, the president told a shaken nation, "Freedom itself was attacked this morning by a faceless coward. And freedom will be defended."[72] The *Us* and *Them* dichotomy that would characterize the coming years was thus established: "We" represented freedom, while, as two linguists noted in their examination of presidential rhetoric, the term "faceless coward" represented "not only the beginning of the dehumanization of the enemy" but also "the antithesis to freedom."[73]

Bush would expand on the theme during a televised address on the evening of September 11. In less than 600 words, he laid the touchstones of America's post-9/11 worldview: "A great people . . . saw evil" and "responded with the best of America,"[74] the president said, setting the stage for what, in later speeches, he would call the "war between good and evil."[75] The nation "was targeted for attack because we're the brightest beacon for freedom and opportunity in the world," he told 84 million Americans watching on television, firmly shutting the door on any attempt to understand the motives of the hijackers and creating the first of many enduring myths to emerge from the Bush administration. Together "with all those who want peace and security in the world" Americans would now "go forward to defend freedom and all that is good and just in our world," Bush promised, hoisting once more the banner of American exceptionalism and leaving many overseas wondering why they had, in the past, seen so little evidence of this "resolve for justice and peace." Instead of "a bright beacon," many Arabs and Muslims glimpsed the long shadow of "the giant with its *animus dominandi*" that was planning once more "to flex its muscles in the Middle East."[76] It was this difference in perceptions that Osama bin Laden so effectively exploited.

In language and worldview, George W. Bush and Osama bin Laden were mirror images, standing at opposite poles of religion and ideology; each equally convinced of the righteousness of his cause; each issuing pronouncements rich with what one scholar called "God-talk."[77] Together, they painted cartoon caricatures of each other and authored a parallel set of narratives of their respective peoples that were, to use Edmund Burke III's description of Cold War dichotomies, "two tunnel-vision histories" that passed but never met. For George W. Bush, Osama bin Laden was "an evil man"[78] who led "a cult of evil"[79] driven by "pure malice"[80] while "daring to claim the authority of God."[81] In bin Laden's eyes, Bush was "the head of global Unbelief" leading a people who "are godless and follow falsehood" and support "the butcher against his victim, and the oppressor against the innocent child."[82] The "evil" that each leader told his followers they were fighting was a looming presence that would become a mainstay of the U.S. president's post-9/11 rhetoric, just as it had long been a fixture of bin Laden's public statements. "Evil," the linguists tell us, is an "archaic word [that] carries with it an emotional jolt from both its ancient beginnings and its current connection to horror."[83] It conveys a sense of "Victorian indignation" that "evokes the moral certainties of a simpler age, when the line between civilization and barbarism was clearly drawn, and powerful nations brooked neither insult nor injury from lesser breeds."[84]

A study of 15 major speeches by George W. Bush between January 2001 and March 2003 found that the themes of evil, security and peril were present in at least one of every 10 presidential paragraphs, and often much more.[85] At first, those responsible for 9/11 were painted as evil incarnate, but it was not long before the definition of evil became all-encompassing. "Anybody who tries to affect the lives of our good citizens is evil," the president was saying by October.[86] Bin Laden, meanwhile, had been setting up the very same dichotomy, packaging ideological and nationalistic concepts in prophetic language with liberal use of Qur'anic allusions.[87]

In structure and framing, the public statements of the warring leaders exhibited a symmetric dualism. "Both men constructed a Manichaean struggle, where Sons of Light confront Sons of Darkness, and all must enlist on one side or another, without possibility of neutrality, hesitation, or middle ground," according to Bruce Lincoln, professor of the history of religions at the University of Chicago.[88] The first phase of this process of polarization reached a crescendo with Bush's September 20 address to a joint session of the U.S. Congress, in which he declared: "Every nation, in every region, now has a decision to make. Either you are with us, or you are with the terrorists."[89] Bin Laden couldn't have agreed more, telling his followers, in a taped statement released in early October, "I say these events have divided the world into two camps: the Hypocrisy-free camp of Belief and the camp of Unbelief from which latter may God protect us and you."[90] This division of the world was, after all, precisely what bin Laden had been preaching for years and was an extension of Qu'tb's division of the world into *dar-ul-Islam*, the lands of Islam, and *jahiliyya*, the lands of barbarism.

THE RHETORIC OF RELIGION AND
THE RELIGION OF RHETORIC

In this mythic confrontation, each leader stood with the Lord at his right hand. Bin Laden believed "Allah has ordered us to glorify the truth and to defend the Muslim land . . . against the unbelievers"[91] and that "God Almighty granted inspiration and success to the vanguard squad of Islam"[92] which struck on 9/11. Bush, meanwhile, was "arguably the most evangelical president in American history,"[93] a man secure in the knowledge that, as he told Congress, in the eternal contest between "freedom and fear, justice and cruelty . . . God is not neutral between them."[94]

In fact, Bush, a born-again Christian who credited Jesus with giving him the power to overcome alcoholism, believed he had been chosen for this battle. During the 2002 election, he told Texas evangelist James Robinson, "I feel like God wants me to run for President." He also had a premonition: "I can't explain it," he said, "but I sense my country is going to need me. Something is going to happen . . . I know it won't be easy on me or my family, but God wants me to do it."[95] That faith had been apparent in his inauguration speech, in which Bush, quoting one of the founders of the republic, assured the nation that he was not alone at the helm, for "an angel still rides in the whirlwind and directs this storm."[96] According to Christian scholar James Barr, this conviction of a God-given mandate was reflective of the "overweening certainty" among fundamentalists that their version of Truth is "absolutely and uniquely right,"[97] which in turn produces a "combustible mixture of militarism, messianic zeal, and machismo."[98]

In a comparison of Bush's October 7, 2001 address, in which he announced the bombing of Afghanistan, and the bin Laden tape released the same day, the University of Chicago's Lincoln saw a mirroring of "narratives in which the speakers, as defenders of righteousness, rallied an aggrieved people to strike back at aggressors who had done them terrible wrongs."[99] Bin Laden's language was overtly religious, invoking the name of Allah seven times in the brief speech, at one point proclaiming, "They have come forth to fight Islam."

> This is a new epic to be added to the epics of Islam, a new battle of faith reminiscent of the great battles of Hittin [against the Crusaders], 'Ayn Jalut [against the Mongols], and the recapture of Jerusalem [by Saladin].[100]

Even for those Muslims who did not agree with his politics, it was, wrote one Islamic scholar, "a compelling performance" in which the exiled Saudi effectively used "words with high religious resonance" to outline his ideological agenda, while "employing structural formulas routinely used in Friday prayers – a device which would have struck the right note with Muslims around the world."[101]

The language of Bush's brief address was less lofty than some of his previous speeches, but, using a strategy of "double-coding" to appeal to his fundamentalist base without offending more secular Americans, this broadcast, too, framed the conflict in religious terms, containing "biblical allusions plainly audible to portions of his audience who are attentive to such phrasing."[102] In his statement that even though "the terrorists may burrow deeper into caves and other entrenched hiding places" American actions would "bring them to justice,"[103] could be heard an allusion to a climactic scene in the book of the Apocalypse, in which the Christ-figure unseals the "scroll of doom" and humankind "hid in the caves and among the rocks of the mountains" to escape God's wrath.[104] Likewise, in Bush's warning that those who side with bin Laden "will take that lonely path at their own peril"[105] could be heard echoes of the Biblical injunction in Job 8:13: "So are the paths of all who forget

God; and the hypocrite's hope shall perish."[106] Even in its closing line, the speech drove home America's claim to divine favor, consciously embellishing on the standard, "God bless America" by substituting instead: "May God *continue* to bless America."[107]

Such framing was not lost on those in the Muslim world whose own worldviews predisposed them to think in apocalyptic terms. However, to many Muslims, the rhetorical battle between Bush and bin Laden was corrupting the language of both religions and, as one distraught Malaysian wrote, transforming the "discourse of rights, democracy and religion" into "a vehicle of war."

> What is blatantly clear for all to see is how the language of politics is being used and abused by politicians – be they dressed in suits or the mantle of the Prophet . . . "Humanity" means much more than what the President of the United States may think, and "Islam" is certainly too big a concept to be grasped by the narrow-minded mullahs of the Taliban and Osama.[108]

No matter that the U.S. president apparently believed he was preaching a message of global unity; within weeks of 9/11, this *Us* and *Them* dichotomy was already beginning to cleave the very fault lines that would doom Bush's stated goal of inclusiveness and fuel bin Laden's aim of polarizing Muslims. Where the Bush administration – and most of the nation – saw a noble cause in America's divine mission "to lift this dark threat from our age and save generations to come,"[109] many Arabs and Muslims saw imperial hubris. "Nothing, nothing can justify this terrorism that melds human flesh with iron, cement, and dust. Nor can anything justify polarizing the world into two camps that can never meet: one of absolute good, the other of absolute evil," wrote Mahmud Darwish, Palestine's most famous poet, in an open letter signed by numerous Palestinian intellectuals considered "moderate" by the Bush administration.[110]

The nation's "deep respect to the opinions of mankind"[111] had been enshrined in the very first line of Thomas Jefferson's earliest draft of the Declaration of Independence. Yet that idea had, quite literally, not survived the rough draft of history and was edited out. Now, in the eyes of much of the world, the underlying concepts were also being jettisoned. After all, America – as it kept telling the world – knew what was best "for all God's children."[112]

RELIGION AND PATERNALISM

From the very start, Bush was careful to insist this was no war against Islam. "The face of terror is not the true faith of Islam. That's not what Islam is all about. Islam is peace," the president said during a September 17 visit to a mosque. "America counts millions of Muslims amongst our citizens, and Muslims make an incredibly valuable contribution to our country."[113] He continued on that theme during a prime-time news conference a few weeks later. "We respect the Muslim culture. We know Islam is a religion that teaches love and peace and compassion."[114] But occasionally, when the president strayed from the carefully crafted script prepared by his speechwriters, glimpses of a very different worldview could be discerned, as during a 2004 question-and-answer session with reporters in the White House Rose Garden, when he unexpectedly blurted out:

> There's a lot of people who don't believe that people whose skin color may not be the same as ours can be free and self-govern. I reject that . . . I believe that people who practice the Muslim faith can self-govern. I believe that people whose skins aren't necessarily – are a different color than white, can self-govern.[115]

It was an off-the-cuff comment thick with Othering. The reference to "people whose skin color may not be the same as *ours*" effectively cleaved the world into *Us* and *Them*,

with *Us* being the white world and *Them* being all those who
"are *a different color than white*." The comment must have
come as a shock to Americans of non-Caucasian ancestry –
expected to be a majority of the U.S. population by mid-
century. The observation that "people whose skins . . . are a
different color than white can self-govern" smacked of
paternalism, while on another level, implicit was the notion
that anyone who disagreed with the president's policies
regarding political change in the Middle East was a racist.
To some Muslims, even the president's characterization of
Islam as a "religion of peace" was arrogant. "I was totally
amazed when I heard George Bush explaining what Islam
means to us," said one Muslim scholar.[116]

Bush once said that it was his personal belief that one
had to accept Christ in order to enter heaven,[117] and that
religious worldview, which divided humankind into those
who were saved and those who were not, was apparent in
the language of salvation and redemption that came to characterize his post-9/11 vocabulary. Evil was something to be
vanquished. The righteous battle had been joined. God's
legions would triumph. Such rhetoric resonated with the
40 per cent of Americans who described themselves as evangelical or born-again.[118] "It's obvious there still remains here
a greater foundation of Christianity than in any other country of the world to my knowledge, and I don't doubt but that
this disposition still influences the political regime," Alexis de
Tocqueville wrote after his travels through the young nation
in the early 1800s.[119] Two centuries later, that foundation
remained intact.

The evangelical Christian core of what G.K. Chesterton
once called "a nation with the soul of a church"[120] had
proven essential to Bush's election and was reflected in the
makeup of his administration. Attorney General John
Ashcroft was an ultraconservative Pentecostal who once told
a Christian audience America was unique among nations

because "We have no king but Jesus."[121] Chief-of-staff Andrew Card was married to a Methodist minister.[122] Political advisor Karl Rove accepted an honorary degree from the controversial evangelist Jerry Fallwell. National Security Advisor Condoleezza Rice, the daughter of a Baptist preacher, had been known to lead prayer services on Air Force One. And the man spear-heading the president's agenda on Capitol Hill, House Speaker Tom Delay, believed "[o]nly Christianity offers a way to live in response to the realities that we find in this world – only Christianity" and blamed the Columbine High School shootings on "school systems that teach our children that they are nothing but glorified apes who have evolutionised out of some primordial mud."[123]

THE POLEMICS OF POLARIZATION

"This crusade, this war on terrorism is going to take a while," the president told reporters on the White House lawn September 16.[124] It was an unscripted, off-the-cuff comment in the midst of a 13-minute question-and-answer session; a perfectly natural choice of words for an American, especially one with a strong Christian vernacular, facing what he knew was going to be a long military campaign. It was also the worst possible reference.

Crusade. Seven letters written in the blood of history. No word better encapsulated the essential disconnect in worldviews between the United States and the world's Muslims. It is extremely unlikely that President Bush was consciously thinking of the invasion of the Holy Lands by the Christian knights of Europe a millennium ago when he referred to his crusade against terror. In the West, the term "crusade" was long-since stripped of its medieval significance and transformed into a generic term for a struggle – military or otherwise. Not so in the Middle East where the mere mention of the word had the power to engender righteous indignation. If "the relations between Christian and Muslim during the Middle Ages were marked by the persistent failure of each to try to understand the other," as British historian Richard Fletcher maintains, things were little better a thousand years later.[125]

"One who has known extreme shame and humiliation may forever struggle to recover a sense of agency and self-respect," observes psychiatrist Robert Jay Lifton, who has written extensively on the psychological basis of war. For Muslims, at the root of that humiliation lay the historical memory of the Crusades, in which tens of thousands of Arabs perished. "Never have the Muslims been so humiliated," says the protagonist of Amin Maalouf's 1984 novel, *The Crusades Through Arab Eyes*, "never have their lands been so savagely devastated."[126] Under the great Kurdish general, Saladin, the Muslims ultimately triumphed, yet there lingers a "bitterness over the relatively primitive Christian Europe initiating a vicious religious and civilizational assault on Arab culture at its height."[127] What came later was even worse. The collapse of the (Muslim) Ottoman Empire and subsequent European colonization of the Middle East; the creation of the State of Israel and exile of the Palestinians; the repeated defeat of the Arab armies; the 1967 War in which the Syrian, Jordanian and Egyptian armies were crushed and Jerusalem and the West Bank were lost; the Israeli invasion of Lebanon; and finally, the massing of U.S. troops in Saudi Arabia for the 1990–91 Gulf War, in which thousands of fellow Arabs were killed as the invading Iraqi army was driven out of Kuwait. These and many lesser humiliations left a deep stain of shame in the hearts of many Arabs. Even today, some Arabs call American Middle East policy *al-hurub al-salibiyya*, the "Wars of the Cross."[128]

This legacy of humiliation burned fiercely in the young scion of the bin Laden family. Pragmatic enough to cooperate indirectly with the Americans in the jihad against the Soviet infidels in Afghanistan, Osama bin Laden had returned to Saudi Arabia in 1989 a cult hero of sorts. He arrived in time to watch the United States mass 300,000 troops on the soil of the Arabian Peninsula, just a few hundred miles from the two holiest cities of Islam, in preparation for the 1990–91 Gulf War. To Osama bin Laden, the arrival of those "Crusader" armies was the final humiliation:

> For some 80 years now, our nation has been tasting this shame and degradation. Its sons have been slain, its blood spilled, its holy places desecrated and indiscriminate killing has been its lot, yet no one has heard its calls for help and no one has responded to them. But then God Almighty granted inspiration and success to a vanguard of Islam, and they dealt America a devastating blow.[129]

In the months after 9/11, George W. Bush would, through his failure to understand Muslim perceptions and sensitivities, inadvertently make a series of gifts to bin Laden. His first was that casual mention of "crusade," of incalculable propaganda value to a man whose organization, known in the West as al-Qaeda,[130] also called itself the World Islamic Front for the Jihad Against Jews and Crusaders,[131] and who, in his 1996 declaration of war referred to the Americans as "Crusaders" 23 times. To bin Laden, the "Zionist-Crusader"[132] aggression in Israel, Lebanon, Iraq and elsewhere was of a piece with the heroic battles of a millennium ago, and so Islam would respond in kind: "I envision Saladin coming out of the clouds," bin Laden told his supporters in a videotape released in 2001. "We will see again Saladin carrying his sword, with the blood of unbelievers dripping from it."[133]

The president's use of the word "crusade" therefore exploded like a thunderbolt through the Muslim world and seemed to confirm bin Laden's central premise. "A spokesman of the Bush administration regretted the utterances but this does not minimize the gravity of the situation as these [comments] reflected the intentions of the West against Muslims," said an editorial in the *Pakistan Observer*.[134] A Turkish columnist put the sense of consternation among Muslim moderates into more colloquial language, using his own variation of the Texas nickname for the U.S. president, Dubya. "'Doubleya' expects to construct a coalition comprising Muslim states to wage a war that he calls a 'crusade' on another Muslim state and he expects Muslims not to get all worked up?"[135]

Yet much of the reaction also focused on the "foolish"[136] nature of the comment. Egypt's *al-Akhbar* newspaper called it "a dreadful mistake" that the U.S. president had corrected through his subsequent visit to a mosque where he declared Islam a religion of peace.[137] Such cautious editorializing was in part due to the influence of the Arab governments that largely controlled the region's media. Most were joining the U.S.-built coalition and had little interest in encouraging anti-U.S. demonstrations. It also reflected a genuine desire on the part of many in the Arab and Muslim mainstream to avoid polarization. The reference to a crusade "is dangerous if he means to declare war on Islam and Muslims in the style of the historically known crusades," the London-based Palestinian newspaper *al-Quds al-Arabi* said in an editorial. "We hope that the U.S. president would avoid making generalizations and give more credit to voices that call for patience so that no harm would be done to innocent civilians who are just as innocent as the American victims."[138] Others reminded the president of the dangers of playing into bin Laden's desire for a religious confrontation. "Bush has made many mistakes in the very few days since the attack on New York and Washington, but perhaps this is the most important one," Sheikh Ahmad Yassin, the leader of the Palestinian Hamas group, told a Spanish newspaper. "I advise Bush not to unleash a religious war. We are against what happened and we are against more innocent people dying in the future.

If he launches himself against Muslims he will have us to face."[139]

The usually moderate Beirut newspaper *an-Nahar* suspected the apparent Bush gaffe might offer a glimpse of the president's hidden agenda. "It is true that a Crusade in the European languages might only mean a campaign to rally public opinion around a certain cause, but in the context of [the September 11 bombings] the investigation of which has focused exclusively on the Arabs and Muslims, this word can only denote a holy Christian war against the Muslims," the paper reasoned in an editorial.[140] Columnist Jalal Arif, writing in Cairo's *Akhbar el-Yom*, was equally cynical: "The American President may have little experience in international affairs. . . . Yet, he could not have deliberately made that mistake."[141] As attitudes polarized in the coming months, such suspicions within the Muslim mainstream would grow and Bush's call to a "crusade" would become a red flag that the forces of extremism would wave in the faces of those who, with suspicion and skepticism, once gave the U.S. president the benefit of the doubt.

Adding to the perceptions of a "Crusade" against Islam were the inflammatory comments of conservative Christian leaders like Franklin Graham, son of Billy Graham, the famous U.S. evangelist and spiritual advisor to presidents, credited with leading Bush to Jesus. The younger Graham, who had given the invocation at Bush's inaugural, denounced Islam as a "very evil and wicked religion,"[142] and televangelist Pat Robertson said Muslims were worse than Nazis.[143] Meanwhile, fellow Christian broadcaster Jerry Falwell, in an interview with the CBS News program *60 Minutes*, labeled the Prophet Muhammad a "terrorist"[144] and the Rev. Jerry Vines, past president of the Southern Baptist Convention, described Muhammad as "a demon-obsessed pedophile,"[145] a comment the president ignored when he addressed that same organization not long after Vines' remark.

Policy advisors close to the White House were capable of comments no less offensive to Muslims. Lawrence Eagleburger, secretary of state under the president's father, told CNN on September 11, "I know this is going to sound awful, but . . . there is only one way to begin to deal with people like this, and that is you have to kill some of them even if they are not immediately directly involved in this thing."[146]

"This is no time to be precious about locating the exact individuals directly involved in this particular terrorist attack," conservative commentator Ann Coulter wrote in a column published on September 13 and quickly quoted around the world. "We should invade their countries, kill their leaders and convert them to Christianity."[147]

Eagleburger was right. Such comments did sound awful to most of the Arabs and Muslims who heard them. But not to bin Laden. For him, it was the stuff of recruiting posters.

5
The Myth of Terror and the Terror of Myth

The cause of [the anarchist's] criminality is to be found in his own evil passions and in the evil conduct of those who urge him on, not in any failure by others or by the state to do justice to him.

President Theodore Roosevelt, Message to Congress, 1901

The themes of good versus evil and America as savior leading "civilization's fight"[1] were quickly repeated and endorsed in a U.S. media that framed the confrontation in mythic terms, with "allusions to tragic victims, brave heroes, sinister evil, and a world changed."[2]

"There are times and issues when right and wrong are colored in shades of gray, when men and women of good conscience may differ," said the Cleveland *Plain Dealer*, "This is not one of them."[3] In the tragedy of September 11, *The New York Times* heard "the opening salvos in the first American war of the twenty-first century," which would be a "war without illusions," against "a malignant threat that can destabilize the underpinnings of the world economy and civil society."[4]

To say the media was compliant with the administration's agenda is not to imply it was inert. The opposite was often true. A study of 84 editorials published in *The New York Times* in the month following 9/11 revealed a proactive pattern of journalistic myth-making in which *The Times* "took on the role of chief priest and state scribe" and "set about mending that fabric with restorative tales of myth."[5]

> The Times lamented the loss of innocence and grieved over a world in which everything had changed. It offered the myth of the Victim, called out for vengeance, and built support for survivors. It constructed and celebrated heroes and bolstered leaders as they responded to the crisis. It mobilized for war and warned of a foreboding future.[6]

This myth-making validated the narratives being produced by White House speechwriters and, by extension, the administration's subsequent military action, but it also exacerbated the growing perception gap between Americans and the world's Muslims. Central to this was the myth of terror.

CONSTRUCTION OF AN ENEMY

"America was targeted for attack because we're the brightest beacon for freedom and opportunity in the world," President Bush explained to the nation in his speech on the evening of September 11. In the coming days, the terrorists would be characterized as "cowardly," "evil" and driven by a hatred of liberty. At no point did presidential rhetoric hint that other motivations might exist. It was an example of what rhetoricians call "strategic misrepresentation,"[7] a distortion of reality that "is likely to occur when one cultural and linguistic voice is given as dominant, and all other voices end up being identified . . . as 'others.'"[8]

This notion that the United States had been attacked precisely because it was the shining "City Upon a Hill" played into the American self-image, but it did little to help the nation's citizens understand what had really happened – or take steps to address the root causes. However, critics of the president maintained that was never really the goal: "Speeches designed to minimize dissent and build unity will necessarily report selectively and slant at least through emphasis."[9]

In the coming weeks, the president relentlessly drove home his message. "These are people that hate freedom,"[10] he told Pentagon employees on September 19, as he toured destruction of that building. "This is a man who hates freedom," Bush said of bin Laden in a meeting with U.S. Muslim leaders.[11] He would grant no quarter to the idea that any form of legitimate grievance lay behind the terrorist action. Asked by a reporter whether bin Laden had political goals, the president shot back: "He has got *evil* goals. And it's hard to think in conventional terms about a man so dominated by evil that he's willing to do what he thinks he's going to get away with."[12] With tens of millions of people around the world watching on television, President Bush later told a joint session of Congress:

> Americans are asking, why do they hate us? They hate what we see right here in this chamber – a democratically elected government. Their leaders are self-appointed. They hate our freedoms – our freedom of religion, our freedom of speech, our freedom to vote and assemble and disagree with each other.[13]

Not so, countered a host of Arab and Muslim voices. "Those who hate America love its freedoms. They hate America because America's hypocritical policies deny them those freedoms,"[14] wrote columnist Humayun Gauhar in the *Nation* of Pakistan. "The war against terrorism is likely to be won or lost in the ongoing battle for the Muslim mind," observed C. Raja Mohan in the *Hindu* of India.[15] But this was a battle the United States began to lose on the first day of the war. Whether Bush's words reflected a failure to understand or a failure to acknowledge to some degree begged the point. The fact was, the United States was engaged in trying to build a global coalition – in which it was essential to include the world's Muslims – without a true picture of its enemy or, most critically, an understanding of the appeal he might have to the populations of the nations that were America's would-be allies. The United States was going to war against an ideological movement reduced to a cliché.

By personalizing the terrorist threat in the figure of Osama bin Laden, President Bush was able to ignore the inconvenient fact that what motivated the al-Qaeda leader was not necessarily the same thing that motivated *every* terrorist or the vast pool of Arabs and Muslims who sympathized with groups such as the Palestinians who also used violence. By lumping together the spectrum of individuals who carried out acts that the president considered "terrorism," Bush was able to create his "good" and "bad" dichotomy without acknowledging the existence of root causes. Terrorism thus became *the* enemy, rather than a tool used by *an* enemy. Such rendering virtually guaranteed the polarization that would follow.

Bin Laden was a very real military threat. But he was an even more potent symbol to disgruntled Arabs and Muslims – and countless others in the developing world – who resented what they perceived as American hegemony. As the al-Qaeda leader told a Pakistani newspaper editor in a handwritten note smuggled out of Afghanistan a few days after 9/11, "If I am killed there will be 100 bin Ladens."[16] It was a boast that would prove all too true even without his death. Despite significant U.S. successes in capturing top al-Qaeda officials and disrupting the group's infrastructure, the first four-and-a-half years of the new millennium would be the most bloody in the history of terrorism, with nearly 500 suicide attacks claiming more than 6,000 lives.[17] Al-Qaeda's relatively formal command structure would be replaced by what has been labeled a "swarming effect" with "actors from many different groups homing in on multiple targets, then dispersing to form new swarms."[18] Disparate groups of Islamist militants in Europe, Africa, the Middle East, South Asia and Southeast Asia came to operate with greater independence and increasing levels of brutality, while bin Laden's own myth grew and anti-Americanism rose. Over the four years following 9/11, the Bush administration would receive from Congress at least $300 billion in emergency spending for what it termed the "war on terror," yet, according to London's authoritative International Institute of Strategic Studies, U.S. actions *increased* the "risks of terrorism to Westerners and Western assets" and served to "enhance *jihadist* recruitment and intensify al-Qaeda's motivation to encourage and assist terrorist operations."[19]

A key reason for the tragedy could be found in the Bush administration's failure – or unwillingness – to understand the thinking of either its enemy or its would-be allies among the world's Muslims. This fatal error was the result of a series of false assumptions about the nature of radical Islamist militancy voiced by Bush administration officials and largely echoed by the media and a corps of self-styled and ideologically motivated terrorism "experts" in those first weeks after 9/11. The decision of an individual to carry out an act of what Americans consider "terrorism" – particularly suicide bombing – was the result of an enormously complex mix of psychological, socioeconomic, cultural, situational and other factors. The phenomenon defies any single explanation. Yet beginning on September 11, 2001, the president and his speechwriters reduced this to a set of simplistic bromides about terrorists, which included:

1. "THEY HATE OUR SUCCESS, THEY HATE OUR LIBERTY."[20]

Rather than hating America's freedoms, the evidence – both the empirical data and the testimony of the Islamist militants themselves – points to a very different conclusion: many *jihadis* are fighting for the very freedoms espoused by the United States. American support for oppressive regimes fuels much of the resentment among Islamist militants and their sympathizers. Many militants – such as the Egyptians convicted in the first World Trade Center attack – have suffered in the prisons of their own regimes. Others have seen friends and loved ones fall victim to systems in which they had no vote – or at least no meaningful vote – and no recourse. They have watched helplessly as the United States propped up authoritarian leaders like Suharto of Indonesia, whom President Clinton once called "our kind of guy,"[21] endorsed or turned a blind eye to the overthrow of democratically elected governments, and split the profits of the Saudi oil fields with the feudal rulers of the House of Saud.

"Osama and his protégés are the children of desperation. They come from countries where political struggle through peaceful means is futile," wrote Malaysian opposition leader Anwar Ibrahim. "These people need space to express their political and social concerns. But state control is total, leaving no room for civil society to grow."[22] The once-popular former deputy prime minister intimately knew of what he spoke. Ibrahim penned the article from his jail cell where he was being held on what were widely seen as trumped-up charges designed to silence and discredit him. As the National Research Council found: "[T]errorism and its supporting audiences appear to be fostered by policies of extreme political repression and discouraged by policies of incorporating both dissident and moderate groups responsibly into civil society and the political process."[23]

It was no coincidence that the majority of the 9/11 hijackers were Saudis, or that one of their leaders, Mohamed Atta, was an Egyptian. Nor was it surprising that the Saudi-originated al-Qaeda and the Egyptian Islamic Jihad, headed by bin Laden's right-hand man, Ayman al-Zawahiri, were the pillars of bin Laden's multinational Islamist alliance. The two Arab countries were run by very different, but equally repressive regimes. The Saudi royal family brooked no dissent; those who opposed the regime were silenced, jailed or executed. According to the 2003 U.S. State Department Human Rights report, Saudi "citizens do not have the right to change their government" and "security forces continued to torture and abuse detainees and prisoners, arbitrarily arrest or detain persons, and hold them incommunicado."[24] Egypt was ostensibly a democracy, but until 2005, President Hosni Mubarak ran unopposed. His regime was propped up by nearly $4 billion in annual U.S. aid,[25] which was, in the eyes of many Arabs, blood money that bought Egypt's peace with Israel. Mubarak's prisons held more than 16,000 Islamists and other opposition figures jailed in numerous crackdowns in the two decades since Islamic Jihad militants assassinated Mubarak's predecessor, Anwar Sadat. Egypt was considered Washington's closest ally in the Arab world, but a Congressional study acknowledged, "There is 'convincing evidence' that Egyptian police use torture to extract confessions, and detain subjects without charge or trial" (in fact, some of the suspected militants rounded up by the United States in Afghanistan and elsewhere were turned over to the Egyptians for just that reason). Islamists, the report noted, were tried in military courts "where the government prevailed and opportunity for appeal was nil."[26] As in Saudi Arabia, the United States held access rights for the use of Egyptian military facilities (many purpose-built by the United States) and the country had, since 1980, played host to the U.S. armed forces' largest joint military exercises in the Middle East.[27] This kind of foreign military presence was closely linked with the emergence of terrorism.

2. "WE'RE FIGHTING PEOPLE THAT HATES [SIC] OUR VALUES; THEY CAN'T STAND WHAT AMERICA STANDS FOR."[28]

"There appears to be no empirical evidence to support the claim that Arabs have a negative view of the U.S. because 'they hate American values,'" a 2004 survey of attitudes in six Arab countries concluded.[29] In fact, much the opposite appeared to be the case. Robert Precht, the lawyer who defended Mohammed

Salameh, an Egyptian convicted in connection with the first bombing of the World Trade Center, found that his client and the three other defendants had a high degree of regard for the American system. "These were people who expressed admiration for Congress and who took pride in the fact that they were taking part in a trial," Precht, then a Legal Aid lawyer who had no previous experience with Islamist militants, later recalled. "It was at odds with the typical terrorist profile."[30]

Polls consistently find that the majority of Palestinians have a favorable impression of U.S. values of equality, the American education system, freedom of the press, economy, and even many aspects of American culture,[31] yet an overwhelming majority of Palestinians support suicide bombings against Israeli targets and almost half refuse to label the attacks of 9/11 "terrorism."[32] Likewise, a survey of public opinion in five Arab and three non-Arab Muslim countries carried out in the spring of 2002 found that while there existed overwhelming resentment of U.S. foreign policy, substantial majorities had favorable attitudes toward American freedom and democracy, the U.S. education system, and even U.S. television and movies.[33] Rather than harboring a hatred of American values and the U.S. system of government, it is a hunger to share in such freedoms that motivates many who carry out acts of terrorism and those who sympathized with them.

3. SUICIDE BOMBERS ARE "FACELESS COWARD[S]."[34]

Many Arabs and Muslims consider suicide bombs the natural response of people facing the vastly superior firepower of a country like the United States or Israel. "Are the Marines *more* brave fighting and trying *not* to die? Is it *more* brave to shoot bombs from the sea?" a Shi'ite militant in Lebanon asked this writer during the 1983 bombardment of Lebanon by the battleship *New Jersey* and other ships of the U.S. Sixth

Fleet. "We have no *New Jersey*. We do not have jet planes. We have many trucks, so we use them. What is the difference between dropping a bomb on a building from the sky and driving it from the street?" The term "suicide bomb" is rarely used among Islamist militants, who prefer "Islamic human bombs," "sacred explosions" and "martyrdom operations," given the Qur'anic injunction against a Muslim purposely taking his or her own life. The bomber is a "martyr" or *shaheed*. "It is well-known that Islam forbids suicide," explains Sheikh Bassam Jarrar, a popular West Bank religious leader. "Suicide is running away, it is weakness and fear of facing life and its troubles. But martyrdom operations are something else. People who carry out such attacks are those who are very brave, braver than others."[35]

Though Americans didn't like to talk about it, the idea of dying to achieve a greater good is not completely alien to the nation's history. Schoolchildren in the United States are taught that Patrick Henry's declaration, "Give me liberty or give me death," was the epitome of patriotism, but to a Muslim ear it might not sound much different from this comment by young man preparing for a suicide mission: "I have become capable of sacrificing myself for my religion and my homeland."[36] Abolitionist John Brown was an "'American terrorist' driven by religious certainty" who gave his life to free the slaves and whose final words were, "the crimes of this guilty land will never be purged away but with blood."[37] The ranks of U.S. soldiers awarded the Congressional Medal of Honor are filled with Americans who willingly died for their country. While critics of such comparisons were inevitably quick to argue that American troops did not knowingly kill noncombatant men, women and children, the 185,000 dead in the Allied fire-bombing of Dresden in World War II,[38] might have disagreed. So, too, the 800,000 casualties of the nuclear attacks on Hiroshima and Nagasaki and the fire-bombings of Japanese cities that preceded them;[39] or the

4 million civilian casualties of the Vietnam War.[40] It was this
kind of double standard that fed resentment, leaving Arabs
and Muslims to wonder by what right Americans bewailed
the deaths of innocents in New York while condoning the
killing of innocents in the mountains of Afghanistan, the
cities of the West Bank and Gaza, and the rubble-strewn
streets of Sarajevo. Bin Laden spoke for many when he
challenged the U.S. president: "What principle makes *your*
blood real blood and *our* blood water?"[41]

4. FIGHTING POVERTY AND POOR EDUCATION IS "THE ANSWER TO TERROR."[42]

There is no doubt that the slums of the Middle East, South
and Southeast Asia provide fertile recruiting grounds for the
foot soldiers of the jihad. One-third of Arabs live on less than
$2 a day and more than 40 per cent are illiterate.[43] However,
the preponderance of individuals coordinating and carrying
out major acts of what most Westerners would call "terrorism"
are well-educated and are not driven by economic deprivation.
Debriefs of Saudi-born al-Qaeda detainees at the Guantanamo
Bay Naval Facility have revealed that many are well-educated
(some with graduate degrees), come from high-status
families[44] and express admiration for such U.S. values as
democracy, free speech, human rights and equality.[45] Fifteen
of the 9/11 hijackers were Saudis, citizens of one of the rich-
est societies on earth, and many of them held advanced
degrees.[46] It was an engineering student from the West Bank
who first proposed the use of human bombs by Palestinians
in the early 1990s, after seeing the success of the tactic in
neighboring Lebanon,[47] and the parents of one of the alleged
2005 London Underground bombers had just bought him a
new red Mercedes.

Data on Palestinian attitudes toward violence indicate that
individuals from the *higher* socioeconomic groups[48] and with

more education[49] are *more likely* to support suicide attacks. In interviews with nearly 250 would-be Palestinian suicide bombers and their families between 1996 and 1999, former relief worker Nasra Hassan found that "[n]one of them were uneducated, desperately poor, simple-minded, or depressed. Many were middle class and . . . Two were the sons of millionaires."[50]

An examination of 129 members of the militant wing of the Lebanese Shi'ite group Hizbullah killed in the 1980s and early 1990s revealed much the same. The poverty rate among dead Hizbullah fighters was 28 per cent compared to 33 per cent for the population, and 47 per cent of the Hizbullah militants had attended secondary school versus 38 per cent in the general population. The figures were particularly significant given that the Shi'ites as a whole occupied the lowest rung of Lebanon's socioeconomic ladder. "The results," Princeton researchers Alan Krueger and Jitka Maleckova reported,

> suggest that poverty is inversely related, and education positively related, to the likelihood that someone becomes a Hizbullah fighter . . . the findings provide no support for the view that those who live in poverty or have a low level of education are disproportionately drawn to participate in terrorist activities.[51]

Rather, the stereotype of suicide bombers as individuals so impoverished they have nothing to live for "may be wildly incorrect."[52] Though counterintuitive on the surface, logic dictated that "although the impoverished have a low opportunity cost in terms of time, they are less likely to become engaged in terrorist organizations because they are less involved politically, and less committed to the objectives of the terrorist organizations."[53]

An examination of the biographies of 400 al-Qaeda members by Marc Sageman, who helped run the Afghan war for the CIA, directly contradicted "the misconception . . . that the

typical al-Qaeda person is somebody who comes from a poor
background, broken family, he's ignorant, immature young
man, no skill, no family, job or responsibility, or weak mind
that's vulnerable to brain washing." In fact, Sageman found,

> three-fourths are from upper and middle-class background. The
> vast majority come from a caring, intact family. Sixty percent
> have a college education. The average age at joining the organ-
> ization is 26. Three-fourths are professional or semi-professional.
> Three-fourths are married. The majority have children.[54]

This pattern was not confined to the Middle East. In
Malaysia, for example, many arrested militants came from
the ranks of the police, the military and the civil service. A
report issued by the government of Singapore, based on
interrogations of members of the Indonesian-based Jamaah
Islamiyah organization arrested for planning an abortive
series of attacks on U.S. interests in that country, concluded:
"These men were not ignorant, destitute or disenfranchised.
Like many of their counterparts in militant Islamic organizations in the region, they held normal, respectable jobs."[55]
Princeton's Krueger reported that after comparing data of
"significant international terrorist events," as recorded by
the U.S. State Department, against the characteristics of the
terrorists' countries of origin, including gross domestic product,
literacy rates, religious divisions, and political and civil freedoms, his team found that, aside from the fact that larger
countries tended to produce more terrorists,

> [t]he only variable that was consistently associated with the
> number of terrorists was the Freedom House index of political
> rights and civil liberties. Countries with more freedom were less
> likely to be the birthplace of international terrorists. Poverty
> and literacy were unrelated to the number of terrorists from a
> country.[56]

Such data would seem to undercut the argument, voiced by
numerous Bush administration officials, that payments made

to the families of "martyrs" constituted a prime motivating factor in their decision to become a suicide bomber.

While poverty *does not* necessarily correlate to an increased proclivity toward terrorism, what *does* correlate is the sense of dashed hopes. Those who have tasted the fruits of economic or political opportunities and have then had those fruits ripped from their grasp seek to avenge that humiliation and right the wrongs. Bin Laden offered a way to do that. "Societies are most liable to tolerate terrorism after people have already begun experiencing increased education, steps toward prosperity and some political opening, but then see their rising aspirations stymied," argues Scott Atran, an anthropologist who studies radical Islam.[57] The 15 Saudi 9/11 hijackers came from a society that had risen to become one of the wealthiest on earth, but in the final years of the twentieth century faced a declining economy and exploding national debt. There was a growing pool of young Saudis who had studied at universities in the United States and Europe – where they were exposed to Western democratic ideals – and returned home to find few prospects for employment and their dreams of prosperity dashed.

Equally potent is the blend of social isolation and lack of economic opportunities that faces the rapidly expanding population of well-educated Muslims in Europe, where second-class status has fed a subculture that draws alienated young men and women into tight-knit circles in which they feed each others' anger and resentment, not unlike the socially marginalized members of a U.S. street gang. A startling 75 per cent of *jihadis* in Sageman's study of al-Qaeda recruits had joined outside the borders of their native land, most while studying abroad, while another 10 per cent had been born in the West of immigrant parents, like the London bombers. They were "literally cut off from their culture and social origins. They were homesick, lonely, and alienated."[58]

Tellingly, the genesis of the 9/11 plot emerged from a *jihadi* cell in Germany.

Palestine, where 157 suicide bombings took place between October 2000 and May 2004,[59] offers a case study in the impact of dashed hopes. The World Bank reported a dramatic drop in living conditions in the West Bank and Gaza between 1999 and 2001. In that same period, support for suicide bombings increased from 26 per cent[60] to 59 per cent.[61] The collapse of the Palestinian economy was not the only factor. Even as their quality of life deteriorated, Palestinians had their hopes for a peaceful resolution of the conflict raised by the Oslo peace accords, then crushed as negotiations for a final settlement bogged down. The result was a dramatic rise in support for the Islamist factions, from 8.5 per cent in August 1999[62] to 35 per cent in March 2004,[63] by which time 77 per cent of Palestinians feared for their own safety.[64] Years of humiliation, curfews and isolation in the Occupied Territories had taken their toll. "Here, our life is full of problems. We Palestinians prefer to die, just kill ourselves, rather than live this worthless life," said one young failed suicide bomber. "We're hollow bodies leading a pointless life. Israelis enjoy their life. They go out at night, they have cafes and nightclubs, they travel all over the world. They go to America and Britain. We can't even leave Palestine."[65]

5. TERRORISTS ARE "PSYCHOPATHS."[66]

Suicide bombings are an apparently irrational act carried out for the most rational of reasons: they are highly efficient. Between 1980 and 2001, suicide attacks accounted for just 3 per cent of what a Congressional report categorized as "terrorist" incidents, but were responsible for nearly half of all the deaths.[67] "I don't know of a single case of a person who is really psychotic," says Ariel Merari, an Israeli researcher who has studied every suicide bombing in the

Middle East since the 1983 destruction of the U.S. Marine Corps barracks in Beirut. He believes that the only "abnormal" thing about suicide bombers is their ability to overcome fear at the critical moment.[68] "They are really quite normal psychologically," agrees Jerrold Post, the man who created and for 21 years ran the CIA's psychological profiling unit.[69] A Congressional Research Service report on suicide terrorism reached much the same conclusion, concluding that suicide bombers are neither "impulsive" nor "crazy."[70] Imprisoned recruiters for Palestinian suicide cells say that potential bombers are turned away if they express strong personal grievances or overt rage, since such emotions can pass, causing the would-be bomber to falter before his mission is complete.[71] Those carrying out such acts need to be rational, level-headed and able to improvise in the event of unforeseen complications during their mission. The organizers of suicide cells claim that they carefully scrutinize potential recruits, seeking out individuals who, in addition to exhibiting piety, demonstrate "self-discipline" and an ability to be discreet.[72]

Hussam Abdo, a 15-year-old would-be Palestinian suicide bomber who became famous when a TV cameraman recorded his dramatic capture at an Israeli checkpoint, told an interviewer that he was initially approached by a friend who asked if he knew of anyone willing to carry out a "martyr operation." "I told him I'll do it. My friend says – really? And I answer – yes I'll do it." He was then taken to a 21-year-old recruiter for the Al-Aqsa Martyr's Brigade. "[H]e asked me a lot of questions. He asked me who I was and why I wanted to do this. I answered all of his questions. I told him I wanted to do it because of my friend who was killed and he agreed to let me do it."[73] That sense of personal injury is a common theme among suicide bombers. A document on the psychology of terrorists widely used within the U.S. intelligence community says of young Palestinians who volunteer to be suicide bombers:

> In almost every case, these potential bombers – who range in
> age from 12 to 17 years – have a relative or close friend who
> was killed, wounded, or jailed during the Israeli occupation.
> Bombers are also likely to have some long-standing personal
> frustration, such as the shame they suffered at the hands of
> friends who chastised them for not throwing stones at the Israeli
> troops during the [first] Intifada.[74]

The implications are chilling in light of the fact that 97.5 per cent
of Palestinian children suffer from Post-Traumatic Stress
Syndrome, nearly 95 per cent have attended a funeral, 83 per cent
have witnessed shooting incidents and 62 per cent have seen a
relative killed or wounded. Many Palestinian suicide bombers
were children during the first Intifada who saw relatives beaten
and humiliated.[75] This combination of terminal degradation
and lifelong exposure to violence creates an atmosphere
in which regard for human life is diminished. "You feel that
you're treated like less of a human being. Not quite like a
human being. And you begin to think of others in that way,"
says Prof. Sari Nusseibeh, a leading Palestinian peace activist,
who has watched support for violence spike each time hopes
for peace seems lost. "And I think this is how people have to
think who go and kill themselves and kill others as they do."[76]

In his interview with the BBC, Abdo was asked whether, as
he donned his explosives-filled belt, he *really* understood "that
you were going to go and murder people, that you were going
to go and cause great suffering to mothers and fathers, that you
were going to be a mass murderer? Did you really know that?"

"Yes," he calmly replied. "Just like they came and caused
our parents sadness and suffering they too should feel this.
Just like we feel this – they should also feel it."[77]

6. TERRORISTS ARE RELIGIOUS "FANATICS."[78]

It is beyond dispute that those militants who carry out acts
of terrorism in the name of Allah harbor a deep commitment

to their religion. They believe they are emulating the Prophet Muhammad, who defended his followers through offensive military action against the Meccans during his exile from that city. The modern *jihadist* embarks on a mission with the absolute conviction that s/he is carrying out the will of God and that not only will s/he go straight to Paradise, but will also reserve a place there for his or her family. Describing the final seconds before he was to die, one would-be suicide bomber, whose belt ultimately failed to explode, told an interviewer, "I was very happy . . . I never felt so calm in my life."[79] This sense of certainty was seen in the expression of serene calm on the face of a Palestinian suicide bomber who blew himself up at an Israeli bus stop (the undamaged head, with its carefully-combed hair, was incongruously attached to the mangled remains of his torso).[80] However, while religion is certainly a motivating factor among those who become suicide bombers, it does not necessarily provide the initial impetus toward militancy. In fact, a study of al-Qaeda members found that only 13 per cent attended *madrasas* (religious schools) and "most of them were not religious when they joined [al-Qaeda]. They became religious in the process of joining and afterwards."[81]

Nor are all suicide bombers radical Islamists – or even Muslims. The decidedly secular Liberation Tigers of Tamil Eelam (LTTE), who are waging an ethnonationalist separatist war in Sri Lanka, were responsible for almost half of the suicide attacks carried out worldwide between 1980 and 2001.[82] Israeli terrorism researcher Ehud Sprinzak points to the Tigers, who were responsible for the assassinations of Rajiv Gandhi and Sri Lankan President Ranasinghe Premadasa, as "the most significant proof that suicide terrorism is not merely a religious phenomenon and that under certain extreme political and psychological circumstances secular volunteers are fully capable of martyrdom."[83] The Tigers are not the only secular group carrying out such acts. Of the remaining suicide bombings in the period cited above, one-third were the work of other militant groups with secular – not religious – orientations, such as the Kurdish PKK, which has been fighting a separatist war against Turkey and Iraq. This is a category Sprinzak calls "rational fanatics."[84] Such suicide bombers act not out of a belief that they will be rewarded in Paradise, but for a mix of nationalistic and pragmatic motives, bolstered by intense indoctrination. Some researchers have labeled this "altruistic suicide," the idea of giving one's life for a greater cause.[85] In many cases, the shift to suicide bombing followed the use of other certain-death tactics, such as the Tigers' "first wave suicide assaults" in which thousands of commandos sacrificed themselves, or the spate of knifings of Israelis in the late 1980s, in which the Palestinian perpetrators were almost always killed. From there, it was a short step to strapping on an explosives-packed vest.

Fanaticism as an explanation for terrorism also ignores politics. The short history of suicide terror campaigns indicates that most seek a specific set of territorial goals and once those are achieved the violence ends. The withdrawal of U.S. and Israeli forces from Lebanon; the creation of a Tamil state in Sri Lanka; the granting of autonomy to Turkey's Kurds; and the temporary withdrawal of Israeli troops from the Occupied Territories in 1994 and 1995; each was followed by a halt to suicide attacks (which, in several cases, resumed after circumstances that brought about the ceasefire changed). Fifty-nine per cent of Palestinians surveyed in 2004 said they supported the continued campaign of suicide bombings, yet the same percentage said they would *oppose* armed attacks against Israel from Gaza if the Israelis withdrew and 72 per cent *supported* reconciliation between the two peoples.[86] Al-Qaeda and its ideological spawn may have more amorphous goals, but demands that foreign forces leave Iraq were a staple of the claims of responsibility as radical Islamist violence spread to Europe.

7. TERRORISTS ARE "BRAINWASHED."[87]

There is little evidence of systematic brainwashing among those who carry out acts of radical Islamist terrorism. However, a culture of martyrdom exists that facilitates the recruitment of suicide bombers. This has been true at least since the 1970s, when Lebanon was the headquarters of Yasser Arafat's Palestine Liberation Organization (PLO) and posters of slain fighters plastered the Palestinian refugee camps. Sports figures, music idols and movie stars are the role models for America's youth. To those who have grown up amid the anger and pain of societies like Lebanon, Palestine and Sri Lanka, the "martyrs of the cause" take their place. The martyr "is like an idol for many young people now," explains psychiatrist Dr. Eyad Sarraj of the Gaza Mental Health Clinic. "It is something to aspire to be. . . . In all my teenage time, my symbols were body-builders and movie stars and singers and people like that. Then it changed," he recalls. "The guerrilla, the fighter, then it was the stone thrower, and today it is the martyr."[88] Would-be suicide bomber Hussam Abdo said of his plans to become a martyr: "It's better than being a singer or a footballer. It's better than everything."[89]

This culture of martyrdom is an essential element in the process of creating a suicide bomber, but it is also a tried and true technique used by insurgent groups and societies at war the world over, including those in the United States. "The manipulators of terrorist youth constantly emphasize the recognition and adulation that the youth's act will bring to them, just as great war leaders and generals try to make their soldiers believe that killing the enemy will bring them recognition as heroes," according to one U.S. expert on violence.[90]

The ritualistic recording of martyr videotapes and the posing for posters are among numerous techniques used to cement commitment and bolster dedication among those

chosen for martyrdom operations. The selection of the youth
comes in several ways. As in the case of Abdo, it might be
through an approach from a friend involved in a militant
group. In others, as in a Singapore cell of Southeast Asia's
Jamaah Islamiyah, scouts attending prayer services led by
radical clerics approach individuals singled out as particularly pious or serious and invite them to take part in religious
discussion groups where their true commitment is assessed.
The first overt step in the recruitment process usually
involves eliciting a *bayt al ridwan* or pledge of fealty – named
for the garden in Paradise reserved for martyrs – to an individual cleric who acts as the spiritual leader of the cell. This
might later be supplemented by another *bayt* to a titular
leader, such as bin Laden, or it may be implied. For example,
the co-founder of Jamaah Islamiyah, Abdullah Sungkar, met
personally with bin Laden in the early 1990s and pledged
bayt to the Saudi,[91] while most of those who carried out
Jamaah Islamiyah's violent actions were graduates of a network of *pesantrens*, or Islamic boarding schools, established
by Sungkar and his fellow cleric, Abu Bakar Ba'asyir, and
had pledged *bayt* to the two Indonesian spiritual leaders or
other clerics under them.[92] In later stages, the recruits are
often asked to carry out small acts demonstrating their commitment to the group, such as reconnaissance or smuggling,
then, through techniques such as deft application of peer
group pressure, their involvement is escalated. The approach
is not unlike that used with Japanese *kamikazes* in World
War II, when pilots were lined up and told to step forward if
they did *not* want to volunteer for a suicide mission.

Once the recruit commits to the operation, the "sacred
drama" of Qur'an reading, taping of messages and the taking
of photographs seals the commitment.[93] Many suicide
bombers then don white garb similar to Muslim burial
shrouds. "At that stage, a person sees himself as already
dead," Israeli researcher Merari explains of the symbolism.

"There is no return for him without really losing any self-respect, the respect of others, but also because his mental state is already focused on killing himself, on being dead."[94] Similarly, members of the Tamil Tigers' suicide unit wear distinctive black robes and have, as *The New York Times* described it, "elevated the suicide attack to the ultimate commitment to the movement."[95]

This psychological manipulation of the would-be suicide bomber plays a factor in sealing commitment. However, studies of those who commit such acts consistently demonstrate that it is impossible to provide a single explanation for the terrorist phenomenon as a whole, since individual suicide bombers are themselves driven by a unique blend of factors that bring them to the point of deciding to give up their lives. Sometimes, the stated reasons are extraordinarily mundane, as in this exchange between Hussam Abdo, the 15-year-old would-be bomber, and his BBC interviewer, who asked why he volunteered for a suicide mission:

> *Hussam*: The reason was because my friend was killed. The second reason I did it is because I didn't want to go to school. My parents forced me to go to school and I didn't feel like going.
> *BBC*: Are you saying that one of the reasons you wanted to become a suicide bomber was because you didn't like your teacher?
> *Hussam*: That and because of my friend Sabih, who was killed.
> *BBC*: It seems extreme that if you don't like your teacher it could partially propel you towards murder and suicide.
> *Hussam*: The thing is my parents forced me to go to school and I didn't want to go.[96]

VISIONS OF THE ENEMY

It is not an exaggeration therefore, to say that every one of the Bush administration's characterizations of the terrorist threat was simplistic or erroneous; grounded in an element of truth, but ignoring the totality of the facts. The enemy created in the mind of the American public was but a caricature of the real enemy. While not all of the above data was available on September 11, 2001, a substantial body of literature on the phenomenon of suicide terrorism already existed – much of it painting a portrait of suicide bombers and their organizers that was very different from the one sketched by the president and his speechwriters. As a 1999 report prepared for the intelligence community put it: "Because terrorism is a multicausal phenomenon, it would be simplistic and erroneous to explain an act of terrorism by a single cause."[97]

Despite such warnings, the Bush administration personalized the terrorist threat in a single individual whom it labeled "evil," thus eliminating any need for an examination of motives. Bin Laden and his ilk, administration officials repeatedly told the country, wanted only to sow destruction.

Bin Laden's ultimate goals today are unclear. Yet it is apparent from even a cursory reading of his early public statements that far from having an "apocalyptic" or nihilist aim of destroying mankind, bin Laden's first priority, at least since the early 1990s, has been to drive U.S. forces from the Arabian peninsula and eliminate the state of Israel. Similarly, al-Qaeda's second-in-command, Ayman al-Zawahiri, was seeking to topple the Egyptian government long before he ever hooked up with bin Laden and turned his attention to Egypt's patron, the United States. There is plenty of room to debate what would have happened if bin Laden's original argument had prevailed and U.S. forces had been prevented from deploying in Saudi Arabia or were quickly ejected after the Gulf War ended. It is possible that, emboldened by the victory, he would still have launched his jihad. What is *not* debatable is the fact that he *did* seek *specific* foreign policy changes and aligned those demands with other grievances that resonated with the wider Arab and Muslim body politic.

The U.S. official who knew bin Laden best, a CIA officer who headed the bin Laden task force until the late 1990s, summed it up this way:

> Bin Laden's genius has been to focus the Muslim world on specific U.S. policies. He's not, as the Ayatollah did, ranting about women who wear knee-length dresses. He's not against Budweiser or democracy. The shibboleth that he opposes our freedoms is completely false, and it leads us into a situation where we will never perceive the threat.[98]

It was the fact that his message was so much in sync with mainstream attitudes in the Arab world and among other Muslims that made bin Laden such a potent force. If President Bush and the majority of Americans had not been distracted by bin Laden's religious rhetoric or deafened by their own preconceived notions, they would have heard a set of tangible and cogent grievances outlined in the al-Qaeda leader's October 7, 2001 tape. Said bin Laden of U.S. sanctions in Iraq:

> A million innocent children are being killed as I am speaking to you . . . for no crime they have committed. We hear no voice denouncing this . . . These days Israeli tanks and armored vehicles wreak havoc in Palestine . . . We hear no voices raised and see no one little finger bent. But when after the passage of 80 years the sword strikes America, Hypocrisy lifts its head and grieves for the murderers who violated the blood and honor and holy places of Muslims.[99]

To Muslims, one Arab professor wrote, the talk "came across as moral in its tone" in contrast to the U.S. president's speech that same day announcing the Afghan war. "He skillfully presents himself as a self-appointed Muslim spokesman to a world which has chosen not to listen.[100] That was not how the U.S. media framed the message. "The speech was brief, unapologetic and inflammatory," reported *The Los Angeles Times*. The *Rocky Mountain News* was even more succinct: "The man is not just a religious fanatic . . . he

is a megalomaniac."[101] *The Atlantic Journal-Constitution*
noted that the address would be viewed through different
prisms: "While Americans are likely to find Osama bin
Laden's speech bizarre and threatening, radicals likely will see
it as pious and warlike,"[102] but the paper ignored any mention of the motivations outlined in the talk. The paper also
joined several leading newspapers in erroneously reporting
that bin Laden's linkage of his jihad to the Palestinian cause
was "a new tack."[103] John Burns of *The New York Times* was
one of the few reporters who focused on substance, noting
that the tape made plain that "two immediate objectives of
bin Laden are the removal of American troops from Saudi
Arabia and a clear Palestinian victory over Israel."[104]

Any reporter – or government official – who bothered to
run a LexisNexis search would have found that this talk of
concrete grievances was nothing new for the al-Qaeda leader.
In 1996, bin Laden told Robert Fisk of the British newspaper
The Independent, "Our country has become an American
colony," referring to U.S. forces there.[105] That same year, his
11,000 word *fatwa*, or religious ruling, offered a detailed
summary of his motivations, goals and intended tactics. His
core complaint was clear from the title itself: "Declaration of
War against the Americans Occupying the Land of the Two
Holy Places."[106] In Palestine and Iraq, Tajikistan and
Kashmir, Chechnya and Bosnia, Somalia and Ethiopia,
Burma and the Philippines, the "aggression" of the "Zionist-
Crusaders alliance" meant "Muslims' blood became the cheap-
est and their wealth as loot in the hands of the enemies."
Chief among the insults to Muslim honor was "the occupation
of the land of the two Holy Places," known to the rest of the
world as Saudi Arabia.

There is a widespread assumption in the United States that
bin Laden has always sought the overthrow of the House of
Saud. In fact, when he first returned home from Afghanistan
in 1989 and began giving talks in mosques and private

gatherings bin Laden's message was largely in accord with that of the Saudi government. He spoke of the great victory of Islam over the infidels in Afghanistan as proof of the righteousness of the strict Saudi interpretation of Islam. The royal family capitalized on this to enhance its own posture and rewarded the bin Laden family with numerous contracts for its vast construction business.[107] All that would change with Iraq's invasion of Kuwait on August 2, 1990. Americans would have a difficult time understanding why some Arabs opposed the U.S. military effort to oust Saddam Hussein's invading forces. However, in the Middle East, the conflict was seen as a continuation of the struggle between the forces of Arab nationalism, represented by Iraq's Ba'ath Party, and the conservative royalist regimes, led by Saudi Arabia. In this view, Saddam was taking on the mantle of Egypt's Nasser, who had confronted the Saudis in the Yemeni civil war of the 1960s, a challenge anathema to an Islamist like bin Laden.

For this reason, bin Laden quickly rallied to the anti-Saddam cause. The victory of his *jihadis* over the Soviets in Afghanistan left him convinced the Iraqis could also be vanquished. He drafted a ten-page memorandum outlining a plan for the defense of the kingdom. It was a sign of the regard in which he was held by the royal family that bin Laden was given an audience with the Saudi defense minister, Prince Sultan, at which he made a plea for self-defense and suggested that the combat-hardened Saudi Afghan veterans be rallied to the cause. He also warned against the consequences of inviting infidel forces to defend the kingdom. Given the fact that the Saudi rulers were guardians of the Muslim holy places, such an invitation, he pointed out, could have a profound impact on both Saudis and their fellow Muslims elsewhere, a belief shared by many of the senior *ulema* or clerics. "At this stage of the crisis," says bin Laden biographer Yossef Bodansky, "Osama bin Laden intervened as a concerned but fiercely loyal citizen."[108]

Fearful for their own survival in the face of Saddam's powerful military and panicked by American warnings of an imminent Iraqi attack,[109] the royal family ignored bin Laden's advice and asked the U.S. to defend them. King Fahd convinced the country's senior *ulema* to temporarily set aside their objections to the presence of U.S. forces on the strength of Washington's assurances that it had no intention of establishing permanent American military bases on Saudi soil. Then-Defense Secretary Dick Cheney insisted his troops "will stay until justice is done but not stay a minute longer."[110] Bin Laden would long remember that promise. His advice rejected by the government, the former Afghan resistance organizer launched a campaign to rally opposition to the American presence, calling for, among other things, a boycott of U.S. goods. However, he parted with other Islamists outside Saudi Arabia – including many of his old Afghan allies – in refusing to condemn the royal family, apparently believing he might still convince them to reverse the decision and order the Americans' expulsion, thus safeguarding their Islamic legitimacy. Instead, the House of Saud, which saw any criticism as treason, turned against him, exerting pressure on both Osama and his family, threatening to drive the hugely wealthy bin Laden construction firm into bankruptcy if the young scion did not back off. Yet bin Laden was not jailed, nor were the threats carried out, in large measure because of his popularity and the government's hope it might still use him.

The crowning blow came after the end of the Gulf War when the royal family announced that it had agreed to the permanent presence of U.S. troops on its soil. To bin Laden, it was the ultimate betrayal and he said so. "The king told lies to the *ulema*," he later charged in his 1996 declaration of war against the United States and the Saudi regime, issued from exile in Sudan. "The King said that: 'the issue is simple, the American and the alliance forces will leave the area in a few months.' Today it is seven years since their arrival and the regime is not able to move them out of the country." After several paragraphs of religiously inspired language, bin Laden shifted tone. Sounding more like a politician than an evil genius, he complained of the weakening value of the Saudi riyal, the skyrocketing national debt, corruption and in-fighting among members of the royal family, government control of the media, the absence of free speech, human rights abuses and the impotence of the military. Bin Laden noted that a reform petition presented to the royal family, "written with soft words and very diplomatic style," had been rejected and its authors harassed and imprisoned:

> [T]he advocates of the correction and reform movement were very keen on using peaceful means in order to protect the unity of the country and to prevent bloodshed. Why is it then the regime closed all peaceful routes and pushed the people toward armed actions?!![111]

Thus, he explained, there was no choice but to strike at "the root of the problem." Lest his supporters have any doubts, bin Laden repeated his core argument, that "to push the enemy – the greatest *Kufr* [infidel] – out of the country is a prime duty." By "country," bin Laden meant the lands from Saudi Arabia to "the Furthest Mosque," the al-Aqsa Mosque in Jerusalem. His degree in business administration and experience in the family construction company was apparent in his orders that the infrastructure of the petroleum industry be spared in any fighting that might occur on Saudi soil, for "the presence of the world's largest oil reserve makes the land of the two Holy Places an important economical power in the Islamic world."

READING MINDS

It was easy, as many scholars, journalists and government officials did, to dismiss bin Laden as a "millennialist" or an "apocalyptic" representative of a new breed of terrorists who, former CIA Director R. James Woolsey told the National Commission on Terrorism, "don't want a seat at the table, they want to destroy the table and everyone sitting at it."[112] Yet such a simplification left out of the equation that critical issue of the root causes that made bin Laden's exhortations so tantalizing to a vast swath of Arabs and Muslims. Ignoring those grievances was to ignore the "hearts and minds" so vital to defeating terrorism. This myopia extended from the highest levels of government down to the frontline.

As he prepared to deploy to Afghanistan where he would serve on the Joint Task Force intelligence staff, Army Capt. Matthew Morgan wrote a piece for *Parameters*, the journal of the U.S. Army War College, a publication widely read in military and national security circles. The editors summarized the article this way: "Morgan takes one inside the mind of the terrorist to distinguish between the 'pragmatic' terrorist of the past and a new generation of fanatic."[113] In the article, Capt. Morgan tells his fellow officers that the "New Terrorism" involves "millennial visions of apocalypse" in which "today's terrorists seek destruction and chaos as ends in themselves."[114] To the average American viewer, the images that filled television screens on September 11 might well have seemed the work of someone who sought "destruction and chaos as ends in themselves." And bin Laden's utterances were wrapped in rhetoric that, to an ordinary listener with a Judeo-Christian worldview, might be considered "millennialist and apocalyptic." However, such language obscured what was, at heart, an Arab – and in some cases Saudi – nationalist agenda. One that, it might be hoped, a military intelligence officer on the frontline of the war on terror who presumed to take his reader "inside the mind of the terrorist," would be able to penetrate. In perhaps the most troubling line of the article, Morgan tells his military and national security audience that "no foreign policy changes by the U.S. government could possibly have appeased the bin Laden radical." It was a conclusion that was both simplistic and ignored the written record.

ALL-PURPOSE BAD GUY

The issue was not whether bin Laden posed a dangerous threat, which he demonstrably did. Rather, the issue was whether, if it had framed the war on terror differently – acknowledging the root causes and taking steps toward addressing them – the United States might have preserved the wellspring of goodwill that existed among the majority of the world's Muslims in the days after 9/11, undercutting bin Laden's ability to broaden his base of support, rather than contributing to the climate of fear and alienation that served bin Laden's goals.

The majority of Muslims opposed terrorist acts. Particularly controversial was al-Qaeda strategist Ayman al-Zawahiri's doctrine of "hitting the distant enemy before the near" and attacking Americans and Europeans on their home soil rather than targeting the despised Saudi and Egyptian regimes or foreign troops in the region. But instead of reaching out to those who opposed al-Qaeda's tactics through a strategy that combined targeted military operations with steps toward ameliorating the many grievances that angered most people in the Middle East and broader Muslim world, the Bush administration turned a deaf ear to those whose support was crucial to undermining the extremists. By "denouncing an enemy that hates us for what we are, not for what we say and do," wrote Robert Kaiser of *The Washington Post*, "President Bush has created an all-purpose bad guy whose existence allows him to sidestep any examination of American policy."[115] This "fact-free approach to Middle East policymaking"[116] was driven by what one former State Department official termed "faith-based intelligence" that played to preconceived notions. In the black-and-white worldview of Capt. Morgan and others who shared his thinking, if terrorists simply hated everything we stood for and sought only apocalyptic destruction, then any search for root causes was pointless self-flagellation. As the Congressionally mandated National Commission on Terrorism so presciently noted in the introduction to its final report, released a year before 9/11, "An astute American foreign policy must take into account the reasons people turn to terror and, where appropriate and feasible, address them.[117] In one of history's great ironies, the introduction was signed by the commission's chairman, Amb. L. Paul Bremer, who would become head of the Coalition Authority ruling Iraq during the U.S. occupation, an event that would spur the bloodiest upsurge in suicide bombings in history. The other great irony was that as the war on terror alienated the world's Muslims and radicalized a vast pool of potential al-Qaeda recruits, it created the very "clash of civilizations" the West was trying to avoid.

6
Enemies, Allies and Other Artificial Constructs

The very concept of objective truth is fading out of the world.
George Orwell

While building its inaccurate portrait of the causes of terrorism, the Bush administration also propagated another myth popular with U.S. presidents: terror does not work. History taught that it did.

"We were an ignored and forgotten people and then overnight the world heard our voice," Bassam abu Sharif, one of the architects of the first wave of Palestinian airplane hijackings, once proudly told this writer. The 1972 Munich Olympics massacre, in which 11 Israeli athletes were killed, rocketed the Palestinian cause "from obscurity to renown."[1] The assault, by a PLO faction calling itself Black September, failed to achieve its immediate objective of freeing Palestinian prisoners held in West Germany and Israel, and most of the commandos were killed, yet it was an unequivocal success. The 24-hour long drama was played out before hundreds of journalists gathered to cover the Olympics and an estimated worldwide audience of 900 million. "[F]rom the purely propaganda viewpoint, [the operation] was 100 percent successful. It was like painting the name of Palestine on a mountain that can be seen from the four corners of the earth," Black September jubilantly announced in a communiqué.[2]

The Palestinian issue was catapulted to the top of the United Nations agenda, where it has remained ever since.

If a picture was worth a thousand words, a single terrorist incident was as valuable as 10,000 speeches. The lesson was not lost on others who would follow; yet they would also demonstrate that terror could be a military, as well as a propaganda tool. "With small means and great faith, we can defeat the mightiest military power of modern times," bin Laden told supporters in a propaganda video entitled *Destruction of the Destroyer Cole*.[3] The truth of that statement has been demonstrated repeatedly in the 30 years since Munich: in Iran in 1980; in Lebanon in 1983; in Somalia in 1993; in Saudi Arabia in 1996, and again in Yemen in 2000. Each time, an American president repeated variations on the same words, an implausible mantra of denial that defied the facts of history:

- "We will never yield to blackmail," President Carter promised in the face of the Iran hostage crisis.[4]
- "Let terrorists be aware that when the rules of international behavior are violated, our policy will be one of swift and effective retribution," vowed Ronald Reagan in his first inaugural address.[5]
- "Foreign policy is not going to be dictated or changed by terror," said then-Vice President George H.W. Bush as he toured the ruins of the U.S. Marine Corps barracks in Beirut.[6]
- "The cowards who committed this murderous act must not go unpunished," said President Clinton in the wake of the suicide bombing of the Khobar Towers military barracks in Saudi Arabia.[7]

Over and over, such bluster quickly gave way to military realities. A month after he vowed to stand fast, Ronald Reagan ordered the Marines to withdraw from Lebanon because, he told the nation, in a comment that reflected the power of terror, "once the terrorist attacks started, there was no way we could really contribute to the original [peace-keeping] mission."[8] Iran would cost Carter the presidency and long after Clinton left office, those responsible for Khobar Towers and the *Cole* were still free.

"The legend about the invincibility of the superpowers vanished" in Afghanistan, bin Laden said in a 1998 interview. Somalia confirmed that. The United States precipitously withdrew after the infamous "Black Hawk Down" incident, in which 18 soldiers were killed, 73 were wounded, a helicopter pilot was held ransom and the bodies of American soldiers were dragged through the streets. When that happened, bin Laden said, "our boys were shocked by the low morale of the American soldier and they realized that the American soldier was just a paper tiger."[9] Defense Secretary Donald Rumsfeld succinctly summed up the problem in an internal Pentagon memo during the Iraq war, "The cost–benefit ratio is against us! Our cost is billions against the terrorists' cost of millions."[10]

Publicly, the White House under George W. Bush maintained the traditional presidential "stand fast" façade in the face of bin Laden's demands after 9/11. Yet in April 2003, as it invaded Iraq, the United States quietly announced the withdrawal of all but 500 of the remaining 10,000 uniformed U.S. forces in Saudi Arabia, shifting the strategic presence to a ring of bases around the region, with Iraq and the U.S. military command in Qatar as its anchors.[11] The move may have been the result of a convergence of geopolitical shifts and changes in U.S. military doctrine, as American officials claimed, but in the Arab world and beyond it was seen as a victory for bin Laden that presaged an eventual American abandonment of the House of Saud.

"To a big extent he's succeeded," Prince Alwaleed bin Talal, a member of the royal family with vast business interests in the United States, told *The Wall Street Journal* shortly after the withdrawal was announced. "He has succeeded in creating a big gap between us."[12] Bin Laden had predicted as much in his 1996 interview with Robert Fisk of *The Independent*, telling the reporter, "I believe that sooner or later the Americans will leave Saudi Arabia and that the war declared by America against the Saudi people means war against all Muslims everywhere. Resistance against America will spread in many, many places in Muslim countries."[13]

BLOWBACK

It was not lost on Arabs and other Muslims that the forces the United States engaged as the first bombs fell on Afghanistan in early October 2001 were, in many ways, a creation of the United States. Al-Qaeda and its supporters in the Taliban were children of the Afghan jihad, America's successful campaign to turn Afghanistan into the Soviet Union's Vietnam.

"Arabs and Muslims have not created the bin Ladin phenomenon or his terrorists," wrote an Egyptian columnist. "They did not train, finance, arm and unleash them against Arab and Islamic states to corrupt and terrorize them after their first mission in Afghanistan against the Soviets ended."[14] Others argued that the very the notion of jihad had been moribund since the tenth century until the Americans revived it to inspire the Afghan uprising against the Soviets.[15]

"America has created the evil that is attacking it," Taliban leader Mullah Muhammad Omar responded in the face of U.S. demands that he turn over bin Laden.[16] Mullah Omar knew of what he spoke. The Clinton administration had supported the Taliban's move into Kabul after the Soviet withdrawal from Afghanistan; the presence of the ultra-conservative Islamists restored order and guaranteed the country would remain hostile to Moscow and friendly to America's allies, Pakistan and Saudi Arabia. The Taliban also conveniently agreed to sign a deal with U.S. oil companies for a new pipeline from Turkmenistan. As Gilles Kepel notes: "For a long time, the Taliban reaped the benefits of American indulgence, while Saudi Arabia, which had spent a fortune dislodging the Soviets from Afghanistan, found itself in close ideological agreement with the rulers of Kabul."[17]

Radical Islamist violence was a classic example of what the intelligence community termed "blowback," the tendency of some operations to shift direction and burn their creators. With active recruitment by the Pakistani and Saudi intelligence services, upwards of 35,000 *jihadis* from across the Muslim world had flocked to join the Afghan war.[18] The conflict solidified Pakistan's position of influence among Muslim countries and served the Saudi goal of "turning the ire of the militants against the Soviet Union and away from the American protector," while undermining Iran's Khomeini in the Saudi–Iranian struggle for regional leadership.[19]

Most of these foreign *jihadis* passed through the border regions of Pakistan, where a young Saudi named Osama bin Laden helped some of them acclimate and added their names to his growing database of Islamist militants committed to the cause. Relatively few of these foreigners actually saw much combat in Afghanistan, where their presence was largely resented by the Afghans. But they did receive combat training at camps set up by bin Laden and his allies. Their tour complete, these newly minted *jihadis* returned home, where they would emerge as the leaders of homegrown militant Islamist groups from Algeria to Indonesia, eventually forming the backbone of bin Laden's jihad. By most accounts, bin Laden did not work directly with the Americans. "We didn't even know his name," claims Marc Sageman, a former CIA operative who helped run the Afghan war out of Pakistan.[20] Whether or not that was literally true, bin Laden was demonstrably a product of the American–Saudi jihad against the Soviets. So, too, were the Taliban and

fundamentalists like Gulbuddin Hikmatyar, head of a key
U.S.-backed *mujahideen* group who is today on the FBI's
"Most Wanted" list of terrorists, with a $25 million bounty
on his head. When American priorities changed after
the Soviet withdrawal and eventual onset of the 1990–91
Gulf War, these erstwhile spawn of U.S. foreign policy
were orphaned, sparking a massive backlash against the
U.S. among Islamist groups. "The *mujahideen* used to be
America's blue-eyed boys during the Afghan jihad. They
would be invited to the White House and be decorated. But
now they have been labeled as terrorists," complained Hafiz
Said, the fiery leader of one militant Pakistani Islamist
group.[21]

In the aftermath of the anti-Soviet jihad, Pakistani society
suffered the twin effects of a radicalization of its own Islamist
parties and the militarization of the border regions. As one
Pakistani writer reminded the U.S. after 9/11:

> The people of Afghanistan have been the first victims of this
> terrorism. Pakistan continues to suffer from the fallout of the
> Afghan jihad, including [a] Kalashnikov culture, drug trafficking,
> smuggling, rising crime, over 2.5 million Afghan refugees and,
> more importantly, sectarian killings and random bombings.[22]

The 2001 U.S. bombing of Kabul and the resulting
overthrow of the Taliban prompted another exodus of Sunni
jihadis for whom Afghanistan had been a safe haven. Many
crossed the border into Pakistan. They brought with them
the specter of suicide bombs. Pakistan had not previously
had a "martyr culture;" for the most part, its cleric still
interpreted the Qur'anic injunction against suicide to mean
the condemnation of "human bombs." But as Pakistani
researcher Nasra Hassan wrote of the arrival of suicide
bombing in her native land:

> Maddened and humiliated by defeat in Afghanistan, Pakistan's
> *jihadi* leaders changed their philosophy. They had condemned as

sinners those bombers who died by their own hand; now they switched support to homegrown operations based on an imported idea. Foreign jihadis brought the technique; Arab clerics escaping from Afghanistan preached its virtues; Pakistani merchants and smugglers provided funding; and local zealots supplied the bombers.[23]

The element of "blowback" from the actions of outside powers stretched even deeper into Pakistani history. Many of the modern-day *jihadi* leaders are products of the *madrasas* (religious boarding schools) of Pakistan, where, in the 1980s, an estimated 100,000 foreign Muslims studied. In 2002, Pakistani President Pervez Musharraf announced a crackdown on the schools, which, he charged, "propagate hatred and violence" and "produce semiliterate religious scholars."[24] A large portion of these schools were funded by Saudi charities and blended Saudi Arabia's fundamentalist Wahabi brand of Islam with the teachings of Deobandism, the authoritarian pan-Islamic sect of the subcontinent. Beginning in the late 1980s, according to Zachary Abuza, an expert on Asian Islamist networks, veterans of the Afghan war and the Pakistani *madrasas* – often one-and-the-same – returned to Southeast Asia and began setting up a network of radical *madrasas* on the Pakistani model. These centers blended in with the tens of thousands of private religious boarding schools that already existed in the region. The new networks became the base for militant Islamist groups that would emerge in the 1990s, including Jamaah Islamiyah, the organization responsible for the October 2002 Bali nightclub bombings, which claimed more than 200 lives, the subsequent attack on the Jakarta Marriott and abortive plots against other U.S. and Western targets.

If the United States had only itself to blame for the blowback from Afghanistan, it had the British to thank for the legacy of the *madrasas*. In the mid-nineteenth century, Britain had decided to create a system of education for the wealthy, urban children of its Indian colony in order to "create a class of persons Indian in blood and color but English in taste, in opinions, in morals and intellect."[25] The *madrasas*, which had been vital centers of learning under India's Muslim rulers, were sidelined, their scholars persecuted and, in some cases, the buildings themselves razed. It was left to the urban poor to support the collapsing *madrasa* system until several Muslim revivalist movements emerged, including the fundamentalist Deobandi School. By the mid twentieth century, the *madrasas* of what had by then become Pakistan mainly focused on rote learning and dogmatic interpretations of Islam. They became the focal point of emergent political parties, such as the Deobandi-led Jamiat Ulema-e-Islam, which made numerous failed attempts to gain political power. With the advent of the U.S.-backed war on the Soviets in Afghanistan, many of the *madrasas* were quickly converted into military training grounds, with the World Bank estimating that by the year 2000 as many as 20 per cent of the schools had a military training element.[26] Pakistani economist Waleed Ziad has observed that "these impoverished students readily became cannon fodder in Afghanistan," ultimately forming the foundation of the global *jihadist* movement against the United States.

It was an ideology spawned by British colonial hubris, adopted by resentful Pakistani Islamists for "short-term political gains . . . fueled by the frustrations of a disaffected lower class,"[27] and cynically manipulated by U.S. foreign policy. It would mature into the greatest threat to global stability in the early twenty-first century.

ONE MAN'S TERRORIST

Afghanistan was just one example of the truth of the old saw: one man's terrorist is another man's freedom fighter. When the United States spoke of terrorism, Arabs and Muslims immediately thought of the actions of America and its Israeli

ally. One of the most lethal terrorist attacks of 1985 was
a car bomb that killed 80 Lebanese in a botched CIA-
engineered attempt on the life of Hizbullah spiritual leader
Muhammad Hussein Fadlallah, whom the United States
blamed for sanctioning the Marine barracks bombing.
Likewise, Ali Akhbar Mohtashamipur, who as Iranian ambassador in Damascus in the 1980s was widely believed to have
been the architect of anti-American terrorism in Lebanon,
lost his right hand and several fingers when he received a
booby-trapped Qur'an in the mail, which, he told this writer,
he was sure was a present from the CIA.[28]

Ronald Reagan had famously called the Afghan *mujahideen*
and the Nicaraguan contras "freedom fighters"[29] and said
the contras were "the moral equivalent of the founding
fathers."[30] Yet the Afghan *jihadis* whom Reagan received in
the Oval Office pioneered the tactics used by the "terrorists"
who would later attack American forces in Iraq and the
Nicaraguans were implicated in numerous massacres of
civilians, including children and nuns. "We know the difference between terrorists and freedom fighters, and as we
look around, we have no trouble telling one from the other,"
Reagan's secretary of state, George Shultz, once said.[31]
Things weren't quite so clear to the rest of the world.

After the United States handed over power in Iraq to interim
Prime Minister Ayad Allawi, news broke that Allawi once
ran a CIA operation against the regime of Saddam Hussein
that included numerous car bombs set off on the streets of
Baghdad. He was not the first to transition from terrorist
leader to chief of state. Former Israeli prime minister Yitzak
Shamir was chief of the infamous Stern Gang, responsible for
a series of acts of terrorism during the Israeli struggle for
independence against the British. At the time, sounding much
like the Palestinians he would later confront, Shamir wrote:

> [T]errorism is for us part of the political battle being conducted
> under the present circumstances, and it has a great part to

play: speaking in a clear voice to the whole world, as well as our wretched brethren outside this land, it proclaims our war against the occupier.[32]

The hard drive of a computer discovered in Afghanistan that had been used by bin Laden and his aides contained a primer on the tactics employed by Zionist resistance groups in Israel in the 1940s. It included an admiring account of the activities of former Israeli prime minister Menachim Begin, who headed Irgun Zvai Le'umi, a militant group that bombed Jerusalem's King David Hotel, then the British headquarters.[33] Begin's Irgun, together with the Stern Gang, was held responsible for the 1949 massacre of some 250 Palestinian men, women and children at a village called Deir Yassin, a place that would, to Arabs, become synonymous with Israeli terror. "Arabs throughout the country, induced to believe wild tales of 'Irgun butchery' were seized with limitless panic and started to flee for their lives," Begin wrote in his autobiography, *The Revolt*.

> This mass flight soon developed into a maddened, uncontrolled stampede. Of the almost 800,000 who lived on the present territory of the State of Israel, only some 165,000 are still there. The political and economic significance of this development can hardly be overestimated.[34]

Word of the massacre was spread by the Jewish underground, the Haganah, which used sound trucks to warn Palestinians that "unless you leave your homes, the fate of Deir Yassin will be your fate."[35] The resulting exodus of some 700,000 Palestinians would come to be known as *al-Naqba*, the catastrophe, and would be seared into the collective Arab consciousness. Israel's founding father, David Ben-Gurion, would later proudly observe that by Independence Day "that part of Israel" where Israeli resistance forces were operating "was almost clear of Arabs."[36] To Arabs and Muslims, that early example of what the president of the Arab American

Institute, James Zogby, has called "ethnic cleansing"[37] laid
the foundation for a history of anti-Palestinian violence that,
in their view, can only be labeled terrorism. The U.S. government may have insisted that terrorism was something carried
out by "non-state" players, but few in the Muslim world
agreed. "Terrorism, according to our dictionary, is any violent
method that results in the killing of civilians, since no cause
justifies killing innocents," said Malaysia's former Minister
of Information, Mahmoud Al Sharif.[38]

"A terrorist [is] somebody who does something that you
don't agree with, a freedom fighter is somebody who does
something that I agree with," Ahmed Sattar, one of the
Egyptians convicted in the first World Trade Center bombing, told an American interviewer. "George Washington was
called a terrorist. Menachim Begin [was] called a terrorist.
Anwar Sadat, your hero, was called a terrorist by the British.
So today's terrorist is tomorrow's freedom fighter. Or today's
freedom fighter could be tomorrow's terrorist."[39] Former
U.S. defense secretary Robert McNamara once noted that
if the United States had lost World War II, he and other
American military leaders would have been tried as war
criminals for their firebombing campaigns against German
and Japanese cities in which hundreds of thousands of civilians
perished.[40] Those bombings clearly fit the definition of
terrorism as, "[T]he deliberate creation and exploitation of
fear through violence or the threat of violence in the pursuit
of political change."[41]

Terrorism is, in short, a matter of perspective. While more
than 90 per cent of Palestinians surveyed in a 2001 poll said
they viewed "all Israeli violent acts against Palestinians as
acts of terror," almost as many reported that they did "not view
Palestinian violent acts against Israelis as acts of terrorism."[42]
That equivalency was underscored in a letter sent by the
Palestinian Council to the U.S. Congress on September 12,

2001, in which the Palestinian ruling body, in carefully chosen language, affirmed "our complete condemnation of all forms of terrorism and state terrorism against innocent civilians."[43] For the Palestinians, subject to decades of Israeli occupation, there was no difference between acts of violence carried out by individuals and acts of violence ordered by governments. By specifically including the phrase "innocent civilians," the Council also telegraphed the fact that while it considered the killing of noncombatants to be terrorism, attacks on soldiers and other military targets were the legitimate right of an occupied people.

To Arabs and other Muslims, America's failure to acknowledge that Israeli violence fit the definition of terrorism, while condemning Palestinian actions as exactly that, was just another example of U.S. double standards. Then there were the issues of U.S. bombing raids in places like Lebanon, Afghanistan, Sudan, Libya, Iraq and elsewhere, and the sanctions that resulted in the deaths of thousands of Iraqi children, about which Madeline Albright, then secretary of state in the Clinton administration, famously commented, "we think the price is worth it" to keep Saddam in check.[44] Many Arabs asked whether the U.S. public would be so sanguine if Caucasian children in some European country were dying due to sanctions. The answer was obvious. All this, in the eyes of many in the Middle East, South and Southeast Asia, was as much terrorism as a plane crashed into the World Trade Center. "American terrorism is more dangerous than other terrorisms," said Sheikh Hamed Betawi, the preacher at a mosque in the Palestinian city of Nablus.[45]

It was this broad resentment of U.S. double standards among mainstream Arabs and Muslims that bin Laden so effectively exploited: "They rip us of our wealth and of our resources and our oil. Our religion is under attack. They kill and murder our brothers. They compromise our honor and our dignity and dare we utter a single word of protest against the injustice, we are called terrorists."[46]

TERROR AS A TOOL

Just as the question of who is a terrorist may shift with the political winds, so too does the definition of "good" and "bad" regimes. Another source of anger among Muslims in the months after 9/11 was what they saw as the Bush administration's jettisoning of all other priorities in favor of a hypocritical embrace of an assortment of regimes, from African despots to the ex-Communist thugs of Uzbekistan, that had previously been subject to a cold shoulder. This was most vivid in the case of Pakistani Gen. Pervez Musharraf, who had seized power in a coup, imposed martial law, and was viewed with disdain by the country's Islamist parties. Before 9/11, the United States had in place sanctions against both Pakistan and India for their testing of nuclear weapons. These were quickly scrapped in return for the decision of the two countries to join Bush's antiterrorist coalition.

"America and its western cronies support dictatorships when it suits them and shed crocodile tears for democracy when convenient," said one Pakistani columnist. "If America cannot help Muslims win those freedoms it should at least not hinder them by supporting those who would take them away, who occupy Muslims lands, who grab power through a rigged ballot, the barrel of a gun or monarchy."[47] Membership in the antiterror coalition offered oppressive regimes a license to crush internal dissent. Suddenly, ethnonationalist insurgents and troublesome domestic groups from Chechnya to China were labeled "terrorists" and targeted as part of the global "crusade." The notions of terrorist, enemy and ally had become artificial constructs shaped by Washington to serve the aims of America and its new partners, with little regard for how they were perceived by those who did not control the levers of power.

ULTERIOR MOTIVES

The name chosen by the Pentagon for the so-called war on terror was a demonstration of just how out of touch with Muslim sensibilities was the Bush administration. The announcement that it would be called Operation Infinite Justice caused many across the Muslim world – as well as those in the United States who knew something about Islam – to recoil. Only Allah could mete out "infinite justice," American Muslims and Islamic scholars explained to the White House. The name was quickly changed to Operation Enduring Freedom, giving rise to much grumbling in the Arab and Muslim media about the fact that there was nothing enduring about freedom in the region, nor did they expect Bush's crusade to change that.

"Human nature tells us what is justice and what to do when we see an injustice inflicted upon a community or anywhere else," said Dr. M.S. Bahmanpour of the Faculty of Oriental Studies at Cambridge in early October 2001. "This injustice is not created by us, rather it is created by the people now claiming to be the protectors of justice and having the operations of 'Infinite Justice' and 'Enduring Freedom.'"[48] An added problem for the Bush administration in those first weeks after 9/11 was that many Muslims believed the United States was jumping the gun in blaming bin Laden for the bombings, just as it had initially blamed Muslims for the Oklahoma City bombing carried out by a white Christian right-wing separatist. Where, they asked, was the evidence? Some, like Bahmanpour, saw a Machiavellian motive:

> All those people who are now wandering in Afghanistan are in fact potential recruits for terrorism and they will react and fight back and I am sure the American people know this, but what hidden agenda they have, I don't know.[49]

Many saw it as a gambit by the hawkish neoconservatives who surrounded Bush to create what they firmly believed could be a New American Century, as the blueprint written long before the Bush administration took office was titled, governed by what one of the document's authors called a "benign imperium."[50]

"The United States named its destructive attacks against Afghanistan 'enduring freedom' and raised the slogan of 'justice,'" Jerusalem's *al-Quds* newspaper said in an editorial. "But how can justice be served . . . without presenting conclusive evidence on the role of Afghanistan or the ruling Taliban movement in the attacks in the United States, which were used as pretext to launch this horrible war?"[51] In Buddhist Thailand, thousands of Muslims gathered to demand that the United States refrain from attacking Afghanistan on the basis of "the unproven allegation" that bin Laden was responsible, warning that Islam itself appeared to be the target. "It might be the crusade of the twenty-first century," said one Thai Muslim leader.[52]

The image of a wounded superpower striking out blindly before it had all the facts was a common theme, as in the *News* of Pakistan:

> Revenge and retribution is writ large all across the United States, particularly in the media. The most powerful imperium of all time, long lush with arrogance, has been wounded and humiliated. It seeks to perform rites of blood to restore its self-esteem.[53]

Many across the political spectrum worried that by attacking Afghanistan, the administration was playing right into the hands of those responsible for 9/11. "There is broad agreement that they provide enough grounds for some punitive measures," said *Arab News* of Saudi Arabia. "Now one can only hope that the action will be swift and spare innocents."[54]

In his speech announcing the invasion of Afghanistan on October 7, President Bush warned: "Every country has a choice to make. In this conflict, there is no neutral ground."[55]

The comment bolstered the view that the war on terror masked a broader agenda:

> Maybe there is no neutral ground, but there are treacherous territories. Among President Bush's advisers are people who take the Sept. 11 terrorist attacks as a blank check to move against those countries in the Middle East they don't like. . . . For President Bush to play into the hands of such people with hidden (or Israeli) agenda would be to play into the hands of the very terrorists he wants to decimate.[56]

Suspicions were only exacerbated by comments from leading neoconservatives in the administration who pushed for an expanded war that included toppling Saddam Hussein in Iraq and attacking Hizbullah in Lebanon. Deputy Defense Secretary Paul Wolfowitz called for an expansive policy of "ending states who sponsor terrorism."[57] "If all we do is go after bin Laden, it'll make a mockery of all the president had to say about waging a war on terrorism," observed Pentagon advisor Richard Perle, who said Saddam Hussein should be removed even if he had nothing to do with 9/11. "This is just an added reason for making life as difficult as we can for Saddam."[58] In an article published in the *National Review*, Michael Ledeen, a National Security Council official in Bush Sr.'s administration who has been called "the driving philosophical force behind the neoconservative movement,"[59] proudly boasted: "Creative destruction is our middle name. We do it automatically, and that is precisely why the tyrants hate us, and are driven to attack us."[60]

This unvarnished truth about U.S. foreign policy and the roots of terror was far more accurate than all the president's talk of terrorists hating "our values," yet it was equally reflective of the fundamental difference in perspectives between the United States – and particularly the individuals shaping Bush administration policy – and the people of the Muslim world. Many in the Middle East and Asia heartily agreed with Ledeen's boast that destruction "is what we do best.

It comes naturally to us."[61] But what Ledeen and those he influenced saw as *an attribute*, Arabs and Muslims (and many elsewhere in the world) saw as *the problem*. This American penchant for selective muscle flexing was precisely what they had been complaining about for decades; so, too America's right to decide what constituted a "tyranny." Insisting that striking Afghanistan alone was not enough, Ledeen wrote, "We dealt with the original kamikazes . . . by destroying the country that launched them. We have to do that again."

"One should seriously consider the loud rhetoric of Western leaders of settling the issue of international terrorism (Islamic fundamentalism plus Islamic terrorism) once and for all," a Pakistani analyst advised in response to such comments. "It becomes clear that this war will not be limited only to Afghanistan. Being the only nuclear power of the Islamic world, Pakistan is likely to be the next target of the nefarious designs of this huge and unholy alliance."[62] Others worried that Iraq, Lebanon, Iran, or even Indonesia might be on the U.S. radar screen.

It was *Us* against *Them*, and both sides felt under siege.

Section III

Perceptions of Policy

7
Weaponizing the Media

A nation scared of a satellite station, regardless of its source or color, is a shy and timid nation.

Editorial, *Asharq al-Awsat*

It was not until the bombs started falling on Afghanistan that most Americans first heard the name "al-Jazeera." The American networks were blind in Kabul, their reporters hundreds of miles from the action across the border in Pakistan or in areas of Afghanistan controlled by the Northern Alliance. They were reduced to doing what in the business are called "thumb-suckers," speculative pieces based on information fed back from New York or Washington or bits and pieces picked up from diplomats and the local media, and "informed analysis," which was a polite way of saying "educated guessing."

But al-Jazeera had people – and, more importantly, cameras – on the ground in the Afghan capital. In fact, the channel had maintained a bureau there for the previous two years and was well connected. When the Taliban expelled the few reporters present in Kabul, al-Jazeera was allowed to stay. While CNN correspondents reported that news was "filtering out very slowly because of the lack of communication and infrastructure,"[1] al-Jazeera was feeding satellite images of the bombs crashing down. While ABC News anchor Peter Jennings was admitting "We're just whistling in the wind" as he waited for a Pentagon briefing on what was going on in

Afghanistan, al-Jazeera was reporting from the Afghan Ground Zero. While Bush administration officials spoke of precision air strikes, al-Jazeera cameras recorded scenes of devastation and interviewed civilians who had lost their homes. "We now have an Arab network that competes in newsmaking," the channel's director, Mohammed Jasem al-Ali, told *al-Hayat* newspaper, relishing his scoop. "We were the only channel that broadcast the beginning of the war and its progression live."[2]

With their own cameras shut out of the action, a catfight erupted among the U.S. networks over who could use al-Jazeera's footage. CNN had purchased the rights from the Arab channel, but the other networks claimed "fair use" and simply recorded the footage off the satellite and used it on their own broadcasts. Coverage of the U.S. attack wasn't al-Jazeera's only scoop. Within hours of President Bush's announcement that the attack on Kabul had begun, the channel broadcast a videotaped message from the prime target of the invasion: Osama bin Laden himself. The al-Qaeda leader promised "America will not live in peace" even if he should die in the assault. The channel also rebroadcast an interview it had conducted with bin Laden in 1998 at an Afghan training camp.

Over the course of the previous half-decade, bin Laden had met with several Western journalists, including Robert Fisk of London's *Independent*, John Miller of ABC News and CNN's Peter Arnett. But with the arguable exception of CNN's international arm, he was addressing a largely Western audience in those interviews and doing so through media outlets with a decidedly Western viewpoint. When al-Jazeera went on the air, the al-Qaeda leader suddenly had a means through which he could reach the broad Arab public. Bin Laden clearly understood the power of the media; that had been evident in the years leading up to 9/11 when he continued to meet with reporters, both Western and Muslim, even as the

Taliban pleaded that he keep a low profile in the face of American demands that they turn him over. So as al-Jazeera gained audience, bin Laden increasingly relied on it to spotlight his activities, granting an exclusive interview in 1998 and sending the channel videotapes of training sessions and footage of his son's wedding in the following years. When the bombs began falling on Afghanistan and it was time to exhort the world's Muslims to rise up on his behalf, bin Laden knew where to turn.

"The Al-Qaeda needs a medium to present its point of view and it chose al-Jazeera without fear or hesitation," al-Ali said of the bin Laden message broadcast on October 7. "They brought the tape to our offices as the attacks began and we broadcast it live from Kabul."[3] The White House may have bristled at al-Jazeera's decision to air bin Laden's message, but this was business as usual for any news organization offered exclusive access to one of the world's most newsworthy figures. That had been demonstrated just days before when none other than the Voice of America broadcast an excerpt from an interview with Mullah Omar in which the Taliban leader explained why he was refusing to give in to U.S. demands that he turn over bin Laden. To the then-acting director of VOA, Myrna Whitworth, it was just good journalism:

> News organizations around the world were trying to get Mullah Omar, and the Voice of America got him – that, in a sense, was news itself. And I think we showed who he was, both to his countrymen and to the world ... All that we can do as a legitimate news organization is provide the information and hope that, by providing objective and accurate information, that our audience is able to make reasoned decisions and conclusions, and that, I believe, is our role.[4]

The White House vociferously disagreed. Whitworth and several other VOA executives lost their jobs over the incident. But the Bush administration had no such power over al-Jazeera. Which was precisely what made U.S. officials so angry.

A NEW TELEVISION WAR

With the onset of the U.S. campaign to oust al-Qaeda and the Taliban, the Arabs had their first real TV war. Al-Jazeera's coverage of the early days of the Afghan invasion was a revelation. Viewers in the Middle East were able to sit in their own living rooms and witness what was, in their eyes, the huge disconnect between America's words and its actions. As they heard the U.S. president boast that "we are showing the compassion of America by delivering food and medicine to the Afghan people,"[5] they saw on al-Jazeera images of death, destruction and fleeing refugees. From the early days of the conflict, when Americans watched little more than shots of planes taking off in Europe and so-called experts being interviewed in the United States, to its later stages, when U.S. reporters focused on the activities of American troops on the ground, al-Jazeera's viewers were experiencing coverage that, as the *Columbia Journalism Review* concluded in a lengthy side-by-side analysis, "conveyed far more of the human truth of a massive bombing attack and its effects at ground zero."[6]

It was a more dramatic, more concentrated, version of the same contrast between words and actions that, thanks to al-Jazeera, they had been watching unfold against the Palestinians in the Occupied Territories, thus hardening their attitudes toward both Israel and its U.S. patron. The media-savvy bin Laden played to that. In his October 7 tape, prerecorded for just such a moment, the al-Qaeda leader jettisoned his usual references to Chechnya, Bosnia, the Philippines and Kashmir, and instead focused on the plight of the Palestinians, the Afghans and the children of Iraq. He was the humanitarian concerned for the Arab and Afghan peoples; America was the aggressor.

"If he seems to be several steps ahead of the Western allies in the propaganda war, that is because he very probably is," Rahimullah Yusufzai, an Arab journalist who knew bin Laden well, wrote from Kabul.

> He is saying all the right things, because in millions of homes in many Muslim countries, people can see what is happening in the Occupied Territories via their televisions ... He touches on issues that he knows concern the entire Islamic world, speaking to those who increasingly look to him for leadership.[7]

"In an unconventional war in which propaganda is an essential weapon, an Arab-language television channel is striking with relentless power," read the lead paragraph of an al-Jazeera profile in *The New York Times* two days after the war began.[8] The Pentagon had clearly noticed the same thing. It quickly launched a counteroffensive. The first target: the American media. All of the U.S. networks had rebroadcast in their entirety the October 7 bin Laden message and an earlier statement by one of his aides. Now, in a conference call with network news executives, National Security Advisor Condoleezza Rice warned that the tape might contain hidden messages, demanded that it be pulled, and insisted that only brief excerpts of any future tapes be aired. "The phone call was a discussion among citizens about the national interest," CBS News president Andrew Heyward told *Variety*. "We're talking about a situation that's bigger than any of our competitive concerns."[9] A CNN spokesperson said the cable channel would take the advice of "appropriate authorities" to avoid showing anything that might aid terrorist attacks.[10] British broadcasters rejected similar pressure from the Blair government. "I think it's right that people do get to see and hear the man who is at the centre of this crisis and believed to be behind these attacks," said the head of BBC News, Richard Sambrook.[11]

The decision by the U.S. networks to accede to White House pressure was the first in a series of steps that would produce a world in which Americans would witness the war on terror and invasion of Iraq through a distorted lens. The result was a fundamental disconnect in understanding and perception. "Americans alone should not be denied the opportunity to hear from this man, however heinous his crimes may be," Charles N. Davis, co-chair of the Society of Professional Journalists Freedom of Information Committee, said at the time. "Pressure from the government to limit coverage, especially when it's aimed at suppressing 'propaganda,' simply creates propaganda of our own."[12]

Even as it brought the U.S. networks to heel, the Bush administration simultaneously struck at other information war targets. The Taliban's Pakistan office, which was providing Western journalists with a steady diet of newsworthy quotes, was shut down by America's Pakistani allies and administration officials mounted a war of words against al-Jazeera, accusing the channel of serving as the al-Qaeda chief's propaganda mouthpiece. Rumors began to circulate that al-Jazeera was being paid off by al-Qaeda. Elements of the American media joined the chorus of denunciations, leaving al-Jazeera executives bemused by the hypocrisy of their U.S. colleagues, who, they reported, had in the past bid tens of thousands of dollars for the rights to al-Jazeera's 1998 bin Laden interview. "Any organization that was able to obtain such a scoop would not hesitate to accept it," the channel's chief executive, Hamad bin Thamer, told a news conference, referring to the most recent bin Laden tape. Few journalists in the audience would have disagreed. "We will continue in a high professional manner . . . [to present] opposing viewpoints [and] to cover events when and where they occur."[13]

Journalistic independence would have its price. Just days later, ten minutes after its news team received a warning to clear their offices, two 500-pound bombs slammed into the building housing al-Jazeera's bureau in Kabul. Only one detonated, but it was enough to level the building, temporarily halting the station's Afghanistan coverage and forcing it to resort to running CNN footage.[14] At the time, U.S. officials insisted the incident was an accident. "We would not, as a policy, target news media organizations," a spokesman for the U.S. Central Command said.[15] Only later, in a letter to the Committee to Protect Journalists, would Gen. Tommy Franks, commander of U.S. operations in Afghanistan, confirm the attack had been deliberate. The building, he wrote, was "a known al-Qaeda facility."[16] As evidence, Franks claimed that a key bin Laden deputy, Muhammed Ataf, had been killed in the bombing. No other substantiation was produced. Weeks later, the Pentagon would again claim it had killed Ataf, this time with a Hellfire missile fired from an unmanned CIA drone elsewhere in Afghanistan.

The weaponization of the media had begun.

TARGET: AL-JAZEERA

The destruction of al-Jazeera's Kabul bureau would be just the first in a pattern of such attacks on the media in the coming years. Al-Jazeera's Baghdad bureau was likewise bombed during the Iraq invasion, killing one of its senior reporters and temporarily knocking the Baghdad feed off the air. Moments later, the neighboring office of Abu Dhabi television was also hit. American officials called the bombings an "accident,"[17] but al-Jazeera staffers knew the channel's executives had given Washington precise coordinates for the offices in Iraq to prevent just such a tragedy – just as they said they had done in Kabul. "I will not be objective about this because we have been dragged into this conflict," one of the channel's Baghdad correspondents, Majed Abdel Hadi, said on the air, noting that four unexploded bombs had earlier fallen on a hotel that was the base for al-Jazeera's crew in the southern city of Basra. "We were targeted because the Americans don't want the world to see the crimes they are committing against the Iraqi people."[18] During the subsequent U.S. occupation, the al-Jazeera bureau in the Iraqi city of Ramadi was raided and its news team detained. Eventually, more than 21 al-Jazeera staffers were arrested and, at least briefly, jailed by U.S. military authorities. The U.S. military consistently denied it was specifically targeting al-Jazeera or other journalists, but insight could be found in a directive issued by the General Counsel of the Department of Defense: "Civilians and civilian property that make a direct contribution to the war effort may also be attacked, along with objects whose damage or destruction would produce a military advantage because of their nature, location, purpose, or use . . ."[19]

There were also other, more subtle, measures taken to silence these outlets. Not long after 9/11, al-Jazeera's New York correspondent was stripped of his credentials to cover the New York Stock Exchange. Later, the U.S. Internet provider that hosted the channel's English-language website – which was getting millions of page views a day, many from Americans seeking an alternative view of the war on terror – pulled the plug. In the autumn of 2003, Spanish authorities, working with their U.S. counterparts, arrested Tayseer Allouni, al-Jazeera's Kabul correspondent during the Afghan invasion. The reporter, who had been based in Kabul for two years before the war and present when American planes bombed the bureau, was charged with having ties to al-Qaeda. Interrogators demanded to know how he managed to arrange an October 2001 interview with bin Laden. Allouni's interview, which was never aired, was at the center of a largely unreported episode that provided interesting insight into the ambiguous relationship between bin Laden and al-Jazeera – and the American media. On October 21, 2001, Allouni was blindfolded and driven to a meeting with bin Laden somewhere in or near Kabul. Al-Jazeera had received advance warning that bin Laden wanted to do the interview and had submitted a set of questions, including six provided by its production partner, CNN, which had been contacted separately by bin Laden's people and agreed to participate. But when Allouni arrived in bin Laden's presence, he was handed a new list that included only a few of the original questions submitted. Once the interview was complete, Allouni sent the tape back to al-Jazeera headquarters in Qatar where news executives decided not to air it. Over the course of the next two months, rumors of its existence circulated in the Middle East and Europe. In November, British Prime Minister Tony Blair quoted some of bin Laden's comments in the interview, saying they were made on "a tape circulating among al-Qaeda supporters." In mid-December, *The New York Times* reported that the tape was actually an al-Jazeera interview. A spokesman for the channel refused to say whether it was an interview or a tape provided by bin Laden. Still the channel did not air it.

CNN had received a copy of the tape, but under the terms of its production agreement with al-Jazeera was not allowed to use it until the Qatar-based station had done so. On January 31, 2002, CNN decided it had waited long enough. It ran a short excerpt from the hour-long interview in which bin Laden, for the first time, specifically addressed U.S. claims that he was responsible for the attacks of 9/11. "America has made many accusations against us and many other Muslims around the world. Its charge that we are carrying out acts of terrorism is unwarranted," the al-Qaeda leader said. He then clarified that seeming denial: "If inciting people to do that is terrorism, and if killing those who kill our sons is terrorism, then let history be witness that we are terrorists." Killing civilians, he added, is "permissible in Islamic law and logically."[20]

The interview in Kabul had taken place just one day after Vice President Dick Cheney met with the emir of Qatar and urged that al-Jazeera "act in a more responsible and representative way" or risk being labeled "Osama's outlet to the world." Cheney issued a "blanket request" to the Qatari leader, who was also al-Jazeera's main patron, not to give bin Laden a "platform or to use the Arab press to spread propaganda." Said one U.S. official traveling with Cheney, "We didn't want them to help bin Laden and his merry band of freaks."[21] Had the emir and al-Jazeera buckled to U.S. pressure in withholding the interview? It was possible. Or had the channel kept the interview secret because to air it would have confirmed bin Laden's responsibility for 9/11. Some critics muttered darkly that was the case. Al-Jazeera itself had another explanation: that it was exercising precisely the kind of journalistic responsibility its critics claimed it lacked. The conditions under which the interview had been conducted "did not represent the slightest level of objectivity and professionalism," the channel said in a statement. Allouni had been under "strong psychological pressure, which prevented him from carrying out (the interview) in a professional way."[22] "Bin Laden's people wanted it all or nothing: either we air the entire interview or none of it. And our answer was none," said al-Jazeera's Washington bureau chief, Hafez al-Mirazi. "We're not going to be intimidated by someone who pressures us to broadcast an interview we don't want to broadcast."[23] The channel announced that it was severing its relationship with CNN for "illegally" broadcasting a segment of the interview.

In many ways, the U.S. campaign against al-Jazeera and other Arab news outlets was counterproductive. If, in fact, al-Jazeera did kill the interview because of U.S. pressure, the suppression ultimately undermined American interests. When the interview was conducted in late October, the U.S. assault on Afghanistan was at its height and many Muslims were still saying there was no definitive evidence of bin Laden's direct involvement in 9/11, thus no justification for the invasion. The interview would have confirmed bin Laden's involvement in his own words at a time when it would have had maximum positive impact.

The appearance that al-Jazeera was being deliberately targeted also had a negative effect on Muslim opinion, particularly within the region's media. There is nothing that galvanizes journalists more than attacks on their own. After the missile destroyed the Baghdad bureau, al-Jazeera broadcast endless tributes to its "martyr" Tariq Ayoub, the reporter killed by American bombs (al-Arabiya did much the same for a slain cameraman, Ali Abd al-Aziz, the following year). Bumpers between programs carried his image set against heroic music; colleagues recalled him in paeans to his bravery. Other media in the Middle East and wider Muslim world took up his cause. "The message we take from Tariq's killing makes CENTCOM spokesman Vincent Brooks' statement seem quite ironic: 'We bomb locations with precision, and we pay attention to locations where journalists are present,'" wrote Sultan al-Hatab in *al-Ra'i*, a Jordanian newspaper.[24] Reported BBC correspondent Rageh Omar, who had witnessed the attack from across the river: "We were watching and filming the bombardment and it's quite clearly a direct strike on the Al-Jazeera office. This was not just a stray round. It just seemed too specific."[25] Several Arab and Muslim media outlets recalled that during the Kosovo war the U.S. had bombed Serbian television, explaining afterwards that the station was a legitimate target because it had been broadcasting enemy propaganda. To the Middle East's media and its audience, the implications of these latest attacks were clear: the United States might claim it was waging the war to bring "values" like democracy and a free press, but it was murdering reporters in the process.

The conflict between the Bush administration and the Arab media would continue unabated throughout the U.S. occupation of Iraq. When Deputy Defense Secretary Paul Wolfowitz accused al-Jazeera of "inciting violence" and "endangering the lives of American troops," the channel's Baghdad bureau chief issued a scathing reply charging that his staff had been "subject to strafing by gunfire, death threats, confiscation of news material, and multiple detentions and arrests, all carried out by U.S. soldiers."[26] The merits of the American accusations against al-Jazeera and the veracity of U.S. claims that the pattern of attacks constituted a series of "accidents," were, to a degree, irrelevant. Seen from the Arab world, the verbal and physical assault was yet more evidence of U.S. bullying and hypocrisy.

"The stations that are showing Americans intentionally killing women and children are not legitimate news sources," Brig. Gen. Mark Kimmitt told reporters, referring to al-Jazeera, al-Arabiya and other Arab channels.[27] Arabs countered that it was those Western outlets that failed to show such images that were illegitimate, presenting a sanitized version of the war that bolstered support at home. "This is not anti-Americanism," said Hassan Fadlallah of Hizbullah's al-Manar channel, which claimed to have a policy of not airing the kind of up-close graphic images frequently seen on al-Jazeera. "It reflects reality and American policy either in Palestine or Iraq."[28] In fact, some Arab media, including al-Jazeera and the main London-based pan-Arab newspapers, avoided loaded terms like "martyr" in their news coverage, copying their Western rivals in using "suicide bomber" and "insurgent."

"We reflect what happens on the ground from the Arab perspective as much as say, CNN reflects the American perspective," explained Jihad Ballout of al-Jazeera.[29] Jon Alterman, a leading American expert on Arab satellite television, agreed: "If you're saying Arab media is anti-American, you're wrong. If you're saying Arab media is pro-American, you're wrong."[30] There was no doubt al-Jazeera in particular was sensational, in the tradition of American local TV newscasts with their mantra, "If it bleeds, it leads."

The bloodiest and most graphic images were the mainstay of its newscasts, reporters in the field wore their hearts on their sleeve; the bumpers between commercials were montages of American tanks, missiles exploding and wounded children. Its talk shows, meanwhile, were the venue for sensational screaming debates. Critics pointed specifically to Feyssal al-Qassem's *The Opposite Direction* program, which one Western-trained Arab journalist called "vile, loud and messy."[31] The program's mission was to give voice to all opinions. That included the most extreme, such as one guest who repeatedly and vociferously claimed the beheading of hostages in Iraq was justified by the Qur'an. But al-Qassem also devoted much time to denouncing Arab leaders whom he called "symbols of corruption and backwardness and tyranny."[32] Another thorn in the side of the U.S. authorities was Egyptian cleric Yusuf Qaradawi, who frequently fulminated against "infidel" concepts like democracy on his program *Sharia and Life*. Largely missing from U.S. government criticism of al-Jazeera, however, was a distinction between the news broadcasts and the talk shows. Qaradawi's show was itself an example of the degree to which al-Jazeera *did* allow all opinions. His denunciations of democracy were loud and frequent even though al-Jazeera's *raison d'être* was democratic change in the Middle East. As American television had learned long ago, screaming debates and gripping pictures meant higher ratings. Few would describe CNN's *Crossfire* or Fox's *Hannity and Colms* as being fair and balanced, yet that was precisely the standard critics applied to al-Jazeera's talk shows. Guests on the American programs may not have advocated beheadings, but to an Arab viewer, demands for bombing and assassination campaigns and the dismissal of civilian casualties as collateral damage were no less outrageous.

As in America, ratings were king. "The competition is pushing us to show strong images and use strong language to

have more viewers than other TV stations," said Elie Harb of
the somewhat more sedate Lebanese Broadcasting Company
(LBC). And, as in America, the Arab debate shows were
stage-managed for maximum effect. "It's like pornography,"
one well-known al-Jazeera host told researcher Jon Alterman,
appealing to the basest instincts of the viewer. Geraldo
Rivera in Arabic. Yet in stark contrast to the airwaves of its
Western counterparts, al-Jazeera kept fluff and entertainment
news to a minimum, knowing that its viewers' interest in
current affairs substantially exceeded the already high
threshold of Arabs in general.[33]

Al-Jazeera also opened its airwaves to a parade of Bush
administration figures, including National Security Advisor
Condoleezza Rice, Secretary of Defense Donald Rumsfeld,
Secretary of State Colin Powell and several top generals.
Each of those interviews was nonconfrontational and
respectful – and all aired without editing. Indeed, a U.S. journalist taking the same approach would be accused of toadying
up to the administration. Characteristic of the tone was the
opening portion of Rumsfeld's February 2003 interview with
Jamil Azer, his second appearance on al-Jazeera:

> *Azer*: Sir, there are lots of questions which we feel they might be
> sort of like critical of the United States but we feel that
> al-Jazeera's audience would like to know your views about.
> It isn't that we are trying to find fault or anything like that.
> *Rumsfeld*: Fair enough. If I hear a question that has a premise
> in it that's inaccurate I'll state that and say that – good.[34]

A study conducted by researcher Muhammed Ayish of the
American University in Sharjah identified commitment to
news and issues of concern to viewers as traits that distinguished al-Jazeera from Western news organizations.[35] In
fact, al-Jazeera had more international correspondents than
all the U.S. networks combined. Even its U.S. reporting
sometimes eclipsed that of the American networks. During
the 2004 Republican and Democratic national conventions,

al-Jazeera carried three hours of live coverage a night, compared to just an hour each for ABC, CBS and NBC.

At the conclusion of Condoleezza Rice's 2001 al-Jazeera interview, she was asked, "Overall, how do you perceive Al Jazeera as a credible or independent media?" Rice's reply: "If I did not have respect for Al Jazeera, I would not be doing this interview. I think it's important that there be a network that reaches broad Arab audiences. And the United States believes in freedom of the press."[36] In Arab eyes, that commitment was already proving hollow.

The American offensive against al-Jazeera and its imitators was tacit recognition that the battlefield of the information war had dramatically changed since the first Gulf War. Accustomed to dominating the discourse, the U.S. was now forced to adjust to the fact that a new, largely unfettered media voice was drowning out White House attempts to write the storyline of its war on terror. Information warfare was an integral part of the training at the U.S. military academies and, as noted in an earlier chapter, control and manipulation of the media had long been tools of war. A month after the Afghan invasion was launched, the White House set up the Coalition Information Center, a precursor to the White House Office of Global Communications, and hired as consultant self-described "information warrior" and "perception manager" John Rendon, a former Democratic party campaign manager who had orchestrated the PR campaign for the Kuwait government-in-exile during the first Gulf War.[37] The CIC would seize on the plight of Afghan women as the cause célèbre of the Afghan invasion, a tactic CIC spokesman Jim Wilkinson later called "the best thing we've done." Not everyone agreed. Many reporters outside the United States saw the women's campaign as a patent example of obfuscation to hide America's true motives (an approach repeated later in the shifting justifications for the invasion of Iraq).

"Ever since the Afghan conflict began the only 'authentic' sources of information have been the regular briefings at the Pentagon in Washington," complained *Indian Express* columnist Saeed Naqvi. "The U.S. has made it clear that propaganda would have to be an integral part of the strategy to combat terrorism."[38] Naqvi also warned the United States against what many Arabs and Muslims suspected was in the cards:

> Now that the international community is embarked on the historic reconstruction of Afghanistan, the U.S. must be seen to be there helping the process and not fly away to Iraq with its B52s. This will only accentuate the self-destructing image of a Goliath run amuck.[39]

Leading Islamists meanwhile, bore no illusions about the nature of the U.S. threat or the role played by the Western media. The head of Jordan's Islamic Action Front, Sheikh Hamza Mansoor, told an Islamist summit in Lahore that organized attacks were being made on Islam not only through military and political action, but also via "information technology channels."[40] It should have been no surprise then that, just as the Americans were apparently targeting Arab journalists, U.S. journalists would soon find themselves in the crosshairs of Islamist militants.

ELECTRONIC TOOLS OF TERROR

If Osama bin Laden had needed a model that demonstrated the power of television as a tool of war, he could easily have found it in Lebanon. Hizbullah had effectively exploited the Western media to publicize its suicide bombings, kidnappings and hijackings against American targets. As it consolidated its power after driving out the U.S. Marines, the group established its own television operation, al-Manar TV, aimed at opinion closer to home. The station, the signal of which could be picked up in Israeli homes, became an important weapon in the struggle against the Israeli occupation in South Lebanon.

Camera crews regularly accompanied guerrillas of the Lebanese resistance during their attacks on Israeli troops. Video of the ambushes, car bombings and frontal attacks was broadcast on al-Manar. The station also ran photo galleries of dead Israeli soldiers with the words, "Who is next?" in a deliberate campaign to undermine Israeli morale. "It is well known that the most advanced weapon is psychological warfare, and we use the media as part of this warfare," said Hizbullah chief Sheikh Hassan Nasrallah.

> We use real pictures, we don't act out the campaigns or the victories, we show you scenes of Israelis weeping and screaming like children, scenes of our fighters taking the most difficult military bases, scenes of martyrdom operations. We show you the last testimonial of the brother who is ready to leave this world. We film all of these realities and offer them to the nation.[41]

Al-Manar used the same approach during the Iraq war, leading the State Department to add the station to its Terrorist Exclusion List in late 2004 for what a spokesman called "disgusting programming that preaches violence and hatred."[42] Most of the mainstream Arab television outlets did not take such an overtly propagandistic approach to coverage. However, the fact that they were showing the violent and unblemished reality of what was taking place on the ground in Iraq, along with the comments of bin Laden and others who opposed the war, had a powerful effect on opinion in the region.

The television revolution in the Middle East was paralleled by an explosion of online information sources, which not only created a new public sphere for the free exchange of views among Muslims around the world, but also enabled Islamists and other dissidents direct access to populations they would have been unable to reach through traditional media.[43] One example was Saad Faqih, a Saudi surgeon-turned-dissident who hosted a daily three-hour antigovernment call-in program over the Internet and satellite radio and television from his base in London. Faqih, who was later implicated in an assassination plot against Crown Prince Abdullah, was among 18 Saudis imprisoned in 1993 after authoring a blueprint for reform. Following his release, he went into exile in London, formed an opposition group and established a web site to reach other potential supporters. Such "cyber-Islamic environments"[44] produced virtual communities that helped to enhance the sense of connection and shared identity among Muslims around the world. Content frequently included religious teachings, revolutionary exhortations, training manuals on everything from bomb-building to kidnappings, and even *jihadi* computer games, in which Israeli and American troops replace the Arabs who are targets in many such Western games. "Other people use the Web for stupid reasons, to waste time," said Omar Bakri, a radical Syrian cleric based in London. "We use it for serious things."[45] The strategic use of the Internet allowed the militants to begin reducing their dependence on state sponsors as they relied more on each other.

Militant Islamists could not only reach out to each other on the Web, they could also reach out to the media. That was vividly apparent when the kidnappers of *Wall Street Journal* reporter Daniel Pearl distributed their demands, and eventually photos of his beheading, via email, with the untraceable address kidnapper@hotmail.com.[46] The brutal beheading of the American journalist was itself an example of the degree to which the media had become weaponized. In past decades, U.S. reporters covering the Middle East had always prided themselves on interviewing militants and extremists of all stripes, whether that was the PLO, Kurdish nationalists, *Hizbullahis*, operatives of al-Dawa or Saddam Hussein. However, as the U.S. media became identified with Bush administration policy for reasons discussed earlier, reporters were shorn of the always-thin armor of neutrality. Besides, the militants now had other ways to communicate their messages and were no longer dependent on foreign reporters. In a tape aired on al-Jazeera and other Arab channels in April 2004, bin Laden specifically included the Western media in his list of targets, telling followers that "the leading media companies" were among "the tools used to deceive and exploit peoples" and thus "pose a fatal threat to the whole world." The Western media was now fair game.[47]

Arab satellite television was a useful tool, but even Arab editors could not always be relied on to communicate all that the militants hoped to communicate. There was no such problem with the Internet. Threats and claims of credit for terrorist attacks regularly appeared on Islamist web sites, which themselves just as regularly disappeared, either because authorities had shut them down or because they fell victim to cyber attacks by Western intelligence agencies. Some sites, employing proxy servers – Internet providers that were little known but still accessible to the public – frequently shifted locations in a cat-and-mouse game with authorities. One of al-Qaeda's first sites, maalemaljihad.com (Milestones of the Holy War), was set up using a Chinese web-hosting company in an attempt to put it out of reach of Western authorities.[48] Another site, run by al-Qaeda's media arm, the Center for Islamic Studies and Research, shifted between hosts in Malaysia, Texas and Michigan over a single six-month period. Alneda.com, said to be al-Qaeda's main line of communications with its followers, was eventually hijacked by the American operator of a series of pornographic websites, who put up a graphic announcing: "Hacked, tracked and now owned by the USA. Webpage offline to preserve Public Safety and Homeland Security." Sites run by the Islamist Azzam Publications suffered the same fate. Each new site Azzam created carried a link to an online Islamic bookstore to which it directed visitors for information on future URLs "if this site goes down."[49]

When the militants of Jamaah Islamiyah blew up a pair of nightclubs in Bali killing over 200 people, they claimed credit on behalf of the Afghan people on an Indonesian website that went dark soon after.[50] Not incidentally, Jamaah Islamiyah's operations chief, an Indonesian known as Hambali, began his career as head of al-Qaeda's media branch. Some sites, like alneda.com, were said to be directly connected with al-Qaeda. Others were associated with an array of Islamist parties, charities, educational institutions and individuals. Experts said that the number of such sites had exploded in parallel with the growing influence of al-Qaeda, going from a few dozen in the late 1990s to more than 4,000 by 2004.[51]

"The Internet in many ways parallels al-Qaeda operations," according to Josh Devon, an analyst at the SITE Institute, a Washington terrorism research center. "Like the Internet, al-Qaeda is a loose, decentralized, network of independently operating cells."[52] So fleeting were some of these sites, and so murky were their origins, that it sometimes led to accusations among them that one or another was a front for various Western intelligence agencies. This was the claim against one of the slickest, a site called JihadUnspun.com. Said one rival site:

> The "front" behind Jihadunspun.com is supposedly a middle-aged Canadian businesswoman who is said to have accepted Islam after 11 September 2001. The Muslims can draw their own conclusions from this, bearing in mind the tenfold increase in the budgets and manpower of Western intelligence agencies in the post-September-11th World.[53]

The Internet offered the extremists what British researcher Gary Bunt has termed a "digital sword" for their "e-jihad."[54] The result was a "netwar" pitting Western computer experts against their counterparts among the Islamists, such as Mohammad Naeen Noor, an al-Qaeda computer hacker whose August 2004 arrest led to the unraveling of several al-Qaeda cells around the world. Noor was a key player in the al-Qaeda communications system, running a network of web sites and email addresses in Turkey, Nigeria and north-west Pakistan, that passed encoded instructions between operatives.[55] As the CIA intelligence chief for the Near East and South Asia explained, "In today's globalizing world, terrorists can reach their targets more easily, their targets are exposed in more places, and news and ideas that inflame people to resort to terrorism spread more widely and rapidly than in the past."[56]

One study of Yahoo discussion groups by a private intelligence contractor found many inquiries about vacations in the border region between Pakistan and Afghanistan, a lawless region dominated by militant Islamist groups where bin Laden was believed to be hiding. The respondents assured the would-be vacationers they would receive a warm welcome.[57] Internet chat rooms were not only a venue for recruitment. They were also used by al-Qaeda operatives to pass messages and orders. According to trial transcripts, individuals involved in the so-called Millennium plot to bomb Los Angeles airport used web-based discussion groups to communicate with planners in Jordan.[58]

Some legitimate sites were unwitting accomplices to terror, as al-Qaeda computer experts hid instructions in otherwise innocent content and photos using a technique known as "steganography." This tactic was used, for example, to pass messages to operatives involved in a 2002 attack on Israeli tourists at a Kenyan resort.[59] The cat-and-mouse game over alneda.com eventually led Western investigators to a small educational consultancy in the Netherlands, where they found alneda.com hidden in the subfiles of the company's own web site, unbeknownst to the firm's officials. "People are mistaking [al-Qaeda's] competence because they think of these men as living in caves and primitive, which is far from the truth, indeed," says Michael Wilson, a private counterterrorism analyst.[60]

This "crossroads of radicalism and technology," as it was
described in the 2002 U.S. National Security Strategy report,
created an unprecedented challenge to Western intelligence
agencies, but militant Islamists also used more prosaic communications tools to spread their messages. In the 1970s,
smuggled audiotapes of sermons by the Ayatollah Khomeini
passed from hand to hand and were played in mosques and
private homes to build support for the Iranian revolution.
Recordings of countless clerics – radical and otherwise –
were commonly available in the *souks* (marketplaces) of the
Middle East. That was still the case when bin Laden came on
the scene. More than 250,000 audio cassettes of his speeches
were sold in Saudi Arabia alone following the *jihadist* victory
in Afghanistan, and his 1996 declaration of war against the
U.S. also spread through the vast network of cassette vendors
in the region.[61] However, by the 1990s, these audio sermons
had also migrated to the Internet, where they were joined by
a new genre, the *jihadi* video. The first of these pseudo-
documentaries were produced in Afghanistan, where cameramen accompanied *mujahideen* and packaged inspirational
programs set to music, which were duplicated and distributed across the Muslim world. From Bosnia came a wave of
similar tapes, these depicting graphic scenes of Muslims
killed or maimed at the hands of Serbs, as well as military
operations by the small cadre of Arab *jihadis* who had
arrived to aid the Bosnian Muslims. Some of these tapes,
such as the classic *Martyrs of Bosnia*, were shot and produced
by an Egyptian known as Sam Reda, who was working for a
Saudi production company.[62] After Bosnia, Reda applied for
a job with al-Jazeera and was turned down, then suddenly
appeared in the Indonesian capital Jakarta as the jihad
against Christians in the Maluku Islands and Sulawesi was
heating up. He approached the local al-Jazeera bureau,
applied for a job and was again turned down, then rented a
large home in an expensive suburb of the capital. There he

set up a video-editing suite and began turning out videos of the new Indonesian jihad, which was serving as a training ground for militants in the region. Reda's operation was eventually raided by Indonesian authorities and shut down, but in an age of cheap digital video cameras and laptop editing software, plenty of other amateur producers remained at work, producing videos with titles like *India's War against Islam* on the Kashmir conflict and *Russian Hell* on the conflict in Chechnya. These videos were intercut with Disney cartoons and wildlife documentaries to hide the true content from customs officials as they were smuggled across borders,[63] but many were also posted on an array of Islamist web sites.

Jihadi videos would become a staple of the Iraqi resistance. American authorities were enraged when portions were aired by al-Jazeera and some other Arab channels. At one point, an angry Defense Secretary Donald Rumsfeld accused al-Arabiya of being in collusion with those attacking U.S. forces. "Al-Arabiya news channel has never aired any footage of an attack against coalition forces. Its reporters have never been in close proximity to such attacks. Nor have they cooperated with any persons with a view to filming such an attack," the channel angrily replied in a statement released to the media.[64] Video was also the weapon of choice for militant groups in Iraq and Saudi Arabia as they sought to publicize the kidnappings of foreign workers beginning in the spring of 2004. In a reprise of the Pearl execution in Pakistan, contractor Nicholas Berg was beheaded on camera, setting off a series of copycat kidnappings and killings. Both Western and Arab news organizations struggled with how to handle this new attempt to weaponize the media, balancing good taste, ethics and the fact that with a 24-hour all-news cycle, as Fox News executive John Stack put it, they had "a tremendous void to fill."[65] Not incidentally, audiences around the world were riveted – driving home the effectiveness of this new tactic in generating attention. Whenever such stories broke, traffic to Internet news sites spiked. The Malaysian Internet provider hosting an Islamist site that posted the Berg execution video, Acme Commerce Sdn. Bhd., had to pull the plug when traffic overwhelmed its servers.[66] Most of the major U.S. networks and Arab channels stopped just short of showing the actual executions, but it was impossible for them to ignore the incidents entirely. "If people can't watch, we've lost our ability to convey information," argued NBC News president Neal Shapiro.[67]

As the Black September terrorists had demonstrated in Munich, the media was a powerful weapon. The needs of the terrorists for publicity closely matched the needs of the media for news. Yet in an age of instant info-tainment, the boredom threshold among television audiences and – in particular – news executives themselves, was low. By the summer of 2004, the kidnappings were beginning to get less play, both in the United States and the Arab world. Said al-Jazeera spokesman Jihad Ballout, "It's nothing new anymore that hostages are being taken. This is becoming somewhat monotonous."[68]

8
Prism of Pain: Palestine

Great Britain is prepared to recognise and support the independence of the Arabs in all the regions within the limits demanded by the Sherif of Mecca.

> Letter from British High Commissioner Sir Henry McMahon
> to Ali Ibn Husain, Sherif of Mecca, 1915

In the immediate aftermath of 9/11, Israel's supporters in the United States mounted a concerted effort to quash any suggestion that anger over the plight of Palestinians and U.S. support for Israel may have had anything to do with the bombings. "Israel Isn't the Issue," read the headline of a *Wall Street Journal* opinion piece by Norman Podhertz of the conservative Heritage Foundation, a consistent defender of the Jewish state.[1] Added David Harris, executive director of the American Jewish Committee: "Only those reaching for the most complicated or conspiratorial theories would reach the conclusion that Israel is somehow central to the story."[2]

The campaign to divert attention from the impact U.S. policy toward Israel had among Arabs and Muslims manifest itself in two ways: statements like those above further sensitized the antennae of government officials and newspaper editorial writers, exacerbating the traditional reluctance to criticize Israel for the many reasons of politics and culture outlined earlier. At the same time, those who did imply even an indirect connection between U.S. Israel policy and the tragedy of 9/11 were quickly denounced as anti-Semites. This writer encountered both faces of that campaign.

Appearing on a September 17, 2001 National Public Radio special about 9/11 and U.S. foreign policy, I suggested that if the United States took steps to "eliminate the oozing wound of the Palestinian crisis" it would undercut the resentments upon which bin Laden and other radicals fed. My fellow guest, Graham Allison, a former assistant secretary of defense in the Clinton administration, gingerly acknowledged that the Palestinian conflict was an issue, but insisted anti-American terrorism "wouldn't be all that substantially affected" by its solution. Rather, he said, the real conflict in the Middle East was between "the forces of modernization against medievalists and against traditional cultures."[3] A few days later, I presented a similar argument about the central role of the Palestinian issue in Arab and Muslim perceptions on the *David Brudnoy Show*, the top-rated talk radio program in New England. The host, who had strong pro-Israeli views, politely debated the issue with me and we ultimately agreed to disagree. However, after the interview ended and I could no longer respond, Brudnoy remained on the air and proceeded to denounce me as an anti-Semite. Nor did he stop there. I had mentioned that I was moderating a panel discussion that evening at a Unitarian Church on Harvard Square. Brudnoy said the choice of venues wasn't surprising, given what he claimed were the anti-Israeli and pacifist attitudes of Unitarians in general.

Such a seemingly extreme reaction to suggestions that the Palestinian crisis played a role in fomenting anti-American violence reflected a deep concern within the U.S. Jewish community that there could be a backlash. "The bombings," warned the *Baltimore Jewish Times*, "could have huge implications for a U.S.–Israel relationship that some may blame for provoking the terrorists."[4] The *Jewish Exponent* of Philadelphia noted much the same in a September 20 article entitled, "The Blame Game: Will Americans Now View Israel as a Friend or a Liability?"[5] "There is a danger of people saying, 'If we didn't support Israel, those people would have no reason to dislike us,'" said Shoshana Bryen, special projects director for the Jewish Institute for National Security Affairs (JINSA). The move to head off any identification of U.S. policy toward Israel with the roots of animosity driving anti-American terrorism was not confined to the U.S. mainland. After Dewi Fortuna Anwar, an Indonesian political researcher and presidential advisor, published a column in the *Jakarta Post* suggesting such a link, the U.S. ambassador to Indonesia, Robert Gelbard, wrote to the paper denouncing her "anti-Semitic and misinformed comments."[6]

This acute level of defensiveness largely shut down the opportunity to re-examine the role of American policy toward Israel in shaping Arab and Muslim perceptions. The irony was that while Israel's supporters in the United States were dismissing linkage between Palestine and Muslim anger, some Israelis themselves saw the bombings as a clarion call. Wrote Israeli peace activist Uri Avnery: "The world must at long last treat the festering wound of the Israeli–Palestinian conflict, which is poisoning the whole body of humanity."[7] His voice was lost in a cacophony of abnegation emanating from official circles in the United States and Israel.

No matter how vociferous the denials among Israel's defenders, they could not change reality; Palestine was, as Shibley Telhami put it, "the prism of pain" through which Arabs saw the world.[8] "Nothing has shaped the Arab mood since the post-World War II [period] more than the developments concerning Palestine," agreed Egypt's ambassador to Indonesia, Ezzat Saad el Sayed.[9] Others were even more pointed in their conclusions. "Israel was the real [party] responsible for this bloody tragedy," Jalal Duwaydar of Egypt's *al-Akhbar* newspaper wrote in a column published September 12. "Washington has sacrificed all its interests, values, resolutions of international legitimacy and principles of international law merely to consolidate the Israeli occupation and injustice."[10] It was just one of many such comments across the region and beyond – and precisely what Israel's supporters feared. "That event must be used as a lesson, especially for President Bush and America," the head of Ikhwanul Muslimin Indonesia, the Indonesian branch of the Muslim Brotherhood, said of 9/11. "America has played its role and used its veto [in the UN Security Council] to support Israel although Israelis do whatever they want in Palestine."[11]

Neoconservatives within the Bush administration would later claim that "the road to Jerusalem runs through Baghdad."[12] In other words, overthrow Saddam, put the fear of U.S. military might into the minds of other Arab states, and the Palestinian conflict could be solved. It was a fatally flawed strategy that betrayed the ignorance – or conscious denial – of Middle East realities among the neoconservatives who authored it. Looking back, Gen. Anthony Zinni, the one-time commander of U.S. forces in the region, whom President Bush had appointed Middle East envoy in 2002, told an audience, referring to the Iraq invasion: "I couldn't believe what I was hearing about the benefits of this strategic move. That the road to Jerusalem led through Baghdad, when just the opposite is true, the road to Baghdad led through Jerusalem. You solve the Middle East peace process, you'd be surprised what kinds of others things will work out."[13] Yet the administration's official line *did* accurately reflect one reality: the existence of a Washington mindset in which every aspect of U.S. Middle East policy was calculated on the basis of how it would affect Israel. In a twisted way, the neocons were right: all roads in U.S. Middle East policy *did* lead to Jerusalem.

There is much debate over bin Laden's sincerity regarding the Palestine issue. Just as Israel's supporters downplayed the role of the Israel–Palestine conflict in motivating terrorism, mainstream Palestinian leaders, too, questioned bin Laden's commitment to their struggle as they tried to distance themselves from the al-Qaeda leader in order to avoid becoming a target of America's wrath. Yet one of bin Laden's early known influences was a militant Palestinian Islamist scholar, Sheikh Abdallah Yussuf Azzam, whom he briefly met at university in Saudi Arabia and whose close disciple he became after Azzam set up one of the first *jihadi* training centers in Pakistan. At least from the mid-1990s, after he went into exile, opposition to the occupation of Jerusalem and concern for the plight of the Palestinians had been a consistent element of bin Laden's public statements. For example, in 1998 he sent this message to an Islamist conference in Pakistan: "At this moment, Israel and the United States are dominating Palestine and other holy places in such a way that *mujahideen* are being killed and besieged and Muslims have been economically ruined."[14] No matter whether it was a cause of convenience for bin Laden or a central concern, his rhetoric about the Palestinian struggle, combined with the graphic coverage of the Palestinian crisis by al-Jazeera and other Arab media, brought the issue front-and-center in the succeeding years.

THE ISRAELI–AMERICAN "US" AGAINST THE MUSLIM "THEM"

In the immediate aftermath of 9/11, Israeli leaders sought to use the tragedy to link Israel's war against the Palestinians firmly with America's war on terror. "The fight against terrorism is an international struggle of the free world against the forces of darkness that seek to destroy our liberty and our way of life," Prime Minister Ariel Sharon said on September 11, using language that would become the staple of Bush administration rhetoric. "I believe that together, we can defeat these forces of evil."[15] Asked by *The New York Times* what the attacks meant for U.S.–Israeli relations, former prime minister Benjamin Netanyahu replied, "It's very good," then quickly edited himself, adding, "Well, not very good, but it will generate immediate sympathy" and "strengthen the bond between our two peoples."[16] Writing in the *Jerusalem Post*, Israeli journalist Uri Dan (who also served as Israel correspondent for *The New York Post*), saw the attacks of 9/11 as ushering in a new era in which "the U.S. will join Israel in a totally new approach to the war against terrorism [which] will obligate special, more drastic steps to be taken by both countries, both individually and with greater coordination than ever before."[17]

Exactly what some Israeli officials hoped such a putative new relationship might mean was evident 24 hours after the attacks of 9/11. The Sharon government launched the largest Israeli incursion into the West Bank in a year, as the *Evening Standard* of London reported, "knowing [Israel] will not be condemned by the international community in the aftermath of the terrorist strikes on New York and Washington."[18] Yasser Arafat, Sharon told Secretary of State Colin Powell, was "our bin Laden."[19]

At first, Bush administration officials refused to take the bait. Recognizing that it was critical to build a solid coalition with Arab and other Muslim countries, the president, Powell and others distanced themselves from Sharon's comments and made clear their displeasure at the new Israeli military offensive, calling on both sides to "do everything they can" to "jump-start" negotiations.[20] "No matter what you might think about the crisis in the Middle East, this is not the way to solve it," said Powell.[21] To underscore its sensitivity to the dangers that Arabs and Muslims might perceive the American response to 9/11 as a U.S.–Israeli campaign, the White House specifically left the Palestinians off its list of terrorist groups to be targeted in the war on terror and opened conversations with Arafat, who had quickly denounced the 9/11 attacks and signaled his cooperation.

This issue of what constituted a terrorist group would become a political football deftly manipulated by Sharon. In his September 20 Congressional address, President Bush vowed that the "war on terrorism" would continue "until every terrorist group of global reach has been found, stopped and defeated."[22] When Bush gave the speech, he still hoped to include as many Arab and Muslim countries as possible in his new antiterror coalition. The deliberate choice of the phrase "of global reach" to describe the terror groups being targeted was a pragmatic move meant to reassure these potential Arab and Muslim allies that the United States distinguished between al-Qaeda and more localized groups such as the PLO, Hamas, Hizbullah and others, which many in the Middle East looked upon with sympathy or favor. That language was chosen on the basis of what was in America's strategic interest. Many at the White House, the State Department and the Pentagon still wanted to strike back at Hizbullah for the slaughter of Americans in Beirut, but there was a tacit recognition that in the bigger picture, it was – for the moment, at least – more important to build a broad coalition against al-Qaeda than to get even.

As part of this new pragmatic approach that sought to reposition the U.S. relationship with the Muslim world, the administration also revisited the thorny issue of the Palestinian conflict. In early October, after President Bush remarked that "The idea of a Palestinian state has always been part of a vision, so long as the right to Israel to exist is respected,"[23] Sharon immediately accused the United States and its allies of trying to "appease the Arabs at our expense": "Do not repeat the dreadful mistake of 1938, when enlightened European democracies decided to sacrifice Czechoslovakia for a 'convenient temporary solution.' Do not try to appease the Arabs at our expense. Israel will not be Czechoslovakia."[24]

The White House labeled Sharon's comments "unacceptable,"[25] but in the process merely confirmed what Arabs and Muslims already knew: "Israel can have no better or stronger friend than the United States and [no] better friend than President Bush," White House spokesman Ari Fleischer told reporters.[26] To many in the Middle East, it was just more evidence of the impermeable bond between the United States and Israel. "As the White House spokesman has said, the United States is Israel's best ally and friend in the entire world," wrote columnist Ahmad Al-Jindi in Cairo's *al-Akhbar*.

> Consequently, we must not expect any complications to come out of this crisis [between the U.S. and Israel], or any impact on the special relationship binding the two countries, regardless of how angry Bush is with Sharon, or what tone he employs to express that anger.[27]

"Lest anyone forget," added the *Jordan Times* in an editorial,

> Israel's Environment Minister Tzachi Hanegbi also helpfully pointed out that the Congress is more pro-Israeli than the Knesset in saying that the president should be "fully aware of the unprecedented level of support Israel has in . . . the Congress, and it will therefore be very hard to pressure Israel."[28]

Acknowledging that the dispute was likely little more than "a scratch" in U.S.–Israeli relations and that "experience has taught us that such scratches heal rapidly," as the Sharjah-based daily *al-Khaleej* observed,[29] many Arab media outlets were nonetheless hopeful the United States would continue to move toward a more evenhanded approach to the Palestinian conflict. That was bolstered by a November speech on U.S. Middle East policy given by Secretary of State Powell, in which he painted a picture of Palestinian *and* Israeli suffering, noting that, "Both sides will need to face up to some plain truths about where this process is heading" and "make hard compromises."[30] Yet U.S. resolve to take a new evenhanded approach to the conflict had already begun to fray. The first public sign came in late October when the *Jerusalem Post* reported that President Bush had explicitly told Israeli foreign minister Shimon Peres that he now considered Hizbullah a terrorist organization of global reach, "making it clear for the first time that the Iranian-backed group would be targeted in the next phase of the U.S.-led war on terrorism."[31]

Any remaining Arab and Muslim hopes of U.S. parity in the Middle East were dashed with Sharon's visit to the White House in early December. Through the autumn, the Bush administration had publicly kept up its pressure on the Israeli leader to resume negotiations with Arafat, with whom Washington had opened a dialogue. Gen. Zinni, the new Middle East envoy, was dispatched to mount a concerted effort to move talks forward. The diplomatic initiative was recognition that the United States could not afford to have the Palestinian crisis undermine efforts to bring Arab and Muslim countries into the antiterror coalition. However, as Sharon arrived in Washington for what was expected to be a round of meetings in which he would face strong pressure to compromise with Arafat, suicide bombers from the Palestinian Islamist group Hamas struck in Haifa and Jerusalem, killing 26 people and injuring more than 150 in retaliation for the earlier Israeli assassination of a leading Hamas official. During an emergency meeting with Sharon at the White House, President Bush denounced the "horrific acts of murder" and demanded that Arafat reign in the radicals.[32] It was the first in a series of pivotal events that would have a serious negative impact on Arab and Muslim perceptions. Washington made clear that the burden for achieving peace now rested firmly on Arafat's shoulders.[33] Less than 24 hours later, with Sharon back home, Israel launched a major assault on the Occupied Territories. Helicopter gun-ships pounded positions around the Palestinian leader's headquarters

and targeted the security infrastructure of the Palestinian
Authority. Much to the chagrin of America's would-be Arab
allies, the Bush administration resolutely refused to denounce
the latest violence. Israel "obviously has the right to defend
itself," White House spokesman Ari Fleisher told reporters.
"The President understands that very clearly."[34] Colin
Powell said the crisis was "a moment of truth" for Arafat
and demanded that the Palestinian leader arrest those
responsible for the suicide bombings, which, he said, were
not only "dastardly acts of terror, they were attacks against
his authority."[35]

For the Arab world, the timing of the new Israeli offensive –
the day after Sharon was welcomed at the White House –
and the tone of the U.S. response were evidence of an
American "green light" for Sharon's plan to use the U.S. war
on terror as cover for his own expansionist goals.
"Washington gave Israel the green light to launch more
attacks against targets in the West Bank and the Gaza Strip,"
charged the *Syria Times*.[36] "The White House has justified
these crimes by saying Israel has the right to defend itself,"
noted *al-Watan* of Saudi Arabia.[37] This perception was
driven home by Sharon himself, who, in a nationwide speech
the night after returning from Washington, echoed
President Bush in declaring Israel would wage a "war on
terror . . . with all the means at our disposal."[38] Singling out
Arafat, who he claimed had "chosen the path of terror,"[39]
Sharon promised that Israel would "pursue those responsible,
the perpetrators of terrorism, its supporters and those who
send them. We will pursue them until we catch them, and
they will pay the price."[40] The parallels between Sharon's
speech and the language that President Bush had been using
since 9/11 was so apparent that the Associated Press distributed a story headlined, "Sharon Echoes Bush in Anti-terror
Speech," which compared quotes from the two leaders.[41]
Former secretary of state Lawrence Eagleburger complained

that Sharon was "piggy-backing off our own war," noting that, from the perspective of U.S. interests, "this link to Israel is – can be a problem."[42] Under any circumstances, this psychological linking of America's war on terror with Israel's conflict with the Palestinians was an impediment to winning Arab and Muslim support for the U.S.-led coalition. The fact that it was Ariel Sharon with whom the president was perceived to be siding made matters infinitely worse. Sharon was, without match, the most hated man in the Arab world. His career was seen as one long string of bloody and aggressive actions against Palestinians and other Arabs, most famously the 1982 massacre of hundreds of Palestinian and Lebanese Shi'ites in the Sabra and Chatilla refugee camps in Beirut. The slaughter was carried out by Israeli-allied Christian Phalangist militiamen allowed into the camps by Israeli forces under the command of then-defense minister Sharon, who was found culpable for the massacre by an Israeli investigating commission and forced to resign.[43] The Arabs weren't alone in their disdain for Sharon. Philip Habib, the Reagan administration envoy who brokered the U.S.-guaranteed deal under which PLO forces withdrew from Beirut weeks before the massacre, had this to say of the then-Israeli defense minister: "Sharon was a killer, obsessed by hatred of the Palestinians. I had given Arafat assurance that his people would not be harmed, but this was totally disregarded by Sharon, whose word was worth nothing."[44]

That was the view of a top U.S. government expert on the Middle East. The Arab and Muslim perception of Sharon was even more negative. To them, he was both "the butcher of Beirut" and the man who in 2000 deliberately provoked the second Intifada by visiting the sacred grounds of al-Aqsa Mosque, one of the holiest places in Islam, with a full contingent of bodyguards. The move broke a longstanding agreement between Israeli and Palestinian leaders and sparked riots that soon spread into a full-scale Palestinian revolt, destroyed the peace process and led to Sharon's election as prime minister. Yet despite President Bush's apparent tilt toward Sharon in the autumn of 2001, many in the Middle East continued to give the United States the benefit of the doubt. Lebanon's *ad-Diyad* saw the latest Israeli assault on Palestinian targets as a direct challenge to Bush's stated "vision" of a Palestinian state. "Sharon wanted to abort the idea, so he spilled all his anger on the most important symbols of the state," said the paper, referring to the attacks on Arafat's compound and the infrastructure of the Palestinian Authority.[45] Jordan's *al-Arab al-Yawm* said Sharon's attempt to equate Israel's struggle against the Palestinians with America's war on terror was doomed: "The general is mistaken. The Palestinian Authority is not Taliban and Arafat is not the Mullah Omar and neither is the general in the same position as President Bush."[46] Yet the reservoir of goodwill for the United States among Arabs and Muslims was quickly draining.

In the coming months, from the perspective of the Muslim world, the Bush administration slid inexorably into the Israeli camp, even as the president dispatched envoys to the Middle East because, he said, "we fully understand that in order to be effective in our fight against terror . . . we need others to join us."[47] Both the media and leaders in Arab and Muslim countries warned the United States that it was undermining its own interests. "The United States's support for the current Israeli policy is a strategic blunder,"[48] Iranian foreign minister Kamal Kharrazi wrote to UN secretary general Kofi Annan in a letter responding to President Bush's State of the Union speech, which had labeled Iran a member of the "axis of evil."[49] "Such U.S. policy undermines the global resolve to embark on a real and comprehensive war on terrorism," Kharrazi said.[50]

Pressure on Arafat, who had been under virtual house arrest in his Ramallah compound since December, continued to build. In early February 2002, against the backdrop of Palestinian suicide bombings and Israeli attacks in the Occupied Territories, Sharon was back at the White House, being welcomed by the president as "a good friend" who shared "our mutual desire to rid the world of terror."[51] Though he stopped short of acceding to Sharon's request that the United States cut ties to the PLO, the president promised, "We will continue to keep pressure on Mr. Arafat to convince him that he must take serious concrete, real steps to reduce terrorist activity in the Middle East."[52] Numerous observers across the Muslim world all responded with the same question: "If Palestinian violence is seen as terrorism, what then is Israeli aggression?"[53] The comments of Malaysia's *New Straits Times* reflected a widely shared perception of deliberate American myopia:

> Palestinian self-rule areas are being razed by Israeli bombing as retribution for one-man suicide attacks on Israelis. Yasser Arafat has been confined to Ramallah for the last two months while Ariel Sharon visits President George W. Bush for the U.S.'s blessing on the carnage that Israel is inflicting.[54]

Noted the Syrian government newspaper *Tishrin*: "During the meeting between Bush and Sharon, the U.S. 'F-16s' and 'Apaches' continued to drop their bombs on Palestinians without any discrimination, killing, destroying and causing terror everywhere in the occupied West Bank and Gaza."[55] What was evident to Arabs and Muslims was also becoming apparent to some Americans. *The Christian Science Monitor* observed that "in the wake of The war on terrorism, the yellow 'caution' lights the United States once flashed at Israel have largely turned green."[56]

> And the sea of green – on everything from Israel's isolation and virtual imprisonment of Palestinian leader Yasser Arafat, to its comparison of the struggle with Palestinians to the war on terrorism – is drawing into question the ability of the U.S. government to be a balanced arbiter in one of the world's most dangerous conflicts.[57]

Despite such perceptions at home and abroad, the Bush administration continued its tacit support for Israel's steadily escalating military campaign in the Occupied Territories and the isolation of Arafat. There are various explanations for why the administration diverged from its initial arm's-length association with Sharon immediately after 9/11. These include Bush's personal chemistry with the Israeli leader, which dated back to 1998 when Sharon took the then-Texas governor on a helicopter ride over the West Bank; the president's antipathy for terrorism in all its forms; and the influence of Elliot Abrams, whom Bush appointed in December as his top National Security Council advisor on the Middle East. Abrams, who had been convicted in the Iran-Contra scandal and pardoned by Bush's father, was an ardent Zionist with little first-hand experience in the Middle East, a fact that caused considerable consternation among Arab leaders.

A fourth explanation involves Bush's personal relationship with Arafat. In January 2002, the Israeli Navy intercepted the *Karin-A*, a cargo ship loaded with 50 tons of heavy weapons and explosives bound for the Occupied Territories. Arafat initially told the United States he had nothing to do with the shipment. However, the Iranian-organized cargo was in fact destined for Arafat's military units. When Bush discovered Arafat was lying, he reportedly lost all confidence in the Palestinian leader.[58] This personalization of the Palestinian issue was similar to the way in which the president had embodied the war on terror in the persons of Osama bin Laden and Saddam Hussein. His antipathy toward Arafat and growing friendship with Sharon would define the American president's approach to the Israel–Palestine conflict in the coming months. "Mr. Arafat has heard my message. I can't be any more clear about it, that he must do everything in his power to reduce terrorist attacks on Israel," President Bush said with Sharon standing at his side. "At one point in time, he [Arafat] was indicating to us that he was going to do so, and then all of a sudden, a ship loaded with explosives show[s] up that most of the world believes he was involved with."[59] Many observers in the Arab and Muslim world saw the shipment as an attempt by the Palestinian Authority, which had no advanced weaponry, to defend itself against the relentless assault by Israelis powerful military. Others argued that Israel's systematic destruction of the PA's security infrastructure had stripped Arafat of the means to crack down on suicide cells. Egyptian Foreign Minister Ahmed Maher said Arafat, under siege in his compound, had been "humiliated" by the Israelis and it was thus a "contradiction" for the United States and Israel to expect him to take actions possible only for a powerful leader. The Egyptian diplomat also pointed to the inherent imbalance of U.S. policy: "You cannot make demands of Arafat without requiring anything of the Israelis."[60]

While Arafat remained under political and physical siege at his headquarters in Ramallah, Sharon became a frequent visitor to Washington. He was back at the White House in early February, where he declared the time had come to replace Arafat with new Palestinian leadership. At a separate Washington, D.C. news conference, Israeli Defense Minister Benjamin Ben-Eliezer claimed that in a private meeting Vice President Dick Cheney had said of Arafat, as far as the vice president was concerned "you can go ahead and hang him."[61] U.S. officials vociferously denied Cheney had ever said such a thing and Ben-Eliezer apologized, but in terms of Arab and Muslim perceptions, the damage had already been done. The idea that the U.S. had given a green light for the assassination of Arafat was underscored when, soon after Sharon and Ben-Eliezer returned to Jerusalem, Israeli jets bombed a Palestinian security complex a few hundred yards from Arafat's compound. The action was part of a continuing escalation of the violence, punctuated by Palestinian suicide bombings and Israeli air raids and ground attacks in the

West Bank and Gaza, which also hit UN facilities. So ferocious were the Israeli attacks that the State Department eventually issued a rare criticism of the Jewish state: "Though we understand the need for Israel to take steps to ensure its self-defense, we're seriously concerned about Israeli attacks over the past several days."[62] Arabs and Muslims welcomed the comment, but noted that it was carefully couched in language that betrayed what they saw as America's inherent bias.

As the weeks wore on, anger in the Arab and Muslim world mounted as Israeli troops invaded Nablus and Gaza City; launched air, ground and seaborne assaults on Palestinian areas across the Occupied Territories; and sealed off five West Bank cities. Even when Arafat arrested three men accused of assassinating Israeli interior minister Rahavam Ze'evi, a key Israeli demand, Arabs and Muslims heard the United States blame Arafat for the upsurge in violence, while only mildly rebuking Sharon as "unhelpful."[63] When Sharon responded to an American call for both sides to "consider their actions and the consequences very carefully" by announcing he would seize Palestinian lands to set up new buffer zones and defeat the "terrorists,"[64] while Arafat simultaneously reiterated his December call for Palestinians to cease attacks on Israelis, State Department spokesman Richard Boucher said only, "Israel's right to defend herself is clear."[65]

PERCEPTION AND REALITY

The right or wrong of U.S. policy toward Israel is, in the context of this book, immaterial. The issue is one of perception. Arabs and Muslims saw American statements and actions as concrete evidence of the inherent link between the U.S. war on terror and Sharon's campaign against the Palestinians. By the end of February 2002, as a new wave of suicide bombings prompted yet another round of Israeli attacks, the death toll in the 17 months of violence had reached more than 1,000 Palestinians and 288 Israelis.[66] From the perspective of Arabs and Muslims, the lopsided figures were further evidence of the inherent unfairness of American criticism of Arafat. That was only reinforced in the coming months as Israel mounted the largest invasion of the Occupied Territories since the 1972 Arab–Israeli war, with what appeared to Arabs and Muslims to be tacit U.S. approval. From an American perspective, the administration was genuinely working for a fair and equitable solution. President Bush sketched out a "roadmap to peace,"[67] endorsed a Saudi plan for a broad Arab–Israeli settlement, and dispatched the head of the CIA and his special Middle East envoy, Gen. Zinni, to the region; but to Arabs and Muslims, the rhetoric that accompanied these putative peace initiatives sent a clear message that it was the Palestinians who must bend to America's will, even though most of the blood being shed was theirs.

March 7, 2002 offered a snapshot of what Arabs and Muslims saw as America's blind support for Israeli violence. Newspapers across the Middle East reported enthusiastically on a comment the day before that seemed to signal a shift in Bush administration attitudes toward Sharon, who had declared he would "hit hard" against the Palestinians and only negotiate after they had been "beaten."[68] "If you declare war against the Palestinians thinking that you can solve the problem by seeing how many Palestinians can be killed, I don't know that that leads us anywhere," Powell said in Congressional testimony. *The New York Times* reported that the comment resulted from a reassessment at the White House, where

> in the past two days, as scenes of carnage and helicopter attacks have played across the television sets in the West Wing, senior administration officials decided they needed to rein in Mr. Sharon. The alternative, one official said, was that "Sharon would feel free to conduct a full-scale war, declared or undeclared."[69]

Sharon responded immediately, insisting that, referring to Arafat, "the one who initiated this war has the power to stop it, but he continues to prefer the war of terrorism."[70] There was no respite to the violence. And if televised images were having an impact in the West Wing, the effect in the Muslim world was even more intense. On March 7, viewers of al-Jazeera and other channels in the Middle East saw scenes of Israeli tanks and troops invading the West Bank refugee camps of Nor Shams and Tulkarm and seizing a UN school, while other units attacked Arafat's Ramallah headquarters, where he was meeting with a European Union envoy, as well as Palestinian police stations across the West Bank, killing eight and wounding more than 20. They also saw reports that Israeli troops had assassinated a leader of Islamic Jihad, shot four Palestinians at roadblocks and killed two others, including a UN employee, who were traveling in an ambulance; and they viewed scenes of the aftermath of Israeli air attacks on Palestinian government buildings in Bethlehem and Gaza City, which wounded eight, along with reports that a lone Palestinian teenager had attacked a Jewish settlement in Gaza, killing five Israeli teens and wounding 20 others.

The following morning, side-by-side with accounts of the violence, newspapers carried stories from Washington reporting that at the height of this bloodshed, President Bush had essentially repudiated Powell's tough words for Sharon. At a news conference in Washington, Bush had told reporters that he was "deeply concerned about the tragic loss of life and escalating violence in the Middle East," then, without mentioning Sharon, continued, "I once again call upon Chairman Arafat to make maximum effort to end terrorism against Israel, which undermines the prospects for peace."[71] Under questioning from reporters, the president had several opportunities to criticize Israeli tactics or Sharon himself, but each time declined, shifting the burden of responsibility back to Arafat. Asked whether he thought that "Ariel Sharon, engaging in his current policies, has become an obstacle to peace," Bush reshaped Powell's earlier firm message to Israel:

Well, I read the Secretary's comments, and it sounded like he had pretty tough words for all parties. He's concerned about the level of violence, like I am. He made it clear that Chairman Arafat needs to do a better job of reducing violence, of using his leadership role to reduce violence.[72]

Bush made no direct reference to Sharon, then repeated, "Chairman Arafat must do everything he can to reduce the violence, to stop the spread of violence. We don't believe he's doing enough."[73] Asked why he was "only talking to one side in this conflict" and why he did not "reach out to Chairman Arafat," Bush said he was confident "we've got ample amplification to both parties," then added, "I fully understand the Israelis' perspective that they want to defend themselves. That's why I've constantly called on Mr. Arafat to do a better job of reining in those who would wreak havoc on Israel."[74] The response was a torrent of angry comment across the Arab world. "The American administration, which is supposed to be an impartial broker in the peace process, has blatantly aligned itself with the aggressive side," charged Qatar's *al-Rayah* in an editorial entitled "A Condemnable American Position."[75] American efforts to end the violence were prompted only by "concern for Israel and a quest to rescue [the Jewish state] from the embarrassing situation in which it finds itself," said *al-Khaleej* in the United Arab Emirates.[76] Reporting on the deaths of another 40 Palestinians on March 8, Saudi Arabia's *al-Watan* said the United States did not have "the political will to halt the massacres" and, noting mounting White House pressure on Iraq, warned that the simultaneous visits by Gen. Zinni and Vice President Cheney to the region were "serving as a sedative to open the way for other plans."[77]

The siege of Ramallah. The assault on Jenin, which left more than 50 Palestinians dead and some 4,000 homeless in what Amnesty International would later label Israeli "war crimes."[78] The blockade of Bethlehem's Church of the Nativity by Israeli forces, who had trapped a group of Palestinian fighters in the birthplace of Jesus. Day after day Arabs and Muslims saw on their television screens and the front pages of their newspapers images of Israeli tanks and Palestinian bodies, as they heard and read statements from the Bush administration that grew increasingly critical of Arafat and more closely identified with the Israelis. Each time the administration seemed to finally reach its breaking point with the Israelis, such as the president's early April declaration that "enough is enough,"[79] it quickly settled back into what Arabs and Muslims saw as a pro-Israel tone. Particularly shocking to them was the administration's adoption of terminology favored by Sharon, such as "homicide bomber,"[80] which the president and his spokesman began using in mid-April to refer to what were more commonly known as suicide bombers. The shift in language came as Powell met with Arafat in his battered Ramallah headquarters, ending – for the moment – the administration's boycott of the Palestinian leader. Yet any positive feeling toward the United States that the Arafat meetings might have produced within the Arab and Muslim body politic were dissipated when President Bush welcomed Powell back to Washington by endorsing Sharon as "a man of peace," said he understood why Israel continued to lay siege to Ramallah, and appeared to directly align his war on terror with that of Sharon. "It is essential that we continue to work to fight terror. There will never be peace in parts of the world unless we're willing to rout out terror," he told reporters, referring to the conflict in Israel. "And that's why we will be engaged not only there, but around the world where we fight terror. This is the calling of our time, to fight terror."[81]

Critics at home and abroad were stunned. "To have Sharon, the butcher of Sabra and Chatilla, believed by many

Israelis to be a war criminal, named a 'man of peace' by President Bush may be one of the worst misstatements any president has ever made," wrote former Congressman Paul "Pete" McCloskey, Jr. "Those words could only infuriate the very people who were most likely to volunteer as suicide bombers against us. Worse, they cause the entire Muslim world to view the United States as the willing abettor of Sharon's more recent acts of brutality in the occupied territories."[82]

Weeks later, as Israeli armor and aircraft continued operations in the Occupied Territories and the siege of the Church of the Nativity dragged on, Sharon was back at the White House, where President Bush once more praised his desire for peace and told reporters, "I have been disappointed in Chairman Arafat. I think he's let the Palestinian people down. I think he's had an opportunity to lead to peace and he hasn't done so."[83] Sharon took the opportunity to again identify Israel's fight with that of the United States, explaining, "We need to act against terror worldwide,"[84] feeding directly into the Arab suspicion that the war on terror was, as the radicals claimed, a Zionist–Christian conspiracy against Islam. By Sharon's next White House visit a month later, the Palestinian death toll in the Intifada had reached 1,600, including some 300 children, and Arafat was again politically isolated and still physically besieged by Israeli armor. Once more, images of a smiling George Bush welcoming his "friend" Ariel Sharon were juxtaposed on Arab and Muslim television screens with Israeli tanks and Palestinian dead. Once more Arafat was criticized by the president as an impediment to peace, even as television viewers across the Muslim world saw him a prisoner of the Israeli armor that ringed – and continued to shell – his wrecked headquarters, a beleaguered Arab David facing the Israeli Goliath and its American patron. By month's end, as the violence continued unabated, President Bush was standing in the Rose Garden demanding that Arafat, who was elected president of the Palestinian Authority in 1996 with 87 per cent of the vote, be replaced by a "new Palestinian leadership."[85] This time, he expanded the circle of responsibility for ending the violence to the Arab world as a whole, still omitting any mention of Sharon. The president, whom the *Jerusalem Post* later called "Israel's best friend ever in the White House,"[86] insisted that Arab countries must "stop the flow of money, equipment and recruits to terrorist groups seeking the destruction of Israel." For good measure, he added: "Arab states will be expected to build closer ties of diplomacy and commerce with Israel, leading to full normalization of relations between Israel and the entire Arab world." Bush took a major step in endorsing the eventual formation of a Palestinian state, but at the same time seemed to equate support for Palestinian militants with support for the Islamist radicals targeting the United States: "I've said in the past that nations are either with us or against us in the war on terror."[87] If anyone still doubted the administration's position, National Security Advisor Condoleezza Rice told NBC's *Meet the Press* that if the Palestinians reelected Arafat to the presidency of the Palestine Authority, there would be "consequences."[88] She and other administration officials refused to rule out the use of force. To Arabs and Muslims, it was more hypocrisy from an administration demanding democracy in the Middle East. "In words and deeds, Bush has demonstrated that by 'foes' he means those who see things from an angle different from the American perspective," said Egypt's *al-Gomhuriya* newspaper.[89] Even Israeli Foreign Minister Shimon Peres, who together with Arafat and Yitzak Rabin won the 1994 Nobel Peace Prize for negotiating the Oslo peace accord, was "reportedly so revolted" by the president's speech "that he could not listen to the end."[90] Writing in the *Jordan Times*, journalist Rami Khouri gave the U.S. president credit for acknowledging the eventual necessity of a Palestinian state, but said this "heavily camou-flaged substantive core" of Bush policy "was so heavily tilted and burdened by Bush's pro-Israeli statements that it has been largely lost."[91]

9
Rewriting the Script: Iraq

I knew very well that it was enough to . . . deprive [a person] of hearing or sight, for the world to undergo immediate transformation . . . Another world? Not really. The same world rather, but seen from another angle.

Jacques Lusseyran, *And There Was Light*

There was a certain irony in the fact that my last glimpse of American television before boarding a flight to the Persian Gulf in the early days of the Iraq war was that of Fox News commentator Bill O'Reilly, on an airport monitor, fulminating about the BBC's "disgraceful" coverage.[1] This from the channel whose reporters gushed that "liberty" was sweeping through Iraq[2] and whose anchors dismissed as "ridiculousness" the idea that some Arabs might consider the Americans to be invaders.[3] If critics argued that Bush and bin Laden were mirror images, then Fox was al-Jazeera's ideological doppelganger, walking point for America's media commandos as they prepared the psychological ground for the troops. The BBC, meanwhile, was fighting a rearguard action to defend journalistic independence.

I was reminded of that again when I turned on the television in my hotel room in the United Arab Emirates 24 hours after leaving Boston. The BBC was showing footage of a Baghdad market where, a short time before, at least 58 Iraqi civilians had been killed and scores more wounded by an explosion. The BBC's anchor reported that it was not yet clear what had caused the blast, which had occurred during a U.S. bombardment of the Iraqi capital, but speculation included an errant American missile or Iraqi anti-aircraft fire. Al-Jazeera was showing the same footage, emphasizing close-ups of the dead and wounded and clearly pointing the finger of responsibility at the United States. CNN, meanwhile, appeared to be downplaying the mass casualties, leading the broadcast hour with a report about pro-Saddam *fedayeen* "terrorizing civilians" in Basra, and emphasizing the fact that U.S. troops were trying to protect the "liberated" Iraqis. When it finally got around to mentioning the scores of dead Iraqi civilians in the Baghdad market a full 15 minutes into the newscast, CNN anchor Wolf Blitzer conducted an on-camera discussion with another reporter in which the two twisted themselves into knots pointing out all the reasons the disaster might *not* be America's fault.

The BBC was, as reporters in the trenches like to say, committing journalism, providing a fair and balanced account of the tragedy. The other two broadcasters had become defenders of their respective nationalistic causes; al-Jazeera taking on the mantle of the Arab people, just as CNN supported the American war effort by emphasizing a story that implicitly painted the United States as protector of the Iraqi people and downplaying a humanitarian disaster that was also a U.S. public-relations fiasco.

CNN's stance was emblematic of the jingoism that had taken root in the U.S. media since 9/11 as news organizations responded to the tidal wave of patriotism that swept the country, as well as the machinations of a highly efficient White House communications machine. That jingoism was evident in the fervor with which U.S. media organizations had painted the news in red, white and blue; evident in the media's failure to challenge unsubstantiated White House claims of Iraqi weapons of mass destruction, investigate dissenting views in the intelligence community or question widespread infringements of civil rights; and, as noted earlier,

evident in the sorry scene of Dan Rather, one of America's
most influential news anchors, declaring on national television:
"George Bush is the president. He makes the decisions
and . . . wherever he wants me to line up, just tell me
where."[4] Was it any wonder that during the Iraq invasion
many "embedded" reporters would drop any pretense of
detachment and use the pronoun "we" when describing the
U.S. units with which they were traveling?

"Every government is run by liars and nothing they say
should be believed," the famous American counterculture
journalist I.F. Stone once said. It was an adage to which, at
least since Vietnam, most U.S. reporters had traditionally
subscribed. But post-9/11, the American media's adversarial
relationship with the government – and particularly the
military – had largely been set aside. One survey of U.S. news
coverage in the last three months of 2001 found that less
than 10 per cent of reporting was critical of the government's
viewpoint.[5] Objective journalism had been transformed into
patriotic journalism. It was *Us* against *Them*, but this time,
instead of government officials, *They* were the amorphous
Islamic Other. In this war, the soldiers of objectivity had
crossed over to the traditional enemy – the government – for
the duration.

With opinion in the Muslim world against the United
States even before the invasion was launched, columnist
Ellen Goodman wondered in print "how we got from there
to here."[6] The bigger question for reporters and editors
should have been: where were *they* while the ground of
global opinion shifted? For many, particularly Washington
insiders, the answer was that they were front and center,
reading their lines from a carefully crafted script. In return
for front-page bylines and top-of-the-broadcast billing, they
were dutifully serving as unquestioning conduits for well-
choreographed Bush administration leaks about weapons of
mass destruction, a claim that Deputy Defense Secretary

Paul Wolfowitz would eventually admit was a "bureaucratic" device to give the administration an excuse to attempt to reshape the Middle East.[7] Emblematic of that insidious partnership was a September 2002 front-page article in *The New York Times* headlined, "U.S. Says Hussein Intensifies Quest for A-Bomb Parts."[8] Written by Michael R. Gordon and Judith Miller, the story was part of a carefully crafted administration effort to bolster support for an invasion of Iraq. The previous day, in a news conference at Camp David with British prime minister Tony Blair, President Bush had told reporters that a new report from the UN's International Atomic Energy Agency found that Iraq was six months away from building a nuclear weapon. "I don't know what more evidence we need," said Bush. In reality, the IAEA had issued no such report, but the president's claim went virtually unchallenged in the U.S. media. *The Times* article, meanwhile, cited unnamed administration sources as claiming Iraq had purchased "thousands of specially designed aluminum tubes" for use in nuclear centrifuges, and quoted Iraqi defectors as claiming Hussein had "also heightened his efforts to develop new types of chemical weapons." Buried deep in the article was a CIA assessment that it would take Iraq five to seven years to develop enriched uranium for use in nuclear weapons and that there were "no signs" Iraq was trying to acquire such a supply. The story generated its own headlines around the world, bolstering the administration's case for war.

The "you-scratch-my-back" nature of the relationship between *The Times'* reporters and the administration was underlined by the fact that the article appeared on a Sunday. The timing enabled Vice President Dick Cheney to go on NBC's *Meet the Press* later that morning and cite *The Times* article – for which his own administration had been the source – as seemingly independent evidence of Iraq's quest for weapons of mass destruction. "There's a story in *The*

New York Times this morning," Cheney told NBC's Tim Russert. "And I want to attribute *The Times*," he repeated to drive home the idea that this was supposedly independent and objective information dug up by the nation's leading newspaper, rather than the spoon-fed disinformation it later proved to be. Not incidentally, access to the supposed Iraqi defector cited in the article had been arranged by Ahmed Chalabi, an exiled Iraqi dissident whom the CIA had long ago jettisoned as unreliable, but who worked closely with neoconservatives in the Pentagon to generate support for a war in Iraq. Chalabi – convicted of bank fraud in Jordan – would serve as the primary source for a long string of *Times* articles. After the invasion, one of the reporters who wrote the original piece, Judith Miller, would use a steady stream of false intelligence fed to her by Chalabi to lead U.S. weapons inspectors on an odyssey across Iraq that would ultimately prove futile but would ensure a series of front-page articles for Miller and serve Chalabi's interests.

If most Americans were naive about such manipulation of information, other U.S. reporters certainly were not. After all, they had given prominent play to White House aide Andrew Card's cynical comment in the summer of 2002 about the packaging and selling of the war: "From a marketing point of view, you don't introduce new products in August."[9] By slavishly reporting the administration's statements without question, the Washington press corps became a mouthpiece for the administration, reprising the media's role in past conflicts as "propagandists and myth makers"[10] More sinisterly, that symbiotic relationship gave dominance to the rhetoric of violence, creating a climate in which the country could seamlessly slip into war with little discussion or debate. As columnist Robert J. Samuelson predicted of his fellow journalists in the autumn of 2001, by falling prey to the patriotic fervor, "[w]e will become (and already partly have become) merchants of fear."[11] Dissenting media voices, which argued that the watchdog role of the press was a cornerstone of democracy, were accused of being unpatriotic. "People have to watch what they say and watch what they do," warned White House Press Secretary Ari Fleischer in a line that seemed to turn on its head the set of democratic principles that the administration said it was fighting to defend.[12]

When, in the early days of CNN, Ted Turner ordered his team to substitute the word "international" for "foreign,"[13] it gave rise to much talk of the globalization of news and the emergence of what might be called borderless journalism by individuals who transcend national attachments. Some observers went so far as to write of the emergence of a new "world news order" in which journalism was "charged with the responsibility of contributing to the establishment of a worldwide discourse that would be sensitive to the different perspectives."[14] Aspirations toward such an independent line made the BBC the journalistic whipping boy of conservatives like Bill O'Reilly on both sides of the Atlantic. "If Iraq proved anything, it was that the BBC cannot afford to mix patriotism and journalism," said BBC director general Greg Dyke. "This is happening in the United States and if it continues, will undermine the credibility of the U.S. electronic news media."[15]

War is ugly. Smart or otherwise, bombs kill. Limbs are torn asunder. Flesh is peeled from the bone. The raw images of conflict are frightening, shocking, nauseating. It is humankind at its most savage. During the first "television war" in Vietnam, some viewers complained about the graphic coverage. The sight of mutilated soldiers on the news at dinnertime made them lose their appetite. But ultimately, those images turned the U.S. public against the war. American viewers saw little of that horror during the invasion of Iraq. It was a war the whole family could love.

That was precisely as the administration had planned. What the Bush administration had *not* counted on was the dramatic impact of Arab television. Americans may have been blinded to the other side of the conflict, but viewers in the Arab world and beyond had a ringside seat.

MANAGING THE MESSAGE

No longer did the U.S. enjoy the same dominance over words and images that it held over military power. Stories like the July 2002 U.S. strafing attack on a wedding party in central Afghanistan that killed 48 civilians and wounded another 117, including children, took on a life of their own, streaking around the world despite the best efforts of Pentagon officials to provide a different version of events.[16] Estimates that Afghan civilian deaths were as high as 9,000[17] were made even worse by the widely reported comment by the overall U.S. commander, Gen. Tommy Franks, that "we don't do body counts,"[18] which many commentators seized on as evidence of "the different worth attached to American as opposed to Muslim lives."[19] Meanwhile, images of Israeli tanks and Palestinian dead on the West Bank and Gaza gave the lie to President Bush's claims that Ariel Sharon was "a man of peace." When American forces rolled into Iraq, these disparate conflicts seemed to blur. "Every day we see these terrible parallels – American tanks facing Iraqis, Israeli tanks facing Palestinians," wrote Jihad Al Khazen, the former editor in chief of *al-Hayat*, the largest-circulation Arabic-language daily. "For peace, for the future of the region, there is a sense among Arabs that everything has been brought to a dead end [by the White House]."[20]

Not only had al-Jazeera changed the television landscape, but it had inspired other media with its aggressive new style built on sensational images, American-style sets and graphics, and boisterous – sometimes outlandish – debate. This al-Jazeera effect was seen in the launch of similar news channels in the United Arab Emirates, Iran and elsewhere; the beginnings of a heightened assertiveness on the part of the print media in the region; and a loosening of the reigns on state-run broadcasters in countries that disapproved of America's intentions in Iraq. In response, the Bush administration prepared an unprecedented multimillion-dollar effort to manage the message in Iraq and prevent a replay of Afghanistan, where its storyline had been hijacked by the Arab media. "It was an orchestrated effort [that] began before the war," USAF Colonel (Ret.) Sam Gardiner, a former lecturer at the U.S. Army War College, reported in a study of information warfare techniques used in the conflict.[21] In the lead-up to the assault on Baghdad, a highly choreographed message management strategy was put in place. The day would begin with a predawn conference call in which White House spokesman Ari Fleischer briefed the U.S. networks and wire services. Not long after, another conference call would link key civilian and military spokespersons in Washington, London and at the Central Command media center in Qatar, setting out the thematic story lines for the day. Meanwhile, administration officials took turns fanning out on the U.S. morning network shows and making themselves available to domestic and international print reporters. The briefing in Qatar was timed to coincide with mid-day U.S. newscasts and evening European broadcasts, while the afternoon Pentagon briefing was designed to provide material for the U.S. evening newscasts. A nightly compendium of talking points and quotes from key officials was sent out to U.S. embassies around the world overnight, to make sure everyone was "on message" early the next day. The goal was to "fill every information void in the 24-hour worldwide news cycle, leaving little to chance or interpretation."[22]

The second prong of the strategy involved creating realities on the ground. U.S. policymakers had seen the dramatic impact of CNN's broadcasts from Baghdad during the 1990–91 Gulf War, which included reports on civilian casualties and

stories that contradicted the official U.S. version of events.
They were determined to avoid a repeat this time. Word went
out to the major networks: the initial U.S. air attack on
Baghdad – the so-called "shock and awe" – would be so
devastating that it would be far too dangerous for American
reporters to remain there. In addition, electronic counter-
measures would mean it would be impossible for the networks to transmit pictures or for their reporters to
communicate (which proved not to be true). There was, in
short, no reason to stay. All of the major networks took note
of the warning and ordered their teams withdrawn, much to
the chagrin of some veteran war correspondents. Only CNN
remained, hoping to reprise its coup of the 1990–91 Gulf
War, but it was soon expelled by the Iraqis in favor of al-
Jazeera and its new competitors, al-Arabiya and Abu Dhabi
TV. The U.S. networks – and the American people – were
thus rendered largely blind in the Iraqi capital, dependent on
a handful of freelancers, information and footage provided
by the Pentagon and, ironically, feeds from the Arab network
cameras that recorded the "shock and awe" of the American
bombardment from Baghdad's ground zero. But those cameras also provided footage of the impact on civilians, a story
U.S. planners had hoped would be hidden from view, which
was why so many red flags were raised among news organizations, human rights groups and the Arab public at large
when an American missile scored a direct hit on the al-Jazeera
bureau.

Al-Jazeera specialized in an up-close, in-your-face
approach to covering the Muslim world's first television
wars. Dead babies, wounded children, screaming mothers
dominated the channel's coverage of Iraq, Afghanistan and
Palestine. Almost nothing was too gruesome to show: close-
ups of open wounds, limbs torn asunder, people collapsing in
agony. But those pictures were largely ignored by the U.S.
networks. Where audiences watching al-Jazeera and the

other Arab broadcasters saw bleeding children and destroyed homes, Americans experienced the war as a Hollywood extravaganza on the small screen, billed in advance by the White House as certain to evoke "shock and awe." In America, tanks charged across the screen in real time as breathless embedded reporters mouthed platitudes to the valor of U.S. military might. On al-Jazeera, innocent civilians died. One conflict, two faces; each reflected in a rival bloodshot lens.

This most highly covered and – seen from the U.S. side – most sanitized of conflicts was the result of the administration's brilliant tactic of "embedding" hundreds of reporters with military units in the field and making them agree to strictures on what they could say and when. It was an approach pioneered with great success by the British during the Falklands War, a fact that did not escape American notice. "In spite of a perception of choice in a democratic society, the Falklands War shows us how to make certain that government policy is not undermined by the way a war is reported," Lt. Commander Arthur Humphries wrote in the *Naval War College Review* in 1983. "Control access to the fighting, invoke censorship, and rally aid in the form of patriotism at home and in the battle zone."[23] White House image makers knew human nature: when your life depends on the people you are covering, it is only natural to develop a bond. In short, you become one of the gang. Some reporters appeared on camera in full combat gear – helmet, camouflage, flak jacket and American flag patch on the shoulder. Journalist as GI Joe. "Toy soldiers," veteran British reporter Robert Fisk disparagingly labeled them.[24] The vast majority of the "embeds" had never seen war. Many had never been outside the United States, pulled directly from Main Street to the turret of a Main Battle Tank. Some couldn't even pronounce the name of the country they were covering – "EYE-rak." Context was lost. Accuracy went wanting.

How many times did we learn from some breathless reporter that Basra had fallen, only to find out, yet again, it had not? As an editorial in Britain's *Financial Times* put it, "Few conflicts . . . have produced such confusion, or so many spectacular news stories one day that seem strangely to disappear into the swirling Iraqi dust the next."[25] On American television, bloodshed was kept to a bare minimum. U.S. viewers did not see badly wounded Americans writhing in agony or the body bags being shipped home. And what of the Iraqi civilians? Did no one die under those missiles?

While the print media also felt the effect, television was the most overtly impacted by government efforts to control the message. The fact that all the U.S. networks pulled their staff correspondents out of Baghdad on the recommendation of the Pentagon only exacerbated the reliance on official sources and images. Veteran Middle East television correspondents were largely prevented from doing what they do best, ferreting out the truth under dangerous and difficult conditions. Their absence – coupled with self-censorship that prevented use of some Arab TV footage – made this, in the U.S. at least, a one-sided television war.

A study of coverage by embedded reporters at the U.S. networks during three of the first six days of the war revealed a bloodless view of the conflict. While 21.3 per cent of the reports aired showed weapons being fired, not a single broadcast showed human impact. "None of the embedded stories studied showed footage of people, either U.S. soldiers or Iraqis, being struck, injured or killed by weapons fired," the Project on Excellence in Journalism reported.[26] A content analysis of photo coverage in *The New York Times* found much the same.[27] Meanwhile, facts became elusive. "Most of us were so busy trying to get a front seat at the war that there was a lack of focus on the bedrock truth of what was being said," recalled Jay Weiss, an ABC News producer who was embedded with the Marines.[28] Meanwhile, images of death and destruction dominated the Arab media, epitomized by a photograph of a young girl bleeding from her eye that appeared in many Arab media outlets. The caption on one popular website: "My dead mother is liberated and so am I."[29]

These two very different perspectives on the war were magnified by the cultural lens through which journalists reported the conflict; the coverage on each side naturally shaped by the worldview of the man or woman crafting the story. "For different reasons, Arab and American broadcasters provide a distorted, incomplete picture of the war in Iraq – while accurately reflecting emotional and political sentiments on both sides," Rami Khouri of Beirut's *Daily Star*, wrote in the early days of the war.[30] Just as CBS News anchor Dan Rather told CNN's Larry King, "When my country's at war, I want my country to win; there is an inherent bias in the American media,"[31] Arab journalists felt the same. American journalist-scholar Abdallah Schleifer reported that an Arab correspondent covering events at the U.S. military command headquarters in Doha, Qatar told him that "he put his duty to his people, to the Arab nation, above his duty as a journalist."[32] Did that mean al-Jazeera and its counterparts were toeing the Iraqi line?[33] Donald Rumsfeld and the U.S. military command certainly drove that message home in their almost daily verbal attacks on the network for its "pattern of playing propaganda over and over and over again," but the channel didn't seem to have many fans in the Baghdad regime either. As American tanks closed on the capital, Iraqi Information Minister Saeed al-Sahaf snapped, "I warn al-Jazeera: stop your American propaganda."

MEDIA AND THE NATIONAL INTEREST

Where the American media's mirroring of the sense of moral superiority and patriotic intervention that gripped the country had fed public support for the conflict, coverage in the Muslim world was framed by the long-standing political and cultural factors outlined in earlier chapters and a deeply cynical view of U.S. motives that had been nurtured by American rhetoric and actions regarding Iraq for more than a decade. Arab and Muslim journalists remembered well the comment of President Bush's father, George H.W. Bush, that he would "bomb Iraq back to the stone age."[34] They had reported on claims that upwards of 500,000 Iraqi children had died as a result of UN sanctions and that hundreds of thousands more were suffering from disease and malnutrition.[35] They had heard the president tell British journalists a full year before the invasion, "I made up my mind that Saddam needs to go, that's about all I'm willing to share with you."[36] And they had listened with skepticism to mounting U.S. rhetoric about the link between secular Saddam Hussein and Islamist terrorism. In fact, the same post-9/11 rhetoric and policies that produced a patriotic, anti-Saddam fervor in the United States, had exactly the opposite effect in the Muslim world, galvanizing opposition and framing the conflict as an imperialist imposition of U.S. will.

None of this background made it any less galling to U.S. officials that al-Jazeera and its brethren were drowning out their own attempts to shape attitudes in the region, whether through CNN and Fox News – which by the Iraq war was also available by satellite in the Middle East – or, after the occupation began, on al-Iraqiya, the newly renamed Iraqi national television channel operated by American contractors with the help of U.S. military psychological operations teams. Yet the fact remained, it was the administration's failure to grasp how its own words and actions had contributed to the atmosphere of suspicion and disdain that had brought attitudes to the point where the United States was unable to communicate its message with any credibility. Even the administration's attempts to use al-Jazeera itself to reach out to Arab and Muslim viewers often went badly awry thanks to the contradiction between American words and actions evident to anyone with a television. Two weeks into the U.S. bombing campaign in Afghanistan, during which al-Jazeera viewers had seen countless images of death and destruction, Secretary of Defense Donald Rumsfeld went on the station and admitted to only one incident in which "a round of munitions actually went amiss and did in fact kill possibly four people and injured several people." As for the rest, Rumsfeld pointed to Taliban anti-aircraft fire "that kills people on the ground when it comes back down" and "the various tribes" that were "all shooting at each other."[37] National Security Advisor Condoleezza Rice spent much of her 16-minute interview with the channel assuring viewers that the United States was committed to resolving the Palestinian crisis and would urge Israel to "relieve the financial and economic pressures on the Palestinian people," but within hours those same viewers were watching Israeli tanks rolling through the West Bank.[38]

The first two days of December 2002 offered a snapshot of how this kind of mixed message systematically alienated audiences in the Middle East and beyond. In the midst of the White House campaign to convince the world that it was committed to a multilateral solution in Iraq, Richard Perle, chairman of the Defense Policy Review Board, stunned British members of parliament by announcing that even if UN weapons inspectors gave Iraq "a clean bill of health," it would not stop a U.S. invasion.[39] Meanwhile, in Israel, Ariel Sharon repudiated an earlier statement by his own UN ambassador, Yahuda Lancry, that his government accepted the vision of "two states living side by side in peace and security."[40] In Washington, the Bush administration imposed formal sanctions on the Palestinian Authority and simul-taneously announced the appointment of ardent Zionist Elliot Abrams as the president's top National Security Council advisor on the Middle East. Stepped-up military action accompanied these political developments. U.S. jets bombed southern Iraq in a raid the Saddam Hussein government said killed four people and wounded 27. Israeli troops opened fire on a group of stone-throwers, killing an 18-year-old student, and injuring 27 others, including 17 children. At least 50 tanks, backed by helicopter gunships, mounted an assault on a village in Gaza. A former Israeli education minister charged that the government was applying Nuremberg-style laws to Israel's Arab citizens. And the UN World Food Program claimed that, in an earlier raid, Israeli forces had purposely blown up a Gaza warehouse containing more than 500 tons of food destined for 40,000 needy Palestinians.[41] All this in two days – just part of an endless barrage of stories that fed the Muslim perception that the United States and Israel were involved in a grand conspiracy against Arabs and Islam.

Therefore, when Secretary of State Colin Powell stood before the UN General Assembly and outlined his case for war against Iraq in early February 2003, media in the United States and the Muslim world reported the event through completely different frames. American newspaper columnists and editorial writers – liberals and conservatives alike – hailed the speech under such headlines as "The UN Gets the Truth,"[42] "Powell's Smoking Gun,"[43] "I'm Persuaded,"[44] and "A Winning Hand for Powell."[45] Arab newspaper coverage reflected a deep sense of skepticism. "Powell unconvincing at UN," reported *Arab News*;[46] "A U.S. show full of special effects and stunts," said Jordan's *al-Arab al-Yawm*.[47] Indonesia's *Suara Merdeka* demanded that Powell hand over his evidence and pointed to the "contradiction" inherent in Bush administration policy.

> The United States is of the view that, with or without an excuse, Saddam Hussein must be eliminated because he is a danger to the world. The majority of the world community sees that as

injustice and is concerned about the deleterious impact if war really breaks out.[48]

Malaysian newspapers quoted Prime Minister Mahathir Mohamad as insisting that the United States had provided no good reason for war. "[T]oo many people are going to be killed, merely because you want to change the government of the country," he said, addressing himself to President Bush via the media.[49]

IMAGES OF WAR

When U.S. bombs and missiles began falling on Baghdad a few weeks later, the war of liberation envisioned by many Americans was greeted with anger and fear in the Muslim world, not out of any love for Saddam Hussein, but out of a conviction that America's motives were anything but pure. "The world's most modern center of civilization is attacking the world's oldest one, with its eye on the latter's oil wealth," charged *al-Riyadh* of Saudi Arabia.[50] The government-dominated Egyptian media reported on the outbreak of hostilities with ambivalence, reflecting Egyptian president Hosni Mubarak's mixed feelings about the conflict, caught between the billions of dollars in U.S. aid his country received, his dislike of Saddam, and his Arab nationalist impulses. "Saddam Hussein will renew the tragic scenario of his war in Iran and Kuwait only to guarantee safety to himself and his family at the expense of his oppressed people," observed Samir Ragab, editor in chief of the pro-government daily *al-Gomhuriya* and long-time Mubarak confidant, while Syrian newspapers predictably echoed the Assad regime's vehement opposition. "Baghdad is burning," wrote government-owned *al-Thawra*, "Iraqi territories have become a place for catastrophe unleashed by American–British war machines. The volume of killing and destruction, which they claim is liberating Iraq, has abandoned human and civilized values."[51] But the rhetoric was not confined to those hostile to the United States. Across the region, even in countries long considered among America's strongest Arab allies, newspapers wrote of a "return to the law of the jungle"[52] and a "total defeat for the values of humanity."[53] Talk of American "values" that had so dominated the discourse from Washington in the previous 18 months made such comments all the more damning. Overnight, even many staunchly pro-American commentators turned against U.S. policy. "There is an inevitable result for this war," wrote Galal Dewidar of Egypt's *al-Akhbar*. "It is to increase hatred towards anything American because of the U.S. rush into war without authorization from the [UN] Security Council. This will push the world into further chaos."[54] Meanwhile, from Cairo to Jakarta, tens of thousands of Muslims took to the streets in protest as once-apolitical clerics issued a flurry of fatwas condemning the invasion by what one newspaper called "the new Mongols."[55]

In the media of the Muslim world "shock and awe" was greeted with fear and loathing. Some newspapers began running photo galleries of the dead, akin to the portraits of 9/11 victims carried in many U.S. papers. "We are not siding with Saddam," said Gameel George, the managing editor of Egypt's *al-Akhbar*, "but we *are* siding with the Iraqi people."[56] The Bush administration immediately began claiming bias. Al-Jazeera, Saudi-backed al-Arabiya and Iran's al-Alam (both of which went live a month before the invasion), and Abu Dhabi television were singled out for particular scorn. Coverage by the Arab channels was distinguished from that of their American counterparts both in the framing of stories – where America's NBC News, for example, titled its war coverage "Target: Iraq," al-Alam used the slogan "War for Control" – and, most critically, in the fact that their camera teams could go where U.S. TV crews could not.

When that explosion in a crowded Baghdad marketplace killed at least 58 civilians during a U.S. air strike in the first days of the conflict, the Arab channels provided vivid and compelling footage of the dead and wounded and linked the tragedy to the American bombardment. In contrast, CNN buried the story deep within its newscasts, using brief clips of al-Arabiya's footage, concentrating on official U.S. denials of responsibility and emphasizing the possibility that the blast had been caused by an errant Iraqi anti-aircraft missile.[57] In fact, the United States later admitted it had dropped "precision-guided" bombs on Iraqi anti-aircraft positions in the neighborhood, aware that "civilian damage" was "possible."[58] That CNN's team was hundreds of miles from Baghdad, embedded with U.S. troops, is likely to have contributed to its on-side approach, which was in sharp contrast to that of the few print and radio reporters who had stayed behind in Baghdad. "Whatever coalition military chiefs say about the cause of the tragedy, every individual [whom] reporters spoke to in [the neighborhood] believe emphatically it was a deliberate attack on civilians," Bob Graham of the London *Evening Standard* reported.[59]

> The battle for the hearts and minds of people in this area, which is home to mainly non-Iraqi Arabs – Palestinians and Egyptian immigrants – has been long lost. So deeply entrenched is the distrust of American and British reasons for entering the war – along with barely-concealed hatred of the coalition countries – that any words from Washington and London are immediately disbelieved.[60]

When al-Jazeera aired Iraqi TV footage of a group of dead and wounded American prisoners, U.S. officials – and many Americans – were outraged. "Horror Show," screamed the *New York Daily News*.[61] "A Video War Crime," charged the *Denver Post*.[62] The commander of U.S. forces in Iraq, Lt. Gen. John Abizaid, said al-Jazeera's broadcasting of the footage was "absolutely unacceptable" and called the images "disgusting."[63] CBS was the first to air the pictures in the U.S., rolling the tape during an interview with Rumsfeld on the Sunday morning interview program *Face the Nation*. The secretary of defense expressed shock and immediately said, "The Geneva Convention indicates that it's not permitted to photograph and embarrass or humiliate prisoners of war."[64] Many in the U.S. media struck a similar tone. "They are horrifying pictures, and we are not showing them on MSNBC," anchor John Siegenthaler said. "Why would al-Jazeera put them on television?"[65] "They are extremely, extremely disturbing images," agreed NBC anchor Matt Lauer.[66] "They are utterly, utterly gruesome," declared Fox News reporter Greg Palkot.[67] "Is there not a line between sanitizing the news and simply putting something on TV because it is gruesome?" CNN's Aaron Brown asked.[68]

The media and public in the Middle East – and much of the rest of the world – couldn't understand what all the fuss was about, particularly since, just the day before, U.S. television had shown videotape of Iraqi POWs and military casualties. The same had been true in Afghanistan and elsewhere. In fact, as a veteran of dozens of conflicts, I cannot think of a single war from which my television reports did not include dead bodies. As a young correspondent covering the Iran–Iraq war in the early 1980s, I had regularly used footage of dead Iraqi and Iranian soldiers and civilians, and had even interviewed Iranian POWs held in Iraqi camps. Bodies have littered my reports from Zimbabwe, Zaire, Chad, Lebanon and an assortment of other countries. Nor were those images confined to non-Americans. U.S. diplomats and servicemen killed and wounded in terrorist bombings; the body of a Navy diver murdered by the hijackers; statements coerced from kidnapped Americans, including one of my friends; these and many more such scenes have been a central element of my reporting and that of war correspondents around the world.

Suddenly, with the capture of the first U.S. POWs of the Iraq war, a tradition of American journalism was scrapped overnight as the White House imposed a new standard. Americans, who had enjoyed two centuries of press freedom, may have instantly accepted the idea that showing POWs was unconscionable, but such government-imposed strictures were rejected out of hand by Arabs and Muslims who had just recently begun tasting press freedom. "Our viewers and the world at large have the right to see the other view," Jihad Ali Ballout, a spokesman for al-Jazeera, told Western reporters. "It is a reflection of reality. The reality of war is horrible. Sometimes people miss this."[69] Some American reporters – particularly experienced war correspondents – shared that belief. But they came up against the strong strain of patriotism and outrage that ran through the mainstream U.S. media. A live on-air exchange between ABC *Good Morning America* anchor Charles Gibson and *Nightline* anchor Ted Koppel, who was reporting from Iraq, epitomized this confrontation. "Any time that you show bodies, it is simply disrespectful," said a clearly upset Gibson. "The Geneva Convention [says] prisoners of war must, at all times, be protected, particularly against acts of violence and public curiosity." Koppel, who covered Vietnam as a young reporter, countered that "we have often shown dead bodies . . . both with enemy dead and the dead of Americans." The *Nightline* anchor pointed out that his own report the previous evening had shown Iraqi POWs. As Gibson shook his head in disagreement, Koppel went on to argue that media self-censorship, carried out because news outlets were "ginning up patriotic feelings," was a mistake:

> I feel we do have an obligation to remind people in the most graphic way that war is a dreadful thing. . . . Young Americans are dying. Young Iraqis are dying. To turn our faces away from that is a mistake. . . . To sanitize it too much is a dreadful mistake.[70]

In fact, photos of the so-called "American Taliban," John Walker Lindh, strapped to a board naked and blindfolded after his capture in Afghanistan, had been widely circulated in the U.S. media with little protest. Likewise, the administration had voiced no objection to a photo of an Iraqi prisoner on his knees that ran on the front page of many newspapers.[71] To much of the world, this was hypocrisy. After President Bush said he expected Iraq not to abuse the POWs, "just like we'll treat any prisoners of theirs that we capture, humanely,"[72] *The Independent* of London observed that "Bush's words rang just a little hollow" since the 600 prisoners captured in Afghanistan and held at the Guantanamo Bay Naval detention facility "in total legal limbo" had been shown by the U.S. media "in conditions that seemed designed to humiliate, confined to metal cages, led hooded and blindfolded to interrogation sessions that were not, and could not, be monitored."[73] London's *Daily Mail* was even more pointed in its parallel: "Sickening: But what the hell does America expect when it treats PoWs like this?" read a headline that ran above photos of U.S. POWs juxtaposed against al-Qaeda suspects at Guantanamo Bay.[74]

The Bush administration bristled at such comparisons. "There are two different situations here," White House spokesman Ari Fleischer told reporters. "You have the war against terrorism and then you have this additional conflict."[75] It was an interesting distinction given the administration's insistence that the invasion of Iraq was *part* of the war on terror. Arabs and Muslims saw it as another example of double standards Some commentators in the United States, meanwhile, complained that Saddam Hussein was not playing fair. Said Robert Maginnis, a retired Army lieutenant colonel: "He's using al-Jazeera, Fox News, CNN to try to manipulate the people so that he can persuade their governments to put pressure on our government to back down."[76] And so he was. When a U.S. Apache helicopter was downed by heavy anti-aircraft fire and the two pilots were captured one day after the initial POWs tapes, Iraqi TV showed footage not only of the prisoners, but also of Iraqi farmers dancing beside the wreckage and holding rifles aloft. "A small number of peasants – brave peasants – shot down two Apaches," said Information Minister Saeed al-Sahaf.[77] It was a David and Goliath image designed to appeal to Arab nationalist impulses by crafting a portrait of the Iraqi underdog standing up to U.S. imperialist might.

But the United States was not to be left behind in the war of words and images. That was evident in the hero myth built around Private Jessica Lynch, a member of the same unit as those POWs and slain Americans shown in the initial Iraqi TV footage. The opening salvo in the U.S. government's propaganda campaign came in early April with the release of dramatic night-vision videotape of a helicopter-borne raid by Navy SEALS and Army Rangers on an Iraqi hospital where the 19-year-old was being held. "America is a nation that does not leave its heroes behind," Jim Wilkinson, a Central Command spokesman in Qatar, said in an interview with CNN,[78] which like all the American networks, made extensive use of the footage. The campaign picked up the following day with a *Washington Post* story, headlined, "She Was Fighting to the Death."[79] Quoting unnamed Pentagon officials, the *Post* reported that when Lynch's unit was ambushed after making a wrong turn in the desert, the maintenance company private "continued firing at the Iraqis even after she sustained multiple gunshot wounds and watched several other soldiers in her unit die around her." When she ran out of ammunition, the paper reported, Iraqi forces closed in and Lynch was stabbed in hand-to-hand combat. "She did not want to be taken alive," *The Post* quoted the official as saying.[80] Lynch was reported to be in "stable" condition at a U.S. military hospital in Germany, with broken arms and a broken leg in addition to the gunshot and stab wounds. There was also talk of rape.

It was an inspiring story that galvanized the nation and seemed destined to become a made-for-TV movie. "Brave young Jessica Lynch survives captivity – and torture – to become a hero of the Iraqi war," gushed *People* magazine, which featured Lynch on its cover superimposed against the Stars and Stripes. The only problem was that almost none of the story was true. The fabrication began to unravel when the BBC interviewed staff at the Iraqi hospital where Lynch had been treated. "There was no [sign of] shooting, no bullet inside her body, no stab wound," said Dr Harith a-Houssona.[81] He said her only injuries were a few broken bones apparently sustained when her vehicle overturned in the ambush. As for the dramatic rescue, hospital staff said they had put her in an ambulance and driven her to U.S. lines once American forces moved into the area, but were turned back at gunpoint before they could explain who their passenger was. "It was like a Hollywood film," another doctor, Anmar Uday, said of the rescue. "They cried 'go, go, go,' with guns and blanks without bullets, blanks and the sound of explosions. They made a show for the American attack on the hospital – action movies like Sylvester Stallone or Jackie Chan."[82] Col. David Rubenstein, commander of the Army hospital at Landstuhl, Germany, where Lynch was taken for treatment, confirmed that evidence did "not suggest that any of her wounds were caused by either gunshots or stabbing."[83]

After her recovery, Lynch herself was almost as bitter toward the U.S. government as she was toward the Saddam regime. "They used me as a way to symbolize all this stuff," she later complained in a television interview of the U.S. myth-making effort. Filming the rescue for publicity purposes, she said, was "wrong."[84]

> I'm not about to take credit for something I didn't do. I did not shoot, not a round, nothing . . . I went down praying to my knees. And that's the last I remember. From the time I woke up in that hospital, no one beat me, no one slapped me, no one,

nothing . . . I'm so thankful for those people because that's why I'm alive today.[85]

In a lengthy criticism of the initial coverage, *The Post*'s ombudsman, Michael Getler, concluded that the newspaper's reporting had been "thin" and relied too much on anonymous official sources.[86] Arab and Muslim audiences came to a different conclusion. To them, it was just more evidence that the U.S. media was a tool of the American war machine and could not be trusted; one more reason to watch al-Jazeera and its rivals. When the American channels were endlessly looping the Lynch rescue video in those first days of April, Iran's al-Alam showed extensive clips of wounded Iraqi civilians being treated or dead lying in the streets; the Syrian Space Channel aired scenes of wounded children, destroyed buildings and archive footage of dead U.S. soldiers, as well as reports on antiwar demonstrations around the world; and Lebanon's al-Manar television ran footage of President Bush talking about bringing freedom to the Iraqi people intercut with footage of wounded children, dead adults and wailing relatives, and a caption that read "Freedom: The American Way."[87] The Lynch story was barely mentioned in the Arab world; what mattered far more to Arabs and other Muslims glued to televisions was the death and suffering of Iraqi civilians at the hands of the Americans who had allegedly come to set them free.

The deification of Jessica Lynch demonstrated how the media on both sides had been turned into *political* weapons to stir up popular support. The U.S. military's so-called "Operation Thunder Run" was an example of how the media was also employed as a *military* weapon. At dawn on April 5, as U.S. units took up positions on the outskirts of the Iraqi capital, a column of tanks from the Third Infantry Division's Second Brigade made a surprise 25-mile dash through the southern portion of the city, all the more dramatic because it was witnessed live around the world through the cameras of an embedded U.S. network television team. The purpose was not to secure new positions or destroy Iraqi units. Instead, the operation, reported at the time as "a daring raid" in which American tanks sliced "through the city,"[88] was purely psychological. "The main intent . . . was to get the story out," the unit's commander, Col. David Perkins, told a conference at the Army War College five months later. "I don't know why anyone would want anything other than that."[89] The logic was simple; the military knew Hussein and some of his top aides were monitoring U.S. operations via satellite TV, a key reason embedded reporters were not allow to give away their positions. The sight of U.S. tanks racing through the streets of Baghdad, planners thought, would be a psychological blow that might even cause some Iraqi commanders to retreat or surrender. "We've turned the media into a mechanism for communicating information from the action to the consumer, including the enemy," Army Brig. Gen. Vincent Brooks, a member of the Joint Chiefs of Staff, told his fellow officers at the Army War College conference.[90]

PLAYING TO THE SCRIPT

Days after Thunder Run, the U.S. information war would reach its crescendo with live television coverage of the toppling of Saddam Hussein's statue in Firdos Square, which the chief operations officer for the land war command, Maj. Gen. James Thurman, called the crowning achievement of the embedded media program: "I felt chills in my body. The signal that sent, it's powerful."[91] Newspapers around the world ran the iconic photo of the regime's collapse. U.S. papers large and small hailed it as a triumphant moment. "Iraqis Go Wild in Baghdad," reported the *Advocate* in Baton Rouge.[92] "Euphoric Iraqis Topple Symbols," said the *Boston Globe*.[93] The image also appeared on the front pages of newspapers across the Muslim world, but many of those publications cropped it differently, clearly showing the U.S. tank that pulled down the statue. Others used a photo taken moments prior to the actual toppling, when an American soldier draped the U.S. flag over Saddam's head, before an officer more attuned to PR ordered him to take it down, replacing it with a pre-1991 Iraqi flag, which someone *just happened* to have on hand. Even that was quickly taken away.

Television footage of the statue's toppling and other scenes of celebration were endlessly repeated on all of the U.S. networks. "The republic of fear is conquered. Saddam rules no more," John Gibson of Fox News exalted.[94] Some, like Harry Smith of CBS, tried to put the images of celebration in context. In a city of five million, "there's not 1,000 people, there are not 5,000 or 10,000" gathered to witness the event; "it's somewhere – somewhere in the hundreds," he said.[95] CNN noted that one of its correspondents had been reporting live from a vicious firefight moments before the statue toppled,[96] an indication that the Americans were not being universally welcomed, and a Fox News correspondent said U.S. forces were encountering both "pockets of resistance" and "pockets – *pockets* – of jubilation."[97] But such attempts at contextualizing the story were generally overwhelmed by the way in which a collection of isolated scenes were woven into a mosaic that fit the administration's storyline. "Scenes of free Iraqis celebrating in the streets, riding American tanks, tearing down statues of Saddam Hussein in the center of Baghdad are breathtaking," an enthusiastic Secretary of Defense Rumsfeld told reporters. "Watching them, one cannot help but think of the fall of the Berlin Wall and the collapse of the iron curtain."[98] Many reporters were no less ecstatic. "It feels like Paris 1944, if you've seen the movies, in terms of widespread jubilation," reported Bob Arnot of NBC News,[99] a medical doctor with little experience covering wars and too young to have been even a twinkle in his father's eye at the liberation of Paris.

This journalistic cheerleading was not the result of some grand conspiracy between the media and the White House. Rather, it was the almost inevitable product of a combination of effective message manipulation on the part of the administration and the inherent tendency of the media to simplify complex events. The Bush administration had been predicting Iraqis would embrace U.S. troops as liberators, now – albeit in an extremely limited way – it was happening on the ground. "These are the symbols of the regime. So [it was] almost as symbolic to see this coming down as it was to see a U.S. Marine holding the Iraqi flag; an Iraqi man holding up the U.S. flag," CBS News correspondent Lara Logan reported from beside the fallen statue. "There is this initial moment of euphoria. It's exactly what the coalition leaders had been hoping for."[100]

For the U.S. media, the script had been written in advance; the pictures now conveniently completed the story. The ultimate evolution of this reduction of news to theater could be seen on MSNBC. The cable channel, which had on at least one occasion during the day told viewers that the statue had been pulled down by Iraqi citizens themselves, edited all of the fits and starts out of the tape, making the statue's fall appear to be one seamless movement, with no sign of the American tank.[101] What was destined to become the war's signature image had been little more than a photo opportunity created for the media by the American military, with the rent-a-crowd provided by U.S.-backed Iraqi exile Ahmed Chalabi and the actual toppling done by an American tank crew. But few reporters were willing to risk being labeled unpatriotic or biased by dwelling on that.

The media in the Muslim world had no such hesitation. The Saudi press reported scornful claims that those toppling the statue were "not real Iraqis."[102] "It does not mean anything," said media-savvy Saudi banker Tariq al-Zuhayr, "it was just a clip."[103] On al-Jazeera, a narrator providing commentary over the footage noted that "a few young Iraqis" working with U.S. troops tried to pull down the statue. When their rope broke, he explained, the Americans took over. "The scene was set and the dividing line between truth and reality disappeared to a great extent,"[104] the reporter told his audience. "The American soldier who approached on the back of a tank did not have the presence of mind to remember that he was on non-American soil," he continued, over footage of the soldier placing the American flag over the face of the Saddam statue in a classic tableau of conquest:

> . . . maybe it was a deliberate insult, or maybe he acted out of ignorance. All the excuses are uglier than the sin itself. In any case, that was the scene which history will record. But then there was still the problem of interpreting the scene. Was it an American soldier strangling an American dictator, or a foreign invader chopping off another head?[105]

Just as the U.S. media saw the toppling of the statue as highly symbolic, so too did al-Jazeera. But there the similarity ended:

> A final moment brought another development, which perhaps sent a slight fear into the hearts of the Marines. The statue toppled, but it did not fall fast. Even after it fell, he still had his feet left implanted in the reinforced Iraqi cement in the heart of Baghdad.[106]

Rumsfeld and Pentagon image-managers were certain the symbolic overthrow of the tyrant would give confidence to the Iraqi people and provide inspiration to others in the Middle East, a view many in the U.S. media appeared to share. "These pictures are the purest gold that the administration could imagine," Fox News anchor Brit Hume enthused.[107] In terms of U.S. domestic public opinion, that may well have been true. However, symbols exist in the eye of the beholder. "What Americans see as a man beating

Saddam's picture with his shoe is an image that means something very different to us," explained Hani Shukrallah, managing editor of Egypt's *al-Ahram Weekly*. "We see people who are mad at their own leaders who have brought us to this. They may want Saddam out. But in a few weeks, they will be doing the same thing to a picture of George Bush."[108]

All the Arab satellite channels accompanied their coverage of the toppling of the statue with extensive reports on civilian casualties. "Why has the U.S. military killed my children?" a wailing mother shouted at the camera in a frequently-aired al-Arabiya report that showed parents crying over dead children in crowded Baghdad hospitals.[109] "The Americans came to our country to control our oil," said an unidentified man in an al-Jazeera profile of a family that lost its father and three daughters in a U.S. air raid. "When we see our children, our families and relatives killed at their hands, we want to fight them in Baghdad. You should tell this to Bush, the American people, the Europeans and the whole world."[110] Ending the piece, the reporter concluded: "The question remains: For what have thousands of civilians paid with their blood over the past weeks? And will the Iraqis really reach the end of their suffering after two decades of wars and sanctions?"[111]

Across the Muslim world, newspapers and broadcast commentators asked much the same question. "For the Iraqi people to be rid of a tyrant only then to be vulnerable to exploitation by the conservative Zionist junta who have taken over the White House is merely for them to be thrown from the frying pan into the fire," said the *Arab News*, returning to the familiar theme of the U.S.–Israel alliance. "Baghdad has fallen, Saddam is on the run and his Ba'ath party has disintegrated. Good riddance to them all. But now those who were against the war must double their protests against an American occupation."[112] With the exception of Kuwait, where Saddam Hussein was despised for his 1990 invasion of that country, even those Muslim media outlets that were pleased to see Saddam's ouster were quick to insist the ends did not justify the means. "Iraqis' relief at what is possibly the nearing end of both the war and the regime does not mean that this aggression was ever just or right, nor that a U.S. occupation is welcomed," said the *Jordan Times*. "It does not mean, most of all, that all the suffering and death brought about by this war was 'for a good cause.'"[113] U.S. allies Saudi Arabia, Egypt and Jordan all called for a quick American exit from Iraq. Saudi foreign minister Saud al-Faisal expressed concern about the "collapse of security, chaos, theft, and looting"[114] and Osama el-Baz, a top advisor to Egyptian president Hosni Mubarak, made the point that "The idea of imposing democracy from outside is not supported by Egypt or any Arab country."[115]

Largely missed in the Bush administration's portrait of the victory was the impact it had on the broader Arab psyche. To the president and the neoconservatives who surrounded him, the toppling of Saddam Hussein's statue was, as White House spokesman Ari Fleischer described it, "an expression of the power of freedom that we're seeing in the streets of Baghdad with the Iraqi people who yearn to be free."[116] Vice President Dick Cheney could only shake his head and let his voice trail off in amazement that he was watching scenes of "liberation and still the U.S. is subject to criticism from our friends in the region."[117] In the Arab world, the U.S. invasion had struck a nerve, serving as a reminder both of the region's weakness in the face of Israel and the United States, and, on an even deeper level, the failure of Arabs to confront their own demons. "This chapter is a setback for all of us in the Arab world," news analyst Qassam Jaffir said on al-Jazeera. "It hit us like an earthquake. We denied the reality [of Saddam's rule] for too long. We should have made the change ourselves rather than have the American tanks do it for us."[118] The schizophrenic nature of this response to the fall of Saddam was summed up by Mahmoud Ahmed Youssef, a 26-year-old Jordanian software designer: "I know that he was a dictator, a tyrant. But his defeat, I believe, leaves all Arabs weaker – the fall of Baghdad is a terrible humiliation."[119] In the non-Arab Muslim world, there was less a sense of shame than a sense of anger. A Gallup poll released the day the statue was toppled found that 85 per cent of Pakistanis wanted Saddam to remain in power and, in a harbinger of the radicalizing effect of the Iraq war, 69 per cent favored action against U.S. interests in Pakistan.[120] The speaker of the Indonesian parliament, Amien Rais, said that while his countrymen did not like Saddam Hussein and were "relieved" to see him fall, "Mr. Bush has treated the Iraqi people as subhuman."[121]

EXCEPTIONALISM IN IRAQ

"The citizens of Iraq are coming to know what kind of people we have sent to liberate them. American forces and our allies are treating innocent civilians with kindness."[122] President Bush said those words as U.S. units rolled into Baghdad in early April; there is little doubt that he believed them. His worldview left little room for the idea that Americans could be considered anything less than "liberators" or that they would act with anything other than "kindness" toward "innocent civilians." So when he staged his dramatic arrival aboard the USS *Abraham Lincoln* on May 1 to declare "Major combat operations in Iraq have ended,"[123] it should have been no surprise that he once more sketched a portrait of Americans as a chosen people carrying out God's Will. "In the battle of Iraq, the United States and our allies have prevailed," the president declared, standing in full flight suit beneath a banner that proclaimed, "Mission Accomplished." With his talk of the "noble cause" and "advance of freedom," the president once more waved the flag of American exceptionalism. "We stand for human liberty," he told the thousands of sailors aboard the carrier and millions around the globe watching this ultimate photo opportunity. "We have fought for the cause of liberty and for the peace of the world."[124] Estimates compiled by the media and private groups put Iraqi civilian deaths from the war by that date as high as 7,200,[125] but the president made only the most glancing of references to the suffering of Iraqis, in part, perhaps, because his Pentagon was steadfastly refusing to count civilian casualties. Instead, the president honored the 171 American and British troops who had died, employing the same black-and-white rhetoric that had been used to justify the invasion: "Their final act on this Earth was to fight a great evil and bring liberty to others."[126] The conscious omission of Iraqi deaths only confirmed the belief among Arabs and Muslims that Bush devalued non-American lives. As further evidence that they remained the Other, the president reemphasized the fundamental *Us* and *Them* dichotomy that had characterized America's approach to the Middle East since 9/11. "Any person, organization, or government that supports, protects, or harbors terrorists is complicit in the murder of the innocent, and equally guilty of terrorist crimes,"[127] Bush said, refusing to acknowledge that some of those he called "terrorists" were "liberation fighters" to many in the Arab world.

As Bush spoke, Secretary of State Colin Powell was enroute to Damascus where he would attempt to pressure the Syrian regime to dissolve the Lebanese group Hizbullah and withdraw support for Hamas and other Palestinian groups, all seen by many Arabs as fighting for a just cause. Powell would also press the Syrian government to stop providing aid to fleeing Saddam regime loyalists, a charge that Washington had failed to substantiate. Nowhere in the criticism of Syria was there any acknowledgement that the Assad regime had provided the CIA with critical intelligence on terrorist groups after 9/11 (and, it would later emerge, was one of several countries where U.S. forces were bringing suspected terrorists detained elsewhere to be tortured at the behest of American interrogators). In Arab eyes, the hypocrisy was underlined by the fact that both Bush and Powell were silent about an Israeli assault on the Gaza Strip then underway that was already being called "a major blow"[128] to the administration's new "roadmap to peace." That plan had been handed to Israeli and Palestinian negotiators just 24 hours before, with a call from the president for both sides to "end the violence and return to a path of peace."[129]

If all of this wasn't enough to leave Arabs and Muslims shaking their heads in wonder at America's imperial hubris, there was the comment by the newly appointed U.S. administrator in Baghdad, Lt. Gen. Jay Garner, who exulted to reporters: "We ought to be beating our chests every day. We ought to look in a mirror and get proud and stick out our chests and suck in our bellies and say, Damn, we're Americans."[130] Such arrogance served as a potent weapon for those who preached violence against the United States. Among those was Iran's Ayatollah Jannati, who called for an intifada in Iraq. "These [Americans] behave as if they are the guardians of some orphan children whose evening meal should be prepared as a morsel by someone else and put in their mouths," he said during a Friday prayer service broadcast on Iranian radio the day after the president's speech.

> These American wolves respect nothing. They neither accept the international conventions, nor the resolutions of the United Nations and the principle of the UN. They are not committed to the democracy that they repeatedly lie about. The helpless people of Iraq . . . have no option but to resort to Intifada and martyrdom-seeking operations.[131]

Much the same could be heard in sermons broadcast from mosques across the Middle East that Friday after the president declared major combat operations had ended.

At al-Aqsa Mosque in Jerusalem, Sheikh Muhammad Hussein compared "the recent Anglo-American occupation of Iraq under the veil of liberation" to the invasion of the Tartars, while at the Grand Mosque in Sana'a, Akram Abd-al-Razzaq al-Ruqayhi thanked God for the recent rains and prayed, "O Lord, deal with the enemies of Islam, including the Zionists and Americans. Shake the land under their feet, instill fear in their hearts, and make fate turn against them." From Medina, the second-holiest place in Islam, Saudi television broadcast the sermon of Sheikh Salah al-Budayr, who said the "painful blows, successive defeats, and tragic disasters to which we are exposed day after day" were "due to our disavowal of our pledge to God," and prayed, "O Lord, whoever wishes us, our country, and other Muslim countries evil, busy him with himself, turn his plot against him, kill him with his weapon, torture him, and make his plot destroy them."

In retrospect, the sermon that fateful Friday which best demonstrated the vast gulf in perceptions between Americans and Arabs – and that held the most potential to reshape future events – was broadcast by al-Arabiya television from the Grand Mosque of Fallujah, deep in the heart of what would become known as the Sunni Triangle. There, the city's Grand Mufti, Sheikh Jamal Shakir al-Nazzal, began his sermon with a prayer to God "to reconcile us with the invading forces, the people of the Book."[132] Denouncing the "corrupt and oppressive" regime of Saddam Hussein, the cleric then addressed himself to the Americans, charging that they had committed an "unjustifiable crime" when U.S. forces in Fallujah opened fire on an anti-American demonstration on April 28 in what *The Los Angeles Times* reported as "a melee marked by misunderstanding, confusion and seething anger" at the presence of American troops.[133] The situation had then been made worse the day before the sermon when U.S. forces killed two more and wounded

18 others taking part in a demonstration protesting the earlier killings. Addressing his followers, Sheikh Jamal demanded: "More than 20 people killed in our town without any provocation? Why are American tanks and armored cars still roaming our streets? Do we have military units here? We do not have anything of the kind other than God and His prophet." Repeatedly ordering that "our youths and men must absolutely not stage any demonstrations," Sheikh Jamal continued:

> We should strive to save the lives and blood of our people and maintain the security of our town. God willing, we will negotiate with the Americans. And, if they erred in what they did to us, they must not repeat that error. They must withdraw their forces to outside the walls of our town. They must leave the map of this blessed town.[134]

Ominously, he added, "We seek the well-being of our town and people. The responsibility for what has happened rests with the American command." History records that a year later Fallujah would become the headquarters of the insurgency and a powerful new symbol of Muslim resistance to American hegemony.

Bush had won the battle of Baghdad; but in the process, he was losing the war of ideas.

Section IV

Hearts and Minds

10
Beyond the Middle East

In every age there have been people who considered that an individual had one overriding affiliation so much more important in every circumstance to all others that it might legitimately be called his "identity."
Amin Maalouf, *In the Name of Identity*

Eight days after 9/11, Megawati Sukarnoputri, president of the most populous Muslim country on earth, sat beside George Bush in the White House Oval Office and condemned terrorism, declaring her support for the United States in its time of need. "Indonesia has always been against violence. Anything that relates to violence, including acts of terrorism, we will definitely be against it,"[1] she told reporters. The two leaders pledged to lead their countries into "a new era of bilateral cooperation based on shared democratic values and a common interest in promoting regional stability and prosperity."[2]

Three years later, as President Bush prepared to visit Indonesia, her successor as president, Abdurrahman Wahid, declared: "The U.S. is not a good friend. It will push you aside, threaten you, and harm you if you don't follow its line."[3]

Much had changed in 36 months.

Just as the onset of suburban sprawl in the 1950s disrupted the sense of cohesive identity that once characterized American city-dwellers, the arrival of the new fragmented channels of communication, such as al-Jazeera and the Internet, changed how Muslims around the world saw the United States – and themselves. Marshall McLuhan's global village – a place where all eyes turned to the same apocryphal TV screen – was relegated to history. The narrative once written in the United States now had competing storylines as Americans and the world's Muslims gathered around distinctly different electronic public spheres, witnessing two versions of political reality as reflected in the bloodshot lenses of their respective media. In the months and years after September 11, the U.S. media had shown Americans a world in which they were valiantly fighting for democracy and freedom; the newly aggressive media of the Middle East and Asia conveyed images of a world in which Islam was under siege. As a result, just as Americans had – for a time after 9/11 – united in the face of the external terrorist threat, the diverse peoples who practiced Islam around the globe experienced a dramatically heightened sense of Islamic identity, bound together by their digitally enhanced and near-universal sense of outrage.

In his well-known theory of imagined communities and national identity, Benedict Anderson defined a "nation" as an "imagined political community" that "has finite, if elastic, boundaries." "Imagined," because its members "will never know most of their fellow members [and] yet in the minds of each lives the image of their communion;" a "community" because it is "always conceived as a deep, horizontal comradeship."[4] Among Muslims, who already experienced elements of a shared worldview, that sense of "horizontal comradeship" was dramatically enhanced in the post-9/11 era as they viewed the actions of the American Other through the lens of their newly evolved shared media. This was not the birth of a "new" or completely "imagined" community; Muslims were already bound together in the Islamic *ummah* or community, which had existed since the days of the Prophet Muhammad. Nor did it mean that they abandoned their separate national identities as Moroccans or Bangladeshis or Malaysians. Rather, the sense of Muslim identity, their kinship for coreligionists suffering in Afghanistan, Palestine, Iraq and elsewhere, and for each other, was magnified to a degree never before witnessed, forming a global overlay that transcended political, ethnic and racial divides and bound them together in a globally encompassing *Us* that exceeded in geographic scope even the great Caliphate of old.

Indonesia was a vivid example of this metamorphosis. It was, fittingly, the place where Anderson had developed his theories; an archipelago nation of more than 12,000 islands and 300 language groups united by an ideology and language manufactured for precisely that purpose. It was also, not incidentally, home to more practitioners of Islam than the entire Arab world. The religion had arrived in Indonesia gradually in the ships of traders via South Asia over the course of several hundred years. A notable characteristic of Islam in Indonesia was that the dominant form through much of that period was Sufism, a strain far less doctrinaire than orthodox Sunni Islam – and particularly the Wahabi brand of the Saudis – that would later spread elsewhere. These teachings blended easily with the esoteric beliefs indigenous to Java and the other islands of the archipelago, as well as the Buddhist and Hindu civilizations that had preceded the arrival of Islam. What emerged was a uniquely Indonesian syncretism, a blend of Islam and Javanese mysticism with touches of other Eastern religions. Later waves of Arabs brought with them an "orthodox" version of Islam more closely attuned to the teachings in Arabia. So, too, did the Indonesian Muslim students attending the Islamic universities of Saudi Arabia and Egypt, and, with the advent of modern transportation, the increasing numbers of Indonesians taking part in the *Hajj* pilgrimage to Mecca. Two competing strains of Islam would emerge in Indonesia: the Islam of the *abangan*, who continued also to honor Javanese traditional beliefs; and that of the *santri*, whose approach was closer to the "pure" Islam of the Middle East. Yet, despite this, the Arab world lay far to the West and its impact was finite. As the twentieth century came to a close, Indonesian Islam still retained its unique character.

Nor did the politics of the Middle East too deeply intrude on the Muslims of Indonesia. They were certainly aware of the Arab–Israeli conflict, and, on some level, sympathized with their fellow Muslims of Palestine. At the UN, Indonesia consistently voted with the Muslim block against Israel, but the plight of the Palestinians was far from top of mind. The average Indonesian was focused instead on issues closer to home. As the twenty-first century dawned, that involved surviving amid the country's economic and political turmoil, and, for Muslims of a more political bent, carving out a place for political Islam in the post-Suharto era. Distance was one reason for this attitude toward Middle East politics. But there was also a more deep-seated psychological aspect. Arabs in Indonesia had long been considered an Other. They were not marginalized to the degree of the Chinese, who were resented for their economic clout and inevitably became the target during periodic outbreaks of violence, but Arabs *were* seen as different. Those whose ethnic roots in the Middle East lay several generations back were still commonly referred to as *orang Arab*, "Arab people," a subgroup intrinsically apart from the majority of the population, whose antecedents were largely Malay. For the average citizen, the violent politics of the Middle East was an *Arab* issue; *they* were Indonesians.

All that would soon change thanks to the policies of the Bush administration and the recent restructuring of the global village.

PALESTINE AS A MARKER OF IDENTITY

In the year 2000, a Pew survey reported that 75 per cent of Indonesians had a "favorable view" of the United States.

In the spring of 2002, that figure still stood at 61 per cent. But by the spring of 2003 the situation had essentially reversed, with 85 per cent of Indonesians surveyed reporting a negative view.[5] Equally significant, in a country where the Israeli–Palestinian conflict had never been more than a tertiary issue, 68 per cent of those polled in 2003 listed Yasser Arafat as the world figure in whom they had the *most* confidence. Osama bin Laden came in third at 58 per cent, slightly trailing King Abdullah of Jordan, another major player in the Israel–Palestine dispute.[6] The Middle East was suddenly at the top of the Indonesian agenda. "There is no other problem which Muslims identify with more than the Israel–Palestine conflict," Jusuf Wanandi of Indonesia's Center for Strategic and International Studies wrote that same year.[7] It was a huge psychological shift.

When the first Palestinian Intifada broke out in December 1987, Indonesians barely noticed. The initial mention of the crisis in the country's largest-circulation daily, *Kompas*, came nine days after the uprising began in the form of a small photograph from the Associated Press buried deep inside the paper. The caption read: "Beaten – Israeli soldiers on Tuesday hit and kicked a Palestinian youth who was violently protesting in the Gaza Strip. The protests, which have been occurring since 8 December, also broke out on the Western side of the River Jordan."[8] The fact that Israeli troops had killed at least 17 Palestinians by that date was not mentioned. Over the coming days, riots in South Korea and stories about the scandal involving presidential candidate Gary Hart and model Donna Rice dominated the paper. Another four days would pass before *Kompas* again mentioned the crisis. As two million Palestinians went on strike, shutting down Israel's economy, widespread rioting continued and sympathy attacks on Israeli troops broke out in Lebanon, the paper ran a short wire service article on its foreign page about Arab condemnation of Israeli actions in the Occupied Territories,[9] then printed another small wire service story the following day.[10] With the shooting deaths of three Palestinians by Israeli forces, bringing the death toll for the two weeks of violence to at least 22, the Intifada finally made it to the front page of *Kompas* on December 23, the same day the paper wrote its first editorial on the emerging conflict. While U.S. editorials evocatively described the "clash of dreams and realities" in the Occupied Territories that had left as casualties "Arab lives and Israeli conscience,"[11] *Kompas* confined itself to a dry history lesson of the past 40 years that failed even to mention Israel's 1973 conquest of Jerusalem, site of Islam's third most holy mosque, which had been declared the Jewish capital. Quoting a political science professor from Hebrew University, the paper dryly explained that there were "basically two opinions" regarding the Gaza Strip and what *Kompas* called "the West Bank of the Jordan River." "One thought is the territorial school of thought and the other is more of a sociological school of thought." Without betraying any opinion on the subject, the paper blandly explained, "[t]he Arab population" of those areas occupied by Israel "think that these areas that they reside in are theirs."[12]

Not only was the newspaper silent about its own opinion of the violence or the plight of the Palestinians, so too was the Indonesian government and the country's Muslim community. During this period in late December 1987, the White House had sharply rebuked Israel for "harsh security measures and excessive use of live ammunition" against Palestinian civilians in those opening days of the Intifada,[13] but *Kompas* reported no similar concerns from the presidential palace of the world's largest Muslim country. Palestine, it seemed, was a land far, far away. Over the coming days, the crisis would remain on the front pages of U.S. newspapers and serve as grist for American editorial writers and columnists, with talk of "inhumane conditions" for detainees[14] and the danger that, if it did not resolve the plight of the Palestinians, "Israel will become another South Africa."[15] A headline in the *San Diego Union-Tribune*, for example, asked, "Has Israel Lost Its Democracy?"[16] However, *Kompas* neither posed compelling questions nor cast its lot with its fellow Muslims. Nor, apparently, did its readers. Not a single letter to the editor published between December 9 and December 24 mentioned the Palestinians.

Ten months later, in October 1988, when at least 18 Palestinians were killed and more than 150 were injured by Israeli forces after they prevented Jewish extremists from placing a cornerstone for a "Jewish third temple" on the grounds of al-Aqsa Mosque, *Kompas* exhibited only slightly more interest. A small article headlined "Israel Shoots Palestinians" made the bottom corner of the front page, but it was dwarfed by a four-column photograph that took pride of place on the page, showing Israeli soldiers fitting children with gas masks in anticipation of missile attacks from Iraq, which was then occupying Kuwait, an image likely to evoke sympathy for Israelis. With al-Aqsa Mosque closed to Muslims and ringed by Israeli troops, a *Kompas* editorial still showed little solidarity with the Palestinians, noting only that, "[w]hoever is to blame" for the violence, "the Israeli police have already killed 22 Palestinians and this event can easily cause other bigger events" in the Middle East "and even the whole world of Islam."[17] An Indonesian picking up the paper three days later would have assumed the crisis had passed. Newspapers in the United States continued to report on Israel's refusal to allow entry to a team sent by the UN Security Council to investigate the shootings, but *Kompas* had turned its attention elsewhere. Even a demand from President George H.W. Bush that an investigation into whether a massacre had occurred be "fully implemented" and a warning from Secretary of State James Baker that Israel was in danger of being compared to Saddam Hussein in blocking a UN investigating team[18] passed without mention in *Kompas*.

Coverage could not have been more different when, in the spring of 2002, Israel launched its assault on the Occupied Territories in the midst of the so-called al-Aqsa Intifada. Images of Israeli tanks on the West Bank dominated the front page of *Kompas*, news articles quoted Indonesian political figures as denouncing the violence and editorials attacked Israel and praised the Palestinian "martyrs." "The Indonesian government strongly condemns the Israeli military aggression in Ramallah," read the lead of a front-page story on April 2, 2002.[19] "An unstoppable wave of censure" had erupted in Indonesia, the paper reported the following day.[20] The criticism from the administration of President Megawati Sukarnoputri, which came in stark contrast to the silence of the Suharto regime in the first Intifada, was driven by domestic politics, as was the cooling of her initial enthusiasm to support the U.S. war on terror. Across the ideological spectrum, Indonesians were enraged by the violence unfolding in the Occupied Territories. Where, in the first Intifada, the Palestinians were portrayed as *They*, a sense of *We* now infused the coverage.

A poll conducted in Indonesia by Zogby International in the late spring of 2002, in the midst of the largest Israeli military operation in the West Bank and Gaza Strip since the 1967 war, found that 65 per cent of Indonesians rated Palestine as "the most important" or "a very important" issue. Not even those surveyed in Saudi Arabia gave it more importance. At the same time, 78 per cent had an "unfavorable" view of U.S. policy toward the Palestinians and 66 per cent supported an independent Palestinian state.[21] A distant "Arab" event had been transformed into an Islamic cause galvanizing non-Arab Muslims half a world away. "Palestine's struggle is a struggle along God's ways which should be supported by all Muslims since Israel's Zionism of unbelievers have declared war against the Muslim community," Majalis Ulamaa Indonesia, the leading Islamic clerics organization, declared.[22] Talk of "crimes against humanity" and "Israeli unbelievers and their terrorizing acts" filled the media. Highly publicized meetings were held in Parliament and the presidential palace. The speaker of Parliament called for the government to "react in a very strong and clear way" and the vice president met the Palestinian ambassador to Indonesia to offer his support.[23] The connection between Indonesians and the Palestinians was driven home on another level as well, with Indonesian commentators drawing analogies to their own country's colonial struggle and pointing out that Megawati's father, Indonesia's first president, Sukarno "himself was a very tough leader who fought several forms of colonialism."[24]

Equally significant, political observers were quick to link Israel's actions to those of the United States. Using the American war on terror as an excuse to crush the Palestinians, said analyst Dewi Fortuna Anwar, was "a dirty way to conquer a political opponent." If the U.S. failed to rein in the Israelis, she said, it would confirm that "the U.S. view of terrorism is one-sided," thus undermining the antiterror coalition.[25]

Why had this dramatic shift taken place? Part of the answer could be found in the restructuring of McLuhan's global village. According to Goenawan Mohamad, founding editor of the magazine *Tempo* and one of the most respected figures in Indonesian journalism, when it came to international news, the government generally did not dictate how the media covered foreign stories, so newspaper editors in the Suharto era "took their lead" from state-run television, which gave almost no attention to the first Intifada.[26] The stories that did air in that period were brief clips from U.S. television networks. By the time the second, or al-Aqsa Intifada, broke out, several things had changed. Suharto's forced resignation in 1998 had ushered in an era of *reformasi*, in which most government regulations were removed and the country witnessed the birth of a vibrant media sector, with the number of publications growing from 260 to more than 800, television channels increasing from six to 29, and the population of journalists rising from some 6,000 to more than 25,000.[27] At the same time, al-Jazeera had come to the fore in the Middle East, providing a new perspective on the conflicts of that region. CNN and other Western television networks had supplied the footage of previous conflicts. When the United States attacked Afghanistan, Indonesian TV stations turned to al-Jazeera for their coverage. This new view of war had the same profound effect on Indonesian audiences as it had among Arabs.

A Gallup poll conducted in December 2001 and January 2002 found that 89 per cent of Indonesians surveyed called U.S. military action in Afghanistan "morally unjustified"[28] and the suspicion that America was engaged in a crusade against Islam began to take root. Many Indonesians retained their generally positive view of the United States, but their sense of identification with fellow Muslims in the Middle East was growing, as was their interest in once-distant events. When Israel invaded the West Bank and Gaza in the spring of 2002, Indonesian television provided extensive coverage via the cameras of al-Jazeera, and the print media followed suit, further politicizing the Indonesian body politic. Coverage of the U.S. invasion of Iraq a year later was all-pervasive. One of the aggressive new channels, the *Kompas*-owned TV-7, stayed on the air 24 hours a day to cover the conflict, carrying al-Jazeera's reporting live and unedited, complete with Bahasa Indonesia translation, from 11 p.m. until 11 a.m. every day. The result was new antipathy for both the United States and the U.S. media. One American Ph.D. student who was doing research in a small Indonesian village at the time recalls that he felt a perceptible shift in attitudes toward him as his hosts gathered around the television each evening and sat for hours transfixed by scenes of violence and devastation beamed live from the Middle East.

"We believe al-Jazeera more because what they said about the war is true," said Suhendro, a Jakarta businessman and mosque leader, who divided his viewing between Western channels and al-Jazeera. "They showed us how Iraqi civilians have become the victims of the war. Children, mothers, old people, civilians killed and injured because of their war. I see them losing their hands and legs and other body parts. Scenes I will never see on CNN."[29]

A STUDY IN ALIENATION

Indonesians weren't the only non-Arab Muslims who grew angry as they watched U.S. policy unfold on their television screens each day. One need only look across the Strait of Malacca to Malaysia, where, in his final speech to the Organization of the Islamic Conference, outgoing prime minister Mahathir Mohamad denounced the West's "open support for Israeli intransigence and terrorism" against the Palestinians and charged that Western powers "use their media to hide their misdeeds and spread lies."[30]

It had not always been thus. In the wake of 9/11, the United States had no stronger Muslim ally than Mahathir. He condemned Islamist violence and was welcomed in the Oval Office as someone about whom the president said, "We share a deep concern about terror." The Malaysian leader's early support for the American war on terror was not entirely altruistic. The Malaysian capital, Kuala Lumpur, had become a back office for al-Qaeda and its regional offshoots. Now that the United States wanted him to roll up these militant networks, Mahathir had an excuse to crack down as well on pesky domestic political opponents among the more moderate Islamist parties. After years of listening to Washington lecture him about human rights, the restraints were off. Besides, the ultimate goal of the radicals was the creation of an Islamist empire in Southeast Asia, so they were as much a threat to him as to the United States. Mahathir may have had an ulterior motive in cooperating with Washington in Southeast Asia, but he also became a leading antiterrorist voice on the international stage, a Muslim political moderate speaking out against the radical threat. His credibility was based not just on the fact that he was the leader of a devoutly Muslim nation, but also that his message of moderation was aimed at both sides – the radicals and Washington. His denunciations of terrorism were coupled with criticisms of U.S. policy in Israel, Afghanistan and elsewhere.

In January 2003, with the U.S. invasion of Iraq all but inevitable, Mahathir made a plea for sanity at the World Economic Summit in Davos, Switzerland, arguing that "out-terrorizing the terrorists will not work, but removing the causes for terrorism will." The Malaysian leader expressed regret that the rules "in our modern and sophisticated global village" resembled those of the Stone Age, with both sides driven by fear and revenge. What was required, he said, was

> a new mind-set if we are going to put an end to this Third World War. We need . . . a victory where both sides will win. . . . If we overcome our anger and hatred, our craving for revenge, our unlimited greed, we can manage the world and achieve trust and eventually good governance.[31]

The speech received a five-minute standing ovation from the world's business and political leaders gathered at Davos, but it fell on deaf ears at the White House. The Bush administration was happy to use Mahathir to drum up support for the war on terrorism and to pressure reluctant Muslim leaders like Indonesian President Megawati Sukarnoputri to make good on promises to cooperate with Washington, but the administration was less interested in his policy advice. By the time Mahathir stepped down as Asia's longest-serving leader in the fall of 2003, his patience with Washington had worn thin. Two years of Bush administration Middle East policy had left the Malaysian leader – and his people – alienated and angry. However, Mahathir represented more than just an example of how Washington failed to acknowledge the concerns of even its moderate Muslim allies.

No story better illustrated the way in which the world-views of reporters themselves exacerbate the perception gap between audiences in the United States and the Muslim world, or the double standard driving U.S. policy, than reaction to the outgoing prime minister's parting speech before the summit of the Organization of the Islamic Conference. As President Bush embarked on his whirlwind tour of Asia in October 2003, Mahathir appeared before the leaders of the world's Islamic countries and denounced the U.S. invasion of Iraq as a "cowardly and imperialist" act. However, the Malaysian reserved his greatest criticism for his colleagues, charging that the failure of Muslim leaders to help their peoples unite and adapt to the modern world was responsible for the "feeling of hopelessness" that spawned terrorism. "If we are to recover our dignity and that of Islam, our religion, it is we who must decide, it is we who must act," he told the assembled leaders.

> We are now 1.3 billion strong. We have the biggest oil reserve in the world. We have great wealth. . . . We are familiar with the workings of the world's economy and finances. We control 50 out of the 180 countries in the world. Our votes can make or break international organisations. Yet, we seem more helpless than the small number of *Jahilliah* converts who accepted the Prophet as their leader. Why?[32]

Mahathir blamed "literal interpretations" of Islamic traditions and "superficial interpretations of the Qur'an" for discouraging modernization. "Islam is not just for the seventh century A.D., Islam is for all times. And times have changed," he declared. Literalism had left the region mired in "backwardness and weakness" that allowed it to be exploited by colonial powers.

> And so we find some of our people reacting irrationally. They launch their own attacks, killing just about anybody including fellow Muslims to vent their anger and frustration . . . But the attacks solve nothing. The Muslims simply get more oppressed. There is a feeling of hopelessness among the Muslim countries and their people.

Yet in the face of humiliation at the hands of the West and the oppression of the Palestinians, he said, Muslim leaders stood by impotent:

> Is there no other way than to ask our young people to blow themselves up and kill people and invite the massacre of more of our own people? It cannot be that there is no other way. The 1.3 billion Muslims cannot be defeated by a few million Jews.

Mahathir reminded his listeners that in the struggle to regain Mecca, the Prophet Muhammad used diplomacy and compromise, abjuring revenge. Modern Muslims, he said, must do the same: "We sacrifice lives unnecessarily, achieving nothing other than to attract more massive retaliation and humiliation." The first step, he said, was for Muslims to abandon their centuries of divisiveness and unite in a common cause:

> We are actually very strong – 1.3 billion people cannot be simply wiped out. The Europeans killed six million Jews out of 12 million. But today, the Jews rule this world by proxy. They get others to fight and die for them.

The time had come, he said, to "call a truce" that would allow discussions over even the most intractable issues, including Palestine. "Even among the Jews, there are many who do not approve of what the Israelis are doing. We must not antagonize everyone. We must win their hearts and minds."

The speech was front-page news around the world. And once more, audiences in the West and Muslim countries were exposed to two completely different stories. For Muslim journalists, Mahathir's bold slap at Islamic leaders and radical Islamists was the lead. "Malaysian PM Wants Islamic People United," reported Indonesia's *Republika* newspaper.[33] "Learn from the Israelis, Muslims Told," said the *Hindu* of India, which has one of the world's largest Muslim populations. Western coverage, meanwhile, focused on what was widely reported as an anti-Semitic slur. "Malay PM Calls Jews Puppet Masters," screamed the *New York Daily News* in a headline that typified U.S. media treatment of the speech.[34] "Malaysia's Casual Anti-Semitism," was the headline over Slate.com's summary of coverage, compiled by a former editor of the *Jerusalem Post*.[35] "Muslim PM Seeks 'Final Victory' Over Jews," reported Canada's *National Post*.[36] "Prime Minister Mahathir bin Mohamad of Malaysia lashed out Thursday against what he described as the Jewish subjugation of Muslims, urging a gathering of Muslim leaders to help harness the Islamic world's collective brainpower to turn the tide," the American-owned *International Herald Tribune* reported under the headline, "Mahathir tells Muslims to unite against Jews."[37] In an editorial entitled "Message of Hate," the *Toronto Star* said that by wielding "a poisonous spike of anti-Semitism, the outrageous Malaysian leader succeeded only in promoting the vicious kind of hatred on which terrorism thrives."[38] When French President Jacque Chirac blocked a European Union resolution condemning Mahathir two days later, *The New York Post* headlined the story, "Weasel Gags EU over 'Jew' Slur."[39]

Tellingly, almost every one of the initial accounts of the speech appearing in North American newspapers – from the *San Diego Union-Tribune* and New York's *Newsday* to the *Chicago Tribune* and the *Houston Chronicle* – was written by one of two reporters, Rohan Sullivan and Slovodan Lekic. Both men worked for the Associated Press. Two years into the war on terror, U.S. newspaper editors still did not think

it worth covering a summit that brought together most of the
leaders of the Muslim world, so they all relied on the AP.
It was an indication of both the economic realities of American
journalism and the lack of interest in nonradical Muslim
voices. It also demonstrated what happens when media
diversity is reduced, since the headlines across the country
accurately reflected the framing of the articles themselves.
Sullivan's lead read, "Malaysian Prime Minister Mahathir
Mohamad said at a summit of Islamic leaders Thursday that
'Jews rule the world by proxy' and the world's 1.3 billion
Muslims should unite, using non-violent means for a 'final
victory.'" Lekic was even more incendiary: "In a blistering
attack on Israel and bullying criticism of the Islamic world,
Malaysian Prime Minister Mahathir Mohamad told a summit
of Muslim leaders Thursday that Jews ruled the world and
recruited others 'to fight and die for them.'"

Not even *The New York Times* thought it worthwhile to
show up for the summit. The nation's supposed newspaper of
record first reported on Mahathir's comments in a brief item
written in Brussels, where the EU had criticized the comments.
It was headlined, "Malaysian Attacks Jews,"[40] and was
followed up the next day with an editorial entitled, "Islamic
Anti-Semitism."[41] *The Washington Post* did send a reporter
to the summit, but his lead did not provide any more context
than those written half a world away: "Prime Minister
Mahathir Mohamad told a summit of Islamic leaders on
Thursday that Jews control the world through their influence
over major powers and must be resisted by Muslims."[42] The
lead was a reminder of the degree to which the media plays
to its audience. The stereotype about Jew-hating Muslims
was much more likely to get attention among American readers
than a story about Muslims criticizing Muslims. *The Wall
Street Journal* offered another example of how media
shape the news. The *Journal* publishes various regional
editions around the world. All used one of the same AP stories.

But each framed the story in a way designed to appeal to its local readers. The headline in the *Journal*'s Asian edition stressed the conciliatory nature of the speech: "Malaysian Prime Minister Seeks Muslim Unity. Non-Violent Victory."[43] But back in the States, readers of the U.S. edition were offered a very different take: "Malaysia's Mahathir added to evidence of anti-Semitism against him, telling an Islamic group 'Jews rule the world' and incite wars by others."[44]

A speech that might have provided a peg for a deeper media examination of the complex currents of thought in Muslim politics, or an exploration of potential topics around which the two sides might begin a dialogue, instead unleashed a torrent of distortion, oversimplification and cliché that could only confuse news consumers trying to understand a vital and complex topic. Emblematic was a deeply flawed article in the *Week in Review* section of the following Sunday's edition of *The New York Times*, entitled "Radical Islam Gains a Seductive New Voice." In the piece, which, bizarrely, carried the heading "DON'T TREAD ON US," reporter David Rohde portrayed Mahathir as the public face of a broader movement in the Muslim world that is a "much more nebulous enemy" of the United States than the "religious zealots." "Political Islam is a sophisticated mixture of fundamentalism and nationalism that can foment acts of violence against Western targets," Rohde wrote from New Delhi. "It is an ideology that persuades some alienated young Muslims, whether deeply religious or not, to join what they see as an epic struggle against an evil empire."

Or is it? The term "political Islam" is not shorthand for terror, but describes the movement among Muslim political thinkers engaged in the complex task of translating traditional Islamic concepts into modern democratic idiom. "I didn't know I was the enemy," Ulil Abshar-Abdalla told me, only half in jest, after he read *The Times* article. As head of Indonesia's Liberal Muslim Network, he was at the forefront of the effort to bring democracy based on Islamic values to the world's largest Muslim country. No matter what you thought of Mahathir – who had a history of inflammatory statements about Israel and Jews – it was a huge distortion of his comments to lump him in with those who "foment acts of violence against Western targets," as did Rohde's article. Likewise, while it was understandable that many Jews, and others, would be offended by Mahathir's claim that Jews "rule the world by proxy," this was, in fact, the view of many – if not the majority of – Muslims around the world. To denounce it, to ignore it, was not to change it. As the Advisory Commission on Public Diplomacy reported, "Public opinion in the Arab and Muslim world cannot be cavalierly dismissed."[45]

But were Mahathir's comments on Jews the whole story, or even, in context, the *real* story? Or did the media fan the fires of confrontation by seizing on two inflammatory lines in a speech of more than 4,000 words? Did reporters miss a peg for substantive reporting on an important address that offered deep insight into the thinking of Muslim leaders – even America's ally, Afghan President Hamid Karzai hailed it as "eloquent" – and contained an important message of nonviolence and reconciliation? Mainstream American media coverage contained no such context and the U.S. government wasted no time joining in the chorus of Western condemnation. White House spokesman Scott McClellan made it a point to tell reporters traveling with the president that Bush had "pulled Mahathir aside" at the Bangkok APEC summit and told him the comments were "wrong and divisive," while National Security Advisor Condoleezza Rice called them "hateful" and "outrageous." Bush himself told reporters he "didn't yell" at the Malaysian leader, which did nothing to lessen Muslim perceptions of American arrogance on a trip designed to build bridges. Compounding Muslim anger was the administration's muted reaction to news breaking at the same time that one of America's top commanders had publicly disparaged Islam, saying Islamist radicals were trying to destroy America "because we're a Christian nation." Lt. Gen. William Boykin, the deputy undersecretary of defense, had repeatedly been videotaped in full uniform making speeches to Christian groups in which he called himself a "warrior in God's kingdom" doing battle against the forces of Satan. In one speech, Boykin, who had been U.S. commander in Somalia, recalled that one of the Somali warlords had said on CNN that Allah would protect him. "Well, *you* know what I knew, that my God was bigger than his," Boykin told his audience. "I knew that my God was a real God, and his was an idol."[46]

It would be hard to imagine a more offensive comment coming from a U.S. official or the news coming at a worse time, in the midst of a trip designed to allay Muslim fears that Islam was being targeted in the war on terror. A few members of Congress called for Boykin's resignation – or at least suspension – and Donald Rumsfeld announced there would be an internal probe of the speeches, but the president and White House staff remained silent, and Boykin remained on active duty (and would remain so long after the controversy passed). Days after he publicly rebuked Mahathir, the president finally made his first comment on the Boykin affair, only after the Muslim clerics with whom he briefly met in Bali took him to task for the general's statements. "I said, 'He didn't reflect my opinion. Look, it just doesn't reflect what the government thinks.' And I think they were pleased to hear that," Bush told reporters.[47]

Even if the Indonesian clerics were "pleased," as unlikely as that might have been, much of the rest of the Muslim world was not. "While they condemn Dr. Mahathir when he speaks about the Jews and other injustices inflicted on the poor and the Muslims, there are no such condemnations or reaction when the Muslims are called terrorists," wrote a columnist in Malaysia's *New Straits Times*.[48] "Nobody moved to question Boykin about his attack on Islam," said Egypt's *al-Ahram*. "Doesn't that mean that what happened to [Mahathir] is in itself extremist and racist?"[49] Mahathir's remarks had been condemned around the world, Aouni Kaaki wrote in Beirut's *Asharq*, but the "provocative anti-Islam remarks made by a prominent U.S. Army general are yet to receive such condemnation."[50] "Muslims try to extend their hands in peace and friendship but they gain nothing but insults and regret," agreed an Egyptian columnist. "Western leaders have disregarded all OIC Summit recommendations to focus instead on Mahathir Mohamad's remarks . . . Those very leaders, however, could not move a finger in protest at the remarks made by a top U.S. aid, in which he described the war on terror as a crusade, a war between Christianity and Islam."[51]

Despite Muslim protestations to the contrary, there certainly was a torrent of criticism of Boykin in the American media, but a distinction made by the editorial director of CBSNews.com summed up the general attitude: "General Boykin is a fluke . . . Prime Minister Mahathir is no fluke."[52] The comment brought to mind Edward Said's observation, "covering Islam is a one-sided activity that obscures what 'we' *do*, and highlights instead what Muslims and Arabs by their very flawed nature *are*."[53]

Mahathir himself was unrepentant, throwing oil on the fire by telling a Bangkok newspaper that the reaction to his comments "shows that they [Jews] control the world." He said the Western media had completely ignored his condemnation of violence against Israel: "I even quoted the Qur'an, which says that when the enemy offers to make peace, you must accept. I told Muslims you must accept even if the terms are bad. You have to negotiate. This is the teaching of Islam."[54] Shortly after those words were published, the U.S. Senate voted to restrict military aid to Malaysia, even though Mahathir was stepping down as prime minister within just a few days. The fact that he was voluntarily relinquishing power in a manner that embodied exactly the kind of democratic change the White House was demanding of Muslim nations went largely ignored in the din.

11
Brand America

Public diplomacy is . . . an essential foreign policy element to stop people from coming here to kill us.

              Lee Hamilton, Vice-chair, 9/11 Commission

When the U.S. government launched its $100 million answer to al-Jazeera in early 2004, the move offered vivid evidence that American message managers still did not truly understand the nature of the Arab information revolution.

Al-Hurra was a television version of the Voice of America; a satellite broadcaster whose mission was to communicate "accurate, balanced and objective news"[1] – particularly about American policy – directly to the Arab viewer without the filter of the Arab media. The concept could not have been more flawed. Al-Jazeera's popularity stemmed directly from the fact that, in a region where the media had always been government controlled, it was largely independent. The idea that the U.S. government would try to counter al-Jazeera's influence with yet another government-controlled broadcasting station quite simply made no sense. "The era of this kind of media ended with the fall of the Berlin Wall and the Soviet bloc," said an editorial in the pan-Arab daily *al-Quds al-Arabi* the day after al-Hurra's launch, "yet it appears there are some in the U.S. administration who want to transport us back some 40 or 50 years."[2]

Al-Hurra's status as a mouthpiece for the U.S. government was etched in stone with its very first program. For the opening broadcast, President Bush granted an interview to al-Hurra's Washington bureau chief. Rather than tackling head-on the grievances of the Arab world, Bush repeated the administration's usual pronouncements about democracy and American largesse. It was not lost on the Arab audience that not once did the al-Hurra interviewer ask about the plight of the Palestinians and not once did the president raise the subject. Nor were the questions of alleged Iraqi weapons of mass destruction or Israeli nuclear weapons raised. Any lingering doubts about al-Hurra's lack of independence were erased in the final moments of the broadcast. As the interview ended, the two men stood up and the president, in the manner of an employer to his employee, shook the interviewer's hand and said, "Good job." That such an encounter took place was of no surprise. What was shocking was that Washington's message managers would be so oblivious to its impact on the Arab audience that they would have actually put the exchange on the air. For *al-Quds al Arabi*, the encounter "brought to mind official Arab channels broadcast by regimes mired in dictatorship."

"Our competitive edge in the Middle East is our very dedication to truth and free and open debate," Kenneth Tomlinson, chairman of the Broadcasting Board of Governors (BBG), the U.S. government agency that created al-Hurra, told Congress two days before the launch. "And we will stand out like a beacon of light in a media market dominated by sensationalism and distortion."[3] Yet even those who welcomed the arrival of a new satellite voice were disappointed in what they found. "We expected to see news broadcasts that were not opinionated nor censored, programmes that formed an awareness, programmes that explained the American political system to the Arab world," wrote one Arab commentator. "Anyone who knows the American media or who has worked in Washington will be shocked watching this satellite channel broadcasting at its present standard."[4]

A month after al-Hurra went on the air, the leader of Hamas, Sheikh Ahmed Yassin, was assassinated by the Israelis. Millions of Palestinians jammed the streets of the Occupied Territories for his funeral. Across the Muslim world, all eyes turned to Palestine. Al-Jazeera, al-Arabiya and other Arab satellite channels carried the funeral live. Al-Hurra broadcast a cooking show. "Al-Hurra, like the U.S. government's Radio Sawa and Hi magazine before it, will be an entertaining, expensive, and irrelevant hoax," predicted Rami Khouri, editor of Beirut's *Daily Star*, referring to other official U.S. government media organs developed for the Arab world. "Where do they get this stuff from? Why do they keep insulting us like this?"[5] To many Arabs, the insult was embodied in the channel's very name, al-Hurra, which translated as "The Free One," implying that if al-Hurra was free, no other broadcaster could say the same, even though al-Hurra was directly government-financed and controlled, while al-Jazeera was semi-independent. Or perhaps, Arabs speculated, the name referred to the notion that the United States was free and the Arabs were not. Either was equally offensive.

If Arab intellectuals were insulted by al-Hurra's paternalistic positioning, conservative clerics were outraged. Saudi Supreme Court judge Sheikh Ibrahim al-Khudairi issued a *fatwa* declaring, "It is religiously forbidden to watch the station, participate in it or support it. It must be boycotted."[6] Sheikh Abdul Rahman al Sudais, prayer leader at Mecca's Grand Mosque, said al-Hurra was part of a "war of ideas" against Muslims. Satellite stations that "claim to speak in the name of freedom and independence," he said, "are sowing intellectual chaos and destroying the correct thinking of the *ummah* and its cultural heritage."[7]

KILLING THE MESSENGER

The Bush administration argued that the dramatic rise of anti-American attitudes in the Muslim world was the product of a biased media that had distorted its message. "My solution is to change the channel," Brig. Gen. Mark Kimmitt told reporters in Baghdad.[8] But was it that simple? A comparison of the anti-Americanism of al-Jazeera viewers with the attitudes of those who watched CNN International and the BBC concluded that the source of news had only a "slight buffering effect" on anti-American sentiments among viewers.[9] More importantly, the study found that "for both types of networks, increasing levels of attention to coverage of the U.S. leads to stronger anti-American attitudes."[10] In other words, the more those Arabs questioned in the survey watched television – no matter which network – the less they liked what they saw: "For the Muslim public, the difference in media effects for receiving news through either al-Jazeera or a Western network is a matter of degree, not direction."[11]

Part of the reason was that Arabs weren't just watching one station, Arab or Western. With hundreds of satellite channels at their fingertips, many beamed from the United States, Arabs channel-surfed just like viewers the world over. "The image of Arabs sitting at home all day watching al-Jazeera and hating Americans is as real as Americans sitting at home watching Fox and hating Arabs," said pollster and lobbyist James Zogby. "But they aren't the majority."[12] The highest-rated show on Middle East television was the Arabic version of *Who Wants to be a Millionaire?*, just one of the many remakes of U.S. reality programs. American TV series, movies and even Italian soft porn crowded the dial. As might be expected, those who said they turned primarily to Arab TV for their news about America generally had *less favorable* attitudes toward the United States, but that was not universally true. Saudi viewers of Arab TV felt *more positively* toward most aspects of the United States than did others in their society, and in the UAE, a Zogby poll found "favorable attitudes toward American freedom and democracy actually *increased* among those who have learned about the

U.S. from Arab television."[13] The clear implication was that anti-Americanism arose not from *the way* in which Bush administration policies and actions were portrayed, as the White house claimed, but from the policies and actions *themselves*. "There is no point in saying this is a problem of communications, blah, blah, blah," Yenni Zannuba Wahid, the daughter of former Indonesian President Abdurrahman Wahid, told the U.S. Advisory Group for Public Diplomacy. "The perception in the Muslim world is that the problem is the policy toward the Israeli–Palestinian conflict and Iraq."[14]

As documented throughout this book, media in the U.S. and Muslim world provided very different windows on the post-9/11 conflicts. Yet, even when they were watching the same words and pictures, audiences in the U.S. and the Muslim world often interpreted them in opposite ways. The Arab interpretation was, in part, due to preexisting biases that caused "individuals to select considerations from TV news that only confirm existing anti-American attitudes."[15] In short, Arabs and Muslims perceived U.S. policy statements and actions in the context of their worldview, no matter who was doing the framing. "The most important thing we learn from the news, wherever it comes from, whether it's CNN or al-Jazeera, is that civilians are suffering the most," Joko Haryanto, an Indonesian businessman, said during the U.S. invasion of Iraq.[16] So when President Bush claimed "the Middle East is where you find the hatred and violence," as he did in a U.S. television interview,[17] Americans heard it as an innocuous and self-evident observation, while Arabs had no doubt he meant *they* were violent. When he couched those comments within the frame of Judeo-Christian values, Americans barely noticed, but Muslims saw it as proof he was targeting their faith. And when President Bush made a casual comment about a "crusade" against terror, U.S. audiences heard a synonym for "campaign," but among Muslims – and particularly Arabs – it reopened wounds that had festered for a millennium. "It is difficult to understand how the U.S., with its advanced research centers and clever minds, explains away Arab hatred as a product of a demagogic media and not due to its biased policies and propensity to abuse Arab interests," observed the Egyptian daily *al-Ahram*.[18] "The Americans think that we hate them because we don't receive accurate information about the reality of American politics," added a Palestinian journalism professor on the West Bank. "This is not true. America's image is ugly because American policies and actions are ugly."[19]

Within months of al-Hurra's launch, American officials were issuing cheery pronouncements about the station's success. "Al-Hurra has quickly established itself as a player among satellite stations in the Middle East," Norman Pattiz, the founder of America's Westwood One radio network and head of the BBG's Middle East Committee, said in announcing the results of a BBG-commissioned poll that claimed that 29 per cent of satellite-equipped homes in seven Arab countries were watching the station.[20] Another BBG-commissioned survey late in the year claimed a "weekly viewership" of 39 per cent among Syrian adults.[21] But such polls made no distinction between individuals who paused briefly on al-Hurra out of curiosity while channel-surfing and those who used it as a primary source of information. Independent surveys later that same year painted a much grimmer picture. The Arab Advisors Group found that only 16 per cent of Saudi, 4.6 per cent of Egyptian and 1.3 per cent of Jordanian satellite viewers said they watched al-Hurra, versus the 71 to 88 per cent responses drawn by al-Jazeera. None of those questioned in a six-nation Brookings survey said al-Hurra was their first choice for news and less than 4 per cent chose it as their second choice.[22] *Asharq al-Awsat* reported that a separate poll commissioned by the U.S. embassy in Egypt found al-Hurra viewership at just 1.2 per cent.[23] The news was even worse when it came to trust. "Our product is credibility in news and information," Pattiz had said in issuing that April press release, "if we don't have that, we're dead in the water."[24] The BBG's own numbers showed that more than half of al-Hurra's viewers thought the station reliable, but the catch was that these were *al-Hurra viewers*, a self-selected sample of the small percentage of the people who regularly tuned into the station, not Arab television viewers *as a whole*. For example, less than 20 per cent of the total pool of Saudis polled said they thought al-Hurra trustworthy. Al-Jazeera's figure was 69 per cent. "Viewers in Saudi Arabia have little trust in al-Hurra News Channel," the Arab Advisors Group reported. "In contrast, al-Jazeera and al-Arabiya news channels have much higher credibility amongst a much larger viewer base."[25] Amb. William Rugh, the former U.S. diplomat who literally wrote the book on the Arab media, was no more impressed: "When I watch al-Jazeera coverage, most of it appears to be quite professional." The same, he said, could not be said for al-Hurra. "If it's avowedly a propaganda arm, that's fine, but it claims to be a fair and balanced news organization."

Somewhat more successful in terms of attracting an audience and gaining a modicum of respect was Radio Sawa. A pet project of Westwood One founder Pattiz, the station used U.S. commercial radio strategies to reach out to Arabs under 30, who made up at least 60 per cent of the region's population. An ACNielsen survey funded by the BBG in early 2004 reported that Radio Sawa, with an annual budget of $22 million, was the number one rated station in Casablanca and Rabat. Overall, it reported, 38 per cent of adults in five Middle East countries were listening to the station, with 80 per cent judging its brief newscasts "very or somewhat reliable."[26] The numbers were impressive, but there were two problems. First, there was access. Radio Sawa's strength was that it was an FM station, which meant a clear signal right there on the car radio, unlike the VOA's shortwave Arabic service, listened to by barely 1 per cent of the region's population before it was shut down to free up budget for the new station. But that FM signal was also Radio Sawa's Achilles' heel. Some of the most important countries in the region, such as Saudi Arabia, Egypt and Syria, refused to give Radio Sawa a frequency. It may have had a sizable audience in Morocco, but audiences in much of the Middle East couldn't hear it at all. Then, there was the issue of those newscasts, brief though they were. Many Arabs said that when the news came on, they reached for the dial. Even official Washington was skeptical of Pattiz's numbers. A top official of the General Accounting Office told Congress: "Despite such results, it remains unclear how many people Radio Sawa is actually reaching throughout the entire Middle East because audience research has only been performed in select markets."[27]

A 2004 draft report by the State Department's Inspector General, leaked to *The Washington Post* because pressure from the BBG caused its release to be shelved, concluded that Radio Sawa had failed to meet its mandate of promoting democracy and pro-American attitudes. The station was "so preoccupied with building an audience through its music that it has failed to adequately measure whether it is influencing minds."[28] Most damning, a panel of Arabic-language experts said Radio Sawa's programming did not begin to match that of al-Jazeera for quality. Some Arab parents, they reported, banned their children from listening to the station, not because of any perceived U.S. propaganda or opposition to popular music, but because its broadcasts contained such poor Arabic grammar. The Inspector General even accused BBG's board of governors, whose mandate was to communicate American freedoms to the world, of interfering with and intimidating Radio Sawa staffers whom his team tried to interview.

AFTER THE COLD WAR

"How is it that the country that invented Hollywood and Madison Avenue has allowed such a destructive and parodied image of itself to become the intellectual coin of the realm overseas?" the chairman of the House International Relations Committee, Congressman Henry Hyde (R-Ill.), asked in mid-2002.[29] The answer lay in an endemic failure of vision. With the collapse of the Berlin Wall, the structures of U.S. public diplomacy – the official mechanisms through which the United States reached out to the world – were systematically dismantled. Perhaps it was hubris; the United States was, after all, now the sole superpower. Perhaps it was exhaustion; after 50 years of worrying about Mutually Assured Destruction (MAD), the nation wanted to take a break from the cares of mankind. Or maybe it was simply dollars and cents; public diplomacy took a big chunk of change. Whatever the real reason, the nation's leaders no longer saw much point in spending time or money explaining themselves to the rest of the globe. In 1991, under President George H.W. Bush, the budget for the main body coordinating public diplomacy, the United States Information Agency (USIA), came under the ax. The Muslim world was particularly hard hit. The USIA mission in Indonesia, for example, was cut in half.[30]

Cultural and educational exchanges had always been a critical part of public diplomacy, building bridges of understanding with students, academics, policymakers and future leaders from around the world. It was in just such a program that a young Arab named Anwar Sadat gained his first exposure to the U.S. He went on to sign the Camp David peace agreement with Israel as president of Egypt. "I've always found that the world leaders who are most cooperative with the U.S. are those who have taken part in exchange programs," observed Lee Hamilton, the vice-chair of the 9/11 Commission and long-time chairman of the House International Relations Committee.[31] But between 1995 and 2001 those exchanges were slashed by almost half. During that period, the USIA itself disappeared, dismembered and absorbed into the State Department and the new Broadcasting Board of Governors, the latter directed by part-time private-sector executives and political appointees. Operations focused on monitoring and influencing the foreign media were divided between the State Department's intelligence bureau and a domestically focused Public Affairs bureau, guaranteeing a lack of cohesion and cogent analysis of the international media's impact on foreign policy.

Around the world, USIA libraries and cultural centers were shuttered. These centers were once the first point of contact with the United States for millions of foreigners. There they could read American newspapers and magazines, absorb books about American culture, history, law and government, watch movies that gave new insights into the country, hear speakers, or just hang out and talk with Americans. Javid Nazir, the former editor of Pakistan's *Frontier Post*, recalls that when he was growing up there was a USIA library in every major city in Pakistan. "It was a joy for us to go there and learn about this great country." By September 11, 2001, not a single USIA library was left in Pakistan. "Now young people learn about America through television or the mosque, and each is equally distorted," a chagrined Nazir told me.[32]

Even after 9/11, the cuts to America's public diplomacy structures continued unabated. International exchanges were further reduced and Congress slashed the international broadcasting budget by a third, silencing Voice of America (VOA) and Radio Free Europe (RFE) and Radio Liberty (RL) broadcasts to several parts of the world. VOA was designed to generate support for U.S. policies abroad and promote an appreciation of U.S. culture. It was founded in 1942 to counter Nazi propaganda. Along with news and current affairs broadcasts, programs like Willis Conover's nightly jazz show, which ran for 40 years, drew millions of listeners around the world with what he called "the music of freedom."

Conover "proved more effective than a fleet of B-29s," as an obituary put it. For two hours each night he "would bombard Budapest with Billy Taylor, strafe Poland with Oscar Peterson and drop John Coltrane on Moscow."[33] The mission of Radio Free Europe and Radio Liberty, created in the 1950s, was to substitute for a free press in Communist countries of Eastern Europe, providing balanced coverage of developments behind the Iron Curtain and beaming that news back to the people of the Soviet bloc. Radio Free Asia would come later, with the same mission for China. VOA's TV arm, WORLDNET, was launched in 1983, but was never much more than a closed circuit operation that provided mostly talk programs and interactive teleconferences for audiences invited into U.S. embassies abroad. Radio Marti and its sister service, TV Marti, were designed to do for Cuba what VOA and RFE/RL were doing for the Soviet Union and Eastern Europe, but it quickly fell prey to domestic politics and became a tool of Miami's Cuban exile community.

A reassessment of the efficacy of these various operations was long overdue. But to some critics, the BBG's rapid diversion of resources to the Muslim world and simultaneous elimination of VOA's Arabic service had the feeling of action for action's sake. Among members of the BBG's board of governors, firsthand knowledge of the Muslim world, or of international broadcasting for that matter, was, to say the least, thin. Chairman Kenneth Tomlinson had been Ronald Reagan's appointee as director of VOA for two years, but otherwise had spent most of his career at *Reader's Digest*. Others on the board included the CEO of the Spanish-language Telemundo broadcasting group, a Hispanic Republican talk show host, a lobbyist, a political consultant, the chairman of a cable television company, radio station executive Pattiz, and then-National Security Advisor Condoleezza Rice, the only one with real foreign policy experience. In a 2003 report to Congress, the Government

Accountability Office (GAO) warned that the BBG lacked a "strategic vision" for coordinating international broadcasting with the nation's long-term foreign policy needs.

Six months later, the GAO raised another red flag. The BBG had proposed the elimination of a staggering 17 separate language services in Central and Eastern Europe, even though some of those countries did not yet have their own free and stable media.[34] VOA staffers, meanwhile, sent a petition to Congress protesting the "piece-by-piece" dismantling that was "virtually killing" the organization by reducing broadcasts and launching new services like Radio Sawa "with virtually no accountability" and limited editorial content.[35] The *coup de grâce* came with a spring 2005 announcement that the VOA's overnight news operation was being moved to Chinese-controlled Hong Kong in order to save about $300,000 a year. After the Cold War, the U.S. had taken a short-term approach to public diplomacy. Now it was in danger of repeating the same mistake, in spades.

HAPPY MUSLIMS

The members of the BBG were not the only Middle East neophytes directing America's outreach to the world's one billion Muslims. Enter Charlotte Beers, a former Madison Avenue advertising executive hired weeks after 9/11 to repackage Brand America. She lasted just 17 months in office. Her brainchild was the "Shared Values" campaign, a $15 million series of TV commercials – she called them "mini-documentaries" – about Muslim life in America. These Happy Muslims ads were meant to show that the peoples of the United States and the Muslim world had many values in common, such as love of family, and that Muslims in America were well treated and free to practice their faith. "I have never gotten disrespect because I am a Muslim," Kashmiri-American paramedic Farooq Muhammad of

New York City said in one spot. "That's the beautiful thing about the United States, that you can be of any faith and practice your faith freely . . . We are all brothers and sisters." Toledo schoolteacher Rawia Ismail painted a similar rosy picture in her spot, "I didn't see any prejudice anywhere in my neighborhood after 9/11."

Launched in October 2002, the ad campaign was killed before the end of the year. Critics dismissed the ads as good-news propaganda. Nowhere in the one- and two-minute spots was there any acknowledgement of isolated attacks on Muslims after 9/11 or the sense of defensiveness that pervaded the American Muslim community – all of which Muslims abroad were seeing reported in their own media and on the Internet. Nor was there any mention of U.S. policy. "It was like this was the 1930s and the government was running commercials showing happy blacks in America," said Youssef Ibrahim, a member of the Council on Foreign Relations.[36]

The failure of the producers to understand the cultures in which they were trying to communicate was underscored when the ads were released in Indonesia, the first country in which they were aired. At a preview hosted by the U.S. ambassador, Indonesians immediately asked why all four Muslims profiled were Arabs. The producers quickly scrambled and put together a fifth commercial featuring an Indonesian journalism student at school in Arizona.

Egypt, Lebanon and Jordan all refused to run the spots. The U.S. government didn't even try to get them on the air in Saudi Arabia. Some $5 million was spent buying airtime on pan-Arab broadcaster MBC and private stations in Pakistan, Kuwait, Malaysia and Indonesia, but the spots missed the mark entirely. "How it treats Muslims at home is not an issue," a top Malaysian politician said while the ads were airing in that country. "The issue is the U.S. administration's overall policy toward the Muslim world."[37] The intent might have been to reach "the masses," as a State Department spokesman put it, but even at the bottom of society, viewers were perplexed about the relevance to them. "Life looks good in the U.S., but most Muslims don't live in the U.S.," an Indonesian newspaper quoted one Jakarta prostitute as saying.[38] As the spots were launched in Indonesia, a far more powerful message was being sent by a U.S.-inspired Indonesian government crackdown on Islamists following the bombing of a Bali nightclub that killed 200 people, mainly Westerners. One widely circulated conspiracy theory claimed the CIA carried out the bombing to give it an excuse to strike back at Indonesian Muslims. If they believed that, said one Australian expert on Indonesia, "what credence are they going to give to some highly-packaged advertisement like this?"[39]

Even many American advertising executives thought the campaign laughable. Public diplomacy "is not about ads or catchy slogans, it's about actions," the chairman of the global advertising firm DDB Worldwide told Congress in a ringing indictment of the spots.[40] As poll after poll found, American "values" weren't the issue. Distaste for U.S. policies did not necessarily equate with distaste for other aspects of American society. When asked whether their attitudes toward the United States were based "more on American values or on American policy in the Middle East," more than 75 per cent of Arab respondents in one five-nation poll cited policy.[41] Arabs and non-Arab Muslims alike consistently reported positive attitudes toward the American systems of government, education, economy, and science and technology, evidenced by the traditionally high Muslim enrollment in U.S. universities, which dropped dramatically after 9/11 as students applied – or transferred – instead to schools in Europe and Australia. "It is too difficult to get a visa," Indonesian Ambassador Soemadi Brotodiningrat said with resignation, "why should they bother?"[42]

Instead of "changing misperceptions," as Beers described her goal, the ads only reinforced existing *perceptions* – "mis" or otherwise – and convinced many Muslims the Bush administration was trying to distract from its policy on Palestine and plans for Iraq. "We can see the brutality that goes on against Muslims but the U.S. does not do anything, so it is going to be very hard for them to change their image among Muslims," said Malaysian legislator Syed Azman Syed Ahmad Nawawi.[43] Compounding the damage was the fact that the spots carried the imprimatur of the Council of American Muslims for Understanding, which, it quickly became clear, was nothing more than a front organization set up by the State Department. Then there was the language of the ads themselves, which – because Beers and her team didn't speak Arabic – were originally produced in English and translated into the languages of the target countries. A version of each ad was also produced for print media. Comparing the original English against the Arabic version of the print ad about schoolteacher Rawia Ismail, one Arab researcher for Gallup found it to be incoherent, "inconsistent and often confusing." In the ad, Ismail says she also teaches on Saturdays at an Islamic center. The word "teach" was translated into Arab as *ulaqqen*, which the researcher explained "is loaded with negative connotations about the way Islam is taught as it brings images of forced religious teachings, which does not blend with the theme of the campaign." Why, he asked, "would she need to revert to the most rigid form of religious indoctrination that is, by cramming in, especially in a society that prides itself for tolerance?"[44]

In all, he concluded that only four out of twelve sentences were correctly translated into Arabic. And beyond the distortions of language was a subtle prejudice obvious to his eye but lost on the American producers: "Rawia is not presented as an American, only as a Muslim who lives in America."

When the plug was pulled in December, Beers and her colleagues tried to save face, claiming they had always planned on a temporary halt while the campaign was evaluated and revised. Meanwhile, they said, other aspects, including the Internet outreach, through the web site www.opendialogue. org, would continue. By March, Beers had resigned "for health reasons." Not long after, www.opendialogue.org went dark. The commercials were never revived. The project had been doomed from the start. Anti-Americanism bred and festered in the vast void between the values Americans lived by at home and those they are perceived to operate by abroad. Feel-good ads that ignored Muslim perceptions of U.S. policy were not going to change that.

PSEUDO-NEWS AND RABBIT EARS

Further muddying America's message was a blurring of the lines between legitimate information and propaganda – both at home and abroad. In early 2002, news broke that the Pentagon had established something called the Office of Strategic Influence with the goal of mounting a "perception management" campaign in the Middle East, Asia and Europe that reportedly included the planting of false news items among unwitting foreign journalists.[45] It was another indication of the administration's failure to grasp the nature of media globalization – or its cynical willingness to exploit the new information flow. American law prohibited the government from disseminating propaganda within the U.S., but – given the Internet and the incestuous nature of the media – it was inevitable that propaganda planted with foreign reporters would eventually find its way into American publications. Beyond that, the conscious dissemination of false information threatened to undermine the credibility of the Pentagon and the U.S. government as a whole. In the ensuing uproar, the office was scrapped, but the concept was by no means discarded. Late the same year, the Pentagon signed a $300,000 deal with SAIC, a defense contractor, to develop a "road map for creating an effective D.O.D. capability to design and conduct effective strategic influence and operational and tactical perception-management campaigns."[46] The use of pseudo-news as a weapon of Psychological Operations would be evident in the deification of Jessica Lynch, the toppling of the Saddam statue, military-sponsored pseudo-news web sites, a proposal for Arabic comic books to portray U.S. troops as role models for Arab young, and numerous other stories that crossed the line between information and propaganda.

That is not to say that, in certain situations, media management was not an important element of military strategy. A classic example of Psyops involved Saddam's sons, Uday and Qusay, killed in a shootout with U.S. forces. The death of the pair came on the heels of American criticism of the Arab media for showing the bodies of dead U.S. soldiers. The Pentagon faced a choice: simply announce the deaths of the dictator's sons or display their bullet-riddled bodies and risk charges of hypocrisy. They opted for the latter. After initially releasing a photograph of the two men as they appeared immediately after their death, the Army cleaned and embalmed the corpses, repaired wounds to their faces, shortened Uday's beard and shaved Qusay, who was usually clean-shaven in life, so that they were more readily recognizable. Camera crews were then invited to film the bodies in a Psyops effort to take the wind out of claims that the pair were still alive and leading the resistance and, at the same time, remove the shadow looming over those Iraqis who wanted to cooperate with the Americans. Some conspiracy theorists still believed the bodies were wax dolls,[47] and there was grumbling about the sacrilege of showing dead bodies on television, but the photos appeared on the front pages of newspapers across the region, and most Iraqis – and other

Arabs – were convinced the hated Saddam sons were, indeed, gone. "Now Washington gives itself the right to publish the pictures of Uday and Qusay Saddam Hussein, but no one is talking about a violation of international conventions despite the fact that they show disfigured and charred bodies," grumbled the Saudi daily *al-Watan*, but more common were headlines like, "The End of the Tyrants in Mosul."[48]

An even more spectacular communications success was the capture of Saddam himself in December 2003. Arab enemies and supporters alike were shocked when U.S. officials released footage of the bearded and bedraggled former dictator meekly submitting as an American doctor poked and probed his mouth and ears. Once more, a U.S.-supplied image carefully calculated to be a psychological blow dominated the Arab – and global – media. Newspaper commentators said Saddam resembled "a pathetic hobo from a homeless shelter" and "nothing more than a long-haired tramp, staring absently into the camera."[49] Al-Jazeera mocked him by intercutting the footage of the examination and what America officials called the "rat hole" in which he was captured, with scenes from bombastic prewar speeches in which he commanded his generals to fight to the death. Even those media outlets that framed the capture as, in the words of an *al-Quds al-Arabi* headline, "A New Indignity for the Arabs," were equally appalled that the dictator had given up without a fight. "It would have been far better if he had fought to the end and died as a martyr as his two sons did," the paper's editor wrote.[50] Others wondered "why did he not blow himself up with the explosives belt he was said to wear around him" or shoot himself like Hitler.[51] There were the inevitable rumors of conspiracy. The U.S. version of events was "too perfect, too suspicious," said one Gulf commentator.[52] Some Arabs claimed that the dates on the palm trees seen in the footage of the capture would not have been ripe in December, thus "proving" the capture had actually taken place earlier. But all this was a sideshow. Try as his defenders might to dismiss the images as "mere media propaganda,"[53] the United States had scored an important win in the psychological battle.

The success of these efforts emboldened military propagandists. By the summer of 2004, the military's public affairs and Psyops activities in Iraq were formally combined into a single Strategic Communications Office on orders of the U.S. commander in Iraq, Gen. George Casey, Jr. and against the advice of the chairman of the Joint Chiefs of Staff, who warned of the dangers inherent in blurring truth and falsehood. "Such organizational constructs have the potential to compromise the commander's credibility with the media and the public," Gen. Richard Myers wrote in a memo to regional commanders.[54] The Iraq move set off a fierce debate within the Pentagon. In the process, it became clear that while many in the military had recognized the strategic value of satellite television as a weapon, they had not fully digested the interconnected nature of the globalized media. "Are we trying to inform?" asked Brig. Gen. Mark Kimmitt, who became a familiar face as the military's main spokesman during the Iraq invasion. "Yes. Do we offer perspective? Yes. Do we offer military judgment? Yes. Must we tell the truth to stay credible? Yes. Is there a battlefield value in deceiving the enemy? Yes. Do we intentionally deceive the American people? No." But, as Kimmitt himself admitted, "in a worldwide media environment," the challenge was preventing "that deception from spilling out from the battlefield and inadvertently deceiving the American people."[55] The reality was that battlefield deceptions inevitably *did* deceive both the American people and audiences around the world, undercutting U.S. credibility.

It was all part of a new field of specialization emerging within the military, known in the halls of the Pentagon by the Orwellian title, "Defense Support for Public Diplomacy."

If Public Diplomacy was a practice that "promotes dialogue, the sharing of ideas, and personal and institutional relationships,"[56] these tactics were anything but that. They were certainly effective in manipulating domestic U.S. opinion and, in some cases, sowing confusion on the battlefield, but, for the most part, they had an overwhelmingly negative effect on opinions in the Arab and Muslim world.

Meanwhile, similar information management tactics were being employed at home. Though the news wouldn't break until early in 2005, throughout its first term the Bush administration had been producing its own pseudo-news stories and placing them on local television newscasts. Such segments, known as Video News Releases (VNRs), had long been used by corporations publicizing products and lobbyists pushing a cause. Written and narrated by former television reporters, VNRs exploited the fact that many local newsrooms – like their network counterparts – were underfunded, understaffed and overextended. Properly used, these segments provided additional footage, properly attributed, with which to supplement news stories. More often, they simply ran uncut, as if an actual news story. Sometimes, more insidiously, one of the station's own reporters renarrated the spot to give it a local "feel." A common tool for the public relations industry, their use by the government had been limited, and rarely in the context of foreign policy. The Bush administration produced and distributed hundreds of such spots, which aired on stations in the nation's largest television markets, including many on topics such as homeland security and the supposed positive reaction of U.S. Muslims to the fall of Baghdad. One set of VNRs supported the administration's campaign to focus attention on the plight of Afghan women during the Afghan invasion. A January 2003 White House memo singled out the Afghan series as a "prime example" of how "White House-led efforts could facilitate strategic, proactive communications in the war on terror."[57]

Another group of VNRs emphasized American humanitarian efforts in Iraq. "After living for decades in fear, they are now receiving assistance – and building trust – with their coalition liberators," said the narrator of a piece shot in an Iraqi Shi'ite area.[58] The investigative arm of Congress concluded such spots were "designed and executed" to be "indistinguishable from news stories produced by private sector television news organizations" and thus constituted "covert propaganda."[59] They also appeared to violate the 1948 Smith–Mundt Act, which prohibits the domestic dissemination of American government propaganda (a reason the Voice of America cannot be heard in the United States). In response, a group of Democratic senators introduced the Stop Government Propaganda Act, aimed at making it illegal to distribute any message – via the media, Internet or other medium – that did not "continuously and clearly identify the Government agency directly or indirectly financially responsible for the message."[60]

In Iraq meanwhile, no laws were being violated, but the attitude of CPA officials both flew in the face of a prewar Pentagon blueprint that called for a free, impartial and independent Iraqi media and squandered an important opportunity to at least begin to have America's voice heard in a credible way. SAIC, the San Diego-based information technology firm that drew up the perception-management roadmap, quickly found itself lost on the information highway after it was tapped to take over Iraqi TV and launch the first post-Saddam newspaper. Despite all the talk of strategic influence, American attempts to win hearts and minds would prove inept. The first problem with the new Iraqi Media Network (IMN), as Saddam's government television station was renamed, was that most Iraqis weren't watching.

"For the first nine months of the occupation, we weren't communicating with the Iraqi people," reports Charles Krohn, a veteran military public affairs officer who briefly served as spokesman for the Reconstruction Authority in Iraq. "Instead, media efforts were spent wining and dining U.S. reporters to influence what people back home were thinking."[61] In fact, one of the central problems with Bush administration communications efforts around the war on terror and the invasion of Iraq was that they were carried out with U.S. domestic opinion – not that of the Muslim world – uppermost in mind, evident in such policies as the ban on photographs of the coffins of U.S. war dead arriving back at Dover Air Force base.

With their myopic fixation on manipulating attitudes at home, U.S. officials failed to exploit their most effective communications weapon against what they claimed were the distortions of al-Jazeera and other Arab media: Iraqi television. Under Saddam, satellite dishes had been banned to prevent access to foreign stations. Iraqi TV broadcast only a terrestrial signal picked up through old-style TV antennas. As soon as Baghdad fell, American authorities scrapped the restrictions and $200 satellite dishes blossomed on rooftops across the country. Krohn, a former spokesman for the Secretary of the Army who began his career as a military public affairs officer in Vietnam, says that when he arrived in Baghdad in November of 2003, he discovered that the Iraqi public was avidly glued to their newly accessible satellite channels, yet American-run Iraqi TV was still "transmitting to rabbit ears" – the old set-top antennas common in the age before cable and satellite. "From April 2003 to February 2004, we basically weren't talking to anyone," he recalls.[62] That despite a $4 million a month contract with SAIC.[63] Krohn was even more frustrated when he learned that the U.S. was actually leasing a satellite transponder for IMN, which it wasn't using. The explanation: the contractor had only bought terrestrial rights for the American programming it was retransmitting on IMN, so the signal could not broadcast via satellite. In return for savings of a few thousand dollars, the U.S. was squandering an opportunity to try to win the support of the Iraqi public for its multibillion-dollar war effort. In a further economizing move, those U.S.-purchased programs were supplemented with pirated copies of Hollywood and European films found in the mansion of one of Saddam's sons and aired in violation of copyright.

CPA chief Paul Bremer and his spokesman, a White House appointee named Dan Senor, either ignored IMN or, even worse, put pressure on its reporters to parrot American rhetoric, turning it into, in the words of an American journalist hired to help run the station, "an irrelevant mouthpiece for Coalition Provisional Authority propaganda, managed news and mediocre programs."[64] IMN had the potential to be America's most powerful means of winning the hearts and minds of the Iraqi people. But so irrelevant did Bremer's team apparently consider it that when American forces captured Saddam Hussein, the CPA didn't even bother to tell its own TV station, missing an opportunity to frame the story for the Iraqi viewer. Al-Jazeera, al-Arabiya and every other news channel in the Middle East immediately broke the biggest news since the fall of Baghdad, providing their own extensive commentary, while IMN broadcast an American soap opera.[65] Most bizarrely, some of the training for IMN reporters was turned over to al-Jazeera and al-Arabiya, the very stations U.S. officials were denouncing as biased against them.[66] But the station wasn't completely off the radar screen of American officials. IMN was forced to air CPA news conferences and interviews unedited and was barred from doing its own hiring and firing. Senor also ordered the station to stop the practice of opening the broadcast day with a reading from the Qur'an, a tradition in the Middle East. When North argued that such a move would be seen as offensive to many Muslims, Senor replied that American officials had decided that in Iraq, they wanted a complete separation of Church and state.

By November 2003, with barely one in ten Iraqis tuning in to IMN and two out of three watching al-Jazeera and al-Arabiya, U.S. authorities realized it was time to take drastic measures to revive this important communications conduit. SAIC lost its contract to the Harris Corporation, yet another defense technology contractor, IMN was renamed al-Iraqiya, and, the American advertising agency J. Walter Thompson was hired to mount an ad campaign to convince Iraqis the station was credible. The Pentagon had apparently learned nothing from the Happy Muslims advertising disaster.

For good measure, a U.S. Army Psyops team started work on an Iraqi version of *American Idol*, which included a comedian impersonating Saddam Hussein. "The program was one of those rare, elusive events a Psyop officer dreams about and strives for," two soldiers from the 101st Airborne later reported in a military journal; "an initiative that truly won hearts and minds."[67] Al-Jazeera might have had street cred for its news, but al-Iraqiya had *Talent*.

12
Symbols of Empire

We are dealing with people that are perfectly willing to lie to the world
to attempt to further their case.

Donald Rumsfeld

If a picture is worth a thousand words, there was no
dictionary thick enough – or public diplomacy budget
large enough – to counter the devastating images from
Abu Ghraib prison. Terrorism experts frequently cite
humiliation and alienation as primary drivers of terrorism.
Abu Ghraib was, to paraphrase Saddam's description of the
1990–91 Gulf War, the Mother of all Humiliations.

A pyramid of naked men. A woman soldier holding a
naked prisoner on a leash. A man in a hood with wires
attached to his appendages. Attack dogs cornering a fright-
ened and naked prisoner. These photographs and others
dominated the front pages of newspapers across the Muslim
world in the spring of 2004, examples of what an internal
U.S. Army report termed "sadistic, blatant and wanton criminal abuses" against Iraqi detainees, many of whom were
later released without ever being charged with a crime.

"The Scandal," shouted a headline in Egypt's *Akhbar
el-Yom* over a gallery of pictures of the abuse. "The Shame,"
echoed *al-Wafd*. Al-Jazeera's correspondent in Baghdad
reported that people there "considered the images as an
abuse of the Iraqis' humanity and dignity, which is meant to
humiliate and insult them on top of the occupation imposed
on them." For Muslims, the combination could not have

been more potent: nakedness; sexual humiliation; dogs, considered unclean in Islam. Said Syrian television: "The bizarre and immoral practices of the U.S. occupation become clearer day after day."[1]

The abuse was a sadly inevitable product of America's historic ignorance of, and contempt for, Arabs and Muslims. A linear connection could be drawn from Abu Ghraib back through the portrayal of the Iraq invasion as a war against "evil" to the systematic negation of Arab grievances by the American body politic and the decades of Arab and Muslim stereotyping in the U.S. media. In his *New Yorker* article breaking the Abu Ghraib story, investigative reporter Seymour Hersh quoted one of the men who blew the whistle on the abuse. The soldier's choice of pronouns betrayed the dehumanization that had taken root. "I remember SSG Frederick hitting one prisoner in the side of its ribcage," he recalled. "I saw two naked detainees, one masturbating to another with its mouth open."[2] *Its*. Not "his," not "the man's." Humanity had been stripped away; all that was left was a *thing*. The truth of Edward Said's observation that America looked at the Muslim world in the context of what "we *do*" and what "they *are*" was once more borne out. American officials, such as Deputy Defense Secretary Paul Wolfowitz, institutionalized this mindset among U.S. troops with talk of eliminating "every snake in the swamp"[3] and seeking out enemies in "the uncivilized world."[4]

An Air Force psychological assessment of the Abu Ghraib guards emphasized the degree to which Othering had driven the abuse:

> Soldiers were immersed in the Islamic culture, a culture that many were encountering for the first time. Clearly, there are major differences in worship and beliefs and there is the association of Muslims with terrorism. All these causes exaggerate differences and create misperceptions that can lead to fear or devaluation of a people.[5]

One of the soldiers, projecting his own racist worldview, told investigators that even the guard dogs had come to hate the Iraqi detainees: "They didn't like the Iraqi culture, smell, sound, skin tone, hair color, or anything about them."[6] A cursory glance at the photographs made clear that in the minds of the jailers, Arabs were worse than animals. The Arabs themselves had always suspected such sentiments lay just beneath all the American talk of liberty and equality. A typical editorial said:

> What the US forces did and are doing in Iraq confirms to us what we had always warned of, namely, that the aim of this invasion and occupation was primarily to humiliate the Arabs and Muslims and was never for changing a dictatorship or establishing a model of democracy, justice and human rights.[7]

The smiling visage of Private Jessica Lynch, that poster girl for patriotism created by U.S. military propagandists, had been replaced by the leering image of her evil twin, Private Lynndie England, reveling in the emasculation of a people. Washington dismissed the work of England and her fellow guards as an aberration. "I can't tell you how sorry I am," President Bush said in an interview with Egypt's *al-Ahram* newspaper.

> But this isn't America, that's not – Americans are appalled at what happened. We're a generous people. I don't think a lot of people understand that. So I've got to do a better job of explaining to people that we're for a lot of things that most people who live in the Middle East want.[8]

Few in the region were interested in another lecture on shared values. "It's unbelievable. These are the same old practices of Saddam," said a columnist with Beirut's Syrian-influenced *as-Safir*.[9] Particularly symbolic was the fact that the abuses had taken place in one of the ousted dictator's most notorious torture centers. Others noted that if America could so easily dismiss the deranged acts of its lunatic fringe,

Muslims should not be held accountable for the actions of their extremists. "This white man, who considers himself of a superior race, treats others, whom he considers inferior, with contempt, and he wants to preach to them on morals," *an-Nahar* columnist Sahar Baasiri said of Bush. "How could prisoner torture be an 'incident,' not a systematic method adopted by the U.S. military, when there are 1,800 pictures, CDs, and video tapes?"[10] Abu Ghraib, said Lebanese Shi'ite spiritual leader Muhammad Hussein Fadlallah, was "an outcome of the culture of hate against Arabs and Muslims that Bush and his acolytes promoted."[11] *As-Safir*'s editor called it a product of the "colonial attitude of superiority" on the part of American leaders who, through their words and policies "belittle Arabs and reflect, in such an attitude, their belief that the Arabs are half-wits."[12] At the other end of the Muslim world, members of Indonesian Islamist parties held a rally to condemn the United States. "They claim to be human rights champions, but in fact they are the greatest rights abusers," said one member of the Crescent Star party.[13]

The scandal prompted some who once denounced terrorism to have second thoughts. If the Americans were brutalizing Iraqis, didn't Arabs and Muslims have every right to resort to violence? For many commentators, America's failure to comprehend the damage Abu Ghraib had inflicted on the Arab psyche was a tragedy on a par with the abuses themselves. "We are certain that Osama bin Laden, his deputy Ayman al-Zawahiri and al-Qaeda supporters are the happiest people on earth as they watch the shameful clips because they have given them the best ammunition for recruiting more frustrated young men who are zealous about their religion, creed and honour," wrote Abd-al-Bari Atwan, chief editor of *al-Quds al-Arabi*.[14] It was not long before the extremists themselves responded. "The dignity of the Muslim men and women in Abu Ghraib and others is not redeemed except by blood and souls," declared the hooded executioner of American

Nicholas Berg moments before he beheaded the kidnapped
U.S. contractor in a videotaped ritual that would become a
grim staple of a new brand of terrorist theater.[15] If it was
open season on Iraqis, it would now be open season on
Americans as well. Such tit-for-tat brutality disgusted mainstream Arabs and Muslims, who condemned the executions
as loudly as they condemned Abu Ghraib. "The barbaric
Israeli and U.S. crimes committed against Arabs and
engraved in the memory do not justify the decline of Arab
and Islamic values to such a low level," wrote *as-Safir*
columnist Sateh Nouriddine.[16] There was another, more
pragmatic, criticism as well: in seizing the media spotlight
with such outrages, the *jihadis* were unwittingly serving
American interests by distracting attention from U.S. abuses.

"REMEMBER FALLUJAH"

For America's image in the Muslim world, the Abu Ghraib
scandal could not have come at a worse time. U.S. forces
were locked in combat with Sunni insurgents in the northern
city of Fallujah and with militias loyal to Shi'ite cleric
Muqtada al-Sadr in the south. By the time the Abu Ghraib
story broke, these conflicts were already being portrayed in
the Muslim media as mythological battles in defense of Islam
and Arab honor. America had the *Maine*, Pearl Harbor and
9/11. For Arabs, the rallying cries were Deir Yassin, the 1948
massacre that panicked thousands of Palestinians into fleeing
what is now Israel, and Sabra and Chatilla, site of the 1982
slaughter of hundreds of Palestinians and Shi'ites. Now,
Fallujah, Najaf and Karbala joined the list.

The bloodshed began on March 31, 2004, when four
U.S. security contractors who were escorting a food convoy
for American troops were ambushed in Fallujah, a city of
300,000 in the so-called Sunni triangle north of Baghdad.
Insurgents opened fire on the vehicles when the contractors

became lost and found themselves in the heart of the city, known to be hostile to Americans. The cars were quickly surrounded by a mob. The bodies of the contractors, all Special Forces veterans working for North Carolina-based Blackwater Security Services, were set on fire and dragged through the streets, then hung from a bridge. The horrifying scenes were videotaped by a local cameraman and transmitted around the world. To many in the United States, the sight of a wild mob of Arabs stringing up the charred bodies of fellow Americans confirmed every cliché they had ever heard. U.S. government reaction was swift and firm. The White House vowed to "show resolve in the face of these cowardly, hateful acts." President Bush declared: "America will never be intimidated by thugs and assassins."[17] U.S. military commanders in Iraq demanded that Fallujah residents turn over those responsible for the murders. "If not, we're prepared to go in and find them," promised Army Brig. Gen. Mark Kimmitt.[18]

During Friday prayers in Fallujah two days after the killings, clerics at the city's main mosques berated those responsible, if not for the murders, then at least for what followed. "Islam does not condone the mutilation of the bodies of the dead," lectured Sheikh Fawzi Nameq. "Why do you want to bring destruction to our city? Why do you want to bring humiliation to the faithful?" In another mosque not far from the square where the Americans had died, Sheikh Hamid Saleh was equally stern. "This is childish behavior committed by ignorants who don't know the meaning of life and death," Saleh said. "This is a grave mistake that destroys the reputation of Islam and Muslims."[19]

The administration was determined to show that this would not be a repeat of Somalia. Within days of the Fallujah killings, U.S. forces were massing on the outskirts of the city to begin their assault. Yet this shoot-from-the-hip response was doomed from the start. The idea that those responsible would be turned over – or captured by U.S. troops in a city largely hostile to the American presence – betrayed not only a fatal misreading of the nature of the resistance, but also a failure to truly comprehend the degree to which modern warfare had been altered by the media revolution. In an era in which the enemy sought martyrdom and the unblinking eye of the camera lens was fixed on the battlefield 24/7, the notion of victory was turned on its head. Siege was unsustainable. The more blood shed by the defenders, the more powerful their cause.

Once more, Arab cameras were able to venture where American crews dared not go. Once more, viewers in the Muslim world witnessed a conflict far more bloody than the antiseptic operation seen on American television screens. "The sight of decapitated children, the rows of dead women and the shocking pictures of the soccer stadium that was turned into a temporary grave for hundreds of the slain – all were broadcast to the world only by the al-Jazeera network," Israel's *Ha'aretz* newspaper reported under the headline "Remember Fallujah." So brutal was the assault, said the paper, that "after Fallujah, Israel Defense Forces commanders can feel easier with their consciences."[20]

Minute after minute, hour after hour, day after day, viewers from Morocco to Malaysia witnessed the assault. Voices across the Muslim world denounced the murder of the contractors, the gruesome beheading of Nicholas Berg and the wave of kidnappings and executions that followed – "This madness has to stop," said the *Jordan Times*[21] – but outrage at the deaths of Americans was tempered by the absolutist rhetoric and maximalist military response from the Bush administration that turned the city into a symbol of Arab and Muslim resistance. The "orgy of violence" in Fallujah, coming on the heels of the Abu Ghraib scandal, squandered America's claim to moral superiority: "This is the United States' real image, regardless of its attempt to beautify itself and appear as leader of the free world."[22]

After a full year of what so many Arabs perceived as humiliation at the hands of the Americans with the fall of Baghdad, the media in the Muslim world seized on Fallujah as "one of the greatest battles the Arabs have ever waged against the Crusaders."[23] The myth-making said as much about the pitiful state of Arab self-image as it did about the standoff itself. Arab poets penned paeans to this "Arab Stalingrad" and there were analogies to Karameh, the Jordanian town where in 1968 PLO guerrillas repelled an Israeli force of 15,000 troops. "The battle for Fallujah," wrote one commentator in a Baghdad newspaper, "is reshaping public awareness for a nation stunned and has reformulated the Iraqi, Arab and Muslim character after a long period of loss and fragmentation."[24]

Not all Arabs – or Muslims – bought into the portrayal. Kuwaitis, who had no love-loss for Iraqis after the 1990 invasion of their country, were largely contemptuous of the insurgents. "We do not see any reason why Kuwaiti Muslims should have any sympathy for Fallujah . . . when the brother burns corpses, kidnaps and kills," said *al-Ra'y al-Am*.[25] Added a Saudi commentator: "The price of four Americans, who were killed and then had their corpses mutilated, was hell for tens of thousands of innocent people in Fallujah. Where is the heroism?"[26] But much of the rest of the Middle East – and broader Muslim world – was entranced. "The resistance of Fallujah makes it the mother of all Iraqi towns, an example of resistance and sacrifice," declared London-based *al-Arab al-Alamiyah*.[27] The confrontation was manna from heaven for the Islamist groups seeking recruits. "Despite the obvious gap in technological capability, the Resistance fighters of al-Fallujah have written an epic," said the Iraqi Islamist web site albasrah. net. "With only light arms such as automatic rifles and RPGs they have held back the most powerful army on earth."[28]

The degree to which Fallujah became a symbol of resistance to so many Arabs and Muslims – even the intelligentsia – cannot be understated. Shortly after he returned home from a visit to the United States, a Saudi university professor sent me an email in which he painted a grim picture of the prospects for Middle East peace:

> Please forgive my pessimism, but I am really living these days the trauma of the flattened city of Fallujah (during Ramadan! which is considered a holy month and all wars are prohibited in it even before the advent of Islam). Unfortunately the cultural and political schism is getting larger and larger.

Faced with global condemnation for an increasingly bloody siege that forced hundreds of thousands of people to flee the city as refugees, the United States once more blamed the messenger. Secretary of Defense Donald Rumsfeld dismissed as "outrageous nonsense" reports in the Arab media that hundreds of civilians, including women and children, had been killed in Fallujah, telling reporters in Washington, "I can definitely say what al-Jazeera is doing is vicious, inaccurate and inexcusable."[29] Yet the American media carried similar claims, reporting an April death toll of more than 700 Iraqi dead and 2,800 wounded in Fallujah and more than 1,300 Iraqis killed in the country as a whole.[30] The Fallujah body count came from doctors at the city's main hospital, which would be one of the first targets when U.S. forces mounted a second offensive against Fallujah in the fall of 2004. American officers would be unapologetic about attacking a medical facility. "It's a center of propaganda," one commander told *The New York Times*.[31]

In keeping with the vocabulary that helped make Abu Ghraib possible, America's top general in Iraq dismissed Fallujah as a "huge rats' nest," a term that soon punctuated the dialogue of U.S. troops surrounding the city.[32] But the "rats" would – for the moment at least – win. In the face of international outrage, American commanders eventually halted the offensive, negotiated with the city's leaders, and handed over responsibility for Fallujah to a former Ba'athist general who headed a unit of one-time Saddam Republican Guard loyalists, dubbed the "Fallujah Brigade." The unit would later dissolve at the first sign of trouble.

"The global media disrupted the U.S. and Coalition chains of command," one former U.S. officer later wrote of the Fallujah campaign. "We could have won militarily. Instead, we surrendered politically and called it a success. Our enemies won the information war. We literally didn't know what hit us." His solution: in future operations, U.S. forces must "kill faster" before public opinion could be brought to bear.[33]

ON SACRED GROUND

A few hundred miles to the south, meanwhile, most of the U.S. troops surrounding the cities Najaf and Karbala were blissfully unaware of the degree to which Shi'ites across the Middle East saw their actions as sacrilege. The man arguably most responsible for the presence of American troops in Iraq was, apparently, equally ignorant of the significance of the siege. In a stunning example of the degree to which U.S. Middle East policy was driven by an absence of regional expertise, Paul Wolfowitz, a prime architect of the Iraq war, had once told an interviewer: "The Iraqis are . . . by and large quite secular. They are overwhelmingly Shiite, which is different from the Wahabi of the [Saudi] Peninsula. They don't bring the sensitivity of having the holy cities of Islam on their territory."[34]

No holy places – except, of course, the two most sacred cities of Shi'a Islam. Najaf was the burial place of Ali, the fourth Caliph of Islam, who was also the Prophet Mohammad's brother-in-law and cousin. Ali was both the most revered Shi'a saint and their namesake – "Shi'a" is derived from *shiat Ali*, which literally means the "party of Ali" or "partisans of Ali." According to Shi'a lore, Imam Ali was not the only revered figure enshrined beneath the sacred mosque. There also lay the remains of Adam, the first man. Adjoining the shrine was a plot of land said to have been purchased by the Prophet Abraham and his son Isaac, father of the Arab people. It was now the sprawling Wadi al-Salam Cemetery, where Shi'ites from across the Middle East had been burying their dead for centuries, secure in the knowledge that this resting place would ensure entry to Paradise. Najaf was also one of the most important centers of Shi'a scholarship, where Iran's Ayatollah Khomeini had spent a dozen years in exile and where Muqtada al-Sadr's father, the revered Ayatollah Sadiq al-Sadr, was assassinated. A few dozen miles down the road was Karbala, the infamous battlefield where Ali's son and successor, the Imam Hussein, and 70 of his followers knowingly went to their death in 684 A.D. fighting a vastly larger army of the Sunni Umayyad Caliph, thus forever enshrining the concept of martyrdom in Shi'a doctrine. Neighboring Kufa, where al-Sadr's confrontation with the Americans began, was the site of Imam Ali's assassination. All that history had somehow escaped the notice of Wolfowitz, who also likely missed the symbolism of the fact that the martyred Hussein died fighting what Shi'ites considered an illegitimate regime. "Oppose the oppressor and support the oppressed," Ali counseled in his last Will and Testament.

The confrontation with al-Sadr was provoked, at least in part, by the Americans' determination to control the media message. Al-Sadr's newspaper, *al-Hawza*, had regularly attacked the American "occupation." Coalition Provisional Authority (CPA) head Paul Bremer, variously called a "third-rate intelligence agent" and "Zionist-Christian," was a frequent target of the paper's barbs, particularly after his veto of measures that would have enshrined aspects of Islamic law in Iraq's new constitution. The paper also claimed that some apparent car bombs against civilians were actually the result of U.S. missiles and bombs. In late March, three days before the murder of the American contractors that sparked the battle for Fallujah, Bremer issued an order to shut down *al-Hawza* on the grounds it had "published articles that prove an intention to disturb general security and incite violence against the coalition and its employees."[35] A week later, as violent clashes erupted between U.S. forces and al-Sadr's al-Mahdi Army militia, Bremer declared the Shi'ite cleric an "outlaw." U.S. officials announced plans to enforce a hitherto secret arrest warrant that charged al-Sadr with ordering the death of a pro-American Shi'ite cleric blown up outside the Imam Ali mosque shortly after the United States flew him home from exile in the days following the fall of Baghdad. Brig. Gen. Kimmitt said it was up to al-Sadr to decide whether to give himself up, adding that anyone who incited or executed violence "against persons inside Iraq will be hunted down and captured or killed."[36] That threat would prove as empty as the vow to capture those responsible for the murder and mutilation of the contractors in Fallujah. Ultimately, U.S. authorities would agree to a deal brokered by Iraq's senior Shi'ite cleric under which the two sides disengaged. Al-Sadr would live to flex his muscles again, both militarily and as a power-broker in parliament.

The decision by American officials to take on al-Sadr two months before the transfer to Iraqi self-rule played into the hands of the young firebrand, allowing him to seize the media limelight. U.S. strategists had believed that by eviscerating the al-Mahdi Army, they could neuter al-Sadr's ability to interfere with the coming elections. The gamble went fatally wrong, transforming into a national hero a young thug generally despised by the Shi'ite religious hierarchy. But it could have been much worse. Completely missing from the American calculation was the ripple effect on Shi'a politics across the region. "The Iraqis can decide when, how and where to fight for the liberation of their country," Hizbullah chief Hassan Nasrallah told hundreds of thousands of Shi'ites who gathered in Lebanon to protest the American offensive, "however, when it comes to Najaf and Karbala, the graveyard of Imam Ali bin Abi Taleb and his son Imam Hussein, we consider ourselves directly involved. In wearing our death shrouds, we show the enemies our readiness to fight and die in defense of the holy shrines and sites."

The links between the Shi'a of Iraq, Iran and Lebanon ran broad and deep. They included ties of blood, marriage and education. The clergy of all three countries spent decades studying at the great religious centers of Najaf in Iraq and Qom in Iran, marrying each other's sisters and daughters and forging close personal bonds. The failure of U.S. officials to recognize the interconnected nature of the region's Shi'ite community had been apparent since the early days of the war on terror. Key Bush administration officials who had been involved in the Lebanon debacle of the early 1980s, including Donald Rumsfeld and top Pentagon officers, still longed to pay Hizbullah back for the deaths of 241 servicemen in the Beirut Marine barracks bombing and the resulting humiliation inflicted on U.S. prestige. Yet by 2001, Hizbullah was a very different organization than it had been. In the ensuing two decades, it had evolved into a broad-based civil society organization that had largely left behind its violent past.

Hizbullah was an example of a group that had used – and in this case, pioneered – suicide bombings to attain a specific goal: the expulsion of U.S. and Israeli forces from Lebanese soil. There was no intelligence to indicate the Hizbullah leadership had directly harmed a single American since releasing their last hostage, Terry Anderson, in December 1991.[37] Yet in the months and years after 9/11, the Bush administration would consistently single out Hizbullah as a target, promising Ariel Sharon that America would deal with the Shi'ite organization in "phase two" of the terror war. Sen. Bob Graham (D-Fla.), a strong supporter of Israel, went so far as to label Hizbullah "the A-Team" of terrorism, more dangerous than al-Qaeda.[38] The strategy against Hizbullah completely ignored the potentially disastrous consequences for the America policy in Iraq. The United States had a chance of putting together a viable Iraqi government as long as the resistance was largely confined to the minority Sunni community. A broad-based Shi'ite uprising in Iraq was a nightmare scenario, but one that was almost guaranteed if the United States struck at Hizbullah. Yet the administration continued to ratchet up the pressure on Hizbullah and its patrons in Syria, imposing sanctions on the Damascus regime in the spring of 2004, even as it grappled with the al-Sadr rebellion and the siege of Fallujah.

By that point, ever-present suspicions of an anti-Arab, anti-Muslim U.S.–Israeli conspiracy were already at a fever pitch. When, a week before the Fallujah uprising, Israel assassinated Hamas leader Sheikh Ahmad Yassin and threatened to do the same to Nasrallah of Hizbullah, the Bush administration left the clear impression among Arabs and Muslims that it was giving a green light for murder. Asked if the United States condemned the assassination, White House spokesman Scott McClellan demurred. "What we have said is that Israel has a right to defend herself, but all parties, including Israel, need to keep in mind the consequences of their actions," McClellan told reporters. "Hamas is a terrorist organization. Sheik Yassin is someone who was personally involved in terrorism. That's very well-documented." A total of seven times McClellan was given the opportunity to distance the Bush administration from the assassination, but each time he reiterated that "Israel has a right to defend herself."[39] Hours later, as the ramifications of the implicit U.S. endorsement of the assassination sunk in, the State Department issued a statement of its own indicating that the United States was "deeply troubled" by the killing. It was already too late. To audiences in the Muslim world, suspicions of U.S. complicity had been confirmed. The assassination caused the collapse of an Arab League foreign ministers summit that was to have debated an American proposal to foster democracy in the Middle East. Arab leaders could not afford to be seen to be doing the bidding of the United States when its proxy was carrying out murder with American complicity and while the United States itself was locked in bitter combat with Arab forces.

Day in and day out viewers watched as America's Judeo-Christian forces laid siege to the "heroic" Islamic defenders of Najaf, Karbala and Fallujah. Whole neighborhoods of the three Arab cities were laid waste; pilgrim hotels around the holy shrines were destroyed. Even Western news organizations such as the BBC reported that "bodies littered the streets."[40] Particularly damaging to the U.S. cause were images of American troops firing on the mosques themselves. U.S. officials argued that shelling of the mosques was justified. After all, al-Sadr's men were holed up in there, taking potshots at American troops. Secretary of Defense Rumsfeld triumphantly brandished photos of armed followers of al-Sadr inside the Imam Ali shrine; clear vindication of the U.S. action – in American eyes, at least. Rumsfeld even claimed al-Sadr's own men were responsible for the damage that defaced the sacred golden dome. It was another example of the colossal failure of U.S. officials to recognize that others did not see the world through their eyes. The 100 million Shi'ites – and hundreds of millions of other Muslims – watching the confrontation play out on their television screens had little interest in the fine print of international law. Non-Muslims were laying siege to two of Islam's holiest places. It was as simple as that. Nothing else mattered. Juan Cole, a scholar of Shi'ite Islam, noted at the time:

> An Iraqi public might wince at the sight of AK-47 machine guns in a holy place, but many would also see the image as one of dedicated young Muslims fighting to protect their sacred space

against infidel encroachments. For them, Rumsfeld's photograph is not so much incriminating as it is a matter of pride.[41]

As U.S. armor rolled through Najaf's sacred Wadi al-Salam Cemetery – the Prophet Abraham's "Valley of Peace" – and jet fighters carried out air strikes less than 100 yards from Imam Hussein's shrine in Karbala, no less a figure than Iran's Supreme Leader Grand Ayatollah Ali Khamenei told followers, "The Americans have combined stupidity with shamelessness. They are audacious and unrestrained. They are encroaching upon the people's sanctities and what the people love."[42] Among the thousands of Iraqis who swarmed to the twin sacred cities bearing food and offering their lives were many Sunni Muslims, just as some Shi'ites in Baghdad's slums spoke of volunteering to join the Sunni defenders of Fallujah. The United States had achieved what so many had predicted it could never do: it had united Iraqi Shi'ites and Sunnis – against America.

WHOSE TRUTH?

By mid-May 2004, wide areas of Iraq were in open revolt. Shi'ite militants had seized control of Sadr City, the teeming Baghdad neighborhood named for Muqtada al-Sadr's father that was home to more than 2 million Shi'ites, and U.S. and British forces were locked in full-scale battles on the streets of the capital and key cities in the south. Massive suicide bombs became a daily occurrence; Iraqi Governing Council president Izz al-din Salim was blown apart as he entered the coalition headquarters in Baghdad. Each day brought ever more horrifying scenes of violence into homes across the Muslim world. Even those once inclined to support America's ouster of Saddam and condemn terrorism found it increasingly difficult to defend U.S. policy. One poll found that nine out of ten Iraqis now saw the Americans as occupiers, not liberators. "America's credibility in Iraq is hanging by a thread," said pollster Sadoun al Dulame. "It means the coalition forces are now seen as part of the problem, not the solution."[43] President Bush acknowledged as much in an off-the-cuff comment that left U.S. message managers wincing: "They're not happy they're occupied. I wouldn't be happy if I was occupied either."[44] The perception of an army of occupation using what Britain's conservative *Financial Times* called "disproportionate and reckless force"[45] was under-scored when U.S. troops virtually razed a village in western Iraq, killing more than 40 people. American officers claimed the target was an insurgent safe house, but Iraqi officials, aid workers and others at the scene said the dead, half of them women and children, were guests at a wedding party. Graphic footage of maimed children was transmitted around the world, with reporters reminding viewers that American troops had been involved in an identical wedding-party incident in Afghanistan.

Under siege in Iraq, U.S. officials continued to lash out at the messenger. Secretary of Defense Rumsfeld called al-Jazeera's reports "vicious, inaccurate and inexcusable"[46] and Secretary of State Colin Powell met with the foreign minister of Qatar, where al-Jazeera was based, for "very intense discussions" about the channel's "inflammatory" coverage that was making "the situation more tense, more inflamed and even more dangerous for Americans, for Iraqis, for Arabs."[47]

"We have been showing a lot of blood, there is no denying it," acknowledged al-Jazeera executive Maher Abdallah.

> Is it civilized to kill hundreds of thousands of people to civilize them, but uncivilized to show some of those dead? Will someone explain this to me? How can you kill hundreds of thousands to civilize them and you don't even bother to count the dead? Yet, you expect me to follow suit? When al-Jazeera shows a couple of pictures of dead and mutilated bodies, suddenly we are uncivilized.[48]

A month later, in a fit of pique seen in the Arab world as the height of hypocrisy, the Bush administration pointedly refused to invite Qatar's emir to a G-8 summit in Sea Island, Georgia specifically called to discuss proposals for democratizing the Middle East. Since ousting his aging father in a bloodless coup, Sheikh Hamad had rapidly implemented steps to move his country toward democracy, making Qatar one of the few countries in the region without direct government control of the media. A 2004 constitutional amendment had enshrined press freedom and Hamad had created the first largely independent television station in the Arab world. Now he was being snubbed for doing precisely what the United States was supposedly preaching – creating the structures of democracy. "It's strange, having a summit declaration on democratic reforms and not inviting a country because it has a free press," one diplomat wryly observed.[49]

The summit was a reminder of the extent to which each element of U.S. Middle East policy affected the others. In mid-April, the UN envoy tasked with forming an interim Iraqi administration complained that U.S. backing for Ariel Sharon was making his job in Iraq that much harder. "What I hear [from Iraqis] is that these Americans who are occupying us are the Americans who are giving blanket support to Israel to do whatever they like," said Lakhdar Brahimi:

> I think there is unanimity in the Arab world, and indeed in much of the rest of the world, that the Israeli policy is wrong, that Israeli policy is brutal, repressive, and that they are not interested in peace no matter what you seem to believe in America.[50]

"We don't agree," responded state Department spokesman Richard Boucher, who defended U.S. policy on Israel, then launched into an attack on al-Jazeera for its alleged "pattern of false reporting."[51] Whether *Washington* believed its support for Israel affected Iraqi attitudes was beside the point; the chief UN negotiator tasked with putting together an Iraqi government was telling U.S. officials *it did* – whether *they* liked it or not. The administration might have been able to

distract Americans by blaming the Arab media, but that
would not change the hard realities on the ground. "The
policies and choices of the White House should be revised
and not what the Arab satellite networks are saying," wrote
al-Hayat's political editor.[52]

Perceptions of U.S. policy also played a key role in undermining that G-8 summit from which Qatar was so noticeably
absent. On the table was President Bush's so-called Middle
East Partnership Initiative, a sweeping program to fund
democratic initiatives in the region. Even after the White
House reluctantly included language acknowledging the need
for renewed efforts to resolve the Israel–Palestine conflict,
many Arab leaders wanted no part of the gathering. Egyptian
president Hosni Mubarak said he was "furious" the United
States was trying to dictate to the Arab world. U.S. allies
Saudi Arabia, Jordan, Morocco, Kuwait and Pakistan all
boycotted the summit. Such bluster may well have masked a
desire to delay discussion of democracy on the part of leaders
grown comfortable with authoritarian rule. If so, U.S. tactics
had given them a ready excuse, for even Arabs supporters
of democratization objected to seeing it imposed from the
outside, particularly by those responsible for creating change
through the barrel of a gun in what they saw as a naked bid
to control Arab oil, dominate the region economically and
neuter the threat to Israel. "Why is there a sudden interest in
righting the wrongs of the Arab world? Why now?" asked
Galal Amin, a professor at the American University in Cairo.
His answer: American commitment to political change was a
self-serving recognition that the country's history of support
for dictators had backfired.[53]

The issue of perceptions even came into play around the
rash of beheadings that became the media event of choice for
Islamist insurgents as the spring of 2004 wore on. The horrifying images shocked Westerners, who saw such executions
as barbaric. There is little doubt the kidnappers knew the

bloody videos would both capture the headlines and send a shiver through foreigners working in Iraq. Yet a credible argument can also be made that they saw such a style of execution as highly symbolic; not only was it sanctioned by their interpretation of Islamic law, but it was the same penalty meted out by the hated House of Saud, client-state of the American occupiers.

"LIBERTY"

Two days before the scheduled transfer of power to the interim government of Iraq, U.S. and Iraqi officials met secretly in a room inside the heavily fortified "Green Zone" that housed the Coalition Provisional Authority and signed the documents that handed the trappings of government back to the Iraqis. American officials tried to put a positive spin on the hurried move, but Arabs saw it for what it was, an effort to preempt the expected convulsion of violence on the scheduled transfer date, June 30.

In Istanbul for a summit, President Bush learned the handover was complete when Condoleezza Rice handed him a note that said, "Mr. President, Iraq is sovereign." In response, Bush scribbled, "Let freedom reign!" At a news conference with ally Tony Blair a few hours later, the exultant president declared, "The Iraqi people have their country back."[54] It may have looked that way from where he stood, but not to those within shooting distance of the most powerful military force the Middle East had ever seen. Almost 140,000 foreign troops – predominently Americans – remained, with no plans to leave soon. The United States may have vociferously denied that Iraq was part of an imperial enterprise, but all of the symbols of empire were there for the world to see. "Nothing changes from the past," Iran's *Keyhan* said of the handover, except that the "hateful name of 'occupation forces' has changed to the demagogical name of 'multinational forces.'"[55] Or as a headline in Malaysia's *Utusan* newspaper put it, the "Invader Gets New Clothes."[56]

Not all the reaction was quite so negative. Arab leaders and political commentators generally welcomed what they called the "limited transfer of power" and expressed guarded support for the interim Allawi government, but there was little enthusiasm and even less confidence that Iraq would see true independence or stability in the short term. In some cases, the handover was damned with praise: "Having witnessed the way the allied forces stormed the country, overran major towns and took control of Baghdad last year, how many of us would have expected this power transfer to happen so soon?" asked the *Gulf Times*.[57] To others, it was a fait accompli that they had no choice but to accept. As one Jordanian political observer reminded al-Jazeera's viewers, if surrounding countries didn't do all they could to extinguish the fires of rebellion in Iraq, the "sparks could reach the neighbors themselves."[58] Undermining the new government in Baghdad would only foster regional instability. Warned *al-Hayat*'s editor in chief:

> Neighboring states should be aware that if they use Islamic extremists to undermine post-war Iraq, the outcome will be a rabid generation of militants similar to those Arab fighters who came back from Afghanistan after its liberation from the former Soviet Union. Such a generation would be a disaster to Arab countries.[59]

A year later, President Bush marked the second anniversary of the fall of Baghdad with a speech to U.S. troops in which he proclaimed the ouster of Saddam to be "one of the great moments in the history of liberty."[60] Seen through Arab eyes, the view was – inevitably – very different. As many as 100,000 Iraqi civilians were dead.[61] Fighting once more raged in Fallujah. Muqtada al-Sadr's militias again battled U.S. troops in the south. Terrorists threatened Arab and Western governments alike. Despite elections and talk of liberty, said one Iraqi political commentator, his countrymen continued to face the "usurpation of people's rights, confiscation of their lands and assumption of power over their lives, oppression and injustice for no crime committed or wrong done." To Arabs and their sympathizers in the farthest reaches of the Muslim world, it all looked depressingly familiar: "The Iraqi uprising and the way it is being dealt with by the occupying forces present an exact reflection of the criminal deeds committed by the Israeli occupiers against the Palestinians," said Saudi Arabia's *al-Watan*.[62]

The perception gap had never been wider.

Epilogue
Beyond Us *and* Them

Hate multiplies hate, violence multiplies violence, and toughness multiplies toughness in a descending spiral of destruction . . . .The chain reaction of evil – hate begetting hate, wars producing more wars – must be broken, or we shall be plunged into the dark abyss of annihilation.

Dr. Martin Luther King Jr. (1929–1968)

The red and white banners of Lebanon's anti-Syrian protests in the spring of 2005 were a testament to the transformational power of the Arab media revolution. The color scheme was made for TV by a team of Lebanese advertising executives who, like the tens of thousands who poured into the streets, were inspired by Ukraine's televised Orange Revolution. Arab television coverage of Lebanon in turn was helping to propel embryonic prodemocracy movements from Egypt to Bahrain, whose mantra *kifaya* (enough) became a media catchphrase.

Without al-Jazeera and the new constellation of Arab satellite broadcasters, it is unlikely there would ever have been a "Cedar Revolution," as a White House image-maker quickly dubbed the spontaneous protests that ended Syria's 29-year military presence in Lebanon. The assassination of popular former prime minister Rafiq Hariri was the spark that lit the fires of protest, but plenty of other Lebanese politicians had been murdered in the past, often at Syria's hands. Anyone protesting faced a similar fate. What was different this time was that the Arab world was watching. White House pressure on Syria played a role in giving the protestors a degree of political cover, but far more important was the presence of the Arab television cameras that broadcast every moment of the protests live across the Middle East. It was an unprecedented event: Arabs standing up to a dictatorial regime. Syria had once wiped out a significant portion of the population in one of its own rebellious cities. But that massacre had taken place far from the probing eyes of the world back in the days when Arab reporters did what they were told. Al-Jazeera had changed the rules of the game. The Syrian regime headed by the young Bashar al-Assad recognized that the new media landscape had altered geopolitical realities. So too, did Egyptian president Hosni Mubarak, who hired U.S.-trained Arab TV experts for the 2005 election campaign, the first in which he faced an opponent. Meanwhile, as it began its second term, the Bush administration was still failing miserably to adapt.

"Extraordinary changes in world communication have made international public opinion a key aspect of achieving American foreign policy objectives," according to the 2004 report from the U.S. Advisory Commission on Public Diplomacy.[1] Al-Jazeera was one of the most recognized brands in the world. It reached more than 40 million viewers. Its coverage of the U.S. political process, the elections in Iraq and Palestine, and the Lebanon protests was bursting stereotypes and inspiring change. Yet American officials persisted in attempting to isolate the channel, rather than embracing it. Continued American denunciations of al-Jazeera and other Arab media for providing a supposedly distorted view of the Iraq war and U.S. policy on Palestine sounded much like Nixon administration claims that the American media "lost Vietnam." What the Bush White House did not seem to recognize was that even if the emir of Qatar sold al-Jazeera or shut it down, the genie was out of the bottle. The Arab media would never be the same again.

DEFINING AMERICA

Whether it was through the lens of al-Jazeera and its competitors or the pages of newspapers in Jeddah or Jakarta, the vision of America as seen by Arab and Muslim audiences remained a grim one. A divided populace at home had opened space for more critical coverage of U.S. Middle East policy in the American media, yet that had done little to change the way Americans perceived Arabs and Muslims. And as it persisted in stereotyping them, the United States continued to stereotype itself.

America's newfound enthusiasm for Arab democracy was cautiously welcomed in the region, yet few were willing to forget that the United States had long propped up most of the regimes it was suddenly trying to reform. The perception of hypocrisy did not end there. As the United States was lecturing the world on human rights, it was sending detainees to Egypt, Syria, Pakistan, Uzbekistan and other countries where they could be tortured. While it demanded that Iran give up its nuclear ambitions, America said nothing of Israel's bombs. While it criticized Indonesia for failing to adequately crack down on extremists, it refused access to the witnesses who would have strengthened the government's case in trials of suspected militants. The same administration that screamed so loudly when Iraqi TV showed American POWs, now touted as great public diplomacy an al-Iraqiya reality show in which captured insurgents begged for their lives. And so it went. Meanwhile, Muslims were dying in unprecedented numbers.

"At a time when rumor and myth reach mass audiences in seconds, communicating with foreign publics is vital to the success of our foreign policy," Karen Hughes, President Bush's nominee as undersecretary of state for public diplomacy and public affairs, told her Senate confirmation hearing.[2] Missing from the comment was any acknowledgment that it wasn't just "rumor and myth" that reached audiences in seconds, but also the often-bloody realities of U.S. policy.

The radical Islamists were communicating their version of those realities with ever more sophisticated media techniques. Bin Laden urged followers to mount an education campaign in Europe to take advantage of public opposition to the war in Iraq. "They can make use of the huge potential of the media," he told followers.[3] He also took the first steps toward reinventing his media image, twice proposing cease-fires and explaining that he only turned to violence after watching the 1982 Israeli invasion of Lebanon and subsequent U.S. war with Lebanese Muslims. "I couldn't forget those moving scenes, blood and severed limbs, women and children sprawled everywhere. Houses destroyed along with their occupants and high rises demolished over their residents, rockets raining down on our home without mercy," bin Laden said in a late 2004 video addressed directly to the American people.

> I say to you that security is an indispensable pillar of human life and that free men do not forfeit their security, contrary to Bush's claim that we hate freedom . . . We fight because we are free men who don't sleep under oppression.

The al-Qaeda leader expressed amazement that despite his repeated efforts to explain, Americans still didn't understand "the real causes" of 9/11, "And thus, the reasons are still there for a repeat of what occurred." Abandoning the fiery rhetoric and religious imagery of the past, bin Laden told Americans, "Your security is in your own hands. And every state that doesn't play with *our* security has automatically guaranteed its *own* security."[4] The tape was a propaganda masterstroke, deftly leveraging the dual nature of media in the age of al-Jazeera. Though ostensibly addressed to the American people, the reasonable tone was first and foremost designed to appeal to mainstream Muslims who might not support terrorism but who were growing increasingly bitter at scenes of Arab bloodshed playing out on their television screens every day. This new face of bin Laden as diplomat aided his continued transition from militant commander to the inspirational figurehead for a broad political movement built on a sophisticated understanding of media power. His military capabilities may have been blunted, but his ability to inspire and motivate through the media remained as dangerous as ever. That was evident with each new suicide bombing by disparate groups whose only connection to bin Laden came through a television screen or Internet site.

Bin Laden was not alone in recognizing the media's potential. Captured *jihadi* handbooks contained whole sections on media strategies, including such detailed instructions as how to manage the 24-hour news cycle for maximum impact. Abu Musab al-Zarqawi, the Jordanian-born Islamist insurgent leader in Iraq, began publishing his own Internet magazine, *Zurwat al Sanam* (*Top of the Camel's Hump*), with articles such as "What is al-Qaeda in Mesopotamia?", obituaries of "martyred" fighters and photographs of Bush and bin Laden. Zarqawi's efforts were supplemented by those of another group that called itself the Jihadist Information Brigade. "We, the media department of al-Qaeda in Mesopotamia, declare that we have our own means of publication and that we observe the accuracy and truth of our statements," Zarqawi's group said in one statement denying responsibility for a suicide attack.[5] And just as the Bush administration complained about skewed media coverage of Iraq, so too did the *jihadis*. "Where are the media correspondents in Iraq, and where is the media coverage in Mosul, Anbar, Diyala, Samarra, Basra, and southern Baghdad?" Zarqawi's group asked.[6] At times, it seemed the *jihadis* were matching the American media effort strategy for strategy.

Al-Qaeda's shift from an operational to an inspirational role was driven home by the emergence of the Global Islamic

Media Front (GIMF), which billed itself as the heir to the World Islamic Front for the Jihad Against Jews and Crusaders and proudly proclaimed itself to be an organization that "knows no boundaries."

"Unite, O Muslims of the world, behind the Global Islamic Media Front," its head, who billed himself as Salaheddin II, exhorted followers on a network of Internet sites. "Set up squadrons of media jihad to break Zionist control over the media and terrorize the enemies."[7]

The increased sophistication of the militants' ability to spread their message – combined with saturation coverage of U.S. policy on Arab television – had a predictable result: a continued rise in anti-American terrorism. According to the State Department's own figures, there were 624 "significant" terrorist attacks in 2004, more than triple the previous year.[8] And that did not include Iraq, where attacks were taking place at the rate of up to 70 a day. Those figures were never officially made public. Instead, for the first time since the State Department began issuing its annual *Patterns of Global Terrorism* report, the document was sent to Capitol Hill stripped of all statistics. Then the entire system of compiling the statistics was revised, making it all but impossible to compare figures against previous years. Once more, the Bush administration met uncomfortable realities by employing sleight-of-hand in the media.

LISTENING TO THE WORLD

A forest of trees has been felled to print the mountain of recommendations on the future of America's relationship with the Muslim world issued by think tanks, universities and the government itself. They all reach the same conclusion: America is badly losing the war of ideas. As the Pentagon acknowledged, "Interests collide. Leadership counts. Policies matter. Mistakes dismay our friends and provide enemies with unintentional assistance. Strategic communication is not *the* problem, but it is *a* problem."[9]

There *were* positive signs. As it launched its second term, the Bush administration appeared to be moderating its tone. There was a new recognition of the importance of dialogue. An 11 per cent increase for public diplomacy spending in the administration's 2006 budget was a step in the right direction, but in current dollars, the public diplomacy budget was still less than it was in the mid-1990s and the bulk of the money remained focused on Europe. Another positive sign came from Indonesia, where the massive influx of U.S. aid following the December 2004 tsunami caused some Indonesians to reconsider their negative attitudes toward the United States.[10] Few who knew Southeast Asia expected Indonesian views of U.S. foreign policy to change, but the tenuous shift demonstrated that it might still be possible to return to a time when Muslims separated their feelings about *Americans* from their feelings about *American policy*. However, a few ill-chosen words could reverse such gains, as demonstrated by President Bush's boast that Indonesians "see a different America now,"[11] which simply fed suspicions the aid was an attempt to buy goodwill.

Make no mistake: money *can* help to buy hearts and minds. The Marshall Plan in post-World War II Europe proved that. The fact that poverty prevails in the Middle East and non-Arab Muslim countries is without a doubt a contributing cause of terrorism. The Bush administration's Greater Middle East Partnership Initiative, a multibillion-dollar effort to promote democracy, build a knowledge society and expand economic opportunities should be welcomed, but it also should have been launched in conjunction *with* the so-called war on terror, not deep in its wake. Nor should U.S. officials think that money alone can distract from other policies that are anathema to the world's Muslims. Why do they hate us? First and foremost, to paraphrase the old

Clinton campaign slogan, it's the policy, stupid. But even if those policies are moderated, U.S. efforts to reconnect with the world's Muslims cannot be successful until Washington adjusts to the changed global information landscape. New electronic government mouthpieces like al-Hurra are not the answer. American democracy is built on a free – though often flawed – independent media. Audiences in the Middle East already have access to a wide assortment of credible U.S. programming, if they want it. "We're being assailed with American media. It's everywhere all at once," the author of a popular Baghdad-based web log observed.[12] Instead of wasting hundreds of millions of dollars on government-owned television and radio channels that carry little credibility, the United States should expand its funding for nongovernmental organizations that are building civil society in the Muslim world. And Americans should have the opportunity to watch what *they* watch. Al-Jazeera's new English channel should be given a home on U.S. cable so Americans who are curious can at least have the opportunity to witness events through the Arab lens. They can hate it, they can curse at it, but at least they will understand there is a different view.

Cooperation must replace confrontation. The United States must listen as much as it speaks. Mosques, schools and neighborhood or village gatherings are all places where opinion is shaped. Those venues must be tapped. Instead of focusing on the structures through which messages are communicated, the United States should be concerned with the *content* of the messages themselves. Instead of banning Qatar's emir from democracy-building conferences, America should be embracing him as one of the few Arab leaders actively taking steps toward democracy. Instead of denouncing al-Jazeera for its aggressive coverage of U.S. policy, Washington should be flooding its airwaves with spokespeople fluent in Arabic. Instead of blacklisting Arab journalists, the

U.S. should support programs that enhance their professional skills. Instead of playing "our" media off against "theirs," America should facilitate dialogues between reporters from the United States and the Muslim world. Instead of undermining U.S. credibility with duplicitous Psyops schemes, the United States should forge a cohesive, nonpartisan national public diplomacy strategy informed by deep regional expertise, crafted by communications experts and coordinated by those who understand the big picture of U.S. foreign policy goals. Public diplomacy is too important to leave to individual officers in the field or those who learned about the Middle East by watching *Lawrence of Arabia*. Abu Ghraib demonstrated that American foreign policy can be crippled by the lowliest grunt. Likewise, as various studies have recommended, a quasi-independent Corporation for Public Diplomacy should be considered. Policy *does* matter, but structures must also be established to ensure that a dialogue continues no matter who occupies the White House or whatever the policy of the day.

This is not just about being popular or doing the "right thing" – though both of those would be nice. There are real economic and human costs to America's failure to communicate. The United States has carried the $5 billion a month price tag of the Iraq war virtually alone because it failed to convince allies the invasion was justified. Turkish public opinion prevented U.S. ground troops from crossing into northern Iraq, forcing U.S. commanders to scrap a pincher strategy that might have shortened the war and saved lives. And the pool of *jihadist* recruits is expanding every day. "Our inability to seize the initiative in the 'War of Ideas' with al-Qaeda is perhaps our most significant shortcoming so far in the war against terrorism," Secretary of Defense Rumsfeld once admitted. New headlines every day bear that out.

The United States can no longer say one thing and do another. Strategic communications begins with thinking before speaking. Officials must put every word and action to the perception test, asking themselves, "How will it be heard and seen in the rest of the world?" That does not mean the United States should allow foreign public opinion to dictate its policies. However, American officials must at least be conscious in advance of the impact specific policies will have so that decisions are based on a comprehensive understanding of the long-term strategic implications rather than the product of blinkered, wishful thinking. The United States has always been willing to make strategic compromises when it comes to geopolitical realities. Policymaking in the age of al-Jazeera should be no different.

The new global media environment means information can no longer be "managed." Actions can no longer be hidden. A single *Newsweek* magazine story about the desecration of the Qur'an by interrogators at Guantanamo Bay sparked violent protests across the Muslim world. American officials can no longer devalue and dehumanize, no longer pander to domestic constituencies and expect the world not to notice, no longer blame the messenger for their own mistakes. Slick ads and clever comic books are counterproductive. The United States is not a brand. It represents a set of ideas to be shared – not imposed. Americans must reach out to the majority of the world's Muslims with respect and equality; break down the distinction between *Us* and *Them*; learn to communicate in an era in which the United States no longer writes the script.

Until then, Americans and the world's Muslims will each continue to view the other through a bloodshot lens. And innocent people on both sides will continue to die.

Acknowledgments

Like my own worldview, this book is a product of three decades of interactions with countless individuals in dozens of countries. Grocers and militants, journalists and intelligence chiefs, taxi drivers and heads of state. Some I remember with fondness and gratitude, some with disdain. Many I do not consciously remember at all. They all have my thanks.

Thanks also to the Marsh family whose endowment made possible the two-year appointment at the University of Michigan during which this book was written, and to Michael Traugott, then head of the Communications Studies Department, who selected me for the visiting chair that carries the Howard R. Marsh name. Mike and the permanent faculty of the department always made me feel welcome. My time at Michigan was made all the richer by my other academic homes on campus, the Center for Middle East and North African Studies, the Center for Southeast Asian Studies and the Gerald R. Ford School of Public Policy. Thanks particularly to Marcia Inhorn and Charley Sullivan, friends and academic guides. Likewise to Scott Atran, who graciously welcomed me as a colleague from our first meeting and whose insights into the psychology of terrorism, grounded in the real world, added an important new dimension to my understanding of the phenomenon. Amy Robb was of invaluable help in locating documents that seemed to have disappeared into the ether of the university's impressive but sometimes complex labyrinth of electronic databases.

This book began life as a dissertation. Gary Bunt, my advisor in the Islamic Studies program at the University of Wales, Lampeter, played a crucial role in helping me to bridge the worlds of journalism and academia. He not only ensured the scholarship was rigorous, but also helped a reporter find his academic voice without losing his own.

And then, of course, there is my family. A few words on an acknowledgments page cannot begin to convey my gratitude to them. Aside from being a loving wife and partner, Indira is my eternal reality check, always reminding me when my American slip is showing. I love her more than I can say. Our children Annya, Shantara and Justin continue to amaze me with their ability to adapt to our peripatetic lifestyle, global citizens always ready for the next adventure. My thanks to them for putting up with all the cancelled "Daddy days," the afternoons when I couldn't shoot hoops or kick a ball around and all the times they gave me "just a few more minutes" to complete a thought, or a paragraph, or a page. They constantly make me so proud.

Notes and References

PREFACE

1. Sanger, David. "On High-Speed Trip, Bush Glimpses a Perception Gap." *New York Times*, October 25, 2003.
2. "Kuala Lumpur Declaration on International Terrorism." Kuala Lumpur, April 3, 2002.
3. Liu, Melinda. "The Mahathir Mystique." *Newsweek*, November 3, 2003: 32.
4. Doherty, Carroll. "Mistrust of Americans in Europe Ever Higher." In *Pew Global Attitudes Project*, edited by Andrew Kohut. Washington, D.C.: Pew Research Center for the People and the Press, 2004. 42.
5. "The 9/11 Commission Report: Final Report of the National Commission on Terrorist Attacks Upon the United States." New York: W.W. Norton, 2004.
6. McLuhan, Marshall, and Quentin Fiore. *The Medium Is the Massage.* New York: Random House, 1967. 67.
7. "The War on Terrorism: Terrorism FAQs." Central Intelligence Agency, 2002 (cited February 28, 2004). <http://www.cia.gov/terrorism/faqs.html>.
8. Hoffman, Bruce. *Inside Terrorism.* New York: Columbia University Press, 1998. 43.
9. Al-Sayyid, Mustapha Kamel. "The Other Face of the Islamist Movement." In *Working Papers, Global Policy Program*, edited by Marina Ottaway. Washington, D.C.: Carnegie Endowment for International Peace, 2003. 28.
10. Bin Sayeed, Khalid. "American Dominance and Political Islam." Paper presented at the Conference on Political Islam and the West. Nicosia, Cyprus, October 1997.
11. Esposito, John L. *Unholy War: Terror in the Name of Islam.* Oxford and New York: Oxford University Press, 2002. 55.
12. Fuller, Graham E. *The Future of Political Islam* (first edition). New York: Palgrave Macmillan, 2003. xi.
13. Ibid. xii.
14. Eickelman, Dale F., and James P. Piscatori. *Muslim Politics.* Princeton, N.J.: Princeton University Press, 1996.

INTRODUCTION

1. Lewis, C.S. *The Magician's Nephew.* London: Bodley Head, 1955. 125.
2. Wallace, Anthony F.C. *Culture and Personality* (second edition). New York: Random House, 1970.

3. Kuipers, Ronald A. "Toward a Peaceable Mosaic of Worldviews and Religions." Paideia Project, Boston University, 1998 (cited December 13, 2003). <http://www.bu.edu/wcp/Papers/Reli/ReliKuip.htm>.

4. Naugle, David K. *Worldview: The History of a Concept*. Grand Rapids, Mich.: Eerdmans, 2002. xvii.

5. Roosevelt, Theodore. "The Roosevelt Corollary to the Monroe Doctrine." U.S. National Archives and Records Administration, 1904 (cited March 8, 2005). <http://www.theodore-roosevelt.com/trmdcorollary.html>.

6. Eisenhower, Dwight D. "Inaugural Address of President Eisenhower." History Central, January 20, 1953 (cited June 6, 2004). <http://www.multied.com/documents/Eisenhower.html>.

7. Kennedy, John F. "American University Speech." June 10, 1963 (cited June 5, 2004). <http://www.usembassy.de/usa/etexts/speeches/rhetoric/jfkuniv.htm>.

8. Jefferson, Thomas. "The Declaration of Independence." Library of Congress, National Archives, 1776 (cited June 5, 2004). <http://www.archives.gov/national_archives_experience/declaration.html>.

9. Johnson, Lyndon B. "Annual Message to the Congress on the State of the Union." Lyndon Baines Johnson Library and Museum, 1967 (cited June 8, 2004). <http://www.lbjlib.utexas.edu/johnson/archives.hom/speeches.hom/670110.asp>.

10. Winthrop, John. "City Upon a Hill." 1630 (cited June 7, 2004). <http://classiclit.about.com/library/weekly/aa112600a.htm>.

11. Reagan, Ronald. "City Upon a Hill: The President at the First Annual CPAC Conference." January 25, 1974 (cited June 6, 2004). <http://www.presidentreagan.info/speeches/city_upon_a_hill.cfm>.

12. Nunberg, Geoffrey. *Going Nucular: Language, Politics, and Culture in Confrontational Times*. (first edition). New York: Public Affairs, 2004. 57.

13. Kennedy. "American University Speech."

14. Anthony, Carl Sferrazza. "CNN Newsnight with Aaron Brown." New York: CNN, June 7, 2004.

15. Cigar, Norman. "Nationalist Serbian Intellectuals and Islam." In *The New Crusades: Constructing the Muslim Enemy*, edited by Emran Qureshi and Michael Anthony Sells. New York: Columbia University Press, 2003. 321.

16. Broyles, William. "Why Me? Why Them?" *New York Times*, May 26, 1986, 19.

17. Kennan, G.F. "The Gorbachev Prospect: Review of *New Thinking for Our Country and the World*, by Mikhail Gorbachev." *New York Review of Books* 34, no. 3 (1988): 6–7.

18. Mack, John E. "The Enemy System." *Lancet* (1988): 385–7.

19. Said, Edward W. *Orientalism* (first Vintage Books edition). New York: Vintage Books, 1979. 12.

20. Ibid. 3–4.

21. Said, Edward W. *Covering Islam: How the Media and the Experts Determine How We See the Rest of the World*. New York: Vintage Books, 1997. xxii.

22. Foucault, Michel, Luther H. Martin, Huck Gutman and Patrick H. Hutton. *Technologies of the Self*. Amherst: University of Massachusetts Press, 1988.

23. JanMohamed, Abdul R., and David Lloyd. *The Nature and Context of Minority Discourse*. New York: Oxford University Press, 1990.

24. Ajami, Fouad. *The Dream Palace of the Arabs: A Generation's Odyssey* (first edition). New York: Pantheon Books, 1998.

25. Gerges, Fawaz A. *America and Political Islam*. Cambridge and New York: Cambridge University Press, 1999.

26. "Muslim Official Raps Islamic World." BBC News, June 14, 2004 (cited June 14, 2004). <http://news.bbc.co.uk/2/hi/europe/3805649.stm>.

27. Gregorian, Vartan. *Islam: A Mosaic, Not a Monolith*. Washington, D.C.: Brookings Institution Press, 2003. 2.

28. Sarwar, Ghulam. *Islam: Beliefs and Teachings*. Nottingham: The Muslim Educational Trust, 2000. 13.

29. Ibid.

30. Qu'tb, Sayyid. *Milestones* (revised translation). Indianapolis: American Trust, 1993. 64.

31. Ibid. 64–5.

32. Ibid. 89.

33. Ibid. 62.

34. Eickelman, Dale F., and James P. Piscatori. *Muslim Politics*. Princeton, N.J.: Princeton University Press, 1996. 16.

35. Tibi, Bassam. *The Challenge of Fundamentalism*. Berkeley, Los Angeles and London: University of California Press, 2002. 6.

36. Zurcher, Erik Jan. "The Vocabulary of Muslim Nationalism." *International Journal of Social Language* 137 (1999): 81.

37. Geertz, Clifford. *The Interpretation of Cultures: Selected Essays*. New York: Basic Books, 1973.

38. Juergensmeyer, Mark. *Terror in the Mind of God*. Berkeley, Los Angeles and London: University of California Press, 2000. 10.

39. Gellner, Ernest. *Nations and Nationalism*. Ithaca: Cornell University Press, 1983.

40. Little, David. "Belief, Ethnicity and Nationalism." *Nationalism and Ethnic Politics* 1, no. 1 (1995).

41. Pfaff, William. *The Wrath of Nations: Civilization and the Furies of Nationalism*. New York: Simon & Schuster, 1993.

CHAPTER 1

1. Heilbrunn, Jacob. "The Cool Zionist." *Washington Monthly* 35, no. 7/8: 56.

2. Schafer, David. "Triumph and Catastrophe: Origins of the Israeli/Palestinian Conflict." *Humanist* 62, no. 6: 22.

3. Ovendale, Ritchie. "The Origins of the Arab–Israeli Conflict." *Historian*, no. 76: 20.

4. Neff, Donald. "Truman Overrode Strong State Department Warning against Partitioning of Palestine in 1947." American Educational Trust, October 1994 (cited March 11, 2005). <http://www.washington-report.org/backissues/0994/9409074.htm>.

5. Ratnesar, Romesh. "The Dawn of Israel." *Time* 161, no. 13: A27.

6. Oren, Michael B. "Does the U.S. Finally Understand Israel?" *Commentary* 114, no. 1: 33.

7. Ibid.

8. Gerges, Fawaz A. "The 1967 Arab–Israeli War: U.S. Actions and Arab Perceptions." In *The Middle East and the United States*, edited by David W. Lesch. Boulder, Colo.: Westview Press, 1996. 189.

9. Ibid. 190–1.

10. "U.S. Vetoes of UN Resolutions Critical of Israel." Jewish Virtual Library, March 2004 (cited July 30, 2004). <http://www.jewishvirtuallibrary.org/jsource/UN/usvetoes.html>.

11. Ovendale. "Origins."

12. Findley, Paul. *They Dare to Speak Out: People and Institutions Confront Israel's Lobby*. Westport, Conn.: Lawrence Hill, 1985. 121.

13. Ibid. vi.

14. Ibid.

15. Oren. "Israel."

16. Dechter, Gadi. "President Kerry on Israel." United Press International, 2004 (cited July 9, 2004). <http://www.upi.com/view.cfm?StoryID=20040709-042549-2017r>.

17. Kerry, John. "An Unwavering Commitment to Reforming the Middle East." *Forward*, August 25, 2004 (cited August 29, 2004). <http://www.forward.com/main/article.php?ref=kerry200408251051>.

18. Gauhar, Humayun. "America Is Its Own Worst Enemy." *Nation*, September 30, 2001.

19. "*Soros Blames U.S., Israel for Anti-Semitism*." 2003. <http://worldnetdaily.com/news/article.asp?ARTICLE_ID=35535>.

20. Chesnoff, Richard. "Syrian Prez Goes Nazi." *New York Daily News*, May 28, 2001. 23.

21. Friedman, Thomas L. "After the Storm." *New York Times*, January 8, 2003. A23.

22. Quoted in Kidd, Thomas S. " 'Is It Worse to Follow Mahomet Than the Devil?' Early American Uses of Islam." *Church History* 72, no. 4 (2003): 766.

23. Ibid.

24. Ibid.

25. Ibid.

26. See Friedlander, Dov, and Calvin Goldscheider. "Israel's Population: The Challenge of Pluralism." *Population Bulletin* 39, no. 2 (1984): 3–39.

27. Conversation with the author. Ann Arbor, Mich., October 5, 2004.

28. Albright, Madeleine K. 'Informal talk.' Ann Arbor, Mich., March 12, 2004.

29. Mishkhas, Abeer. "Arabs, West Must Overcome Mutual Stereotypes." *Daily Star*, June 15, 2004.

30. Interview with the author. Dearborn, Mich., 2003.

31. Halliday, Fred. *Islam and the Myth of Confrontation*. London and New York: I.B. Tauris, 2003. viii–ix.

32. Tessler, Mark. "Arab and Muslim Political Attitudes." *International Studies Perspectives* 4 (2003): 175–80.

33. ABC News and Films for the Humanities. *Why the Hate? America, from a Muslim Point of View* (video cassette). Princeton, N.J., Films for the Humanities and Sciences, 2002.

34. Zorthian, Barry. "Public Diplomacy Is Not the Answer." Public Diplomacy News File (Listserv), June 7, 2004 (cited 2004).

35. Mekay, Emad. "Alienation Cuts Both Ways." Global Information Network, February 26, 2002.

36. Ibid.

37. "Finding America's Voice: A Strategy for Reinvigorating U.S. Public Diplomacy." New York: Council on Foreign Relations, 2003.

38. Email to the author. Ann Arbor, Mich., 2004.

39. Sardar, Ziauddin, and Merryl Wyn Davies. *Why Do People Hate America?* Cambridge: Icon, 2002. 171–2.

40. Singh, Patwant. *The World According to Washington: An Asian View.* Cheltenham: Understanding Global Issues, 2004. 9.

41. *Timeline: Birth of a Superpower, Christian Science Monitor*, August, 2003 (cited June 6, 2004). <http://www.csmonitor.com/specials/neocon/timeline/>.

42. Lesch, David W. *The Middle East and the United States: A Historical and Political Reassessment* (third edition). Boulder, Colo.: Westview Press, 2003.

43. Sardar and Davies. *Hate.* 197.

44. Bush, George W. "Remarks by the President in Photo Opportunity with the National Security Team." White House, September 12, 2001. <http://www.whitehouse.gov/news/releases/2001/09/20010912-4.html>.

45. Roy, Arundhati. "The Algebra of Infinite Justice." *Guardian*, September 29, 2001. 1.

46. Ameli, Saied Reza. "Muslim Response to Globalization." 1999 (cited February 2, 2004). <http://www.inminds.co.uk/globalisation-muslim-response.html>.

47. "Arab Big Brother Show Suspended." BBC News, March 1, 2004 (cited March 1, 2004). <http://news.bbc.co.uk/go/pr/fr/-/2/hi/middle_east/3522897.stm>.

48. "Kuwait Bans Concerts Involving Women Entertainers." Arab News (AFP), May 25, 2004 (cited July 6, 2004). <http://arabnews.com/?page=4&section=0&article=45598&d=25&m=5&y=2004>.

49. Quoted in Bodansky, Yossef. *Bin Laden: The Man Who Declared War on America.* Rocklin, Calif.: Forum, 1999.

50. "Ummah Should Seek Guidance from Qur'an, Sunnah." Jamaat-E-Islami Pakistan, December 6, 2003 (cited January 9, 2004). <http://www.jamaat.org/news/pr120603.html>.

51. Haddad, Yvonne Yazbeck. "Islamist Perceptions of US Policy in the Near East." In *The Middle East and the United States: A Historical and Political Reassessment*, edited by David W. Lesch. Boulder, Colo.: Westview Press, 1996. 424.

52. Qu'tb, Sayyid. *Milestones* (revised translation). Indianapolis: American Trust, 1993. 119.

53. Ibid. 120.

54. Ahmed, Akbar S. *Living Islam: From Samarkand to Stornoway.* New York: Facts on File, 1994.

CHAPTER 2

1. Said, Edward W. *Covering Islam: How the Media and the Experts Determine How We See the Rest of the World*. New York: Vintage Books, 1997. li.

2. Shaheen, Jack G. *The TV Arab*. Bowling Green, Ohio: Bowling Green State University Popular Press, 1984. 4.

3. Suleiman, Michael W. "American Mass Media and the June Conflict." In *The Arab–Israeli Confrontation of June 1967: An Arab Perspective*, edited by Ibrahim A. Abu-Lughod. Evanston, Ill.: Northwestern University Press, 1970. 9–30.

4. Said. *Covering Islam*. 109.

5. Ahmed, Akbar S. *Postmodernism and Islam: Predicament and Promise*. London and New York: Routledge, 1992. 186.

6. Said. *Covering Islam*. xvi.

7. Ghareeb, Edmund. *Split Vision: The Portrayal of Arabs in the American Media* (revised and expanded edition). Washington, D.C.: American–Arab Affairs Council, 1983. 186.

8. Ibid. 5.

9. Terry, Janice J. "A Content Analysis of American Newspapers." In *The Arab World: From Nationalism to Revolution*, edited by Fauzi M. Najjar. Wilmette, Ill.: Medina University Press, 1971.

10. See Belkaoui, Janice Monti. "Images of Arabs and Israelis in the Prestige Press, 1966–1974." *Journalism Quarterly* 55 (Winter 1979): 732–8. And Mousa, Issam Suleiman. *The Arab Image in the US Press*. New York: P. Lang, 1984. And Suleiman. "Mass Media."

11. Chafets, Ze'ev. *Double Vision: How the Press Distorts America's View of the Middle East* (first edition). New York: Morrow, 1985.

12. Patai, Raphael. *The Arab Mind*. New York: Scribner, 1976.

13. Lewis, Bernard. *The Political Language of Islam*. Chicago: University of Chicago Press, 1988. 16.

14. Pipes, Daniel. *In the Path of God: Islam and Political Power*. New York: Basic Books, 1983. 179.

15. Said. *Covering Islam*. xvi.

16. Ibid. xxviii.

17. Ibid. 150.

18. Ibid. xi.

19. Mousa. *Arab Image*. 171.

20. Quoted in Tugend, Alina. "Explaining the Rage." *American Journalism Review* 23, no. 10 (2001): 24–8.

21. Mishkhas, Abeer. "Arabs, west must overcome mutual stereotypes." *Daily Star*, June 15, 2004.

22. Said. *Covering Islam*. 108.

23. Goudsouzian, Tanya. "Arab World through the Eyes of the Western Media." Gulf News, April 29, 2002 (cited August 5, 2003). <http://www.gulf-news.com/Articles/news.asp?ArticleID=49382>.

24. "Anti-Islam in the Media." Canadian Islamic Congress. Toronto, 2002. <http://canadianislamiccongress.com/rr/rr_2002_1.php#_Toc32912620>.

25. Karim, Karim H. *The Islamic Peril: Media and Global Violence*. Montreal and New York: Black Rose Books, 2000. 10.

26. Ibid. 9.

27. Noor, F. A. "The Evolution of 'Jihad' in an Islamist Political Discourse." Social Science Research Council, 2001. <http://www.ssrc.org/sept11/essays/noor.htm>.

28. Netanyahu, Binyamin. *Terrorism: How the West Can Win* (first edition). New York: Farrar Straus Giroux, 1986.

29. "Lost in the Terrorist Theater." *Harper's*, October 1984.

30. Hoffman, Bruce. *Inside Terrorism*. New York: Columbia University Press, 1998.

31. "Terrorist Theater."

32. McAlister, Melani. *Epic Encounters: Culture, Media, and U.S. Interests in the Middle East, 1945–2000*. Berkeley, Los Angeles and London: University of California Press, 2001. 222.

33. Schmid, Alex Peter. "Editors' Perspectives." In *Terrorism and the Media*, edited by David L. Paletz and Alex Peter Schmid. Newbury Park, Calif.: Sage, 1992. 111–36.

34. Ibid.

35. Friedlander, Robert. "Coping with Terrorism." In *Terrorism: Theory and Practice*, edited by Yonah Alexander, David Carlton and Paul Wilkinson. Boulder, Colo.: Westview Press, 1979. 212–22.

36. Hachten, William A., and James Francis Scotton. *The World News Prism: Global Media in an Era of Terrorism* (sixth edition). Ames: Iowa State Press, 2002. 57.

37. "A World Transformed: Foreign Policy Attitudes of the U.S. Public after September 11." Chicago: The Chicago Council on Foreign Relations and the German Marshall Fund of the United States, 2002. 11.

38. Pape, Robert A. "The Strategic Logic of Suicide Terrorism." *American Political Science Review* 97, no. 3 (2003): 345–60.

39. Alali, A. Odasuo, and Gary W. Byrd. *Terrorism and the News Media: A Selected, Annotated Bibliography*. Jefferson, N.C.: McFarland, 1994. 11.

40. "American Sympathy toward Israel and the Arabs/Palestinians." American–Israeli Cooperative Enterprise, 2004. <http://www.us-israel.org/jsource/US-Israel/polls.html>.

41. Altschull, J. Herbert. "What is News?" *Mass Comm Review* (December 1974).

42. Koppel, Ted. "Terrorism and the Media: A Discussion." *Harper's*, October 1984. 47.

43. Entman, Robert M. "Framing U.S. Coverage of International News." *Journal of Communication* 41, no. 4 (1993): 6–28.

44. Norris, Pippa, Montague Kern, and Marion R. Just. *Framing Terrorism: The News Media, the Government, and the Public*. New York: Routledge, 2003.

45. Shoemaker, Pamela J., and Stephen D. Reese. *Mediating the Message: Theories of Influences on Mass Media Content* (second edition). New York: Longman, 1996. 219.

46. Norris, Kern and Just. *Framing Terrorism*. 11.

47. Seib, Philip M. *The Global Journalist: News and Conscience in a World of Conflict*. Lanham, Md.: Rowman & Littlefield, 2002. 11.

48. Bush, George W. "Address to a Joint Session of Congress and the American People." White House, September 20, 2001. <http://www.whitehouse.gov/news/releases/2001/09/20010920-8.html>.

49. Allport, Gordon W. *The Nature of Prejudice* (abridged edition). Garden City, N.Y.: Doubleday, 1958.

50. Sciolino, Elaine. "Seeing Green; the Red Menace is Gone. But Here's Islam." *New York Times*, January 21, 1996, 4.1.

51. Aislin. "In the Name of Islamic Extremism." *Montreal Gazette*, 2002 (cited August 5, 2003). <http://www.aislin.com/IMAGES/ISLAMIC-18th.jpg>.

52. Seib, Gerald F. "U.S. Vs. Islam: Ending a Myth Is Hard to Do." *Wall Street Journal*, October 24, 2001, A24.

53. Jamieson, Kathleen Hall, and Paul Waldman. *The Press Effect: Politicians, Journalists, and the Stories That Shape the Political World*. Oxford and New York: Oxford University Press, 2003. 151.

54. McChesney, Robert Waterman, and John Nichols. *Our Media, Not Theirs: The Democratic Struggle against Corporate Media*. New York: Seven Stories, 2002. 91.

55. Kurtz, Howard. "CNN Chief Orders 'Balance' in War News." *Washington Post*, October 31, 2001. C1.

56. Ibid.

57. "Report on International News Coverage in America." U.S.: The Southern Center for International Affairs, 2003.

58. Entman, Robert M. *Projections of Power: Framing News, Public Opinion, and U.S. Foreign Policy*. Chicago: University of Chicago Press, 2004. 2.

59. Anderson, Benedict. *Imagined Communities: Reflections on the Origin and Spread of Nationalism* (second edition). London and New York: Verso, 1991.

60. Hess, Stephen, and Marvin L. Kalb. *The Media and the War on Terrorism*. Washington, D.C.: Brookings Institution Press, 2003. 146.

61. McAlister. *Epic Encounters*. 270.

62. Waisbord, Silvio. "Journalism, Risk, and Patriotism." In *Journalism after September 11*, edited by Barbie Zelizer and Stuart Allan. London and New York: Routledge, 2002. 216.

63. Welch, Maureen, Joseph Campbell, Tyler Foster and Michael Alley. "Media's Role in Shaping Public Opinion on the War in Iraq." Oklahoma City: Department of Defense, Joint Program in Communication, University of Oklahoma, 2003.

64. Johnson, Reed. "Trashing the Media: Veteran Journalists Are Coming to Some Grim Conclusions About Their Industry. Are They Raising Red Flags or Merely Grinding Axes?" *Los Angeles Times*, January 11, 2004.

65. "International News Coverage."

66. *The Late Show with David Letterman* (television). CBS, September 17, 2001 (cited November 3, 2003). <http://www.mediaresearch.org/cyberalerts/2001/cyb20010918.asp>.

67. Engel, Matthew. "US Media Cowed by Patriotic Fever, Says CBS Star." *Guardian*, May 17, 2002.

68. Collins, Scott. Crazy Like a Fox: *The inside Story of How Fox News Beat CNN*. New York: Portfolio, 2004.
69. Quoted in Lapham, Lewis H. "American Jihad." *Harper's Magazine* 304, no. 1820: 7.
70. "International News Coverage."
71. Noelle-Neumann, Elisabeth. *The Spiral of Silence : Public Opinion, Our Social Skin* (second edition). Chicago: University of Chicago Press, 1993.
72. Glynn, C.J., A.F. Hayes and J. Shanahan. "Perceived Support for One's Opinions and Willingness to Speak Out." *Public Opinion Quarterly* 61, no. 3 (1997): 453.
73. Noelle-Neumann. *Spiral of Silence.* 262.
74. Telephone conversation with the author. April 15, 2004.
75. Mooney, Chris. "The Editorial Pages and the Case for War." *Columbia Journalism Review* 42, no. 6: 28.
76. "The Times and Iraq." *New York Times*, May 26, 2004. A10.
77. Younge, Gary. "Now Dissent is 'Immoral'." *Guardian*, June 2, 2003. 15.
78. Quoted in Lapham. "American Jihad."
79. Quoted in Easton, Nina J. "Left in the Lurch." *American Journalism Review* 24, no. 1: 38.
80. Sontag, Susan. "Talk." *New Yorker* 77, no. 28: 32.
81. Carlson, Peter. "Still Pictures That Are Far More Moving Than Words." *Washington Post*, September 25, 2001. C1.
82. "More Sontags." *Weekly Standard*, November 19, 2001. 39.
83. Ivins, Molly. "Update on President Bush's Creative Use of the English Language." In *Morning Edition*. U.S.: NPR, 2001.
84. Lapham. "American Jihad."
85. Higham, Nick. "America Keeps its Blinkers On." *British Journalism Review* 13, no. 1 (2002): 13–18.
86. Fuller, Jack. *News Values: Ideas for an Information Age*. Chicago: University of Chicago Press, 1996. 3.
87. Knightley, Phillip. *The First Casualty: The War Correspondent as Hero and Myth-Maker from the Crimea to Kosovo*. Baltimore, Md.: Johns Hopkins University Press, 2002. 1.
88. Ibid. 43.
89. Ibid. 83.
90. Ibid. 207.
91. Katovsky, Bill, and Timothy Carlson. *Embedded: The Media at War in Iraq*. Guilford, Conn.: Lyons Press, 2003. xi.
92. Quoted in Humphries, Lt. Commander Arthur A. "Two Routes to the Wrong Destination: Public Affairs in the South Atlantic War." *Naval War College Review* 36, no. 3 (1983): 57.
93. Knightley. *First Casualty.* 116–17.
94. Miller, Mark Crispin. *Boxed In: The Culture of TV*. Evanston, Ill.: Northwestern University Press, 1988. 324.
95. Knightley. *First Casualty.* 58.
96. Karnow, Stanley. *Vietnam, a History* (revised and updated edition). New York: Viking, 1991.
97. Knightley. *First Casualty.*

98. Pilger, John. "Torture's Not New but Now It's News." *Daily Mirror*, May 8, 2004, 6.

99. Fuller. *News Values*. 5.

100. Harrison-Hall, Jessica. *Vietnam Behind the Lines: Images from the War, 1965–1975*. Chicago: Art Media Resources, 2002.

101. Pintak, Lawrence. *Seeds of Hate: How America's Flawed Middle East Policy Ignited the Jihad*. London and Sterling, Va.: Pluto Press, 2003. 199.

102. Knightley. *First Casualty*. 484.

103. Roberts, Gene, and Thomas Kunkel. *Breach of Faith: A Crisis of Coverage in the Age of Corporate Newspapering*. Fayetteville, Ark.: University of Arkansas Press, 2002.

104. McChesney, Robert Waterman. *Rich Media, Poor Democracy: Communication Politics in Dubious Times*. New York: New Press, 2000. 51.

105. "The State of the News Media 2004," edited by Amy Mitchell. Washington, D.C.: Center for Excellence in Journalism, 2004. <http://stateofthemedia.org/2004/>.

106. Hazen, Don. "Media Monopoly on Notice." March 1, 2003. <http://www.alternet.org/story.html?storyID=15283>.

107. Safire, William. "On Media Giantism." *New York Times*, January 20, 2003, A19.

108. "Press Release: NBC and Vivendi Universal Entertainment United to Create NBC Universal." New York and Paris: General Electric Company, 2004.

109. McChesney. *Rich Media*. 30.

110. Telephone conversation with the author. May 24, 2004.

111. Fleeson, Lucinda. "Bureau of Missing Bureaus." *American Journalism Review* 25, no. 7: 32.

112. "Bottom-Line Pressures Now Hurting Coverage, Say Journalists," edited by Andrew Kohut. Washington, D.C.: Pew Research Center for the People and the Press, 2004. 64. <http://www.stateofthemedia.org/2004/journalist_survey_prc.asp>.

113. "Public's News Habits Little Changed by September 11." In *Survey Reports*, edited by Andrew Kohut. Washington, D.C.: Pew Research Center for the People and the Press, 2002. 87.

114. Seib. *Global Journalist*. 17.

115. Ibid. 20.

116. Ahmed, Akbar S. *Living Islam: From Samarkand to Stornoway*. New York: Facts on File, 1994.

CHAPTER 3

1. Ayalon, Ami. *The Press in the Arab Middle East: A History*. New York: Oxford University Press, 1995. 111.

2. Ibid. 244

3. Rugh, William A. *Arab Mass Media : Newspapers, Radio, and Television in Arab Politics*. Westport, Conn.: Praeger, 2004.

4. Ibid. 171.

5. Alterman, Jon. "New Media, New Politics: From Satellite Television to the Internet in the Arab World." Washington, D.C.: Washington Institute for Near East Policy, 1998.

6. "Editor of Pan-Arab Newspaper Sentenced to Jail in Absentia." *Dar al Hayat*, April 23, 2004.

7. Ibid.

8. Ayish, M.I. "Political Communication on Arab World Television: Evolving Patterns." *Political Communication* 19, no. 2 (2002): 138.

9. Rugh. *Arab Mass Media*. 7.

10. Amin, H. "Freedom as a Value in Arab Media: Perceptions and Attitudes among Journalists." *Political Communication* 19 (2002): 128.

11. Nawar, Ibrahim. "Freedom of Expression in the Arab World." Arab Press Freedom Watch, 2000 (cited May 25, 2004). <http://www.apfw.org/indexenglish.asp?fname=report\english\spe1001.htm>.

12. Conversation with the author. Ann Arbor, Mich., March 18, 2004.

13. "State of the Arab Media 2001." London: Arab Press Freedom Watch, 2001. 8.

14. Ibid.

15. Amin. "Arab Media." 128.

16. "Freeing the Arab Media from State Control." Casablanca: Arab Press Freedom Watch, 2004.

17. Assaf, Nayla. "Facing Local Restrictions, Mideast Media Finds an International Voice." *Daily Star*, June 15 2004.

18. Sakr, Naomi. *Satellite Realms: Transnational Television, Globalization and the Middle East*. London: I.B. Tauris, 2001. 4.

19. Conversation with the author. May 25, 2004.

20. El-Affendi, Abdelwahab. "Eclipse of Reason: The Media in the Muslim World." *Journal of International Affairs* 47, no. 1: 163.

21. Akhtar, Shakil. *Media, Religion, and Politics in Pakistan*. Oxford and New York: Oxford University Press, 2000.

22. Ingram, Simon. *"Malaysia's Much-Maligned Media."* BBC News Online, November 16, 1999 (cited May 5, 2004). <http://news.bbc.co.uk/1/hi/world/asia-pacific/522848.stm>.

23. Quoted in Vatikiotis, Michael R.J. *Indonesian Politics under Suharto: Order, Development and Pressure for Change* (revised edition). London and New York: Routledge, 1994. 107.

24. Conversation with the author. Ann Arbor, Mich., April 2, 2004.

25. Quoted in Friend, Theodore. *Indonesian Destinies*. Cambridge, Mass.: Belknap Press of Harvard University Press, 2003. 208.

26. El-Affendi. "Eclipse".

27. Amin. "Arab Media." 129.

28. Seventy-eight per cent of Jordanians say they watch entertainment programming. Jordan data from Siwady, Judeh. "Jordan Households Media Survey." Amman, Jordan: Arab Advisors Group, 2005. U.S. data from "Consumers, Media and U.S. Newspapers: Results from the Impact Study." Evanston, Ill.: Readership Institute, Northwestern University, 2002.

29. Packer, George. "Caught in the Crossfire: Letter from Baghdad." *New Yorker* 80, no. 12: 63.

30. Ibid.

31. Quoted in El-Affendi. "Eclipse".
32. Haddad. "Islamist Perceptions of US policy in the Near East." In *The Middle East and the United States: A Historical and Political Reassessment*, edited by David W. Lesch, Boulder, Colo.: Westview Press, 1996.
33. Darwish, Adel. "Anti-Americanism in the Arabic Language Media." *Middle East Review of International Affairs* 7, no. 4 (2003).
34. Rugh, William A. "Arab Media and Politics During the October War." *Middle East Journal* 29, no. 3 (1975).
35. Diamond, M. "No Laughing Matter: Post-September 11 Political Cartoons in Arab/Muslim Newspapers." *Political Communication* 19 (2002): 251–72.
36. Sakr. *Satellite Realms*. 13.
37. "The World through Their Eyes." *The Economist*, February 24, 2005 (cited February 26, 2005). <http://www.economist.com/displaystory. cfm?story_id=3690442>.
38. Williams, Dan. "A Real News Maker." *Jerusalem Post*, July 13, 2001, B2.
39. Kifner, John. "At Arab All-News Channel, Western Values Prevail." *New York Times*, October 12, 2001, B7.
40. El-Nawawy, Mohammed, and Adel Iskandar. *Al-Jazeera: How the Free Arab News Network Scooped the World and Changed the Middle East*. Cambridge, Mass.: Westview Press, 2002. 23.
41. Quoted in ibid. 116.
42. "Kuwait Shuts Down Al-Jazeera Bureau." Reuters, November 3, 2002 (cited July 3, 2003). <http://news.bbc.co.uk/2/hi/south_asia/2395085.stm>.
43. This is the literal translation. It is frequently translated as "The opinion – and the other opinion." See Schleifer, S. Abdallah. "The Sweet and Sour Success of Al-Jazeera." *Journal of Transnational Broadcasting Studies*, March 5, 2001.
44. Soueif, Ahdaf. "Nile Blues." *Guardian*, November 6, 2001, 2.
45. Ibid.
46. Conversation with the author. Ann Arbor, Mich., March 9, 2004.
47. Roth, Wendy D. and Jal D. Mehta. "The Rashomon Effect: Combining Positivist and Interpretivist Approaches in the Analysis of Contested Events." *Sociological Methods and Research* 31, no. 2 (2002): 131.

CHAPTER 4

1. "Terror Attacks in US Widely Condemned." *Nation*, September 13, 2001.
2. "Attacks Denounced." *Jakarta Post*, September 12, 2001.
3. "Raja Zafarul Haq Says the Lack of Information on the Part of the American Secret Agencies Should Make Us Rethink." *Nawa-i-Waqt*, September 12, 2001.
4. "Terror in US." *Arab News*, September 12, 2001.
5. "Jordan Ambassador in US on US Blasts." *Al-Ra'y*, September 13, 2001.
6. "Al-Azhar's Grand Imam Condemns Killing of Civilians." IslamOnline, September 14, 2001 (cited March 12, 2004). <http://www.islam-online.net/English/News/2001-09/15/article2.shtml>.
7. "President Bush Must Draw Lesson from US Destruction." *Khabrain*, September 13, 2001.

8. 'Terror Attacks Widely Condemned.'

9. Quoted in Jorisch, Avi J. "The Language of Terrorism." *Policywatch* 567 (2001).

10. "Grand Imam Condemns Killing." <http://www.washingtoninstitute.org/templateCO5.php?CID=1445>.

11. Azeem, Ashraf. "Under Influence of Jewish Lobby US May Launch Strike against Afghanistan, Palestinians." *Khabrain*, September 12, 2001.

12. Lloyd, John. "The Beginning of a Virtual Revolution." *New Statesman* 14, no. 674: 6.

13. Saddam enjoyed broad support among Palestinians because he had successfully exploited their cause to position himself as an Arab nationalist leader in the mold of the late Egyptian president Gamal Abdel Nasser. There was also no love for the Kuwaitis among the Palestinians, who were treated as second-class citizens in Kuwait.

14. Callahan, Christopher. "Anatomy of an Urban Legend." *American Journalism Review* 23, no. 9: 46.

15. It is important to note that this sympathy for the United States did not translate into Palestinian support for Bush's so-called "war on terror." While Arafat had, as a measure of survival, thrown his support behind it, fully 94 per cent of Palestinians surveyed in December 2001 opposed the U.S. campaign against bin Laden, in large measure because only 16 per cent believed the al-Qaeda leader was responsible for 9/11. See Shikaki, Khalil. "PSR Survey Research Unit Public Opinion Poll No. 3." Palestinian Center for Policy and Survey Research, December 19–24, 2001. <http://www.pcpsr.org/survey/polls/2001/p3a.html>.

16. "Documents and Source Material." *Journal of Palestine Studies* 31, no. 2: 138.

17. Olewine, Sandra. "How Did Palestinians React to the Attacks on the United States?" *Washington Report on Middle East Affairs* 20, no. 8: 16.

18. Ibid.

19. Morin, Richard, and Claudia Deane. "The Poll that Didn't Add Up; Spin on Data Blurs Findings from Gallup's Muslim Survey." *Washington Post*, March 23, 2002, C1.

20. "Survey Finds American Distrust of Muslim World." CNN, May 4, 2002 (cited May 5, 2003). <http://www.cnn.com/2002/US/03/04/u.s.muslim.poll>.

21. Bush, George W. "President's Remarks at National Day of Prayer and Remembrance." White House, September 14, 2001.<http://www.whitehouse.gov/news/releases/2001/09/20010914-2.html>.

22. Ur-Rasheed, Haroon. "Palestinians may be Behind Attack on US Cities." *Khabrain*, September 12, 2001.

23. Faysal, Salman. "Regrettable." *As-Safir*, September 12, 2001.

24. "The United States Is in a State of War." *Al-Quds al-Arabi*, September 12, 2001.

25. "A Human Catastrophe and Denounced Actions." *Al-Ra'y*, September 12, 2001.

26. Arif, Jalal. "A Foolish Blunder." *Akhbar al-Yawm*, September 22, 2001.

27. Abu-Zikri, Wahih. "After the New York and Washington Explosions, Will the United States Change its Foreign Policy?" *Al-Akhbar*, September 14, 2001.

28. Ibid.

29. Al-Rantawi, Urayb. "Arrogance under the Ruins." *Al-Dustur*, September 13, 2001.

30. "Terror in US."

31. Arif, Jalal. "Islam and Arabs are Victims." *Akhbar al-Yawm*, September 29, 2001.

32. Sawalha, Francesca. "Flurry of Diplomatic Activity Expected in Amman Prior to King–Bush Talks." *Jordan Times*, September 23, 2001.

33. Duwaydar, Jalal. "There is No Difference between Israeli Terrorism and the Terrorist Attacks on the United States." *Al-Akhbar*, September 14, 2001.

34. Gauhar, Humayan. "America is its Own Worst Enemy." *Nation*, September 30, 2001.

35. "Terror Attacks Widely Condemned."

36. Sazak, Derya. "Fighting against an Invisible Enemy." *Milliyet*, September 14, 2001.

37. Arif. "Foolish Blunder."

38. Nasir, Gen. Lt. Javed. "Pakistan Should Not Make Decision in Haste, Call OIC Meeting." *Nawa-i-Waqt*, September 15, 2001.

39. "US Campaign against Liberation Movements, Not Just Bin Ladin." *An-Nahar*, September 20, 2001.

40. "United States Should be Ready for Reaction before Attacking Afghanistan." *Khabrain*, September 14, 2001.

41. Awadat, Ibtisam. "Is Islam the Target?" *Star*, September 20, 2001.

42. "Bush's Ultimatum." *Nawa-i-Waqt*, September 22, 2001.

43. Sazak. "Invisible Enemy."

44. "United States Should Review its Policies: Lawyers." *Khabrain*, September 15, 2001.

45. "Terror Attacks Widely Condemned."

46. Hussain, Asim. "Religious Parties Express Sorrow over Attacks in US." *News*, September 12, 2001.

47. "Review Policies."

48. El-Sharif, Osama. "Precipitous Action: Recipe for Disaster." *Star*, September 20, 2001.

49. Atwan, Abd-al-Bari. "A Dangerous US Adventure." *Al-Quds al-Arabi*, September 14, 2001.

50. "Indonesian Reaction to Attack on US." *Jakarta Post*, September 14, 2001.

51. Al-Khuri, Rafiq. "The Day After: The Punishment of States." *Al-Anwar*, September 13, 2001.

52. Niazi, M.A. "The Lion and the Ant." *Nation*, September 14, 2001.

53. Sazak. "Invisible Enemy."

54. Cemal, Hasan. "Is War Easy to Start, but Difficult to End?" *Milliyet*, Islamabad, September 26, 2001.

55. Al-Khuri. "The Day After."

56. Lule, Jack. "Myth and Terror on the Editorial Page: *The New York Times* Responds to September 11, 2001." *Journalism and Mass Communication Quarterly* 79, no. 2: 275.

57. Bush, George W. "Remarks by the President in Photo Opportunity with the National Security Team." White House, September 12, 2001. <http://whitehouse.gov/news/releases/2001/09/20010912-4.html>.

58. Bush. "Remarks at National Day of Prayer."
59. Bush, George W. "President Bush Calls for Action on Economy, Energy." White House, October 26, 2001. <http://www.whitehouse.gov/news/releases/2001/10/20011026-9.html>.
60. Bush, George W. "President Speaks at Veterans Day Prayer Breakfast." White House, November 11, 2001 (cited August 5, 2004). <http://www.whitehouse.gov/news/releases/2001/11/20011111.html>.
61. Kane, John. "American Values or Human Rights? U.S. Foreign Policy and the Fractured Myth of Virtuous Power." *Presidential Studies Quarterly* 33, no. 4: 772.
62. Ibid. 6.
63. Ibid. 3.
64. Ibid. 16.
65. Bush, George W. "Statement by the President in His Address to the Nation, September 11, 2001." White House, September 11, 2001. <http://www.whitehouse.gov/news/releases/2001/09/20010911-16.html>.
66. Alam, Chaklader Mahboob-ul. "The USA and the Muslim World." *Daily Star*, May 24, 2004. <www.thedailystar.net/2004/05/24/d405241501114.htm>.
67. Sowell, Thomas. *A Conflict of Visions* (first edition). New York: W. Morrow, 1987. 24.
68. Hamilton, Alexander, and Clinton Lawrence Rossiter. *The Federalist Papers: Alexander Hamilton, James Madison, John Jay.* New York: New American Library, 1961. 33.
69. Packer, George. "Wars and Ideas." *New Yorker*, July 5, 2004.
70. Sowell. *Conflict of Visions*. 4.
71. Powell, Colin. "U.S. Vision for Middle East Peace, November 19, 2001." *Journal of Palestine Studies* 31, no. 2: 168.
72. It is interesting to note that this line was absent from the official text of the speech posted on the White House web site. See Bush, George W. "Remarks by the President Upon Arrival at Barksdale Air Force Base." White House, September 11, 2001. <http://www.whitehouse.gov/news/releases/2001/09/20010911-1.html>. And Bush, George W. "Remarks by President Bush on Arrival at Barksdale AFB, Shreveport, La. 9/11/01." American Rhetoric, 2001 (cited July 5, 2004). <http://www.americanrhetoric.com/speeches/gwbush911barksdale.htm>.
73. Helfrich, Michele, and Sandi Reynolds. "Day of Infamy: A Social Psychologist and Rhetorician Examine the Effects of Instigative, Patriotic Discourse." *Journal of American and Comparative Cultures* 25, no. 3/4 (2002): 327–32.
74. Bush. "Address to Nation, September" 11.
75. Bush, George W. "President Directs Humanitarian Aid to Afghanistan." White House, October 4, 2001. <http://www.whitehouse.gov/news/releases/2001/10/20011004.html>.
76. Bin Sayeed, Khalid. "American Dominance and Political Islam." Paper presented at the Conference on Political Islam and the West. Nicosia, Cyprus, October 1997.
77. McClay, Wilfred M. "The Soul of a Nation." *Public Interest* 155 (Spring 2004).

78. Bush, George W. "Prime Time News Conference." White House, October 11, 2001. <http://www.whitehouse.gov/news/releases/2001/10/20011011-7.html>.

79. Bush, George W. "President Pays Tribute at Pentagon Memorial." White House, October 11, 2001. <http://www.whitehouse.gov/news/releases/2001/10/20011011-1.html>.

80. Ibid.

81. Ibid.

82. Bin Laden, Osama. "Statement to the Muslim People, October 7, 2001." *Journal of Palestine Studies* 31, no. 2 (2001): 133–4.

83. Helfrich and Reynolds. "Day of Infamy."

84. Nunberg, Geoffrey. *Going Nucular: Language, Politics, and Culture in Confrontational Times* (first edition). New York: Public Affairs, 2004. 41.

85. Coe, Kevin, David Domke, Erica Graham, Sue Lockett John and Vincent W. Pickard. "No Shades of Gray: The Binary Discourse of George W. Bush and an Echoing Press." *Journal of Communication* 54, no. 2 (2004): 244.

86. Bush, George W. "Economy an Important Part of Homeland Defense." White House, October 24, 2001. <http://www.whitehouse.gov/news/releases/2001/10/20011024–2.html>.

87. Nunberg, Geoffrey. "Bin Laden's Low-Tech Weapon." *New York Times*, April 18, 2004, 4.4.

88. Lincoln, Bruce. *Holy Terrors: Thinking About Religion after September 11*. Chicago: University of Chicago Press, 2003. 20.

89. Bush, George W. "Address to a Joint Session of Congress and the American People." White House, September 20, 2001. <http://www.whitehouse. gov/news/releases/2001/09/20010920-8.html>.

90. Bin Laden. "Statement to the Muslim People."

91. "Interview with Osama Bin Laden" (television). ABC News, May 1998 (cited June 15, 2004). <http://www.pbs.org/wgbh/pages/frontline/shows/binladen/who/interview.html>.

92. Bin Laden. "Statement to the Muslim the People."

93. McClay. "Soul."

94. Bush. "Address to Congress."

95. Harris, Paul. "Bush Says God Chose Him to Lead His Nation." *Observer*, November 2, 2003.

96. Bush, George W. "Inaugural Address." White House, January 20, 2001. <http://www.whitehouse.gov/news/inaugural-address.html>.

97. Barr, James. *Fundamentalism*. Philadelphia: Westminster Press, 1978.

98. Stephens, Gregory. "American Myopia: The View from Abroad." *Political News Today*, 2002 (cited July 5, 2004). <http://www.empirepage.com/guesteds/guesteds161.html>.

99. Lincoln. *Holy Terrors*. 27.

100. Bin Laden. "Statement to the Muslim People."

101. Suleiman, Yasir. "Spinning the News." *Mirror*, October 10, 2001, 15.

102. Lincoln. *Holy Terrors*. 30.

103. Bush, George W. "Address to the Nation." White House, October 7, 2001. <http://www.whitehouse.gov/news/releases/2001/10/20011007-8.html>.

104. Lincoln. *Holy Terrors*. 30–1.

105. Bush. "Address to the Nation."
106. *The Holy Bible: King James Version*. Grand Rapids and New York: Zondervan Publishing House, HarperPaperbacks, 1995. 507.
107. Bush. "Address to the Nation." Italics added by the author.
108. Noor, Farish A. "Don't Carry Out this Senseless Bloodshed in Our Name." *New Straits Times*, September 28, 2001, 12.
109. Bush, George W. "Remarks to the Warsaw Conference on Combatting Terrorism." White House, November 6, 2001. <http://www.whitehouse.gov/news/releases/2001/11/20011106-2.html>.
110. Bin Laden. "Statement to the Muslim People."
111. Quoted in Isaacson, Walter. "A Declaration of Mutual Dependence." July 6, 2004. <http://www.nytimes.com/2004/07/04/opinion/04ISAA.html>.
112. Powell. "U.S. Vision for Middle East Peace."
113. Bush, George W. "'Islam is Peace' Says President." White House, September 17, 2001. <http://www.whitehouse.gov/news/releases/2001/09/20010917-11.html>.
114. Bush. "Prime Time News Conference."
115. Bush, George W. "President Bush Welcomes Canadian Prime Minister Martin to White House." White House, April 30, 2004. <http://www.whitehouse.gov/news/releases/2004/04/20040430-2.html>.
116. Bahmanpour, M.S. "International and Islamic Standards of Justice." Paper presented at the Conference on Human Rights, Justice and Muslims in the Wake of September 11. London, October 2001.
117. Aronson, Raney. "The Jesus Factor." May 4, 2004. <http://www.pbs.org/wgbh/pages/frontline/shows/jesus/etc/script.html>.
118. Ibid.
119. Tocqueville, Alexis de, and Arthur Goldhammer. *Democracy in America, Library of America*. New York: Library of America. Distributed to the trade in the United States by Penguin Putnam, 2004. 147.
120. Quoted in Fineman, Howard. "Bush and God." *Newsweek* 141, no. 10: 22.
121. Boston, Rob. "No King but Jesus?" *Church and State* 54, no. 2: 4.
122. Fineman. "Bush and God."
123. Quoted in Steinberg, Jonathan. "One Man and His God." *Financial Times*, June 12, 2004, 26.
124. Bush, George W. "Remarks by the President Upon Arrival." White House, September 16, 2001. <http://www.whitehouse.gov/news/releases/2001/09/20010916-2.html>.
125. Fletcher, R.A. *The Cross and the Crescent: Christianity and Islam from Muhammad to the Reformation*. London and New York: Allen Lane, 2003. 158–9.
126. Maalouf, Amin. *The Crusades Through Arab Eyes*. London: Al Saqi Books. Distributed by Zed Books, 1984. xiv.
127. Lifton, Robert Jay. *Superpower Syndrome: America's Apocalyptic Confrontation with the World*. New York: Thunder's Mouth Press/Nation Books, 2003. 101.
128. Pintak, Lawrence. *Seeds of Hate: How America's Flawed Middle East Policy Ignited the Jihad*. London and Sterling, Va.: Pluto Press, 2003. 175.
129. Bin Laden. "Statement to Muslim People."

130. There are various explanations for the origin of the term "al-Qaeda," which Western intelligence agencies began using in the media after the 1998 embassy bombings in Africa. The term has been variously translated as "the base" or "the foundation" (leading a few observers to speculate that it was somehow inspired by Isaac Asimov's *Foundation* series). Some say it refers to the computer database of *jihadists* that bin Laden developed during the Afghan campaign. Yossef Bodansky, a former director of the U.S. Congressional Task Force on Terrorism, argues that it was never more than the name of a failed charity bin Laden once ran, while terrorist researcher Rohan Gunatara believes that it came from the political concept of *al-Qaida al-Sulbah* (the solid base) formulated by bin Laden's ideological mentor, the Palestinian Abdullah Azzam, which mixes revolutionary vanguardism with Islamic martyrdom. In his 1996 Declaration of War, according to a translation by linguist Flagg Miller, bin Laden tells his followers that a "safe base [*qaa ida aamina*] is now available on Khorusan on the summit of the Hindu Kush," a reference to Afghanistan.

131. Bin Laden, Osama. "Jihad against Jews and Crusaders." Al-Qaeda, February 23, 1998 (cited May 5, 2004). <http://www.fas.org/irp/world/para/docs/980223-fatwa.htm>.

132. Bin Laden, Osama. "Declaration of War against the Americans Occupying the Land of the Two Holy Places." *Al-Quds al-Arabi*, August 1996. <http://www.pbs.org/newshour/terrorism/international/fatwa_1996.html>.

133. Ringle, Ken. "The Crusaders' Giant Footprints: After a Millennium, Their Mark Remains." *Washington Post*, October 23, 2001, C1.

134. "Convene OIC." *Pakistan Observer*, September 22, 2001.

135. Gauhar, Humayun. "America is its Own Worst Enemy." *Nation*, September 30, 2001.

136. Arif. "Foolish Blunder."

137. "Revenge is Not a Substitute for Peace." *Al-Akhbar*, September 19, 2001.

138. "The Voices of Reason are Still Low." *Al-Quds al-Arabi*, September 18, 2001.

139. "Hamas Leader: 'I Advise Bush Not to Unleash a Religious War.' " *Madrid ABC*, September 18, 2001.

140. "U.S. Campaign against Liberation Movements, Not Just Bin Laden." *An-Nahar*, September 20, 2001.

141. Arif. "Foolish Blunder."

142. Kristof, Nicholas D. "Bigotry in Islam – and Here." *New York Times*, July 9, 2002, A21.

143. Mikkelsen, Randall. *Bush Takes on the Christian Right*, Reuters, November 13, 2001 (cited February 5, 2003). <http://middleeastinfo.org/article1607.html>.

144. Simon, Bob. "Zion's Christian Soldiers: The '60 Minutes' Transcript." *Washington Report on Middle East Affairs* 21, no. 9: 68.

145. Kristof. "Bigotry."

146. "Eagleburger Discusses Terrorist Attacks on United States" (television) CNN, September 11, 2001. <http://www.cnn.com/TRANSCRIPTS/0109/11/bn.59.html>.

147. Coulter, Ann. *"This is War."* New Republic Online, September 13, 2001 (cited July 15, 2004). <http://www.nationalreview.com/coulter/coulter091301.shtml>.

CHAPTER 5

1. Bush, George W. "Address to a Joint Session of Congress and the American People." White House, September 20, 2001. <http://www.whitehouse. gov/news/releases/2001/09/20010920-8.html>.

2. Lule, Jack. "Myth and Terror on the Editorial Page: *The New York Times* Responds to September 11, 2001." *Journalism and Mass Communication Quarterly* 79, no. 2: 275.

3. Quoted in Coe, Kevin, David Domke, Erica Graham, Sue Lockett John and Vincent W. Pickard. "No Shades of Gray: The Binary Discourse of George W. Bush and an Echoing Press." *Journal of Communication* 54, no. 2 (2004): 242.

4. "War without Illusions." *New York Times*, September 15, 2001, A22.

5. Lule. "Myth and Terror."

6. Ibid.

7. Campbell, Karlyn Kohrs, and Kathleen Hall Jamieson. *Deeds Done in Words: Presidential Rhetoric and the Genres of Governance.* Chicago: University of Chicago Press, 1990.

8. Descarries, Francine. "The Hegemony of the English Language in the Academy." *Current Sociology* 51, no. 6: 625.

9. Silberstein, Sandra. *War of Words: Language, Politics and 9/11.* London and New York: Routledge, 2002. 14.

10. Bush, George W. "President Pays Tribute at Pentagon Memorial." White House, October 11, 2001. <http://www.whitehouse.gov/news/ releases/2001/10/20011011-1.html>.

11. Bush, George W. "President Meets with Muslim Leaders." White House, September 26, 2001. <http://www.whitehouse.gov/news/ releases/2001/09/20010926-8.html>.

12. Ibid.

13. Bush. "Address to Congress."

14. Gauhar, Humayun. "America is its Own Worst Enemy." *Nation*, September 30, 2001.

15. Mohan, C. Raja. "Global Complications of Prolonged Action against Taliban." *Hindu*, October 9, 2001.

16. Hiro, Dilip. "Bush and Bin Laden." *Nation* 273, no. 10: 18.

17. Atran, Scott. "A Leaner, Meaner Jihad." *New York Times*, March 16, 2004.

18. Atran, Scott. "Strategic Threat from Suicide Terror."AEI–Brookings Joint Center for Regulatory Studies, 2003. 1.

19. Chipman, John. "Press Launch: Strategic Survey 2003/4." International Institute for Strategic Studies, May 25, 2004 (cited July 1, 2004). <http://www.iiss.org/showdocument.php?docID=364>.

20. Bush, George W. "President Launches 'Lessons of Liberty.'" White House, October 30, 2001. <http://www.whitehouse.gov/news/releases/2001/ 10/20011030-7.html>.

21. Chomsky, Noam. "In a League of its Own." *Harvard International Review* 22, no. 2: 68.

22. Ibrahim, Anwar. "Who Hijacked Islam?" *Time*, October 15, 2004 (cited May 25, 2004). <http://www.time.com/time/asia/news/column/ 0,9754,178470,00.html>.

23. Smelser, Neil J., Faith Mitchell, Eugene A. Hammel and Erik D. Smith, eds. *Discouraging Terrorism: Some Implications of 9/11*. Washington, D.C.: National Academies Press, 2002. 2.

24. "State Department Releases 2003 Human Rights Country Reports." U.S. Department of State, February 25, 2004 (cited June 5, 2004). <http://usembassy.state.gov/posts/in3/wwwhwashnews1379.html>.

25. Mark, Clyde. "Egypt–United States Relations." Congressional Research Service, October 10, 2003 (cited July 17, 2004). <http://fpc.state.gov/documents/organization/25431.pdf. 7–8>.

26. Ibid. iii.

27. Garamone, Jim. "Bright Star Shines in Egypt." U.S. Department of Defense, 2003 (cited July 17, 2004). <http://www.defenselink.mil/news/Oct1999/n10261999_9910261.html>.

28. Bush, George W. "President Bush Calls for Action on Economy, Energy." White House, October 26, 2001. <http://www.whitehouse.gov/news/releases/2001/10/20011026-9.html>.

29. Zogby, John, and James J. Zogby. "Impressions of America 2004." Washington, D.C.: Arab American Institute/Zogby International, 2004.

30. Precht, Robert. "Defending Mohammed." Paper presented at the Strategic Importance, Causes, and Consequences of Terrorism Colloquium. Ann Arbor, Mich., March 13, 2004.

31. Shikaki, Khalil. "Attitudes toward the U.S." Ramallah: Palestine Center for Policy and Survey Research, 2004.

32. Shikaki, Khalil. "Public Opinion Polls." Palestinian Center for Policy and Survey Research, July 4, 2004 (cited July 17, 2004). <http://www.pcpsr.org/new/new.html>.

33. Zogby, John. "The Ten Nation Impressions of America Poll." Washington, D.C.: Zogby International, 2002.

34. Bush, George W. "Remarks by the President Upon Arrival at Barksdale Air Force Base." White House, September 11, 2001. <http://www.whitehouse.gov/news/releases/2001/09/20010911-1.html>.

35. Allen, Lori. "There are Many Reasons Why: Suicide Bombers and Martyrs in Palestine." *Middle East Report* 223 (2002).

36. Barr, Cameron W. "A Suicide Bomber's World." *Christian Science Monitor*, August 14, 2001, 1.

37. Blight, David W. "The Good Terrorist." *Washington Post*, April 24, 2005, T1.

38. "Brief History of the U.S. Army in World War Two." U.S. Army Center for Military History, 2004 (cited August 8, 2004). <http://www.worldwariihistory.info/WWII/Europe.html>.

39. "United States Strategic Bombing Survey Summary Report (Pacific War)." Washington, D.C.: Government Printing Office, 1946.

40. "Vietnamese Government Releases Casualty Figures." April 4, 1995. <http://www.rjsmith.com/kia_tbl.html#press>.

41. Nunberg, Geoffrey. "Bin Laden's Low-Tech Weapon." *New York Times*, April 18, 2004, 4.4.

42. Bush. "Action on Economy."

43. "U.S. Working Paper for G-8 Sherpas." *Al-Hayat*, February 13, 2004 (cited March 15, 2004). <http://english.daralhayat.com/Spec/02-2004/Article-20040213-ac40bdaf-c0a8-01ed-004e-5e7ac897d678/story.html>.

44. Atran, Scott. "Individual Factors in Suicide Terrorism: Response." *Science* 304 (2004).

45. Atran, conversation with the author. Ann Arbor, Mich., February 15, 2004.

46. Cronin, Audrey Kurth. "Terrorists and Suicide Attacks." Washington, D.C.: Congressional Research Service, 2003. 8.

47. Hassan, Nasra. "An Arsenal of Unbelievers." *New Yorker* 77, no. 36: 36.

48. Ginges, Jeremy. "Economic Deprivation and Support for Terrorism: Preliminary Data from Lebanon and Palestine." Paper presented at the Strategic Importance, Causes, and Consequences of Terrorism Colloquium, Ann Arbor, Mich., March 12, 2004.

49. Krueger, Alan B., and Jitka Maleckova. "Seeking the Roots of Terrorism." *Chronicle of Higher Education 49*, no. 39: B10. However, the researcher who carried out the surveys, Khalil Shikaki, cautions against making far-reaching conclusions about the correlation: "The truth is that tests are not always consistent on this matter. For example, while support for violence against civilians is correlated with place of residence, gender, occupation, and refugee status, it is not correlated with income or education." Email correspondence with the author. July 21, 2004.

50. Hassan. "Arsenal."

51. Krueger and Maleckova. "Roots."

52. Ibid.

53. Ibid.

54. "New Intelligence in the War against Terror." In *Talk of the Nation* (radio). NPR, 2004.

55. "The Jemaah Islamiyah Arrests and the Threat of Terrorism." Singapore: Ministry of Home Affairs, 2003.

56. Krueger and Maleckova. "Roots."

57. Atran. "Suicide Terrorism."

58. Sageman, Marc. "The Psychology of Al Qaeda Terrorists." Unpublished paper, 2005.

59. "Palestinians Who Carried out Suicide Attacks in Israel and the Occupied Territories During the Al-Aqsa Intifada." Palestine Human Rights Monitor, May 28, 2004 (cited July 19, 2004). <http://www.phrmg.org/PHRMG%20Documents/Suicide%20bombers/Tables/suicide%20attack%20english.htm>.

60. "JMCC Public Opinion Poll No. 31: On Palestinian Attitudes Towards Politics." Jerusalem Media and Communication Centre, March 1999. <http://www.jmcc.org/publicpoll/results/1999/no31.htm>.

61. Shikaki, Khalil. "PSR Survey Research Unit Public Opinion Poll No. 12." Palestinian Center for Policy and Survey Research, June 24–27, 2004. <http://www.pcpsr.org/survey/polls/2001/p3a.html>.

62. "JMCC Public Opinion Poll No. 32: On Palestinian Attitudes Towards Politics." Jerusalem Media and Communication Centre, August, 1999. <http://www.jmcc.org/publicpoll/results/1999/no32.htm>.

63. Shikaki, Khalil. "PSR Survey Research Unit Public Opinion Poll No. 3." Palestinian Center for Policy and Survey Research, December 19–24, 2001. <http://www.pcpsr.org/survey/polls/2001/p3a.html>.

64. Ibid.

65. Roberts, Tom. "Suicide Bombers." In *Wide Angle* (television). PBS, 2004.

66. Cohen, Richard. "We Can't Fight Terror Everywhere." *Washington Post*, November 13, 2001, A31.

67. Cronin. "Suicide Attacks." 12.

68. Simon, Bob. "Mind of a Suicide Bomber." In *60 Minutes* (television). CBS News, 2003.

69. Bumiller, Elisabeth. "Was a Tyrant Prefigured by Baby Saddam?" *New York Times*, May 15, 2004, B9.

70. Cronin. "Suicide Attacks." i.

71. Atran. "Suicide Terrorism."

72. Hassan. "Arsenal."

73. Reynolds, James. "Nobody is Going to Live Forever." BBC News, July 16, 2004 (cited July 19, 2004). <http://news.bbc.co.uk/2/hi/middle_east/3899015.stm>.

74. Hudson, Rex. "The Sociology and Psychology of Terrorism." Washington, D.C.: Federal Research Division, Library of Congress, 1999. 126–7.

75. *Collateral Damage* (Vol. 5, Issue 34). Americans for Peace Now, March 22, 2004 (cited March 30, 2004). <http://www.peacenow.org/nia/peace/v5i34.html>.

76. Roberts. "Suicide Bombers."

77. Reynolds. "Live Forever."

78. Hardy, Michael. "Virginia Services Mark Lives Lost to Terrorism." *Richmond Times–Dispatch*, December 12, 2001, A10.

79. Simon. "Suicide Bomber."

80. Barr. "A Suicide Bomber's World."

81. "New Intelligence."

82. Pape, Robert A. "The Strategic Logic of Suicide Terrorism." *American Political Science Review* 97, no. 3 (2003): 345–60.

83. Sprinzak, Ehud. "Rational Fanatics." *Foreign Policy*, no. 120: 66.

84. Ibid.

85. Mounayer, Mouna, Nabil Issa, Najat Rizk, George Moufarrej and Charbel Rouhana. "The Living Martyr: Hizbollah Unveiled" (film). Princeton, N.J.: Films for the Humanities and Sciences, 2001.

86. Shikaki. "PSR Survey No. 3."

87. Safire, William. "On Being an Ally." *New York Times*, April 11, 2002, A33.

88. Simon. "Suicide Bomber."

89. Reynolds. "Live Forever."

90. Huesmann, L. Rowell. "How to Grow a Terrorist without Really Trying." Paper presented at the Strategic Importance, Causes, and Consequences of Terrorism Colloquium, Ann Arbor, Mich., March 13, 2004.

91. Abuza, Zachary. *Militant Islam in Southeast Asia: Crucible of Terror*. Boulder, Colo.: Lynne Rienner Publishers, 2003. 128.

92. Jones, Sidney. "Jemaah Islamiyah in Southeast Asia: Damaged but Still Dangerous." In *Asia Report*. Jakarta: International Crisis Group, 2003.

93. Lifton, Robert Jay. *Superpower Syndrome: America's Apocalyptic Confrontation with the World*. New York: Thunder's Mouth Press/Nation Books, 2003. 87.

94. Simon. "Suicide Bomber."

95. Waldman, Amy. "Masters of Suicide Bombing: Tamil Guerrillas of Sri Lanka." *New York Times*, January 14, 2003, A1.

96. Reynolds. "Live Forever."

97. Hudson. "Sociology." 15.

98. "How to Lose the War on Terror: A CIA Bin Laden Expert's Lament." *American Conservative*, July 27, 2004.

99. Bin Laden, Osama. "Statement to the Muslim People, October 7, 2001." *Journal of Palestine Studies* 31, no. 2 (2001): 133–4.

100. Suleiman, Yasir. "Spinning the News." *Mirror*, October 10, 2001, 15.

101. "Words of a Megalomaniac." *Rocky Mountain News*, October 9, 2001, A30.

102. Campbell, Colin. "Bin Laden's Message: Militant's Speech Uses Calculated Theatrics, Poetry." *Atlanta Constitution*, October 9, 2001, A12.

103. Ibid.

104. Burns, John F. "Bin Laden Taunts U.S. and Praises Hijackers." *New York Times*, October 8, 2001, A1.

105. Fisk, Robert. "Why We Reject the West – by the Saudis' Fiercest Arab Critic." *Independent*, July 10, 1996, 14.

106. Bin Laden, Osama. "Declaration of War against the Americans Occupying the Land of the Two Holy Places." *Al-Quds al-Arabi*, August 1996. <http://www.pbs.org/newshour/terrorism/international/fatwa_1996.html>.

107. Bodansky, Yossef. *Bin Laden: The Man Who Declared War on America*. Rocklin, Calif.: Forum, 1999. 28.

108. Ibid.

109. Woodward, Bob. "How the U.S. Sold the Saudis on Using America's Military Might." *Toronto Star*, May 4, 1991, B1.

110. Ibid.

111. Bin Laden. "Declaration of War." 29.

112. Morgan, Matthew J. "The Origins of the New Terrorism." *Parameters* 34, no. 1: 29.

113. Ibid.

114. Ibid.

115. Kaiser, Robert G. "The Long and Short of it." *Washington Post*, September 8, 2002, B1.

116. Evans, Leslie. "Government Attacks on Area Specialists Called Disservice to U.S. Middle East Policy." UCLA International Institute, June 29, 2004 (cited June 10, 2004). <http://www.international.ucla.edu/article.asp?parentid=12443>.

117. Bremer, L. Paul. "Countering the Changing Threat of International Terrorism." Washington, D.C.: National Commission on Terrorism, 2000. 2.

CHAPTER 6

1. Hoffman, Bruce. *Inside Terrorism*. New York: Columbia University Press, 1998. 71.

2. Quoted in Dobson, Christopher, and Ronald Payne. *The Carlos Complex: A Study in Terror* (first American edition). New York: Putnam, 1977. 18.

3. Nordland, Rod, and Jeffrey Bartholet. "The Mesmerizer." *Newsweek*, September 24, 2001, 44.

4. Carter, Jimmy. "State of the Union Address." January 24, 1980, A12.

5. Lescaze, Lee, and Lou Cannon. "Reagan Warns against Future Terrorist Acts; 'There Are Limits to Our Patience.'" *Washington Post*, January 28, 1981, A26.

6. Fisk, Robert. "They Can Run and They Can Hide: Suicide Bombers are Here to Stay." *Independent*, September 13, 2001.

7. York, Byron. "Clinton Has No Clothes." *National Review* 53, no. 24: 34.

8. Quoted in Pintak, Lawrence. *Seeds of Hate: How America's Flawed Middle East Policy Ignited the Jihad*. London and Sterling, Va.: Pluto Press, 2003. 199.

9. "Interview with Osama Bin Laden" (television). ABC News, May 1998 (cited June 15, 2004). <http://www.pbs.org/wgbh/pages/frontline/shows/binladen/who/interview.html>.

10. Pape, Robert A. "The Strategic Logic of Suicide Terrorism." *American Political Science Review* 97, no. 3 (2003): 344.

11. Schlesinger, Robert. "US Remaking Look, Locations of Bases Abroad." *Boston Globe*, July 7, 2003, A1.

12. Cullison, Alan, and Andrew Higgins. "One of Many Followers of Al Qaeda Vows to Die for Cause." *Asian Wall Street Journal*, December 31, 2002, A1.

13. Fisk, Robert. "Why We Reject the West – by the Saudis' Fiercest Arab critic." *Independent*, July 10, 1996, 14.

14. Arif, Jalal. "Islam and Arabs are Victims." *Akhbar al-Yawm*, September 29 2001.

15. Ahmad, Eqbal. *Terrorism: Theirs and Ours*. New York, London: Seven Stories; Turnaround, 2002. 34.

16. Quoted in Sardar, Ziauddin, and Merryl Wyn Davies. *Why Do People Hate America?* Cambridge: Icon, 2002. 56.

17. Kepel, Gilles. *Jihad: The Trail of Political Islam*. Cambridge, Mass.: Harvard University Press, 2002. 12.

18. Abuza, Zachary. *Militant Islam in Southeast Asia: Crucible of Terror*. Boulder, Colo.: Lynne Rienner Publishers, 2003. 10.

19. Kepel. *Jihad*. 218.

20. Conversation with the author. Ann Arbor, Mich., February 11, 2005.

21. Shehzad, Mohammed. "Jihad Not a Choice of Socio-Economic Order." March 13, 2004. <http://www.pakistan-facts.com/article.php/20040313121429655>.

22. Taqui, Jassim. "The Fallacy of the Clash with Islam." *Pakistan Observer*, September 2, 2001.

23. Hassan, Nasra. "Al-Qaeda's Understudy." *Atlantic Monthly* 293, no. 5: 42.

24. Prusher, Ilene R. "Musharraf vs. the Mullahs." *Christian Science Monitor*, January 30, 2002, 7.

25. Quoted in Ziad, Waleed. "How the Holy Warriors Learned to Hate." *New York Times*, June 18, 2004, A31.

26. Abuza. *Militant Islam*. 11.

27. Ziad. "Holy Warriors."

28. Interview with the author. May 29, 1985.

29. Reagan, Ronald. "State of the Union Address." Washington, D.C.: White House, 1988.

30. O'Rourke, William. "Insecurities are Showing at White House: Tour Cancellations Another Blow to Public Confidence." *Chicago Sun–Times*, December 11, 2001, 31.

31. Quoted in Ahmad. *Terrorism*. 14.

32. Shamir, Yitzak. "The Ideology of Terrorism." *Israeli Press Briefs* December–January (1987–88): 22–3.

33. Cullison and Higgins. "Followers."

34. Begin, Menachim. *The Revolt*. Los Angeles: Nash Publishing, 1972.

35. Quoted in Zogby, James J. "Remembering Deir Yassin." Arab American Institute, April 13, 1998 (cited October 5, 2003). <http://www.aaiusa.org/wwatch_archives/041398.htm>.

36. Ben-Gurion, David. *Rebirth and Destiny of Israel*. New York: Philosophical Library, 1954.

37. Zogby. "Deir Yassin."

38. Awadat, Ibtisam. "Is Islam the Target?" *Star*, September 20, 2001.

39. "Interview: Ahmed Sattar." PBS, 1999 (cited June 8, 2004). <http://www.pbs.org/wgbh/pages/frontline/binladen/interview/sattar.html>.

40. Morris, Errol. "Fog of War." Sony Pictures Classics, 2004.

41. Hoffman. *Inside Terrorism*. 43.

42. Shikaki, Khalil. "Prs Survey Research Unit Public Opinion Poll No. 3." Ramallah: Palestinian Center for Policy and Survey Research, 2001.

43. "Documents and Source Material." *Journal of Palestine Studies* 31, no. 2: 138.

44. Albright, Madeleine Korbel. *Madam Secretary*. New York: Miramax Books, 2003. 275.

45. Yuliawan, Krisnadi, and Zaenal Dalle. "A Never-Ending Injustice." *Gatra*, September 22, 2001.

46. "Interview with Osama Bin Laden."

47. Gauhar, Humayun. "America is its Own Worst Enemy." *Nation*, September 30, 2001.

48. Bahmanpour, M.S. "International and Islamic Standards of Justice." Paper presented at the Conference on Human Rights, Justice and Muslims in the Wake of September 11. London, October 2001.

49. Ibid.

50. Quoted in Rogers, Paul. "The War on Terror – One Year On." *RUSI Journal* 147, no. 5: 28.

51. "War is Not the Solution." *Al-Quds*, October 8 2001.

52. "Thai Muslim Leaders Issue Joint Statement Opposing US Plan to Attack Afghanistan." *Nation*, September 23, 2001.

53. Burki, H.K. "Has the Clash Begun?" *News*, September 21, 2001.

54. "Afghanistan." *Arab News*, October 8, 2001.

55. Bush, George W. "Address to the Nation." White House, October 7, 2001. <www.whitehouse.gov/news/releases/2001/10/20011007-8.html>

56. "Afghanistan."

57. Strobel, Warren P. "Bush Advisors Split over Strikes on Iraq, How Wide a War on Terrorism?" *Record–Knight Ridder News Service*, September 18, 2001, A21.

58. Ibid.

59. Beeman, William O. "Neoconservative Guru Sets Sights on Iran: Ledeen Leads the Charge for Attacking More Middle East Nations." *National Catholic Reporter*, May 23 2003.

60. Ledeen, Michael Arthur. "Creative Destruction: How to Wage a Revolutionary War." National Review Online, September 20, 2001 (cited April 18, 2004). <http://www.nationalreview.com/contributors/ledeen092001.shtml>.

61. Ibid.

62. "Operation Infinite Justice: Fallout and Repercussions on Pakistan." October 1, 2001 (cited July 17, 2004). <http://www.balochvoice.com/Operation_Infinite_Justice.html>.

CHAPTER 7

1. Hickey, Neil. "Perspectives on War." *Columbia Journalism Review* 40, no. 6 (2002): 40.

2. "Feisty Arab TV Channel Steals the Show." *Deutsche Presse-Agentur*, October 10, 2001.

3. Ahmed, Akbar S. *Postmodernism and Islam: Predicament and Promise.* London and New York: Routledge, 1992.

4. "In with No News." NPR, July 23, 2004. <http://www.wnyc.org/onthemedia/transcripts/transcripts_072304_news.html>.

5. Bush, George W. "Prime Times News Conference." White House, October 11, 2001. <http://www.whitehouse.gov/news/releases/2001/10/20011011-7.html>.

6. Hickey. "Perspectives."

7. Yusufzai, Rahimullah. "War of Words." *Guardian*, October 9, 2001, 4.

8. Sciolino, Elaine. "An Arab Station Offers Ground-Breaking Coverage." *New York Times*, October 9, 2001, B6.

9. Bernstein, Paula. "Nets Jostle for 'Exclusive' Rights." *Variety* 384, no. 9: 50.

10. Kay, Katty. "Secret Signals 'Hidden in TV Tapes.'" *Times*, October 11, 2001.

11. "British News Channels Say They Will Keep Showing Osama Videos." *Deutsche Presse-Agency*, October 11, 2001.

12. Anonymous. "SPJ Says Media Should Carefully Weigh Government Request Regarding Coverage of War on Terrorism." *Quill* 89, no. 9: S3.

13. "Defiant Al-Jazeera Says it Won't Back Off Broadcasting Bin Laden." *Associated Press*, October 11, 2001.

14. Basu, Moni. "Afghans Testing Freedom after Iron Taliban Rule." *Atlanta Journal/Constitution*, November 14, 2001, A21.

15. Wells, Matt. "How Smart was this Bomb?" *Guardian*, November 19, 2001, 8.

16. Jefferson, Thomas. "The Declaration of Independence." Library of Congress, National Archives, 1776 (cited June 5, 2004). <http://www.archives.gov/national_archives_experience/declaration.html>. For more on this incident, see Miles, Hugh. *Al-Jazeera: The Inside Story of the Arab News Channel that is Challenging the West* (first American edition). New York: Grove Press, 2005.

17. As of April 15, 2005, a total of 39 workers had been killed in Iraq since the U.S. invasion. Circumstances of the deaths varied. The majority occurred as reporters and camera crews were caught in crossfire, mistaken for combatants or fell victim to nervous troops. Two of the cameramen died when a U.S. tank fired a round into the Palestine Hotel in Baghdad, headquarters to much of the foreign media, as American forces moved into the city. The attack on al-Jazeera's bureau was seen by many as far more suspicious, given that it was providing coverage of the impact of the U.S. bombing campaign available nowhere else. In early 2005, the long-time chief of newsgathering at CNN, Eason Jordan, was forced to resign when a scandal erupted after he said it appeared that the U.S. military had been deliberately targeting journalists. The Committee to Protect Journalists (CPJ) maintains a running toll of journalists killed in Iraq.

18. "U.S. Warplanes Bomb Al Jazeera Office, Kill Journalist." April 8, 2003 (cited August 5, 2004). <http://electroniciraq.net/cgi-bin/artman/exec/view.cgi/10/582>.

19. Quoted in Payne, Kenneth. "The Media as an Instrument of War." *Parameters* 35, no. 1: 81.

20. "Bin Laden's Sole Post-September 11 TV Interview Aired." CNN, January 31, 2002.

21. "Cheney Warned Al-Jazeera About Bin Laden Tapes." CNN, January 31, 2002.

22. "Angry Al-Jazeera Hits Back at CNN Criticism." Agence France Presse, February 2, 2002.

23. Sullivan, Sarah. "Courting Al-Jazeera, the Sequel: Estrangement and Signs of Reconciliation." *TBS Journal* February 20, 2001. <http://www.tbsjournal.com/Archives/Fall01/Jazeera-special.htm>.

24. Al-Hatab, Sultan. "Tariq Ayoub: Setting an Example." *Al-Ra'i*, April 9, 2003.

25. "U.S. Targets Independent Media in Its War on Iraq." April 16–30, 2003 (cited July 5, 2004). <http://www.muslimedia.com/archives/oaw03/irqwar-jazeera.htm>.

26. Fisk, Robert. "US Moves to Close Down Al-Jazeera TV." *Counterpunch*, August 1, 2003.

27. Neslen, Arthur. "Reality Television." *Guardian*, April 21, 2004, 23.

28. Cochrane, Paul. "Does Arab TV Generate Anti-Americanism?" June 26, 2004 (cited January 9, 2005). <http://www.worldpress.org/mideast/1883.cfm>.

29. Ibid.

30. "Panel Discussion: Is Arab Media a Force for Reform, the Status Quo, or Extremism?" In *Arab Media, Power and Influence*. Washington, D.C.: Princeton University and Rice University, May 4, 2005.

31. Ibrahim, Youssef M. "Is Al-Jazeera Allowed to Advocate Beheadings?" Gulf News, September 28, 2004 (cited Jan 5, 2005).

32. "Force for Reform?"

33. Newport, Frank. "Gallup Poll of the Islamic World." In *Tuesday Briefing*, edited by Lydia Saad and David Moore. Princeton, N.J.: The Gallup Organization, 2002. 44.

34. "Secretary Rumsfeld Interview with Al Jazeera TV." Department of Defense, February 25, 2003 (cited January 22, 2005). <http://www.pentagon.mil/transcripts/2003/t02262003_t0225sdaljaz.html>.

35. Ayish, M.I. "Political Communication on Arab World Television: Evolving Patterns." *Political Communication* 19, no. 2 (2002).

36. "National Security Advisor Condoleezza Rice Interview with Al-Jazeera TV." White House, October 15, 2001 (cited June 5, 2004). <http:// www.whitehouse.gov/news/releases/2001/10/20011016-3.html>.

37. Miller, Laura, and Sheldon Rampton. *The Pentagon's Information Warrior: Rendon to the Rescue*, PR Watch, Fourth Quarter, 2001 (cited August 4, 2004). <http://www.prwatch.org/prwissues/2001Q4/rendon.html>.

38. Naqvi, Saeed. "A Goliath Run Amuck." *Indian Express*, December 7 2001.

39. Ibid.

40. "Ummah Should Seek Guidance from Qur'an, Sunnah." Jamaat-e-Islami Pakistan, December 6, 2003 (cited January 9, 2004). <http://www. jamaat.org/news/pr120603.html>.

41. Mounayer, Mouna, Nabil Issa, Najat Rizk, George Moufarrej, and Charbel Rouhana. "The Living Martyr: Hizbollah Unveiled" (film). Princeton, N.J.: Films for the Humanities and Sciences, 2001.

42. "United States Adds Al-Manar TV Network to Terrorism List." U.S. Department of State, December 17, 2004 (cited March 29, 2005). <http://usinfo.state.gov/xarchives/display.html?p=washfile-english&y=2004&m=December&x=20041217125030sjhtrop0.2467462 &t=mena/mena-latest.html>.

43. Eickelman, Dale F., and Jon W. Anderson. *New Media in the Muslim World: The Emerging Public Sphere* (second edition). Bloomington, Ind.: Indiana University Press, 2003.

44. Bunt, Gary R. *Virtually Islamic: Computer-Mediated Communication and Cyber Islamic Environments, Religion, Culture and Society.* Cardiff: University of Wales Press, 2000.

45. Higgins, Andrew, Karby Leggett and Alan Cullison. "How Al Qaeda Enlisted the Internet in Service of World-Wide Jihad." *Asian Wall Street Journal*, November 11, 2002, A1.

46. "Blithely into a Trap." *Hindu*, September 7, 2003, 1.

47. "Full Text Bin Laden Tape April 2004." BBC Monitoring, April 15, 2004 (cited May 5, 2004). <http://news.bbc.co.uk/1/hi/world/middle_east/ 3628069.stm>.

48. Higgins and Cullison. "How Al Qaeda Enlisted the Internet."

49. Azzam Publications, 2002 (cited August 5, 2004). <http://www.ruhulamin. com/azzam/www.azzam.co.uk/>.

50. Istimata, al-Katibatul Maut al-Alamiya (cited February 3, 2003). <http://www.istimata.co.id>.

51. Bowers, Faye. "Terrorists Spread Their Messages Online." *Christian Science Monitor*, July 28, 2004, 3.

52. Jacinto, Leela. "*Cyber Jihad.*" ABC News, July 15, 2004 (cited August 4, 2004). <http://abcnews.go.com/sections/World/SciTech/cyberterror_alqaeda_ 040715-1.html>.

53. "Statement from Azzam Publications About Jihadunspun.Com." Azzam Publications, November 6, 2004 (cited May 9, 2004). <http://www. islamistwatch.org/main.html>.

54. Bunt, Gary R. *Islam in the Digital Age: E-Jihad, Online Fatwas and Cyber Islamic Environments.* Sterling, Va.: Pluto Press, 2003.

55. Jehl, Douglas, and David Rohde. "Captured Qaeda Figure Led Way to Information Behind Warning." *New York Times*, August 2, 2004, A1.
56. Pillar, Paul R. "Terrorism Goes Global: Extremist Groups Extend Their Reach Worldwide." *Brookings Review* 19 (Fall 2001): 34–7.
57. Doyle, Neil. "Al Qaeda Said to Be Planning on Web." *Washington Times*, June 22, 2002, A6.
58. Ibid.
59. Ward, Olivia. "Global Terror Battle Moves to Net 'Infowars.'" *Toronto Star*, September 7, 2003, A14.
60. Doyle. "Al Qaeda."
61. Miller, Flagg. "On the Summit of the Hindu Kush: Osama Bin Laden's 1996 Declaration of War Reassessed" (lecture). Ann Arbor, Mich., 2005.
62. Conversation with the author. Ann Arbor, Mich., April 2, 2004.
63. Higgins and Cullison. "How Al Qaeda Enlisted the Internet."
64. "Al-Arabiya TV Denies U.S. Charges over Iraq." Reuters, November 30, 2003 (cited January 7, 2004). <http://famulus.msnbc.com/FamulusIntl/reuters11-30-055113.asp?reg=MIDEAST#body>.
65. Steinberg, Jacques. "Kidnappings, Beheadings and Defining What's News." *New York Times*, August 1, 2004, 4.1.
66. "Difficult Task of Internet Policing." *New Straits Times*, May 30, 2004, 9.
67. Smith, Lynn. "Web Amplifies Message of Primitive Executions." *Los Angeles Times*, June 30, 2004 (cited July 18, 2004). <http://www.latimes.com/news/nationworld/iraq/la-et-behead30jun30,1,3359896.story?coll=la-home-headlines>.
68. Steinberg. "Kidnappings."

CHAPTER 8

1. Podhoretz, Norman. "Israel Isn't the Issue." *Wall Street Journal*, September 20, 2001, A16.
2. Tilove, Jonathan, and Miles Benson. "Jewish Leaders Confident that Israel Won't be Blamed for Sept. 11 . . . For Now." *Newhouse News Service*, October 5, 2001, 1.
3. "Geopolitical Region: Is 9/11 a Failure of US Foreign Policy?" In *On Point*, (radio). NPR, 2001.
4. Besser, James D. "Exploding American Complacency." *Baltimore Jewish Times* 262, no. 2: 26.
5. Mono, Brian. "The Blame Game." *Jewish Exponent* 210, no. 13: 10.
6. Quoted in Guerin, Bill. "Indonesia Needs to Come Off the Fence." Asia Times Online, September 19, 2001 (cited July 30, 2004). <http://www.atimes.com/se-asia/CI19Ae01.html>.
7. Avneri, Uri. "Twin Towers." Gush Shalom, September 15, 2001 (cited March 5, 2004). <http://www.gush-shalom.org/archives/article162.html>.
8. Kavanaugh, Michael. "US–Muslim Relations at Worst Point Ever." Pew Fellowships, Spring 2004 (cited June 5, 2004). <http://www.pewfellowships.org/seminars/2004/spring/shibley_telhami.htm>.
9. El-Sayed, Ezzat Saad. "Middle Eastern Perspectives on Terrorism and Relations with the West." *Van Zorge Report on Indonesia* 6, no. 1 (2004): 22–4.

10. Duwaydar, Jalal. "There is No Difference between Israeli Terrorism and the Terrorist Attacks on the United States." *Al-Akhbar*, September 14, 2001.

11. Quoted in Guerin. *Indonesia*.

12. Judis, John B. "The Road to Aqaba." *American Prospect*, July 1, 2003 (cited August 7, 2004). <http://www.prospect.org/print/V14/7/judis-j.html>.

13. Zinni, Gen. Anthony. "Ten Mistakes History Will Record About War in Iraq." *Defense Monitor* 33, no. 3 (2004).

14. Quoted in D'Agostino, Joseph A. "The Enemy: Osama Bin Laden." *Human Events* 57, no. 34: 3.

15. "Sharon: 'Fight against Terrorism and the Forces of Darkness and Evil'." *Middle East News Online*, September 11, 2001.

16. Bennet, James. "Spilled Blood is Seen as Bond that Draws Two Nations Closer." *New York Times*, September 12, 2001, A22.

17. Dan, Uri. "The US Will Respond." *Jerusalem Post*, September 13, 2001, 8.

18. Kiley, Sam. "Sharon Orders New Wave of Attacks on Palestinians." *Evening Standard*, September 13, 2001, 10.

19. Nordwall, Smita P. "'Arafat is Our Bin Laden,' Israeli Says Amid Fighting." *USA Today*, September 14, 2001, A10.

20. Barthos, Gordon. "Courting U.S. Ire on Mideast." *Toronto Star*, September 14, 2001, A28.

21. Ibid.

22. Bush, George W. "Address to a Joint session of Congress and the American People." White House, September 20, 2001. <http://www.whitehouse.gov/news/releases/2001/09/20010920-8.html>.

23. Bush, George W. "President Meets with Congressional Leaders." White House, October 2, 2001. <http://www.whitehouse.gov/news/releases/2001/10/20011002-1.html>.

24. "Sharon's Warning Shot." *Jerusalem Post*, October 5, 2001, A8.

25. Atkins, Ralph, Brian Groom, Alexander Nicoll and David Stern. "US Rebukes Israeli Leader as Coalition Tensions Rise." *Financial Times*, October 6, 2001, 1.

26. Ibid.

27. Al-Jindi, Ahmad. "A Passing Crisis in a Very Special Relationship." *Al-Akhbar*, October 8, 2001.

28. "Theatre of the Absurd." *Jordan Times*, October 7, 2001.

29. "UAE Paper Plays Down US–Israel Slanging Match." AFP, October 6, 2001.

30. Powell. "U.S. Vision for Middle East Peace, November 19, 2001." 166.

31. Zacharia, Janine. "Hizbullah may be Next in the War on Terror." October 24, 2001 (cited May 5, 2002). <www.jpost.com/Editions/2001/10/24/News/News.36823.html>.

32. Schweid, Barry. "Bush Says Burden on Arafat after 25 Die in Suicide Blasts in Israel." *Chicago Sun-Times*, December 3, 2001, 3.

33. Ibid.

34. Cornwell, Rupert. "US Gives Israel Green Light to 'Defend Itself' against Terrorists." *Independent*, December 4, 2001, 5.

35. Ibid.

36. "Mideast Press Hammers Israel." AFP, December 4, 2001.

37. Ibid.
38. Barzak, Ibrahim, and Mark Lavie. "Israelis Launch Strikes." *Tulsa World*, December 4, 2001, 1.
39. Ibid.
40. "Sharon Echoes Bush in Anti-Terror Speech." *Houston Chronicle*, December 4, 2001, 14.
41. Ibid.
42. Hishmeh, George S. "Bush's 'Green Light.'" Middle East News Online, December 5, 2001.
43. Eban, A. *The Beirut Massacre: The Complete Kahan Commission Report* (first edition). Princeton: Karz-Cohl, 1983.
44. McCloskey, Paul N. "Will President Bush have the Courage to Stand Up to Ariel Sharon?" *Washington Report on Middle East Affairs* 22, no. 4: 11.
45. "Mideast Press."
46. Ibid.
47. "President Bush, Prime Minister Sharon Discuss Middle East." Washington, D.C.: White House, February 7, 2002. <http://www.whitehouse.gov/news/releases/2002/02/20020207-15.html>.
48. Lynch, Colum. "Iran Fires Back at Bush for Accusations of 'Evil.'" *Washington Post*, February 6, 2002, A12.
49. Bush, George W. "State of the Union Address." The White House, January 29, 2002. <http://www.whitehouse.gov/news/releases/2002/01/20020129-11.html>.
50. Lynch. "Iran Fires Back."
51. "Bush, Sharon Discuss Middle East."
52. Ibid.
53. "Who's the Terrorist?" *New Straits Times*, February 9, 2002, 8.
54. Ibid.
55. "Syrian Editorial on Bush–Sharon Meeting." BBC Monitoring Middle East – Political, February 9, 2002, 1.
56. LaFranchi, Howard. "US Rethinks Role as Middle East Referee." *Christian Science Monitor*, February 7, 2002, 2.
57. Ibid.
58. Frum, David. *The Right Man: The Surprise Presidency of George W. Bush* (first edition). New York: Random House, 2003.
59. "Bush, Sharon Discuss Middle East."
60. "Arab Anger Mounting, Egyptian Foreign Minister Warns." AFP, February 10, 2002.
61. "Washington Accepts Israeli Minister's Apologies." IPR Strategic Business Information Database, February 11, 2002.
62. "Israeli Planes Keep up Attack but Arafat Wins Propaganda Skirmish." AFP, February 12, 2002.
63. Powell, Sara. "A Chronology of U.S.–Middle East." *Washington Report on Middle East Affairs* 21, no. 4: 100.
64. Lee, Matthew. "US Watches as Three Peace Processes Crumble in a Single Day." AFP, February 21, 2002.
65. Ibid.
66. Hazboun, Ibrahim. "Palestinian Death Toll Surpasses 1,000 in Fighting with Israel." Associated Press, February 28, 2002.

67. Bush, George W. "President, Vice President, Sec. Of State Discuss Middle East." White House, March 7, 2002 (cited October 1, 2004). <http://www.whitehouse.gov/news/releases/2002/03/20020307-12.html>.

68. Sanger, David. "Bush Officials End Support of Sharon's Tough Stance." *New York Times*, March 7, 2002, A8.

69. Ibid.

70. Ibid.

71. Bush. "President Discusses Middle East."

72. Ibid.

73. Ibid.

74. Ibid.

75. "A Condemnable American Position!" *Al-Rayah*, March 8, 2002.

76. "Gulf Press Suspicious About Zinni's Mideast Mission." AFP, March 9, 2002.

77. Ibid.

78. "Israel and the Occupied Territories." London: Amnesty International, 2002.

79. Slevin, Peter, and Mike Allen. "Bush: Sharon a 'Man of Peace.'" *Washington Post*, April 19, 2002, A1.

80. "Press Briefing by Ari Fleischer." Washington, D.C.: White House, 2002.

81. Bush, George W. "President Bush, Secretary Powell Discuss Middle East." White House, April 18, 2002 (cited May 15, 2003). <http://www. whitehouse.gov/news/releases/2002/04/20020418-3.html>.

82. McCloskey. "Will Bush have the Courage?"

83. Bush, George W. "President Bush Meets with Prime Minister Sharon." White House, May 7 2002. <http://www/whitehouse.gov/news/releases/2002/05/20020507-12.html>.

84. Ibid.

85. Bush, George W. "President Bush Calls for New Palestinian Leadership." White House, June 24, 2002. <http://www.whitehouse.gov/news/releases/2002/06/20020624-3.html>.

86. Rosenblum, Jonathan. "Israel's Best Friend Ever in the White House." *Jerusalem Post*, July 5, 2002, B9.

87. Bush. "Palestinian Leadership."

88. Wolfson, Paula. "US Officials Defend Bush Middle East Plan." Middle East News Online: 1.

89. "Cairo Press Review." Middle East News Online, June 26, 2002.

90. Rosenblum. "Best Friend."

91. Khouri, Rami G. "Strict Justice Must Be Your Ideal." Middle East News Online, July 3, 2002, 1.

CHAPTER 9

1. O'Reilly, Bill. "The O'Reilly Factor" (television). Fox News, March 27, 2003.

2. Getlin, Josh. "Fox News' Patriotic Fervor Sets it Apart in Ratings Race." *Los Angeles Times*, April 11, 2003, A16.

3. Rosenberg, Howard. "Objectivity is Lost to Fox News' Barbs." *Los Angeles Times*, April 11, 2003, E1.

4. *The Late Show with David Letterman* (television). CBS, September 17, 2001 (cited November 3, 2003). <http://www.mediaresearch.org/cyberalerts/2001/cyb20010918.asp>.

5. "Return to Normalcy? How the Media have Covered the War on Terrorism." Project for Excellence in Journalism, January 28, 2002 (cited December 2, 2003). <http://www.journalism.org/resources/research/reports/normalcy/default.asp>.

6. Goodman, Ellen. "Bush's PR War." *Washington Post* Writer's Group, March 9, 2003 (cited October 10, 2004). <http://www.postwritersgroup.com/archives/good0306.htm>.

7. Tannenhaus, Sam. "Deputy Secretary Wolfowitz Interview with Vanity Fair." U.S. Embassy Brussels, May 9, 2003 (cited November 7, 2004). <http://www.uspolicy.be/Issues/Iraq/wolfvanityfair.053003.htm>.

8. Gordon, Michael R., and Judith Miller. "U.S. Says Hussein Intensifies Quest for A-Bomb Parts." *New York Times*, September 8 2002, 1.1.

9. Bumiller, Elisabeth. "Bush Aides Set Strategy to Sell Policy on Iraq." *New York Times*, September 7, 2002, A1.

10. Knightley, Phillip. *The First Casualty: The War Correspondent as Hero and Myth-Maker from the Crimea to Kosovo.* Baltimore, Md.: Johns Hopkins University Press, 2002. 526.

11. Samuelson, Robert J. "Unwitting Accomplices?" *Washington Post*, November 7, 2001, A29.

12. Fleischer, Ari. "Press Briefing." White House, September 26, 2003 (cited March 5, 2004). <http://www.whitehouse.gov/news/releases/2001/09/20010926-5.html>.

13. McLeland, Susan. "Ted Turner: U.S. Media Mogul." Museum of Broadcast Communications (cited April 6, 2004). <http://www.museum.tv/archives/etv/T/htmlT/turnerted/turnerted.htm>.

14. Volkmer, Ingrid. "Journalism and Political Crises in the Global Network Society." In *Journalism after September 11*, edited by Barbie Zelizer and Stuart Allan, London and New York: Routledge, 2002. 235.

15. Marr, Merissa. "BBC Chief Attacks U.S. Media War Coverage." Reuters, April 24, 2003 (cited July 15, 2004). <http://uktop100.reuters.com/latest/BBC/top10/20030424-IRAQ-MEDIA-BBC.ASP>.

16. "U.S. Military Should Investigate Civilian Deaths." Human Rights Watch, Kabul, December 13, 2003. <http://www.reliefweb.int/w/rwb.nsf0/2f8f1ccdaad429d49256dfd0005ed77?OpenDocument>.

17. Donohoe, Miriam. "Forgotten Victims of Afghan War." *Irish Times*, September 6, 2002, 16.

18. Knickerbocker, Brad. "A War's Likely Toll on Iraqis." *Christian Science Monitor*, February 7, 2003, 2.

19. Safi, Omid. "What the Pictures Mean." *Post-Standard*, May 13, 2004, A13.

20. Hammer, Joshua, Richard Wolffe and Christopher Dickey. "The 'Road to Jerusalem.'" *Newsweek*, May 31, 2004 (cited June 15, 2004). <http://msnbc.msn.com/id/5040834>.

21. Gardiner, Col. Sam. "Truth from These Podia." Washington, D.C., 2003. <http://www.usnews.com/usnews/politics/whispers/documents/truth_1.pdf>.

22. DeYoung, Karen. "Bush Message Machine is Set to Roll with its Own War Plan." *Washington Post*, March 19, 2003, A1.

23. Humphries, Lt. Commander Arthur A. "Two Routes to the Wrong Destination: Public Affairs in the South Atlantic War." *Naval War College Review* 36, no. 3 (1983): 57.

24. Fisk, Robert. "The War of Misinformation has Begun." *Independent*, March 16, 2003.

25. Nicholson, Mark, and Peter Spiegel. "'Granularity' of Battle Sometimes Lost in Fog of War." *Financial Times*, March 28, 2003, 2.

26. Rosenstiel, Tom, and Amy Mitchell. "Embedded Reporters: What are Americans Getting?" Project for Excellence in Journalism, April 3, 2003 (cited August 29, 2003). <http://www.journalism.org/resources/research/reports/war/embed/>.

27. Artz, Lee. "War as Promotional 'Photo Op': *The New York Times*'s Visual Coverage of the U.S. Invasion of Iraq." In *War, Media, and Propaganda*, edited by Yahya R. Kamalipour and Nancy Snow. New York and Oxford: Rowman & Littlefield, 2004.

28. Conversation with the author. Ann Arbor, Mich., March 2, 2004.

29. Sachs, Susan. "Arab Media Portray War as Killing Field." *New York Times*, April 4, 2003, B1.

30. Khouri, Rami. "For the Full Story, Watch US and Arab TV." *Daily Star*, March 26, 2003.

31. Krull, Steven. "The Press and Public Misperceptions about the Iraq War." *Nieman Reports* (Summer 2004): 64–6.

32. Schleifer, S. Abdallah. "Satellite Television News: Up, Down, and Out." *Transnational Broadcasting Studies Journal*, Spring/Summer 2003 (cited 10 June, 2004). <http://www.tbsjournal.com/Archives/Spring03/satellite%20tv.html>.

33. The charge that al-Jazeera was doing Saddam's bidding was revived almost two years later when the U.S. government's own Arabic-language television channel, al-Hurra, broadcast a videotape alledgedly found in a pile of documents in Baghdad. The tape showed al-Jazeera's general manager, Mohammed Jassem al-Ali, in a meeting with Uday Hussein, eldest son of the Iraqi dictator. On the tape, al-Ali thanks Uday for his support, adding, "al-Jazeera is your channel." While it is quite possible that Jassem was on Saddam's payroll – as noted earlier, there was a long tradition of Arab journalists taking payoffs or shilling for a cause – the encounter should be seen in context. Plenty of American reporters had also cosied up to the Baghdad regime over the years. During the Iran–Iraq War, this writer successfully convinced Iraqi officials that it was in their interest to let CBS and the other U.S. networks keep a long-term presence in Baghdad even as newspaper reporters were forced to leave after a few weeks. Following the invasion of Iraq, CNN's news chief, Eason Jordan, admitted that his organization had purposely suppressed many negative stories about Iraqi excesses in order to stay in the regime's good graces, including the fact that during his own 1995 meeting with Uday, the Iraqi told him that "he intended to assassinate two of his brothers-in-law who had defected and also the man giving them asylum, King Hussein of Jordan." The CNN executive sat on the story but did warn King Hussein. A few months later, the brothers-in-law were lured back to Baghdad and executed. For more on the al-Ali tape, see Dakroub, Hussein. "Al-Jazeera Ex-Manager Tied to Son of Saddam." Associated

Press, January 4, 2005, A15. For details on the CNN story, see Jordan, Eason. "The News We Kept to Ourselves." *New York Times*, April 11, 2003, A25.

34. Baroud, Ramzy. "America, We Feel Your Pain, Do You Feel Ours?" *Middle East News Online*.

35. Hendawi, Hamza. "War Disastrous for Iraq's Children." *Milwaukee Journal Sentinel*, January 27, 2003, A6.

36. Robbins, Carla Anne, and Jeanne Cummings. "How Bush Decided that Iraq's Hussein must be Ousted." *Asian Wall Street Journal*, June 17, 2002, A1.

37. "Secretary Rumsfeld Interview with Al Jezeera." Department of Defense, October 16, 2001 (cited March 3, 2005). <http://www.defenselink.mil/transcripts/2001/t10172001_t1016sd.html>.

38. "National Security Advisor Condoleezza Rice Interview with Al-Jazeera TV." White House, October 15, 2001 (cited June 5, 2004). <http://www.whitehouse.gov/news/releases/2001/10/20011016-3.html>.

39. Younes, Robert. "A Chronology of U.S.–Middle East Relations." *Washington Report on Middle East Affairs* 22, no. 2: 79.

40. Ibid.

41. Ibid.

42. Rosenthal, A.M. "The UN Gets the Truth, and it's Long Overdue." *New York Daily News*, February 7, 2003, 57.

43. "Powell's Smoking Gun." *Wall Street Journal*, February 6, 2003, A18.

44. McGrory, Mary. "I'm Persuaded." *Washington Post*, February 6, 2003, A37.

45. Cohen, Richard. "A Winning Hand for Powell." *Washington Post*, February 6, 2003, A37.

46. Ferguson, Barbara. "Powell Unconvincing at UN." Arab News, February 6, 2003 (cited April 4, 2004). <http://www.arabnews.com/?page=4&section=0&article=22562&d=6&m=2&y=2003>.

47. "Powell Presents the Pretexts for War." *Al-Arab al-Yawm*, February 7, 2003, 1.

48. "Indonesian Paper Says US Must Hand over 'Questionable' Iraq Evidence to UN." BBC Monitoring Asia Pacific – Political, 2003.

49. "Malaysian Premier Insists UN be Allowed to Resolve Iraq Crisis." BBC Monitoring Asia Pacific – Political, February 7, 2003.

50. "Iraq: Arab Media Condemns War." Global Information Network.

51. Ibid.

52. Ibid.

53. Ibid.

54. "Iraq: Anger Boils over in Arab World at U.S. War on Iraq." Global Information Network.

55. Ibid.

56. Otis, John. "Arab Media Accused of War Bias." *Houston Chronicle*, April 5, 2003, 25.

57. Live coverage. CNN International, 2003.

58. Graham, Bob. "America Did It . . ." *Evening Standard*, March 27, 2003, 11.

59. Ibid.

60. Ibid.

61. Kennedy, Helen. "Horror Show Repulses: Iraqi TV Parades Terrified POWs." *New York Daily News*, March 24, 2003, 4.

62. "A Video War Crime." *Denver Post*, March 24, 2003, B7.

63. Leinwand, Donna. "U.S. Blasts Al-Jazeera's Decision to Air Tape." *USA Today*, March 24, 2003, A6.

64. Weisman, Jonathan, and Bradley Graham. "Display of 5 POWs Draws Firm Rebuke." *Washington Post*, March 24, 2003, A1.

65. Kurtz, Howard. "Media's Battlefield Reporting Outpaces Pentagon Officials." *Washington Post*, March 24, 2003, A27.

66. Ibid.

67. Ibid.

68. Deggans, Eric, and Dave Scheiber. "Blitz on Your Screen is Ultimate in Reality TV Series." *St. Petersburg Times*, March 28, 2003, A1.

69. Leinwand. "U.S. Blasts."

70. "Airing News Footage of Prisoners Creates Quandary." *Charleston Daily Mail*, March 24, 2003, B5.

71. Mason, Julie. "Military Critical of Coverage." *Houston Chronicle*, March 25, 2003, 7.

72. Martin, Paul. "U.S. Calls Footage of POWs 'Disgusting.'" *Washington Times*, March 24, 2003, A1.

73. "Let Us Remember the 600 POWs at Guantanamo." *Seattle Post – Intelligencer*, March 25, 2003, B4.

74. Hughes, Chris, and John Clements. "Now Iraq Parades Captured Pilots." *Daily Mirror*, March 25, 2003, 1.

75. Ibid.

76. Rutenberg, Jim. "After Days of Buoyant Images, Reporting Enters a Second and More Ominous Act." *New York Times*, March 24, 2003, B16.

77. Hughes and Clements. "Pilots."

78. Loeb, Vernon, and Dana Priest. "Missing Soldier Rescued." *Washington Post*, April 2, 2003, A1.

79. Schmidt, Susan, and Vernon Loeb. "'She was Fighting to the Death.'" April 3, 2003.

80. Ibid.

81. Kampfner, John. "Saving Private Lynch Story 'Flawed.'" BBC News World Edition, May 15, 2003 (cited November 5, 2003). <http://news.bbc.co.uk/2/hi/programmes/correspondent/3028585.stm>.

82. Ibid.

83. Getler, Michael. "A Long, and Incomplete, Correction." *Washington Post*, June 29, 2003, B6.

84. "Lynch Calls Filming of Rescue 'Wrong.'" *Washington Post*, November 11, 2003, C7.

85. Younge, Gary. "Private Lynch's Media War Continues as Iraqi Doctors Deny Rape Claim." *Guardian*, November 12, 2003, 17.

86. Getler. "Long Correction."

87. McWhinnie, Chris. "Analysis: Iraq – Pictures Speak Louder than Words." BBC Monitoring Middle East – Political.

88. Nelson, Craig, and Robert W. Gee. "Chaos, Fear Reign after Raid." *Austin American Statesman*, April 6, 2003, A1.

89. Morgan, David. "U.S. Army Used Media Cover in Iraq for Own Ends." *Reuters*, September 5, 2003.
90. Ibid.
91. Ibid.
92. Nessman, Ravi. "Iraqis Go Wild in Baghdad: Saddam's Regime Collapses." *Advocate*, April 10, 2003, A1.
93. Barnard, Anne, and Michael Kranish. "Baghdad Falls: Euphoric Iraqis Topple Symbols." *Boston Globe*, April 10, 2003, A1.
94. Gibson, John. "Coalition Forces Control Baghdad" (television). Fox News, April 9, 2003.
95. Smith, Harry, Julie Chen and Hanna Storm. "Reaction in Baghdad to the Toppling of Saddam Hussein's Regime" (television). CBS Television, April 9, 2003.
96. Johnson, Steve. "Powerful TV Image Obscures Details." *Chicago Tribune*, April 10, 2003, 12.
97. Ibid.
98. Gibson. "Coalition Forces."
99. Johnson. "Powerful TV."
100. Smith, Chen and Storm. "Reaction in Baghdad."
101. Johnson. "Powerful TV."
102. Qusti, Ra'id, and Safinaz Murshid. "Exclusive: Saudis Express Mixed Feelings." *Arab News*, April 10, 2003, 1.
103. Ibid.
104. "Al-Jazeera TV Gives Running Commentary on Toppling of Saddam Statue." BBC Monitoring Middle East, 2003.
105. Ibid.
106. Ibid.
107. Johnson. "Powerful TV."
108. Coker, Margaret. "Anger, Disbelief Echo across Region." *Austin American Statesman*, April 10, 2003, A9.
109. Ibid.
110. "Al-Jazeera Gives Running Commentary."
111. Ibid.
112. "Iraqis Must Now Ensure 'Spoils' Not 'Stolen by Their Conquerors' – Saudi Paper." BBC Monitoring Middle East – Political, April 10, 2003.
113. "Jordanian Editorial: Jordan, Egypt and Saudi Call for Iraqis to Rule Iraq." BBC Monitoring Middle East – Political, April 10, 2003.
114. Nickerson, Colin. "Fall of Baghdad a Day of Gloom for Many Arabs." *Boston Globe*, April 10, 2003, A29.
115. Ibid.
116. Hume, Brit. "Bush Administration Reacts to Victory in Baghdad" (television). *Fox Special Report with Brit Hume*. Fox News, 2003.
117. Ibid.
118. Coker. "Anger, Disbelief."
119. Nickerson. "Day of Gloom."
120. Hume, Brit. "Wartime Grapevine." *Fox Special Report with Brit Hume*. Fox News, 2003.
121. "Amien Rais Compares Bush to Joseph Stalin." *Jakarta Post*, May 2, 2003.

122. Bush, George W. "President Discusses Operation Iraqi Freedom at Camp Lejeune." White House, April 3, 2003. <http://www.whitehouse.gov/news/releases/2003/04/20030403-3.html>.

123. Bush, George W. "President Bush Announces Major Combat Operations in Iraq have Ended." White House, May 1, 2003. <http://www.whitehouse.gov/news/releases/2003/05/iraq/20030501-15.html>.

124. Ibid.

125. Jackson, Derrick Z. "US Stays Blind to Iraqi Casualties." *Boston Globe*, November 14, 2003, A19.

126. Bush. "Combat Operations."

127. Ibid.

128. Zaanoun, Adel. "Huge Israeli Raid in Gaza Kills Eight, in Heavy Blow to Peace 'Roadmap.'" AFP, May 1, 2003.

129. Bush, George W. "Statement on the Middle East." White House, April 30, 2003. <http://www.whitehouse.gov/news/releases/2003/04/20030430-4.html>.

130. Schmitt, Eric, and Elisabeth Bumiller. "Rumsfeld Visits Two Cities in Iraq, Meeting Troops." *New York Times*, May 1, 2003, A1.

131. Jannati, Ayatollah. "Jannati Urges Iraqis 'to Drive out the Enemy' from Iraq." Voice of the Islamic Republic of Iran Radio, 2003, cited by Foreign Broadcast Information Service.

132. "Sermons Uphold Shari'a, Iraqi Imam Asks US Forces to Withdraw from Al-Fallujah." *World News Connection*, May 2, 2003.

133. Slackman, Michael. "Tense Standoff between Troops and Iraqis Erupts in Bloodshed." *Los Angeles Times*, April 30, 2003, A1.

134. "Sermons."

CHAPTER 10

1. "Remarks by President Bush and President Megawati of Indonesia in a Photo Opportunity." White House, September 19, 2001 (cited January 7, 2004). <http://www.whitehouse.gov/news/releases/2001/09/20010919-1.html>.

2. "U.S. And Indonesia Pledge Cooperation." White House, September 19, 2001 (cited March 5, 2004). <http://www.whitehouse.gov/news/releases/2001/09/20010919-5.html>.

3. Yamin, Kafil. "After Iraq, View of U.S. Double Standards Sharpens." IPS, April 24, 2003 (cited August 4, 2004). <http://www.ipsnews.net/interna.asp?idnews=17764>.

4. Anderson, Benedict. *Imagined Communities: Reflections on the Origin and Spread of Nationalism* (second edition). London and New York: Verso, 1991. 6–7.

5. "Views of a Changing World." In *The Pew Global Attitudes Project*, edited by Andrew Kohut. Washington, D.C.: The Pew Research Center for the People and the Press, 2003. 19.

6. Ibid.

7. Wanandi, Jusuf. "Southeast Asia's Role in Eradicating Terrorism." *Jakarta Post*, June 4, 2003 (cited April 12, 2004). <http://www.csis.or.id/scholars_opinion_view.asp?op_id=11&id=55>.

8. "Beaten." *Kompas*, December 17, 1987, 8.

9. "Israeli Action Is Roundly Criticized." *Kompas*, December 21, 1987, 8.

10. "Israel Doesn't Care About World Criticism." *Kompas*, December 22, 1987, 7.

11. "Israel Must Act on Gaza, West Bank." *Chicago Sun-Times*, December 23, 1987, 30.

12. "Vicious Outbreak of Conflict between Israeli and Arabs in the Gaza and West Bank." *Kompas*, December 23, 1987, 15.

13. "U.S. Rebukes Israel for Policy on Protesters." *St. Petersburg Times*, December 23, 1987, A1.

14. Bushinsky, Jay. "'Inhuman' Jailings Charged to Israelis." *Chicago Sun-Times*, December 30, 1987, 2.

15. Hoffman, Stanley. "Israel Lets Arab Poisons Fester." *Star Tribune*, December 31, 1987, A11.

16. "Has Israel Lost Democracy?" *San Diego Union-Tribune*, December 30, 1987, B7.

17. "Israel Can Make the Crisis Murky." *Kompas*, October 10, 1990, 15.

18. Reuters. "Bush Wants U.N. Probe of Killings in Jerusalem 'Fully Implemented.'" *Seattle Post-Intelligencer*, October 16, 1990, A2.

19. "Indonesia Strongly Condemns Israel's Military Aggression." *Kompas*, April 3, 2002.

20. "Megawati Expected to Raise Global Criticism on Israel." *Kompas*, April 3 2002.

21. Zogby, John, and James J. Zogby. "Impressions of America 2004." Washington, D.C.: Arab American Institute/Zogby International, 2004. 22–4.

22. "Indonesia Condemns."

23. "Megawati."

24. Ibid.

25. Ibid.

26. Conversation with the author. Ann Arbor, Mich., April 2, 2004.

27. Harsono, Andreas. "Indonesia: Suddenly Free." *IPI Report*, no. 7 (1998): 4.

28. "Gallup Poll of the Islamic World." *USA Today*, February. 27, 2002.

29. Nakashima, Ellen. "In Indonesia, a Wary Worldview: Skeptical of U.S. Media, People Turn to Al-Jazeera." *Washington Post*, April 8, 2003, C1.

30. Mohamad, Mahathir. "Close Ranks, Muslims Urged." *Star*, October 16, 2003 (cited October 19, 2003). <http://thestar.com.my/oic/story.asp?file=/2003/10/17/oic/6507802&sec=OIC>.

31. Kaur, Hardev. "Dr. Mahathir in Davos: World War III Has Begun" *New Straits Times*, January 24, 2003.

32. Mohamad. "Close Ranks."

33. "Friday's Headlines of Indonesia's Major Dailies." *Antara*, October 17, 2003.

34. Bazinet, Kenneth R. "Malay PM Calls Jews the Puppet Masters." *New York Daily News*, October 17, 2003, 34.

35. Schrag, Carl. "Malaysia's Casual Anti-Semitism." October 20, 2003 (cited June 15, 2004). <http://www.slate.msn.com/id/2090080>.

36. Sullivan, Rohan. "Muslim PM Seeks 'Final Victory' over Jews: Malaysian Leader." *National Post*, October 17, 2003, A12.

37. Arnold, Wayne. "Mahathir Tells Muslims to Unite against Jews." *International Herald Tribune*, October 17, 2003, 5.
38. "A Message of Hate." *Toronto Star*, October 20, 2003 (cited April 5, 2004). <http://www.thestar.com/NASApp/cs/ContentServer?pagename= thestar/Layout/Article_Type1&call_pageid=971358637177&c=Article &cid= 1066428608209>.
39. Blomquist, Brian, and Stefan C. Friedman. "Weasel Gags EU over 'Jew' Slur." *New York Post*, October 18, 2003, 12.
40. "Malaysian Attacks Jews." *New York Times*, October 17, 2003, A8.
41. "Islamic Anti-Semitism." *New York Times*, October 18, 2003, A12.
42. Sipress, Alan. "Malaysian Calls on Muslims to Resist Jewish Influence." *Washington Post*, October 17, 2003, A21.
43. "Malaysian Prime Minister Seeks Muslim Unity, Nonviolent Victory." *Asian Wall Street Journal*, October 17, 2003, A4.
44. "The U.S. Won Unanimous U.N. Approval of its Iraq-Rebuilding Plan." *Wall Street Journal*, October 17, 2003, A1.
45. Djerjian, Edward P. "Changing Minds, Winning Peace: A New Strategic Direction for U.S. Diplomacy in the Arab and Muslim World." Washington, D.C.: Advisory Group for Public Diplomacy for the Arab and Muslim World, U.S. House of Representatives, 2003. 17.
46. "Quotes from Gen. Boykin Speeches." NBC News, October 15, 2003 (cited November 15, 2004). <http://www.msnbc.com/news/ 980764.asp?cp1=1>.
47. Entous, Adam. "Bush Distances Himself from General's Islam Comment." Reuters, October 22, 2003.
48. Ross, Sonya. "Religion Mixes into War on Terror." *Oakland Tribune*, October 24, 2003, 1.
49. Ibid.
50. "Mahathir's Speech Drew Condemnation, but Anti-Islamic Remarks Go Unnoticed." BBC, October 20, 2003 (cited December 10, 2003). <http://www.bbcnews.com>.
51. Ibid.
52. Meyer, Dick. "Gods, Generals, Satan, and Jews." CBS News, October 21, 2003 (cited December 5, 2003). <http://www.cbsnews.com/stories/ 2003/10/21/opinion/meyer/main579135.shtml>.
53. Said, Edward W. *Covering Islam: How the Media and the Experts Determine How We See the Rest of the World*. New York: Vintage Books, 1997. xxii.
54. Chuensuksawadi, Pichai. "Mahathir: Jew Comment out of Context." *Bangkok Post*, October 21, 2003, 1.

CHAPTER 11

1. "Mission Statement." Al-Hurra, 2005. <http://www.alhurra.com>.
2. "Editorial Mocks New U.S. Arabic Channel." *Al-Quds al-Arabi*, February 17, 2004 (cited September 15, 2004). <http://www.worldpress. org/Mideast/1808.cfm>.

3. "U.S. Launches Arabic Satellite Television Broadcasts Feb. 14." Broadcasting Board of Governors, February 10, 2004 (cited February 28, 2005). <http://www.bbg.gov/_bbg_news.cfm?articleID=102&mode=general>.

4. Fisher, William. "Winning the War of Ideas." *Jordan Times*, August 8, 2004 (cited November 5, 2004). <http://www.jordantimes.com/sun/opinion/opinion5.htm>.

5. Khouri, Rami. "The U.S. Public Diplomacy Hoax: Why Do They Keep Insulting Us?" *Daily Star*, February 11, 2004.

6. "Saudi Clerics Bash US Funded Arabic Television Channel, Saying Muslims should not Watch it." *Jordan Times*, March 7, 2004.

7. Ghafour, P.K. Abdul. "Haram Imam Blasts Al-Hurra for Causing 'Intellectual Chaos.'" *Arab News*, March 6, 2004.

8. Neslen, Arthur "Reality Television." *Guardian*, April 21, 2004, 23.

9. Nisbet, Erik C., Matthew C. Nisbet, Dietram A. Scheufele and James E. Shanahan. "Public Diplomacy, Television News, and Muslim Opinion." *Harvard Journal of Press/Politics* 9, no. 2 (2003): 26.

10. Ibid. 32.

11. Ibid.

12. "Panel Discussion: Is Arab Media a Force for Reform, the Status Quo, or Extremism?" In *Arab Media, Power and Influence*. Washington, D.C.: Princeton University and Rice University, May 4, 2005.

13. Zogby, John, and James J. Zogby. "Impressions of America 2004." Washington, D.C.: Arab American Institute/Zogby International, 2004. 16–17.

14. Perlez, Jane. "U.S. Asks Muslims Why it is Unloved: Indonesians Reply." *New York Times*, September 27, 2003, A3.

15. Nisbet et al. "Public Diplomacy." 25. Emphasis added.

16. Nakashima, Ellen. "In Indonesia, a Wary Worldview: Skeptical of U.S. Media, People Turn to Al-Jazeera." *Washington Post*, April 8, 2001, C1.

17. Russert, Tim. "Interview with President George W. Bush". NBC News, February 8, 2004 (cited February 9, 2004). <http://www.msnbc.msn.com/id/4179618/>.

18. Quoted in Gubash, Charlene. "Arabs View U.S. Network with Deep Skepticism." MSNBC, February 25, 2004 (cited December 3, 2004).

19. Amayreh, Khalid. "US TV Channel Raises Palestinian Ire." Al-Jazeera, February 15, 2004 (cited August 5, 2004). <http://english.aljazeera.net/NR/exeres/F1AA34B0-1DAA-4A97-BE65-BD54EB703B65.htm?GUID={79A16E4E-BA73-4159-8FF0-EAB2F329EE03}>.

20. "U.S.-Funded Radio and Television Make Significant Gains in Middle East Despite Anti-American Sentiments." Broadcasting Board of Governors, April 29, 2004 (cited February 28, 2005). <http://www.bbg.gov/_bbg_news.cfm?articleID=112&mode=general>.

21. "Alhurra and Radio Sawa Make Their Mark in Syria." Springfield, Va.: Broadcasting Board of Governors, 2005.

22. Slavin, Barbara. "VOA Changes Prompt Staffer Protests." *USA Today*, July 13, 2004, A10.

23. Mawari, Munir. "Washington Plans to Counter Islamic Militancy in Europe by Extending Al Hurra Broadcasts to Europe." *Asharq al-Awsat*, March 9, 2005.

24. "Arabs are Watching US Channel Alhurra – Survey." Reuters, April 29, 2004 (cited January 15, 2005). <http://www.alertnet.org/printable/ htm?URL=/thenews/newsdesk/N29620731.htm>.

25. "Saudi Sat TV and Radio Survey." Amman, Jordan: Arab Advisors Group, 2004.

26. "Significant Gains."

27. Ford, Jess T. "U.S. Public Diplomacy: State Department and Broadcasting Board of Governors Expand Efforts in the Middle East but Face Significant Challenges." Washington, D.C.: General Accounting Office, 2004.

28. Kessler, Glenn. "The Role of Radio Sawa in Mideast Questioned." *Washington Post*, October 13, 2004, A12.

29. DeYoung, Karen. "Bush to Create Formal Office to Shape U.S. Image Abroad." *Washington Post*, July 30, 2002, A1.

30. Johnson, Stephen, and Helle Dale. "How to Reinvigorate U.S. Public Diplomacy." In *Backgrounder*, Washington, D.C.: The Heritage Foundation, 2003. 11.

31. Hamilton, Lee. "American Public Diplomacy and Foreign Policy: Keynote Speech." In *Arab Media, Power and Influence*. Washington, D.C.: Princeton University and Rice University, March 11, 2005.

32. Conversation with the author. Ann Arbor, Mich., April 15, 2004.

33. Thomas, Robert McG. Jr. "Willis Conover is Dead at 75: Aimed Jazz at the Soviet Bloc." *New York Times*, May 19, 1996, 1.35.

34. "U.S. International Broadcasting: Report to the Committee on Foreign Relations, U.S. Senate." Washington, D.C.: General Accounting Office, 2004.

35. Slavin. "VOA Changes."

36. "U.S. Propaganda Pitch Halted." CBS News, January 16, 2003 (cited January 20, 2003). <http://www.cbsnews.com/stories/2003/01/16/ world/main536756.shtml>.

37. "U.S. Muslim Ad Drive Gets Thumbs Down in SE Asia." Reuters, November 7, 2002 (cited December 12, 2002). <http:// www.dailytimes.com.pk/default.asp?page=story_7-11-2002_pg4-5>.

38. "U.S. Propaganda Blitz Not Telling Full Story." November 7, 2002 (cited August 5, 2004). <http://www.laksmana.net/vnews.cfm?ncat= 19&news_id=4191>.

39. Goodenough, Patrick. "U.S. Ad Campaign Gets Thumbs-Down from SE Asian Muslims." November 7, 2002 (cited April 3, 2003). <http:// www.crosswalk.com/news/1170366.html>.

40. Reinhard, Keith. "Testimony before the House Subcommittee on National Security, Emerging Threats, and International Relations." Washington, D.C.: U.S. Congress, 2004.

41. Telhami, Shibley, and John Zogby. "Arab Attitudes Towards Political and Social Issues, Foreign Policy and the Media." University of Maryland/Zogby International, July 23, 2004 (cited July 26, 2004). <http://www.bsos.umd.edu/sadat/pub/Arab%20Attitudes%20Towards%2 0Political%20and%20Social%20Issues,%20Foreign%20Policy%20and% 20the%20Media.htm>.

42. Conversation with the author. March 12, 2005.

43. "*U.S. Propaganda Blitz.*"

44. Fakhreddine, Jihad. "US Public Diplomacy in Broken Arabic." *Global Media Journal* 2, no. 4 (2004).

45. Dao, James, and Eric Schmitt. "Pentagon Readies Efforts to Sway Sentiment Abroad." *New York Times*, February 19, 2002, A1.
46. Schmitt, Eric. "Pentagon and Bogus News: All is Denied." *New York Times*, December 5, 2003, A6.
47. Constable, Pamela. "U.S. Seizes Bodyguards of Hussein; Leader's Two Dead Sons Cleaned up for Display." *Washington Post*, July 26, 2003, A13.
48. Shard, Peter. "Pictures of Saddam's Sons Splashed Across Arab Front Pages." Agence France Presse, July 25, 2003.
49. Turki, F. "The Banality of Saddam Al-Tikriti." December 18, 2003 (cited September 5, 2004). <http://www.arabnews.com/?page=7&section=0&article=36646&d=18&m=12&y=2003>.
50. LaGuardia, Anton, and Gerald Butt. "Tragedy and Humiliation for Arab Nation." *Daily Telegraph*, December 16, 2003, 5.
51. "Saddam Arrest Dominates World Press." BBC News, 2003 (cited March 5, 2005). <http://news.bbc.co.uk/1/hi/world/3320069.stm>.
52. LaGuardia and Butt. "Tragedy and Humiliation."
53. Al-Zaidi, H. "Daily Reports Yemenis Reaction to Saddam Arrest." *Yemen Times*, December 17, 2003.
54. Shanker, Thom, and Eric Schmitt. "Pentagon Weighs Use of Deception in a Broad Arena." *New York Times*, December 13, 2004, A1.
55. Ibid.
56. "Building America's Public Diplomacy through a Reformed Structure and Additional Resources." Washington, D.C.: U.S. Advisory Commission on Public Diplomacy 16 (Fall 2002): 4.
57. Barstow, David, Robin Stein and Anne E. Kornblut. "Under Bush, a New Age of Prepackaged News." *New York Times*, March 13, 2005, 1.1.
58. Ibid.
59. Gamboa, Anthony H. "Letter to Henry Waxman, Committee on Government Reform, U.S. House of Representatives." Government Accountability Office, January 4, 2005 (cited March 16, 2005). <http://www.gao.gov/decisions/appro/303495.pdf>.
60. Stop Government Propaganda Act, 2005.
61. Conversation with the author. November 15 2004.
62. Ibid.
63. North, Don. "Iraq: Project Frustration." *TelevisionWeek*, December 15, 2003, 1.
64. Ibid.
65. Conversation with the author.
66. North, Don. "Iraq Project Frustration: One Newsman's Take on How Things Went Wrong." *TelevisionWeek*, January 22, 2004.
67. Freeburg, John, and Jess T. Todd. "The 101st Airborne Division in Iraq: Televising Freedom." *Military Review* 84, no. 6: 39.

CHAPTER 12

1. "Media Fury at Abuse of Iraqis." BBC Monitoring, May 1, 2004 (cited October 5, 2004). <http://news.bbc.co.uk/1/hi/world/middle_east/3676495.stm>.

2. Hersh, Seymour M. "Torture at Abu Ghraib." *New Yorker* 80, no. 11: 42.

3. Evans-Pritchard, Ambrose. "US Asks Nato for Help in 'Draining the Swamp' of Global Terrorism." *Daily Telegraph*, September 27, 2001 (cited April 3, 2005). <http://www.telegraph.co.uk/news/main.jhtml?xml=/news/2001/09/27/wusa27.xml>.

4. "DOD News Briefing – Deputy Secretary Wolfowitz." Department of Defense, September 13, 2001 (cited April 9, 2005). <http://www.dartmouth.edu/~govdocs/docs/iraq/dod.htm>.

5. Psychologist, USAF Staff. "Ar15-6 Allegations of Detainee Abuse at Abu Ghraib – Psychological Assessment." Washington, D.C.: U.S. Department of Defense, 2004. 3. <http://www.gwu.edu/~nsarchiv/NSAEBB/NSAEBB140/>.

6. Ibid.

7. "Media Fury."

8. Nafie, Ibrahim. "'I'm Sorry.'" *Al-Ahram*, 2004 (cited April 8, 2005). <http://weekly.ahram.org.eg/2004/689/fr4.htm>.

9. Quoted in Blanford, Nicholas. "To Arabs, Photos Confirm Brutal U.S." *Christian Science Monitor*, May 3, 2004 (cited July 5, 2004). <http://www.csmonitor.com/2004/0503/p06s01-wome.html>.

10. "2,000 Dead in Fallujah as U.S.-Led Forces Sweep Area." *Daily Star*, November 26, 2004 (cited April 7, 2005). <http://www.dailystar.com.lb/article.asp?edition_ID=10&article_ID=10449&categ_id=2#>.

11. "Slaughter of American Civilian May Eclipse Iraqi Prison Scandal." *Daily Star*, May 17, 2004 (cited April 5, 2005). <http://www.dailystar.com.lb/mereview.asp?edition_ID=10&article_ID=3815&categ_id=7>.

12. Samaha, Joseph. "Abu Ghraib Abuse is Only the Tip of the US Iceberg." *As-Safir*, May 10, 2004 (cited August 10, 2004). <http://www.dailystar.com.lb/mereview.asp?edition_ID=10&article_ID=3354&categ_id=7>.

13. "Thousands Rally against US Abuses." *Jakarta Post*, May 17, 2004.

14. "2,000 Dead."

15. Williams, Mike. "Video of Man's Slaying Posted on the Internet: U.S. Civilian Beheaded in Iraq." *Palm Beach Post*, May 12, 2004, A1.

16. Nouriddine, Sateh. "Arab Leaders Failed Because They Confronted US–Israeli Policies with Empty Rhetoric." *As-Safir*, May 26, 2004 (cited August 9, 2004). <http://www.dailystar.com.lb/ mereview.asp?edition_ID=10&article_ID=4349&categ_id=7>.

17. Allen, Mike, and Paul Farhi. "Progress is Ongoing in Iraq, White House Says: Civilian Deaths Condemned as Administration Calls for U.S. to Show Resolve." *Washington Post*, April 1, 2004, A20.

18. Chan, Sewell. "2 U.S. Troops Killed: Fallujah Plan Readied." *Washington Post*, April 3, 2004, A19.

19. Ibid.

20. Shohat, Orit. "Remember Fallujah." *Ha'aretz*, April 28, 2004.

21. Morley, Jefferson. "*Mideast Media Gripped by Another Horrible Image.*" Washington Post, May 14, 2004 (cited Aug 5, 2004).

22. "Torture of Iraqi Captives by US Soldiers Stokes Flames of Resentment and Anger." *Ad-Dustour*, May 3, 2004 (cited June 5, 2004).

<http://www.dailystar.com.lb/mereview.asp?edition_ID=10&article_ID= 3164&categ_id=7>.

23. Taheri, Amir. "Culture of Hate." Islam Review, June 22, 2004 (cited April 5, 2005). <http://www.islamreview.com/articles/cultureofhateprint.htm>.

24. Muhawish, Shakir. "BBC Monitoring Iraq Briefing." April 17, 2004.

25. "Arab Press Cheers Falluja 'Victory.'" BBC Monitoring, April 12, 2004 (cited April 4, 2005). <http://news.bbc.co.uk/1/hi/world/middle_east/ 3619267.stm>.

26. "Slaughter of American Civilian."

27. "Arab Press Cheers."

28. Nasr, Muhammad Abu. "Iraqi Resistance Report." Free Arab Voice, April 15, 2004 (cited April 8, 2005). <http://www.albasrah.net/moqawama/ english/0404/iraqiresistancereport_150404.htm>.

29. "Iraqi Casualty Reports by Arab TV Stations 'Outrageous Nonsense': Rumsfeld." Agence France Presse, April 15, 2004.

30. Keath, Lee. "AP Count: Around 1,361 Iraqis Killed in April's Violence." Associated Press, April 30, 2004.

31. Oppel, Richard A., Jr., and Robert Worth. "G.I.s Open Attack to Take Falluja from Iraq Rebels." New York Times, November 8, 2004, A1.

32. Harnden, Toby. "Fallujah Will Be Your Stalingrad, Americans Told." Daily Telegraph, April 26, 2004, 13.

33. Peters, Ralph. Kill Faster! New York Post, May 20, 2004 (cited March 1, 2005). <http://www.defenddemocracy.org/research_topics/research_topics_ show.htm?doc_id=226344&attrib_id=7511>.

34. Macleod, Scott. "Mideast Diary: Iraq's Shiite Awakening." Time, April 24, 2004 (cited April 10, 2005). <http://www.time.com/time/columnist/ macleod/article/0,9565,446545,00.html>. That same level of ignorance was seen in an abortive U.S. plan to have the Turkish military occupy parts of Kurdistan, therefore making real the worst fears of the Kurds, America's allies, and almost certainly setting off a separate conflict.

35. "Closure of Al-Sadr Daily Stirs Protests." Al-Jazeera, March 29, 2004 (cited April 10, 2005). <http://english.aljazeera.net/NR/exeres/AA233B3B-AA8A-466C-A31B-4D6DE7E62DB6.htm>.

36. "Arrest Warrant Issued for Iraqi Shi'ite Cleric Al-Sadr." Coalition Provisional Authority, April 5, 2004 (cited April 10, 2004). <http:// www.iraqcoalition.org/pressreleases/20040405_Sadr_arrest.html>.

37. For more on the evolution of Hizbullah, see Chapter 17 in my previous book, Pintak, Lawrence. Seeds of Hate: How America's Flawed Middle East Policy Ignited the Jihad. London and Sterling, Va.: Pluto Press, 2003.

38. Ibid. 307.

39. "Press Briefing Scott McClellan." White House, March 22, 2004 (cited August 5, 2004). <http://www.whitehouse.gov/news/releases/2004/03/ 20040322-4.html>.

40. "Cleric Urges End to Najaf Battle." BBC News, May 14, 2004 (cited June 5, 2004). <http://news.bbc.co.uk/1/hi/world/middle_east/3713453.stm>.

41. Cole, Juan. "Losing the War of Images." San Francisco Chronicle, May 9, 2004 (cited June 5, 2004). <http://www.sfgate.com/cgi-bin/article.cgi?f=/ c/a/2004/05/09/INGLH6FJJN1.DTL>.

42. "Iran Leader Condemns US 'Stupidity.'" BBC News, May 16, 2004 (cited September 24, 2004). <http://news.bbc.co.uk/1/hi/world/middle_east/3719095.stm>.

43. Sly, Liz. "'America's Credibility in Iraq is Hanging by a Thread.'" Knight Ridder Tribune News Service: 1.

44. "Transcript of Bush's Remarks on Iraq: 'We Will Finish the Work of the Fallen.'" *New York Times*, April 14, 2004, A12.

45. "Making a Hooligan into a Hero: The US Has Turned Moqtada Al-Sadr into an Iraqi Icon." *Financial Times*, May 21, 2004, 16.

46. Allam, Hannah. "In Iraq, Arab Broadcasts Anger U.S. Authorities." Knight Ridder Tribune News Service: 1.

47. Marquis, Christopher, and Eric Schmitt. "U.S. Protests Broadcasts by Arab Channels." *New York Times*, April 29, 2004, A15.

48. Ritchin, Fred. "Mediating Madness." April 5, 2004 (cited April 5, 2005). <http://www.pixelpress.org/madness_text.html.>

49. Weisman, Steven R. "Bush Plan for Group of 8 to Hail Democracy in the Middle East Strains Ties with Arab Allies." *New York Times*, June 6, 2004, 1.14.

50. Schweid, Barry. "U.S. Stands Firm on Concessions to Sharon." Associated Press, April 27, 2004 (cited December 4, 2004). <http://ap.washington-times.com/dynamic/stories/U/US_MIDEAST?SITE=DCTMS&SECTION=HOME>.

51. Ibid.

52. Saghieh, Hazem. "Abu Ghraib Abuse is Only the Tip of the US Iceberg." *Al-Hayat*, May 8, 2004 (cited August 7, 2004). <http:// www.dailystar.com.lb/mereview.asp?edition_ID=10&article_ID=3354&categ_ id=7>.

53. "Ariel Sharon, Osama Bin Laden Hold World Hostage in 'Hellish Alliance.'" *Al-Ahram*, April 14, 2004 (cited August 9, 2004). <http://www.dailystar.com.lb/mereview.asp?edition_ID=10&article_ID=2060&c ateg_id=7>.

54. Knowlton, Brian. "For Bush, a Chance to Change Headlines: U.S.-Led Military Occupation Formally Ends, Iraqi Handover Comes Early." *International Herald Tribune*, June 29, 2004, 1.

55. "Iranian Daily Says Muslims Will Abort 'New Plot' of US Handover in Iraq." BBC Monitoring Middle East:.

56. "BBC Monitoring Quotes from Malaysian Press 30 June 04." BBC Monitoring Newsfile.

57. Ben Aziz, Ammar. "Arab Press Welcomes Power Transfer." CNN, June 29, 2004 (cited March 4, 2005). <http://www.cnn.com/2004/WORLD/meast/06/29/iraq.press/index.html>.

58. "Al-Jazeera TV Programme Participants View US Transfer of Power in Iraq." BBC Monitoring Middle East, 2004, 1.

59. "Those Who Fish in 'Troubled Waters' of Iraq Should Beware of Allawi." *Al-Hayat*, June 30, 2004 (cited September 15, 2004). <http://www.dailystar.com.lb/mereview.asp?edition_ID=10&article_ID=5736&categ_id=7>.

60. Bush, George W. "President Discusses War on Terror." White House, April 12, 2005 (cited April 15, 2005). <http://www.whitehouse.gov/news/releases/2005/04/20050412.html>.

61. Roberts, Les, Riyadh Lafta, Richard Garfield, Jamal Khudhairi and Gilbert Burnham. "Mortality Before and After the 2003 Invasion of Iraq: Cluster Sample Survey." *Lancet* (pre-publication online edition), October 29, 2004 (cited October 31, 2004). <http://image.thelancet.com/extras/04art10342web.pdf>.

62. "Fallujah Shifts from Support to Rebuke of US-Led War." *Al-Watan*, April 13, 2005 (cited April 14, 2005). <http://www.dailystar.com.lb/mereview.asp?edition_ID=10&article_ID=1992&categ_id=7>.

EPILOGUE

1. "2004 Report." Washington, D.C.: United States Advisory Commission on Public Diplomacy, 2004. 2.

2. Hughes, Karen. "The Mission of Public Diplomacy." Senate Foreign Relations Committee, July 22, 2005 (cited July 28, 2005). <http://www.state.gov/r/us/2005/49967.htm>.

3. Bin Laden, Osama. "Full Text Bin Laden Tape April 2004." BBC News, April 15, 2004 (cited April 16, 2004). <http://news.bbc.co.uk/1/hi/world/middle_east/3628069.stm>.

4. Bin Laden, Osama. "Full Transcript of Bin Ladin Speech." Al-Jazeera, November 1, 2004 (cited November 1, 2004). <http://english.aljazeera.net/NR/exeres/79C6AF22-98FB-4A1C-B21F-2BC36E87F61F.htm>.

5. Worth, Robert F. "Jihadists Take Stand on Web, and Some Say it's Defensive." *New York Times*, March 13, 2005, 1.22.

6. Ibid.

7. Agence France Presse (AFP). "Stripped of Havens, al-Qaeda Turns to 'Media Jihad.'" *Daily Star*, Beirut, September 10, 2005.

8. The figures were contained in a draft copy of the annual *Patterns of Global Terrorism* report. See Landay, Jonathan S. "Democrat Requests Probe of Changes in Terrorism Report." Knight Ridder Tribune News Service, September 10, 2005. 1.

9. "Report of the Defense Science Board Task Force on Strategic Communciation." Washington, D.C.: Office of the Under Secretary of Defense for Acquisition, Technology, and Logistics, 2004. 2.

10. "A Major Change of Public Opinion in the Muslim World." Bethesda, Md.: Terror Free Tomorrow, 2005.

11. VandeHei, Jim. "Bush Says Tsunami Aid Benefits U.S." *Washington Post*, March 9, 2005, A3.

12. "American Media . . . Baghdad Burning." April 3, 2005 (cited April 26, 2005). <http://riverbendblog.blogspot.com/archives/2005_04_01_riverbendblog_archive.html#111247654157434704>.

About the Author

Lawrence Pintak is director of the Adham Center for Electronic Journalism at the American University in Cairo. A veteran of 30 years in journalism on four continents, Pintak has contributed to many of the world's leading news organizations.

Pintak covered the Lebanon conflict, the Iran–Iraq War and the birth of modern radical Islamist terrorism as CBS News Middle East correspondent in the 1980s and more recently reported on the overthrow of Indonesian President Suharto for *The San Francisco Chronicle* and ABC News. He won two Overseas Press Club awards for his Middle East coverage and was twice nominated for Emmys. As the Howard R. Marsh Visiting Professor of Journalism at the University of Michigan, Pintak lectured on media and foreign policy. He has also advised numerous governments, corporations and NGOs on international media issues and is senior editor of the *Journal of Transnational Broadcasting Studies*.

Previous books include *Beirut Outtakes: A TV Correspondent's Portrait of America's Encounter with Terror* (Lexington 1988) and *Seeds of Hate: How America's flawed Middle East policy ignited the jihad* (Pluto Press 2003).

Index

Compiled by Sue Carlton